CW01424501

Irish Identities and the Great War in Drama and Fiction

REGENSBURG STUDIES IN BRITISH AND AMERICAN LANGUAGES AND CULTURES

Edited by
Prof. Dr. Udo J. Hebel, Prof. Dr. Edgar W. Schneider
and Prof. Dr. Anne-Julia Zwierlein

VOLUME 53

PETER LANG
EDITION

Martin Decker

Irish Identities and the Great War in Drama and Fiction

PETER LANG
EDITION

Bibliographic Information published by the Deutsche Nationalbibliothek
The Deutsche Nationalbibliothek lists this publication in the Deutsche Nationalbibliografie; detailed bibliographic data is available in the internet at http://dnb.d-nb.de.

Zugl.: Regensburg, Univ., Diss., 2015

Library of Congress Cataloging-in-Publication Data
Names: Decker, Martin, 1982- author.
Title: Irish identities and the Great War in drama and fiction / Martin Decker.
Description: Frankfurt am Main ; New York : Peter Lang, 2016. | Series:
  Regensburg studies in British and American languages and cultures ; Volume
  53 | Includes bibliographical references.
Identifiers: LCCN 2016026930 | ISBN 9783631666890
Subjects: LCSH: English literature--Irish authors--History and criticism. |
  World War, 1914-1918--Literature and the war.
Classification: LCC PR8722.W36 D43 2016 | DDC 820.9/94150904--dc23 LC record available at https://lccn.loc.gov/2016026930

Cover image:
The Steward of Christendom, Mark Taper Forum, Los Angeles, 2013.
Photograph by Craig Schwartz/craigphoto.com. Used with permission.

D 355
ISSN 1615-925X
ISBN 978-3-631-66689-0 (Print)
E-ISBN 978-3-653-06170-3 (E-PDF)
E-ISBN 978-3-631-70142-3 (EPUB)
E-ISBN 978-3-631-70143-0 (MOBI)
DOI 10.3726/978-3-653-06170-3

© Peter Lang GmbH
Internationaler Verlag der Wissenschaften
Frankfurt am Main 2016
All rights reserved.
Peter Lang Edition is an Imprint of Peter Lang GmbH.

Peter Lang – Frankfurt am Main · Bern · Bruxelles · New York ·
Oxford · Warszawa · Wien

All parts of this publication are protected by copyright. Any
utilisation outside the strict limits of the copyright law, without
the permission of the publisher, is forbidden and liable to
prosecution. This applies in particular to reproductions,
translations, microfilming, and storage and processing in
electronic retrieval systems.

This publication has been peer reviewed.

www.peterlang.com

Acknowledgements

Although only my name appears on the cover of this book, its production would not have been possible without the help and support of a great many people to whom I owe my heartfelt gratitude.

This book is based on a dissertation accepted by the University of Regensburg in July 2015. The dissertation was written under the supervision of Prof. Dr. Anne-Julia Zwierlein, to whom I would like to express my deepest gratitude. I have been very fortunate to have had her as an enduring and patient guide through the project, always willing to offer me her expert advice and support while giving me the freedom to explore my own ideas. Furthermore, I would like to offer my sincere thanks to Prof. Dr. Katharina Rennhak (Bergische Universität Wuppertal), who was also very supportive and acted as the co-supervisor for my project. It was also Prof. Dr. Anne-Julia Zwierlein who kindly accepted this study into the *Regensburger Arbeiten zur Anglistik and Amerikanistik* series, for which I am very grateful. Furthermore, I would like to thank the other main editors of the series, Prof. Dr. Udo J. Hebel and Prof. Dr. Edgar W. Schneider.

I am highly indebted to my colleagues and friends at the Department of English and American Studies at the University of Regensburg, specifically Dr. Anna Farkas and Dr. Katharina Boehm, as well as Dr. Sandra Stadler and Dr. Christine Grieb, who read large sections of my manuscript and whose many insightful comments and suggestions – just as their unfailing encouragement – were of vital importance for me. Moreover, I am sincerely grateful for the wealth of constructive feedback I received at colloquia, workshops, conferences and guest lectures in Regensburg, Basel, Mannheim, Zaragoza and Wuppertal.

Finally, and most specially, I would like to express my deepest appreciation to Eva-Maria who has put up with me and my moods during the ups and downs of a long project and without whose love and unshakable support none of this would have ever been possible. This book is dedicated to her.

Contents

I. Introduction

The 2014 centenary of the outbreak of the Great War was accompanied by a substantial programme of commemoration in and on behalf of Ireland. This included not only the participation of President Michael D. Higgins in commemorative events in Liège and Mons, alongside representatives of more than seventy nations, but also acts such as the unveiling of the "Cross of Sacrifice" in Glasnevin cemetery in Dublin, a new monument for the Irishmen who died in the First and the Second World War. This ceremony stood out as a joint Irish and British effort, "infused with military pomp and solemnity" (Murtagh 2014). It featured Irish and British troops as well as appearances and speeches by President Higgins, the Secretary of State for Northern Ireland, the mayors of Dublin and Belfast, ambassadors from several countries, and even British royalty in the person of Prince Edward, the Duke of Kent. Furthermore, on the occasion of the war's anniversary, several new exhibitions about the Irish Great War experience have been organised, for example by the National Library in Dublin and by the National Museum of Ireland. The topic of the Great War has been extensively covered in Irish media, in newspapers, magazines, internet forums, television programmes and political talk shows, frequently in connection with the centenary of the Easter Rising in 2016. The war has also returned to Irish stages, for example, the Abbey Theatre has announced a new production and international tour of Frank McGuinness's seminal play *Observe the Sons of Ulster Marching Towards the Somme* in 2016. Altogether, these efforts suggest that the First World War is fully integrated and accepted as an important event in modern Irish historical and national consciousness.

Importantly, the spirit that has underpinned these acts of public commemoration and historical education in Ireland since the last decade or so is a fairly new one – it is characterised by sympathy and respect for the fallen and by a conscious and explicitly integrative engagement with a chapter of Irish history that had actually been an unwelcome one for decades. In fact, for much of the twentieth century, there had been something like a public amnesia in Ireland concerning the Great War (cf. Ferriter 2005, 132) – a large-scale historical and political marginalisation of the topic and of those Irishmen and Irishwomen involved in it. In a country long dominated by parochial nationalism, by the idolisation of its revolutionary origins and by a widespread desire to cut all ties to the former coloniser Britain, the service of more than 200,000 Irishmen in the British forces during the Great War had been seen majorly as an irrelevant, embarrassing or, at worst, treasonable episode. Silence quickly fell on the subject after the 1920s.

It was only by the 1980s, as old dichotomies began to crumble and as Ireland became more modern, open and heterogeneous, that the views on the Great War began to change. Against the narrow-mindedness and insularity of the past there developed a growing appropriation of a more inclusive sense of Irish national history and identity in official discourses in the twenty-first century, extending to the issue of the Great War. This finds expression, for example, in the words of President Higgins in the aftermath of the 2014 Glasnevin ceremony:

> I think we should use the opportunity of World War One to recognise the catastrophe that war is as well as how easy it is to become trapped in a bubble of warlike thinking. [...]. [T]here is also a huge obligation on those heads of state and representatives of so-ciety to critique their own inherited assumptions of empire and imperial tendency and imperial consequences. [...] [M]y definition of a republic is a republic that includes all of the experiences and all of the vulnerabilities of all of its citizens and these are Irish.
>
> (quoted in Collins 2014)

However, this does not mean that in contemporary Ireland the topic of the Great War has completely lost its potential for controversy. There is still an element of uneasiness about the Irish involvement in the war, which surfaced particularly in the context of the heightened attention to the topic on the occasion of the cen-tenary. For example, the aforementioned ceremony in Glasnevin cemetery was accompanied by the heckling and verbal abuse by a group of radical republicans who disrupted the event by shouting "shame, shame, shame", "Brits out" and "Hig-gins you traitor" (quoted in Murtagh 2014). The 2014 issuing of commemorative stamps by An Post, showing Irish recruitment posters of the Great War, encoun-tered opposition, for example, by Labour TD Eamon Maloney, who objected to the stamps' depiction of John Redmond, leader of the Irish Parliamentary Party and influential campaigner for volunteering, who, according to Maloney, "shamed Irishmen into killing for Great Britain" (quoted in Calnan 2014). Finally, to in-clude an example from a popular mass media context, the reactions of readers to an opinion piece by the historian John Bowman in *The Irish Times* in August 2014 vividly illustrate the still contested status of the Great War in Ireland. In his article, Bowman points out the history of the Irish forgetfulness about "our largest casu-alty list, those Irish who lost their lives abroad during the Great War" (Bowman 2014), and he calls for new efforts of remembrance. The heated debate of readers on the newspaper's website offers an intriguing panorama of attitudes to the topic – even if the representativeness of such forums of course is questionable. The readers' comments, more than 400 in total, range from approval and understanding to scepticism and outright contempt for the Irish soldiers of the Great War (cf. Bowman 2014).[1] For example, a reader named "Simon Lachlan" agrees with Bowman, even favourably contrasting the Irish soldiers of the war with the venerated rebels of the 1916 Easter Rising: "In their own misguided way, they fought for freedom, not clerical dictatorships by the back door". Conversely, "Joe Nolan" wants to remind Bowman that it was not the Irish soldiers but the revolutionaries and republican fighters of the 1910s and 1920s who "paved the way for independence and the freedom to prevent our involvement in such wars". Another reader, "BikeSafeBeSeen", is largely uninterested in the political implications of the topic and calls for a more humane approach, adding a personal note: "I only care to remember my mother's two Irish uncles and her father, how scarred for life he was after 'surviving' the war and how this impacted greatly on her life and ultimately my life". "T Beckett" argues that Irish volunteers were "betrayed, humiliated and conned" to serve in a war that was nothing but "mindless slaughter for no real values". He or she is also uncomfortable with the involvement of Britain in Irish war commemorations: "I'd prefer [...] not to have our tragic war dead leased out to the British associations". Similarly, "Mike Hughes" is tired of "too many Union Jacks around all this stuff", suggesting that the British influence "should be greatly limited" or even restricted to the separate commemoration of unionist soldiers. A user named "Seán Óg Mac Gearailt" attracts much opposition by wondering polemically why "naive (at best) and money-hungry (at worst) individuals who were, by the standard of the day, well-paid as mercenaries for the biggest empire in world history" should be remembered at all. Finally, most vitriolic, "James Kelly" snaps that "[m]isguided or just traitors, on the plus side [the Great War] rid our country of the pus of unionism", and he adds sarcastically that "[w]e'll be celebrating the Black and Tans next".

Such discordant debates about the Great War and the handling of its legacy reveal much about the contemporary condition of Ireland. Firstly, they vividly illustrate the continuous and powerful grip of 'history' in Ireland – the fact that the Irish past and relations to it are constantly re-examined, remaining a vital if contested and fraught source of orientation and identification. As the historian Ian McBride observes, in Ireland "the interpretation of the past has always been at the heart of national conflict" (McBride 2001, 1). McBride also refers to Richard Rose's view of the country as "almost a land without history; because the troubles

---

1   The following readers' comments have been corrected with regard to punctuation and capitalisation.

of the past are relived as contemporary events" (McBride 2001, 1f.). Secondly, the debates surrounding the war and its legacy reveal a condition of a continuous insecurity about the national self, inevitably leading up to questions of identity and belonging: Who qualifies as 'Irish' and as a relevant part in Ireland's national narrative, and who is relegated to the margins of this narrative? How can this narrative be pluralised and how can marginalised identities be reconciled within the context of a changing Ireland; should they even be reintegrated? These questions of course are again centrally determined by the respective politicised approaches to the Irish past and by the interplay of different inherited allegiances and identities – the variations of nationalism and unionism, also including the related religious affiliations and, probably less prominently, aspects like socialism, pacifism or internationalism – or, respectively, the possibility of transcending these positions.

The period problematised in the above-mentioned debates, the age of the Great War and the domestic disruptions in Ireland connected to it – the Easter Rising, the War of Independence, the Civil War – truly was crucial for the formation of new Irish identities and the reformulation or disappearance of established ones. As Sebastian Barry's Irish soldier protagonist in *A Long Long Way* has to realise at the end of the novel, on a French battlefield in 1918, anticipating the obliteration of his class and identity at home: "All sorts of Ireland were no more" (Barry 2006, 286). The changes and turbulences of those years have affected Ireland and concepts of Irish identity to the present day. The narratives constructed around the events of this period – in political discourses, memory and literature – have played an important role in these processes.

It is this nexus that is the starting point of this study. Crucially, in such historical contexts, 'historical' literature is understood not only as merely 'documenting' the past but as mirroring, shaping and challenging discourses, perspectives and ideologies of specific socio-historical situations. As Fredric Jameson argues in *The Political Unconscious*, texts are "socially symbolic act[s]" that "reflect a fundamental dimension of our collective thinking and our collective fantasies about history and reality" (Jameson 1981, 34) and that are both formed and destabilised by (repressed) historical realities (cf. Jameson 1981, 20). Literature, approached by Jameson from the angle of 'genre', serves as "a proving ground for the dominant anxieties and ideals of an age" (Buchanan 2006, 88). This understanding underpins my approach to the Irish war writings that are in the focus of this book.

The overall aim of this study is to investigate the processes of reflecting, constructing, challenging, discarding and re-envisioning Irish identities in representations of the Great War in Irish drama and fiction, from the time of the war to the present day. This can be broken down to several guiding questions and tasks: How do Irish literary works present Irish identities affected by the Great War and its political, social and cultural legacy? In which contexts and discourses are these literary representations of war embedded? Why has there been an obvious need, particularly in recent Irish writing, to recover such identities and how is this revision carried out? How do contemporary literary works deal with the Irish past in their presentation of identities? The focal point of this work, the issue of identity, of course is a rather broad category and, consequently, this project is informed by a comparatively wide range of approaches to the war writings. This includes ideas and theories of nation and national belonging and identification, as well as the closely connected aspects of class, gender and the body. Considering the more recent Irish literary representations of the Great War, the interplay of constructions of memory and constructions of identity also is of great importance.

The fraught history and the difficult status of the Great War in Ireland are very much reflected in the make-up of the corpus of texts that address the topic. Irish Great War literature[2] is a comparatively small and heterogeneous genre, which is slightly surprising – notwithstanding the war's problematic status – considering the impact of the war and the strong tendency for national self-inspection that characterises much Irish writing. Actually, it is not entirely unproblematic to speak of 'war literature' in the case of Ireland. There are only a few texts that correspond to the traditional conventions of the genre with its focus on first-hand experience and grim tales from the battlefields and trenches[3] – there simply is no Irish Wilfred Owen, as there is no Irish Henri Barbusse, Erich-Maria Remarque or Ernst Jünger. The engagement with Irish works of and about the Great War consequently requires an expanded notion of war literature which attributes greater prominence to events and phenomena that lie beyond the immediacy of the battlefield, like the Irish home front, the role of women and the legacy of the war and its relevance for the Irish conflicts of the following years.

The amnesiac tendencies and the limited literary production in Ireland concerning the Great War are also reflected in the long scholarly neglect of the topic. Apart from few quasi-canonical works such as Sean O'Casey's *The Silver Tassie*

---

2   Importantly, my understanding of the concept "Irish Great War literature" does not only mean the writings produced by combatants or onlookers during the war or in its aftermath, but includes all Irish texts in which the representation of the war and its effects plays an important role.

3   The war novels of Patrick MacGill and Liam O'Flaherty do follow the classic formula of war literature, yet, their outlook is not specifically Irish and they rarely ever directly touch on the subject of Irishness or Irish identity.

(1928) or Frank McGuinness's *Observe the Sons of Ulster Marching Towards the Somme* (1985), this study focuses on prose and dramatic writings that have previously attracted little scholarly attention – works like Margaret Barrington's *My Cousin Justin*, Sean Dowling's *The Bird in the Net*, Tom Phelan's *The Canal Bridge* or Dermot Bolger's *Walking the Road*. Poetry will not be covered extensively in my project as there are already two inspiring monographs on the topic by Fran Brearton (cf. Brearton 2000) and Jim Haughey (cf. Haughey 2002) that neatly complement each other, together offering a complete and detailed view of the Irish and Northern Irish poetic responses to the Great War, including aspects of identity. Generally, broader academic interest in Irish Great War writing is a fairly recent phenomenon, as is the historical re-discovery of Ireland's role in the Great War that preceded it in the 1980s, largely beginning in the 1990s and only becoming more substantial since the 2000s. The topic has been integrated as a facet within larger contexts and surveys (cf. Kiberd 1996, Grene 1999, Brown 2011; Johnson 2003 approaches Irish war literature within a cultural geography approach), yet, it is rarely engaged with exclusively and extensively, i. e. critics have rarely addressed a larger part of or the entire spectrum of texts; there is only a small number of larger studies focusing on individual aspects of the topic (cf. Kosok 2007 on English and Irish drama and the war; Taylor 2013 on the war novelist Patrick MacGill).[4] Among the most active and prolific scholars in the field are Terry Phillips, who has produced a series of journal articles and book chapters on various aspects of the topic (cf. Phillips), the historian Keith Jeffery, who repeatedly addresses Irish war writing in his extensive explorations of the Irish history of the Great War (cf. Jeffery), and Heinz Kosok, who is particularly interested in the war in Irish drama (cf. Kosok). Still, despite the pioneering and inspiring work of these and several other scholars, to whom this study is deeply indebted, the topic remains a comparatively open field. There is a considerable number of texts, even within this narrow genre, that have remained almost untouched by scholarly criticism. To embed some of these texts in the greater context of Irish war writing, using the guiding principle of identity and identity politics, is the purpose of this book.

I will begin with three sections that introduce key concepts and backgrounds upon which the following discussion of Irish war drama and fiction is based. The section on the theoretical context provides a concise overview of the spectrum

---

4   Terry Phillips's comprehensive monograph *Irish Literature and the First World War. Culture, Identity and Memory* (Oxford: Peter Lang, 2015) was published after the completion of this study.

of theoretical approaches that informs my interpretations in varying degrees of directness, including, among others, concepts of Stuart Hall, Benedict Anderson, Prasenjit Duara, Maurice Halbwachs, Jay Winter, and Elaine Scarry. The following section on the historical context traces the complex Irish history of the Great War and its legacy from the early 1910s to the present, specifically focusing on the intricate and contradictory interaction of identities and allegiances. Finally, the section on the literary context addresses the issue of writing the war, including an adjustment of the concept of 'war literature' to the Irish situation. Also, the conditions that led to the scarcity of Irish war writing are investigated and a survey of the existing war works is provided, including the responses to the Great War in poetry. The section concludes with a brief look at Easter Rising literature, which could be seen as a recurrent rival discourse to the writing of the Great War.

This is the backdrop against which a selection of Irish war plays and novels are read in the second part of this book. The selection of texts was largely determined by the existing surveys of Irish war writings by Heinz Kosok (cf. Kosok 2007), Keith Jeffery (cf. Jeffery 1994, Jeffery 2000) and Terence Brown (cf. Brown 2011). Due to the overall scarcity and disparity of the genre, the criteria for selection were rather broad: dramatic or prose works that substantially, but not necessarily exclusively, address the First World War and its legacy in all their facets, from both modern and 'historical' Irish or Northern Irish perspectives. Since the focus of this study is not centrally on questions of aesthetics and genre, dramatic and prose works are not approached separately.[5] With the exception of chapter III. 2, the readings are structured chronologically, beginning with two key texts which have been identified, debatably, as the only major dramatic war works "set in Ireland, Irish in theme and subject-matter" (Kosok 2008, 184) to be written until the early 1980s, G. B. Shaw's satire *O'Flaherty VC: A Recruiting Pamphlet* (1915) and Sean O'Casey's *The Silver Tassie* (1928). Both works are underpinned by the shared socialist impetus of their authors. They concentrate on unflattering depictions of the Irish home front during the Great War, investigating class issues as well as the ambiguous transformative power of wartime heroism, and how the war reshapes and complicates concepts of masculine and feminine identities, including, in the case of O'Casey, the consequences of disability.

This section is followed by a chapter focusing on a larger selection of texts that address the multifaceted effects of the Great War on Anglo-Irish identities and on the troublesome dynamics of Irish and Anglo-Irish relationships, offering a

---

5   The only exception to this is chapter III. 2., where thematic parallels suggested the separate grouping of plays and novels.

complex array of allegiances and identities to be examined. The first part of this section concentrates on two plays that present the Great War as a central factor in the most severe challenge to the validity of Anglo-Irish identities during the war and in its aftermath. Lennox Robinson's *The Big House* (1926) is interested in a level-headed and complex presentation of the social and political nuances of the topic, while the other play, Sean Dowling's *The Bird in the Net* (1960) casts a far more unforgiving and stereotypical eye on the subject, picturing the Great War exclusively as a ruthless colonial and class war. The second part of this section features works best characterised as 'Big House' novels, Pamela Hinkson's *The Ladies' Road* (1932) and Margaret Barrington's *My Cousin Justin* (1939). Here, the focus is again on the construction of the Irish home front from an Anglo-Irish and an English angle, and, specifically, on the role of Anglo-Irish women during the war, presenting the recurring theme of feminine passivity and alienation. The final text of this section, Jennifer Johnston's *How Many Miles to Babylon* (1974), represents a link to more recent works about the Great War by adapting a more individualised and psychological perspective, also introducing the war both as an escapist and oppressive space for the Anglo-Irish protagonist of the novel.

The final part of this study investigates 'revisionist' perspectives, the desire to re-construct and re-contextualise Ireland's and Northern Ireland's Great War experience that is manifest in several Irish and Northern Irish prose and dramatic works since the 1980s. The development of the Troubles and the re-discovery of the Great War as an important and complex context for the roots of sectarian violence in Northern Ireland are of great concern for these texts. Frank McGuinness's seminal play *Observe the Sons of Ulster Marching Towards the Somme* (1985) uses the harrowing experiences of Ulstermen at the Somme to challenge, subvert and, eventually, to humanise identity constructions shaped by Orange radicalism and an Ulster cult of death, questioning, as several other texts of this section, the destructive power of memory. Christina Reid's play *My Name, Shall I Tell You My Name?* (1987) does not take us to the Somme but to 1980s' Derry, presenting an investigation of the power of established narratives in forming identities and the clash of conflicting memories of the past from a female Northern Irish perspective. Nicola McCartney's play *Heritage* (1998) is set in the milieu of Irish immigrants in Canada during the Great War, adding another dimension to the political and social complexity of Irish experience in those tumultuous years, continuing and varying the motif of the burden of history, or, "heritage", that runs through the other texts of this section and that has complicated and aggravated Irish relations. Tom Phelan's historical novel *The Canal Bridge* (2005) presents the tragic story of two Irish peasants who join the British army in 1913 to see the wonders of the world and end up as stretcher-bearers on European battlefields. The novel is a call for historical empathy and includes a scathing critique of Irish nationalism and its rhetoric of martyrdom. The final part of this section is reserved for two Irish authors most directly associated with revisionist ideas, Sebastian Barry and Dermot Bolger. In his 2005 novel *A Long Long Way*, Barry consciously sets out to rewrite what he calls a "censored" part of Irish history and "censored" identities, addressing the marginalisation and alienation of Irish soldiers in Ireland in a very illustrative and straightforward manner. The final text to be discussed, Dermot Bolger's memory play *Walking the Road* (2007), is an experimental re-imagination of the life of Francis Ledwidge, who is frequently regarded as Ireland's major war poet. Like Barry's novel, the play underlines the liminal position of Irish veterans by placing a ghostly Ledwidge figure in what appears to be a historical limbo, a space in-between life and death, memory and forgetting – however, unlike the other authors, Bolger also provides a solution to his protagonist's predicament. Altogether, these texts form a multifaceted and intriguing literary response to the Great War and its legacy in which the transformative power and the lasting repercussions of the event for the contested issue of Irish identity become visible.

II. Contexts

II.1 Theoretical Context

As Nuala Johnson observes, in "Ireland the [Great] [W]ar [...] became part of the vehicle through which disparate voices of identity politics found expression" (Johnson 2003, 12). This disparateness is related to the different contexts within which Irish identities have emerged and have been negotiated and challenged, yet, it also highlights the fact that the very notion of 'identity' is in itself highly ambiguous, complex, changeable, and a subject of discourses of politics and power. The cultural critic Kobena Mercer notes how "identity only becomes an issue when it is in crisis, when something assumed to be fixed, coherent and stable is displaced by the experience of doubt and uncertainty" (quoted in Hall 1995, 597) – war evidently represents a context in which such a crisis is provoked. War is an arena in which identities are constructed and deconstructed, thereby paradoxically highlighting two basic aspects of identity: On the one hand, there is the communal dimension of identity, which in war has various facets, from an overarching sense of a national identity to group identities within the general military system, down to collective microcosms such as the emblematic trench communities of the Great War. On the other hand, there is the personal dimension of identity and self-perception, the sense of (pre-war) individuality that might clash with or be transformed by group identities (cf. Korte and Schneider 2002, 2f.) and by the experience of war itself. A further complication is introduced when we consider the community, and with it the communal identity in whose name war is or was waged. While war transforms those who directly take part in it, war also frequently leads to an increase of social pressure and conformity at home, creating a 'home front' that is a vital part of the war effort, blurring the boundaries between civilian and military identities.

In the following, I will provide a brief overview of the theoretical concepts of identity within which my reading of Irish literary representations of the Great War is embedded. 'Identity' is a multifaceted category and related to a wide range of experiences and discourses. The investigation of identities in the context of the Great War and its legacy is especially connected to questions of nationhood, national belonging and nationalism, just as to the dimension of gender and the body, which, in the context of war, also includes aspects of disability. Furthermore, class aspects play a significant role and are recurrently addressed in the war texts to be covered, the Great War representing an arena in which class boundaries are both blurred by communal experience and enforced by military

19

hierarchies, peacetime social structures being transferred to the framework of the military ranks. A central notion underpinning my approach is the idea of the constructedness and fluidity of identities and the nexus of the constitutive inter-dependencies of identity, memory and narratives – narratives of the self, of the nation, of the past. In this respect and, specifically, in the contested Irish context of this project, concepts of historical revisionism play a central role.

II.1.1 'Cultural Identity', the Nation, Nationalism

Conventionally, 'identity' has been associated with a unified and closed concept of a 'true inner self' (Hall 1995, 597); similarly, history, including wars, has also been seen as the outcome of men and women realising their identities or perhaps acting upon 'instincts', following their 'character' – altogether, in such views experience becomes the result of identity. Yet, the understanding of identity underlying my investigation of Irish war writing is based on the very opposite of such notions, it largely follows the concept of 'cultural identity' defined by Stuart Hall, which centrally postulates the constructed, relational and changeable nature of identity.

Hall's concept can be seen as a strategic, positional, postmodern and performative extension of sociological models of identity, opposed to the closed model of what Hall calls an "Enlightenment subject" (ibid.) with an essential and unchanging inner core of identity. In performative sociological models, a subject's identity is only created and formed by the interaction of the individual with 'society', the cultural world outside and the identity constructions this world offers. In this manner, the subject is envisioned as being stitched or 'sutured' into a cultural structure, into a social configuration. Yet, these processes do not result in the formation of a fixed and stable core of identity. Hall and others have pointed out the unstable and flexible condition of modern societies, particularly of those of the late twentieth century which have been identified as 'de-centred', which is characterised by a constant altering of social practices in response to internal and external transforming forces (cf. Hall 1995, 599f.; Hall 1996, 3f.). The interaction between the subject and its cultural structure in those societies consequently is inevitably characterised by change and fragmentation. The conventional notion of the existence of an essential stable core of identity hence becomes untenable. Instead, the subject and, concomitantly, the social landscape with which the subject interacts, are composed "not of a single, but several, sometimes contradictory or unresolved identities" (Hall 1995, 598), the subject being confronted with a confusing array of possible identities to adopt, adapt to or reject. Along these lines, Hall appropriates an understanding of 'cultural identity' that is defined by the subject's flexible formation by and relationship to "distinctive ethnic, racial, linguistic, and, above all, national cultures" (Hall 1995, 596). The sense of the flexible, performative and unfinished nature of identity is underlined by Hall's preference for the term 'identification' over 'identity': "[I]dentification as a construction, a process that is never completed [...,] not determined in the sense that it can always be 'won' or 'lost', sustained or abandoned. [...] [I]dentification is in the end conditional, lodged in contingency" (Hall 1996, 2f.). Hall even calls for a general reconceptualization of 'identity' purely in the sense of a continuous process of identification (cf. Hall 1996a, 344).

Hall connects his concept of identity strongly to the construction of narratives and to the modern subject's relation to social and cultural discourses. Narratives play a critical role in the development and integration of the self (cf. Taylor 2013, 56). The subject tries to accommodate an identity that is inherently contradictory, unresolved and problematic within a coherent narrative. This narrative essentially is a fantasy – as Hall argues, "[i]f we feel we have a unified identity from birth to death, it is only because we construct a comforting story or 'narrative of the self' about ourselves" (Hall 1995, 598). Actually, according to Hall, identities "arise from the narrativisation of the self", from a "suturing into the story" (Hall 1996, 4). Significantly, the fictional nature of these processes does not in any way undercut their effectivity – the narratives of the self are powerful and they constitute the self as much as the social landscape. Thus, Hall also defines identities as "the result of a successful articulation or 'chaining' of the subject into the flow of discourse" (Hall 1996, 5f.).

Identity constructions and narratives, Hall argues, are fundamentally shaped by difference, exclusion and the creation of hierarchies, not by an inherent identical unity – they emerge "within the play of specific modalities of power" (Hall 1996, 4) and are determined by the construction of difference from the "other", from other cultural configurations. Consequently, an investigation of identities requires an investigation of the specific historical, institutional and discursive sites within and, just as important, *against* which identities were formed. In this sense, for example, when Irish identities and constructions of Irishness are examined, the history and discursive power of attitudes of anti-Englishness need to be acknowledged – as Declan Kiberd remarks about Irish identity politics after Irish independence, "Irish people were so busy being not-English that they had scarcely time to think of what it might mean to be Irish. They forgot who they were or might be in their hysterical desire not to be taken for something else" (Kiberd 1988, 37).

A central form of identification, and one of vital importance for the subject of the Great War as an international conflict, is the one concerned with 'the nation', the related discourses of nationalism and the sense of national belonging and obligation produced in the subject which identifies with the construction of the nation. National identity, Patrick O'Mahoney and Gerard Delanty summarise, is the cultural outcome of a discourse of the nation, functioning in various ways – firstly, it distinguishes one group of people from another by creating a collective sense of belonging and a shared system of reference; secondly, it is the basis for distinguishing who should be granted citizenship of a nation-state, thirdly, it shapes the "character and goals of this nation state in a manner supposed to be in the collective interest of all the people" (O'Mahoney and Delanty 2001, 2f.).

There are two interesting paradoxes in the traditional essentialist concepts of the nation and the accompanying discourses of nationalism – loyalty to an ethnic nation – and patriotism – loyalty to a political state. The first paradox is the seemingly persistent overwhelming authority and universality of national identities, which becomes obvious in the fact that to this day the notion of a person not having a nationality commonly seems strange or even inconceivable (cf. Anderson 2006, 5). As Ernest Gellner observes, "[h]aving a nation is not an inherent attribute of humanity, but it has come to appear as such" (quoted in Hall 1995, 612) – a condition that, as will be shown later, has been challenged by more recent discourses of internationalism and post-nationalism. Secondly, the concept of the nation is objectively a modern one, having been popularised in Europe only since the late eighteenth century – yet, in the eyes of nationalists, nations are almost timeless, their roots usually being located by nationalists in a distant past, often including a mythical foundational narrative.

This aspect of a "national" past has been addressed by a number of commentators, among them, prominently, the historian and political theorist Ernest Renan. In his pioneering 1882 speech "What is a nation?", Renan defines the principle of nationality as being founded upon a shared will to live together and as a "daily plebiscite"; more importantly, for my purposes, Renan links the existence of a nation to the shared possession of memories and a rich heritage of common triumph and suffering that reinforces communal solidarity (cf. McBride 2011, 1): "The nation, like the individual, is the culmination of a long past of endeavours, sacrifice and devotion" (Renan 2011, 82). Yet, Renan's emphasis on the 'cult' of the ancestors as the basis of the nation already can be read as a hint at the man-made, the fabricated nature of the nation's past, and thus as an allusion to the constructedness of the nation as a whole. This notion dominates the attitudes of Hall and other theorists of the twentieth century, who reject the idea of the nation as something natural or essential and instead see the construction of a shared national narrative as constitutive for a national community and identity. To return once more to Hall, "a national culture is a discourse – a way of constructing meanings which influences and organises both our actions and our conception of ourselves" (Hall 1995, 613).

One of the most resonant and influential theories of nation and national identity related to the observations of Renan was devised by the political theorist and historian Benedict Anderson. Anderson addresses the difficulty inherent to the task of establishing a sense of community across a people and beyond individual local contacts, investigating how and why individuals began to relate to and identify with other remote individuals in the context of a national community. Anderson defines the nation as "an imagined political community [...]. It is imagined because the members of even the smallest nation will never know most of their fellow-members, meet them, or even hear of them, yet in the minds of each lives the image of their communion" (Anderson 2006, 6). Anderson stresses how the construction of shared narratives and a shared imagined past are what creates nations and keeps them together and he identifies the development of capitalism and print technology as the fundamental steps to allow the formulation, distribution and consolidation of such narratives. According to Anderson, trans-regionally circulating newspapers have promoted the establishment of new languages of power, standardising and, to some degree, democratising communication. These new practices unified people across the land, enabling individuals to imagine through reading the simultaneous existence of their co-nationals and a destiny shared with them, thereby creating a national consciousness (cf. Anderson 2006, 43ff.; Duara 1996, 152f.). Jonathan Rée points out, however, that despite this appealing notion of a national communion through 'ritual' reading, we should not underestimate older unifying ideas of an imagined "communion with old gods, and of relationships, including sexual ones, with military heroes, or, most especially, with kings and queens, princes and princesses. If one wants to explore the nationalist imagination, one needs to look out for wild longings and weird fantasies as well as sensible calculations" (Ree 1992, 3f.). Still, Anderson offers an appealing concept that can also be transferred to the context of war. Just as the subject can be motivated to imagine a national communion with other subjects beyond local contacts through the shared reception of narratives, the subject is invited in a similar manner to position itself along with its imagined compatriots against the imagined community of an enemy nation.

The "imagined" nature of the narrative of the nation, the constructedness of national identities, is of central importance for this project. Historiography, literature, the media and popular culture in this sense become the creative environment within which a set of stories, images, landscapes, scenarios, historical events, national symbols and rituals are fabricated to represent a range of collective experiences, an imaginative reservoir, which gives meaning to the nation, and which sutures the subjects which share these narratives into a national community (cf. Hall 1995, 613). However, it is also important to be aware of the fact that the constructedness of national identities suggested by Anderson, Hall, Gellner and others also occasions the possibility of a re-construction or de-construction – national identities have also been described as fundamentally unstable and elusive. The historian Prasenjit Duara, for example, stresses the idea of "national identity as founded upon fluid relationships" (Duara 1996, 151). Duara problematises the commonly held view of national identity as monolithic, national identity overpowering other forms of identification within a society, such as religion, class, gender or ethnicity, differences being incorporated in a larger identity, thereby creating a single "harmonised monologic voice of the Nation" (Duara 1996, 161f.) – Duara rejects the assumption of a steady and all-encompassing national uniformity, emphasising instead how the nation in fact is an unstable product of an ongoing negotiation and conflict between rival versions of history and alternative identities. As Duara notes "we may speak of different 'nation-views' as we do of 'world-views' which are not overridden by the nation, but actually define or constitute it" (Duara 1996, 161) – there exists not just one national narrative within a nation. Generally, Duara suggests, national identity must be seen as a relational identity, it represents

> a historical configuration which is designed to include certain groups and exclude or marginalise others. [...] [T]he national "self" is defined at any point in time by the Other. Depending on the nature and scale of the oppositional term, the national self contains various smaller "others" – historical Others that have effected an often uneasy reconciliation among themselves and potential Others that are beginning to form their differences.
>
> (Duara 1996, 163)

This assertion by Duara presents a methodical pattern that very closely encapsulates the identity politics and processes underlying and displayed in much of the Irish Great War literature to be interpreted in this project – a contested history of varying forms of Irish nationalism and divergent definitions of Irishness and non-Irishness with a (post-) colonial edge, including processes of marginalisation and an uneasy legacy of a war that had become 'other' in the context of a shifting historical situation.

II.1.2 History, Memory, Revisionism

As just outlined, identities can be characterised as dynamic, relational and fundamentally embedded within specific communal narratives. This also applies to national identities, which centrally rely upon narrative constructions of a common past, effectively, upon collective memory – as Nuala Johnson observes, "memory as re-collection, remembering and representation is crucial in the mapping of historical moments and in the articulation of identity" (Johnson 2003, 2f.). However, the past invoked in the context of identity, the sense of 'history' as a narrativisation of the past, must be seen as a subjective construction, as an attempt to endow past events with coherence and meaning to serve specific needs and solve specific problems of the present – for example, the narrativisation of the past can be used as a coping mechanism, imposing order and structure on unprecedented, traumatic or chaotic experiences. As Walter Benjamin famously argues, "[d]ie Geschichte ist Gegenstand einer Konstruktion, deren Ort nicht die homogene und leere Zeit, sondern die von Jetztzeit erfüllte bildet" (Benjamin 2007, 137). Similarly, Jan Assmann, analogous to theorists like Hayden White and Arthur C. Danto, defines history as "soziale Konstruktion, deren Beschaffenheit sich aus den Sinnbedürfnissen und Bezugsrahmen der jeweiligen Gegenwarten her ergibt, Vergangenheit steht nicht naturwüchsig an, sie ist eine kulturelle Schöpfung" (quoted in Widmann 2009, 29; cf. Widmann 2009 27ff.). In this manner, history and memory must be understood never as authentic or natural; they are dynamic social and cultural artefacts – the recollection of the past, in the words of Ian McBride, "is not simply a matter of filing away and retrieving information, but an active, continuing process" (McBride 2011, 12). These concepts and the consequential notion of a fundamental instability of 'history' also underpin Jacques Derrida's concept of 'hauntology', in which he addresses the convergence of different temporalities that exposes the problematic ongoing negotiation between past and present (cf. Jameson 1999, 38f.) – a theoretical perspective of great importance considering the contested and long unresolved Irish legacy of the Great War.

International conflicts like the Great War also play a central role in the construction of the past as the material of narratives that fuel the myth-making that is a prerequisite for the shaping of national identities (cf. Korte and Schneider 2002, 3). Importantly, the concept of 'myth' should not be automatically equated with the notion of 'deception'. As Samuel Hynes argues, addressing the very context of the Great War, the concept of myth should not be seen as "a falsification of reality, but [as] an imaginative version of it, a story of war that has evolved, and has come to be accepted as true" (Hynes 1990, xi). Similarly, Bernard Bergonzi argues that 'myth' refers to "actions, persons, events, stories, which escape from their historical background and have the continuing power to haunt our imagination [...]. [They are] not necessarily false, but they contain a large element of the unverifiable" (Bergonzi 1986, 8; cf. Löschnigg 1999, 218ff.). Considering the inherent subjectivity of 'history', myths are inescapable and they are functional, creating ideological structural patterns from the past. In the context of Ireland, particularly the myths of the Gaelic nation and the myths constructed around the events of Ireland's struggle for independence have been instrumental in shaping both views on Irish national identity and historical consciousness, even if these views have come under stress as the dominance of Irish nationalism is fading.[6]

Maurice Halbwachs's seminal work *On Collective Memory* (1925) represents one of the first sustained attempts of integrating individual memory and the notion of a "collective" or "social" memory within a theoretical framework. According to Halbwachs, on the one hand, the individual's memories and images of the past are fragmented and ephemeral and thus need to be validated and complemented by the community. On the other hand, the community is centrally determined by the shared memories and the constructions of the past circulating within the community, the collective invocation of the past constituting and strengthening communal identity (cf. Johnson 2003, 3f.; McBride 2011, 6f.) – individual memory is always socially framed (cf. Winter and Sivan 1999, 24). More recent theorists have extended and complicated these basic assumptions, stressing the discursive role of memory in the articulation of identity politics. They prefer the notion of "social" memory over the more neutral and organic "collective" memory and they have introduced further categories of memory, distinguishing between official and vernacular, public and private, elite and popular memory (cf. ibid.; McBride 2011, 11). Jay Winter's concept of 'historical remembrance' represents such a diversification. Appropriating Halbwachs's ideas and processing the memorial practices related to the Great War, Winter's concept emphasises the overlapping of individual and collective memory; historical remembrance is "a way of interpreting the past which draws on both history and memory, and documented narratives about the past and on the statements of those who lived through them" (Winter 2011, 426). Since the topic of Ireland's Great War represents a harshly disputed and long-concealed episode in Irish historical consciousness, such distinctions that diversify the notion of social memory and stress the flexibility of constructions of the past are of great relevance for my project.

The theoretical notions outlined, emphasising aspects of constructedness, flexibility, 'othering' and permanent conflict, belong to postmodernist discourses. The fundamentally unstable sense of identity and history they postulate is at the

---

6   Speaking at the *Theatre of Memory* Symposium on 16 January 2014, President Michael D. Higgins argued that modern Ireland needs "new myths that not only carry the burden of history but fly from it, making something new" (quoted in Humphreys 2014).

heart of a related, frequently disputed, postmodernist discourse – revisionism. Revisionism, in this project its specific Irish version, is a school of thought that seeks to expose and challenge the synthetic, constructed and distorting nature of what has been identified as the (Lyotardian) 'grand narratives' of the nation, in this case the assumption of a single and authoritative version of Irishness. In a fairly polemical essay, Terry Eagleton summarises the principles and attitudes upon which revisionist critics operate, attesting a "nervousness of grand narratives, [a] preference for pragmatic explanations rather than big ideas, [...] [an] emphasis on regionality, complexity, ambiguity, on plurality rather than mono-causality, on heterogeneity and discontinuity, on the role of sheer happenstance in historical affairs" (Eagleton 2000, 1156).[7] Along these lines, revisionism attempts to pluralise and dislocate collective memory.

In the context of Irish history and historiography and even in Irish literature, such attitudes have gained considerable currency since the 1970s. Irish revisionism, Edna Longley explains, again noting the contested nature of the subject, "is a shorthand and quasi-abusive term for historical studies held to be at odds with the founding ideology of the Irish Free State" (Longley 1994, 10), challenging historically dominant nationalist assumptions of Ireland as home to a homogenous and unproblematic Irish people (cf. Longley 1994, 29).[8] The national identity constructed after 1922 indeed was characterised by the desire of conserving the Irish nationalist anti-colonial spirit of the revolutionary generation of 1916, and, as Declan Kiberd remarks, revisionist critics and writers have complained against this "wish to make time stand still, to freeze everything in the state it was just at the moment of independence", pointing out how apparently the native elites had inherited through independence "not a dynamic society so much as a postcolonial museum [...], the sheer effort of removing the occupier having proven so great that [...] there was little left for reimagining the national condition" (Kiberd 1997, 26). Revisionist critics work against this perceived paralysis and unbalanced monotony of identity, memory and history

---

7 Eagleton particularly criticises the scepticism of Irish revisionism towards aspects of class, disapproving of revisionism's "language of difference and identity [that] is abstracted from the material context" (Eagleton 2000, 1157).

8 I am aware of the varying definitions of Irish revisionism and of the much-contested history of this approach, including the backlash of 'post-revisionism' that Diarmaid Ferriter describes as embodied by "a new generation [which,] with the benefit of distance and modernised curricula[,] generally chose to remember what actually happened as opposed to what revisionists thought could have happened, or believed should have happened" (Ferriter 2005, 747).

by re-assessing and revising the established narratives, emphasising the existence of identities and narratives aside of and beyond the nationalist tradition, which also includes a shift from narratives celebrating national heroes to a focus on the victims of history (cf. Wehrmann 2003, 214). Ireland's Great War experience very much represents such a previously concealed episode, a narrative largely relegated to the side streams of 'history'.

Revisionist efforts can be seen as related to a growing sentiment of the nationalist phase of Irish history coming to an end in the late twentieth-century. A related discourse in this context is the more radical notion of a 'post-nationalist' phase, which is connected to the transformative effects of globalisation and immigration also observable in Ireland, introducing new identities to the array of existing ones, thereby destabilising the hold of traditionally established nationalist concepts. National identity within such contexts increasingly becomes a question of negotiation and choice. Post-nationalism, Terry Phillips summarises, "opens up greater prospects for the articulation of the complex transcultural relations between erstwhile coloniser and colonised, relations which are of particular significance of the anomalous condition of Ireland" (Phillips 2007, 71). A conceptual precursor to the conflation and eventual dissolution of national identities that post-nationalism suggests is represented in ideas of internationalism.[9] These ideas are underpinned by the thought of national identity and nationalism as simultaneously local and supralocal, the nation being "premised on the existence of other analogous national units" (cf. Malkki 1994, 61f.). Internationalism represents an attempt at a moral challenge to nationalism and jingoism; yet, unlike post-nationalism, it does not mean a renunciation of the nation. As the sociologist Marcel Mauss argued in 1920, internationalism "does not deny the nation. It situates it. Internation is the opposite of a-nation. Consequently, it is also opposite of nationalism, which isolates the nation" (quoted in Malkki 1994, 55). Taking the form of something comparable to an 'imagined community' of nations, internationalism includes a transculturally shared "mobile set of representations and practices that has globally translatable currency and that is supralocal in its significance" (Malkki 1994, 61). Significantly, many of the concerns of

---

9   There is also a gradation of the concept referred to as "internationality". As Jonathan Rée argues, "[b]y internationality I do not mean what is usually meant by internationalism: a willingness to overlook national interest in favour of the welfare of humanity as a whole" – instead, internationality is "a style of thought and global social organization which tries to generate a plurality of nations, in order that, for any piece of land, and for any human being, there should be a definite answer to the question 'which nation is responsible?'" (Rée 1992, 10).

internationalism have their roots in the experience of war (cf. Malkki 1994, 56), as visible, for example, in supranational laws and institutions such as the Geneva Conventions or the League of Nations, created in response originally to the Battle of Solferino (1859) and, respectively, to the Great War. Internationalist sentiments also frequently occur in literary representations of the Great War, depicting soldiers from opposing nations as united in their experience of the horrors of war, their shared suffering surpassing the petty question of national affiliation – the national and ideological significance inscribed in the bodies of soldiers is overpowered by universal humanity or also by class affiliations shared across the national divide. This sentiment is also taken up by many Irish war works – considering the already complicated identity configurations of the situation in Ireland, this internationalist angle adds an intriguing facet.

II.1.3 War, the Body, Gender, Disability

In the decades leading up to the Great War, national identity increasingly was seen as a psychological phenomenon, involving emotions, instincts as well as individual and group consciousness. Similarly, the expression of national patriotism was no longer considered an expression of the *patrie* but it was increasingly understood as a natural affective disposition to be found in every member of the nation (cf. Sluga 2004, 240) – along these lines, the nation and national identity were envisioned as bodily practices. This complies with the view of the body proclaimed by theorists such as Foucault, Laqueur, Sennett and others, who address the dualism of the body, on the one hand, as a physical manifestation and reality and, on the other hand, as a semantic or semiotic phenomenon – the body as a vehicle of meaning. The body is seen as constructed and shaped by the intersection of a series of essentially disciplinary discursive practices (cf. Hall 1996, 11); it is a social fact, inextricably connected to culture, perception, language, knowledge and social interaction (cf. Dederich 2007, 58). This inscription of the body is understood as inescapable and integral to the embedding of the subject within social structures and hierarchies – as Gabriele Klein summarises, "der Körper ist Opfer von Inszenierungsstrategien, er verfügt nicht über Eigeninitiative, er wird eingesetzt" (Klein 2005, 40). In this manner, the subject becomes "theatrical", its body becoming a canvas or a stage used to represent and perform understandings of the self and of social status, as well as specific ideas and world views. The concept of 'performativity' radicalises these thoughts, suggesting that identities and the body only come into existence as phenomena through performances, also acknowledging performativity's potential of resistance against normative forces.

In this context, war and soldiership represent a performative arena in which bodies are intricately disciplined and charged with symbolic meaning and concepts of military and state identity, finding expression most vividly in military rituals and hierarchy: the wearing of uniforms, the intricate forms of military communication, of command and obedience, the unifying effects of parading, marching, training and fighting – all in the service and protection of the nation. A telling practice of the processes of national identification and projection men and their bodies are subjected to in the military can be found, for example, in the common use of the acronym 'G. I.' – 'government issue' – for American soldiers that became popular during World War II. The phrase, which was originally used to label all kinds of property of the US forces, clearly conveys how soldiers embody the state and it also represents a reification of soldiers as expendable objects in the military campaigns to advance or defend the nation, the cultural configuration for which they stand and have been recruited.

An elucidating attempt to theorise the complex phenomenon of the military, war, its structures and its implications for identities and bodies, is Elaine Scarry's 1985 study *The Body in Pain*. Scarry notes how upon entering the army, the soldier enters a disciplining and unifying corporeal and ideological regime, being

> inextricably bound up with the men and materials of his labor: he will learn to perceive himself as he will be perceived by others, as indistinguishable from the men of his unit, regiment, division, and above all, national group [...] as he is also inextricably bound up with the qualities and conditions [...] of the ground over which he walks or runs or crawls and with which he craves and courts identification.
>
> (Scarry 1985, 83)

War aggravates these conditions. Scarry also stresses the transitions that going to war entails for the subject, "from the condition of multiplicity to the condition of the binary" (Scarry 1985, 87f.), subjects discarding pre-war individuality by entering the military dualism of friend or foe, to "the transition, at the moment of ending the war, from the condition of the binary to the condition of the unitary" (ibid.), soldiers returning to a post-war society that has been analogously shaped by war into a more homogeneous entity. However, as will become obvious in this project, these general patterns do not entirely fit the altogether fairly anomalous Irish experience of the Great War, as this war and its legacy were centrally shaped by contradictory and persistently conflicted Irish contexts. Additionally, Scarry systematises wars as "contests", knowingly confirming the connotation of the term "contest" as "game", emphasising the notion of war as dynamic and unpredictable. Wars, according to Scarry, are contests of bodies, representing rival cultural constructs, aiming for the outperforming or, more precisely, the "out-injuring" of the other (cf. Scarry 1985, 84ff.), even if modern wars seem to be characterised by increasing distance between combatants. Furthermore, wars can also be seen as contests that destabilise and re-define reality. Scarry looks at war as a

> huge structure for the de-realization of cultural constructs and, simultaneously, for their eventual reconstitution. The purpose of war is to designate an outcome which of the two competing cultural constructs will by both sides be allowed to become real, which of the two will (after the war) hold sway in the shared space where the two collided [...]. [T] he declaration of war is the declaration that "reality" is now officially "up for grabs" [...].
>
> (Scarry 1985, 137)

The body and identity politics of war, just as much as those of the related fields of "the nation" and nationalism, are also inextricably connected to aspects of gender. As Anne McClintock suggests, "[a]ll nationalisms are gendered, all are invented and all are dangerous [...] in the sense that they represent relations to political power and to the technologies of violence. Nationalism becomes in this way radically constitutive of people's identities, through social contests that are frequently violent and always gendered" (McClintock 1996, 260) – and these formative social contests frequently operate on bipolar confrontations, pure vs. impure, normal vs. abnormal, healthy vs. degenerate, manly vs. emasculated (cf. Pierson 2000, 43). Ideas of 'the citizen', 'the soldier' or, respectively, 'the Irishman' and 'the Irishwoman', are seen to include specific ideals and discourses of masculinity and femininity, by the way, an aspect rather overlooked in the theories of Anderson, Gellner and others (cf. McClintock 1996, 259; Pierson 2000, 41). Nationalism has been prolific in defining male roles and new formulations of masculinity which are associated with strength, agency and aggression, while women were usually relegated to the passivity of the domestic realm of the family and the home. Women may frequently appear in the iconography and symbolism of the nation (Pearson 2000, 41), yet, the keynote of myths of nation-building has generally been one of male heroism and sacrifice (cf. Horne 2004, 27), which, for example, is also true in the case of Ireland's nationalist iconography – the sacrificial mother figure of Cathleen Ni Houlihan – and nation-building myths – the martyrdom of the rebels of the 1916 Easter Rising. Also, the positive attributes of national masculine ideals have been traditionally pitted against constructions of internal and external enemies frequently imagined as feminised or defined by a diseased aberrant masculinity (cf. Horne 2004, 29).

The military traditionally represents an arena of masculine activity and authority. Particularly during war, official nationalist discourses propagate the image of the resilient, aggressive and robustly masculine soldier. Nirmala Erevelles points out how this can also be seen as an expression of an uneasiness about

31

masculinity, the military existing "in persistent terror of being emasculated", fearing that an "'effeminate masculinity' might undermine loyalty and defense of the nation-state" (Erevelles 2011, 123). Military service has also been strongly associated with an initiation of young men both into manhood and nationhood, the latter particularly in the context of general conscription (cf. Horne 2004, 30f.). John Tosh recounts, for example, how during the French Revolution "the right to bear arms signified not merely a state commitment to the *levée en masse*, but a new and highly public constituent of universal masculinity" (Tosh 2004, 48). This notion was also evident at the outbreak of the Great War. Informed by belligerent social and cultural discourses and escaping peacetime *ennui*, the "generation of 1914"[10] rushed to arms for a variety of reasons and motivations, yet, as George Mosse suggests, "the quest for masculinity cut across them all" (Mosse 1985, 115). The Great War was commonly taken as an invitation to manliness, a test of courage, maturity, leadership and prowess. It became a reference point of manhood for later generations who did not participate in it (cf. Meyer 2009, 1) – in the words of George Orwell, "[y]ou felt yourself a little less than a man because you had missed it" (quoted in Mosse 1985, 114).

Yet, eventually, the Great War also proved paradoxical concerning established notions of wartime masculinity and femininity. On the one hand, the unprecedented scale and the technologically advanced intensity of warfare provoked a crisis of the ideology of heroism. Death in war increasingly appeared as random and individual agency as futile and irrelevant (cf. Tylee 2004, 304) – as Samuel Hynes observes, "[o]nce the soldier was seen as victim, the idea of the hero became unimaginable" (Hynes 1990, 215). The Great War dehumanised soldiers and created identities incompatible to pre-war configurations, alienating men from the societies for which they went to war, consolidating their affiliation with the homosocial sphere of the trenches and myths of wartime camaraderie. On the other hand, the Great War effected a transformation of concepts of femininity, the absence of men at home destabilising the patriarchal hold, increasing female independence and agency, including female sexuality.[11] The first total and fully industrialised war required the complete involvement of the social fabric into the war effort, making necessary the large-scale admission of women into

---

10 It should be added here that the notion of the "generation of 1914" or, in an English context, the "lost generation", very much reflects the attitudes and war experiences of articulate and educated middle-class soldiers, frequently serving as officers. The representativeness of their views has been questioned in more recent research. See chapter II. 3.

11 Some contemporary observers noted how women "reacted to the war experience with a powerful increase in libido" (Gilbert 1983, 436).

professional life, particularly into manufacturing, and, to a smaller degree, also into the military environment, women serving in the war as nurses, ambulance drivers, doctors or messengers. This created a widely felt sense of female empowerment, even a liberation of long-repressed female discontent (cf. Gilbert 1983, 433), yet, the extension of concepts of femininity by the war – which was also frequently renounced as a masculinisation in wartime media – could not be upheld beyond the end of the war, the post-war phase being characterised by a return to pre-war conservatism (cf. Grayzel 2003, 113ff.).

A final aspect to be added is the physical transformation of bodies and thereby of identities that war entails, specifically the experience and perception of deformation and disability – conditions magnified particularly by the Great War, which produced an entire generation of physically and mentally traumatised men (cf. Bourke 1996, 31). As a corporeal experience, military service, on the one hand, may condition and regularise soldiers' bodies and alter the way they are perceived by others through physical exercise, training and marching. On the other hand, the wounds, scars, disfigurements and amputations as well as traumata and psychological damage suffered in war mean a drastic alteration of perspectives – for the affected soldier there is no longer a pre-war body on which to project images of a peaceful pre-war identity, instead the damaged or disabled body becomes a permanent reminder of the losses suffered (cf. Taithe and Thornton 1998, 8), both in the eyes of the affected and the public. The war disabled may be frequently regarded by the public with empathy and gratitude for their sacrifice in the post-war period,[12] still, they cannot escape the 'contamination' of their identities by their condition. Theorists of disability have observed how disabled people are seen as representing a permanently diminished state of being human (cf. Decker 2014, 159). Tobin Siebers even suggests that the feelings of sympathy and grief directed at the disabled "expose the idea that they are dead – even though they may insist that they are not dead yet" (Siebers 2009, 161).

Disability and deformation are also problematic considering the dimension of gender. Masculinity, Raewyn Connell argues, "is almost always thought to proceed from men's bodies" (Connell 1995, 45) and the "constitution of masculinity through bodily performance means that gender is vulnerable when the performance cannot be sustained – for instance as a result of physical disability" (Connell 1995, 54). The intact male body is the central prerequisite for enacting

---

12 This of course also depends on the popularity and the success of the war – for example, disabled veterans in Ireland after the Great War fell on particularly hard times. See chapter III. 2 on O'Casey's *The Silver Tassie*.

'true' masculinity, a concept that values strength, potency and control and denies weakness, dependence and vulnerability – the very attributes conventionally assigned to the disabled as well as to women. Masculinity as an ideological and psychological process relies on the absolute separation from and superiority to the otherness embodied by the disabled (cf. Shakespeare 1999, 58) – consequently, the response of disabled men to the emasculating, disempowering effect of their condition frequently is fraught with difficulty, particularly when the narrative of the war they fought in is rendered irrelevant for the society they live in – as is the case considering Ireland and the Great War.

From these considerations and developments, the image of war as a powerful transformative force emerges, establishing, processing, reforming and deconstructing identities in manifold ways. In the following chapter, I will outline the specific historical conditions of Ireland's Great War – a history characterised by a complex and contradictory interplay of identities and affiliations and in which all of the aforementioned processes can be seen at work.

II.2 Historical Context

> Then came the Great War. Every institution, almost, in the world was strained. Great Empires have been overturned. The whole map of Europe has been changed. The position of countries has been violently altered. The modes of thought of men, the whole outlook on affairs, the grouping of parties, all have encountered violent and tremendous changes in the deluge of the world. But as the deluge subsides and the waters fall short we see the dreary steeples of Fermanagh and Tyrone emerging once again. The integrity of their quarrel is one of the few institutions that has been unaltered in the cataclysm which has swept the world.
>
> (Winston Churchill, quoted in Larkin 2014, 211)

This 1918 statement by Winston Churchill is exemplary of a widely held external view of the condition of Ireland after the First World War, a view that, Hilary Larkin notes, is dominated by a sense of "the dreary parochial 'sameness' of the Irish Question" (Larkin 2014, 211). Millions die, empires fall, borders are redrawn, economies crash, landscapes and cities are devastated, a generation of soldiers returns, often traumatised, crippled or disfigured – and Ireland, having voluntarily sent about 200,000 men to the battlefields, 35,000 of which were killed (cf. Orr 2008, 76), remains the same? An island forever occupied with domestic quarrels that appear to be insular, petty, even ridiculous, in the face of the unprecedented magnitude of bloodshed, destruction and political upheaval of the Great War? Churchill's observation, evoking a sense of puzzled disillusionment, is certainly comprehensible, yet, it is, as Larkin shows convincingly, distorted by a fairly reductive and one-sided understanding of the historical situation (ibid.) – this is a shortcoming, as will be shown in the course of this work, which was prevalent in the views on Ireland and the Great War for much of the twentieth century.

What Churchill and others ignored in their (re-)constructions of Ireland's Great War experience and its aftermath is the multitude of interdependencies, both stimulating and repellent, between Irish domestic concerns and English, or, rather, European politics of war – something that might be labelled, in accordance with Hilary Larkin, the "national story" and the "international story", two strands of history which are highly interconnected (ibid.). Ireland's Great War experience is intricately tied to the complex divisions that had been running through Irish society for centuries and have fundamentally determined discourses of Irish identity. As Adrian Gregory and Senia Paseta note, "Ireland was never a simple dichotomy and the war played on a wide range of competing ideologies and agencies" (Gregory and Paseta 2002, 4) – the war and its aftermath really became a battleground for rivalling ideas of Ireland and concepts of Irishness. In various ways the war represented an opportunity to demonstrate different degrees of nationalist hostility and unionist loyalty to Ireland's position in the British Empire, the 'Irish Question'. The Great War indeed came to provide the decisive context for the achievement of Irish independence, as it "ultimately cemented the notion of 'two Irelands'. [...] It is impossible to ignore this ultimate polarisation, nascent in 1914, formalised in 1920" (ibid.). The war, in the words of Terence Denman, "prepared the way for the convulsions of 1916 to 1922" (Denman 1992, 16), that is, the Easter Rising, the War of Independence and the Irish Civil War – events that would soon dominate both Irish historiography and political consciousness, marginalising the monumental European conflict in which these happenings were embedded. The Great War, John Horne summarises, would "define and dramatize four varieties of statehood in Ireland: unionist, Ulster unionist, nationalist and republican" (Horne 2008a, 10), it would mark "the definitive failure of unionism on the island as a whole, and thus of that historic attempt to include Ireland in a British nation that had bedevilled Anglo-Irish relations since 1800" (ibid).

In the following, I will provide an overview of Ireland right before the outbreak of the Great War, during the conflict and in its aftermath, outlining the historical and social context in which the formation, transformation and decline of various forms of Irish identities occurred. The section will conclude with a brief look at the role of the Great War in independent Ireland with special emphasis on official and unofficial efforts of commemoration up to the present day and the politics of identity underlying those efforts.

Ireland before the Great War

The years leading up to the outbreak of the Great War in the summer of 1914 are characterised by a steady increase of political tension in Ireland. Diarmaid Ferriter notes how "it seemed like a giant vacuum existed in Ireland, into which a variety of organisations and movements were being sucked" (Ferriter 2005, 110). The crucial issue at the time was the question of Home Rule, Irish self-government within the British Empire, and by May 1914, after years of difficult negotiations, rearrangements and postponements, it seemed like a new era of Irish independence was about to begin. The third Home Rule bill, which had already passed parliament and then only required royal assent to become law, would have given Ireland its own legislature with an Irish government taking care of most domestic affairs – a solution that actually would have been accept-able for a majority of the Catholic Irish (cf. Denman 1992, 19).

Yet, by this time, the political struggle in Ireland between nationalists, who supported Home Rule, and unionists, who rejected it and insisted on Britain's complete authority over Ireland, was about to erupt into a violent confrontation. In July 1914, an alarmed King George V. observed how the "cry of civil war [was] on the lips of the most responsible and sober-minded of my people" (quoted in Pennell 2008, 38). Diarmaid Ferriter traces this culmination of domestic hostilities and the distinct military sharpness of the situation both to the growing cult of militarism that was virulent throughout Europe at the time and, more specifi-cally, to Ulster unionism, which had given the lead in politicising and militarising the masses over the question of Home Rule (cf. Ferriter 2005, 113f.). Unionists abhorred the consequences of Home Rule, perceiving it as a fundamental threat to unionist identity. Home Rule to them was 'Rome Rule' – an independent Dub-lin government was envisioned as an oppressive Catholic regime. Consequently, fears of religious discrimination against the Protestant minority were at the heart of much unionist propaganda.[13] The three years before the outbreak of the Great War subsequently saw a relentless political campaign that would stress the idea of Protestant communal unity and the proud heritage of a shared Protestant past, which centrally included the celebration of iconic Protestant military accom-plishments such as the Battle of the Boyne of 1690.[14] The radical nature of this

---

13 In this context, Diarmaid Ferriter particularly mentions unionist concerns about the possible introduction of the *Ne Temere* papal decree, which demanded that children of mixed marriages be brought up as Catholics (cf. Ferriter 2005, 120; Denman 1992, 19).

14 See also chapter III.3.1 on Frank McGuinness's *Observe the Sons of Ulster Marching Towards the Somme* for a more detailed discussion of the role of war in unionist poli-tical consciousness and identity.

phase, leaving "no stone unturned, no pole unadorned and no tree unclimbed" (Ferriter 2005, 120) in the fight against Home Rule, undermined any potential for moderation and compromise in Irish politics and fuelled the radicalisation and militarisation of the nationalist side. In September 1912, almost half a million Ulstermen and Ulsterwomen signed the Ulster Solemn League and Covenant, promising to oppose and prevent the introduction of Home Rule by all means possible. In January 1913, the Ulster Volunteer Force (UVF) was founded under the leadership of Edward Carson, head of the Ulster Unionist Party. The UVF quickly grew to be a fully equipped private army, 100,000 men strong by early 1914, organised on a professional military basis with an experienced officer corps and armed with 40,000 rifles and ammunition largely purchased in Germany and smuggled to Ireland – at this point a far more impressive striking force than the British army in Ireland (cf. Fitzpatrick 1995, 1027).

The large-scale mobilisation and militarisation of unionism did not remain unmatched by Irish nationalism for long. In November 1913, members of various nationalist organisations, including the Gaelic League, Sinn Féin and the Irish Republican Brotherhood, united to form the Irish Volunteers. By early summer 1914, the group was largely under the control of John Redmond, leader of the Irish Parliamentary Party. The Irish Volunteers were 150,000 to 180,000 men strong – however, they were not as well-equipped or well-trained as the rival unionist army (cf. Denman 1992, 20) and encountered greater obstacles than the UVF in their attempts to obtain weapons and ammunition from the Continent.

It was such an attempt of gun smuggling and a tragic incident connected to it that would eclipse the news of the outbreak of the Great War in Ireland (cf. Pennell 2008, 38). On 24 July 1914, the Irish Volunteers managed to land 900 rifles and 29,000 rounds of ammunition from Germany in Howth – a small coup compared to the cunning delivery of 25,000 rifles and three million rounds of ammunition to the UVF at Bangor and Larne three months earlier. In the aftermath of the Howth operation, British soldiers opened fire on a crowd of nationalist civilians suspected of gun running on Bachelor's Walk, Dublin, killing four and wounding up to 50. The killings caused public indignation throughout Ireland and the day of the funeral of the victims, 29 July 1914, became a day of national mourning, the funeral procession being watched by 200,000 people (cf. ibid.). The anger at the tragedy on Bachelor's Walk, the frustration within the nationalist community and the absolute willingness to fight for their interests and confront their unionist opponents was officially voiced by Redmond in the House of Commons: "Let the House clearly understand that four-fifths of the Irish people will not submit any longer to be bullied, or punished, or shot, for conduct which is permitted to go scot-free in the open light of day in every country in Ulster by other sections of their fellow countrymen" (quoted in Pennell 2008, 38). On the same day as the Bachelor's Walk shootings, the British Prime Minister, Henry Asquith, informed the Commons of the Austrian ultimatum to Serbia (cf. Denman 1992, 20) – still, the outbreak of a civil war in a heavily militarised and polarised Ireland seemed to be more imminent than a conflict on the Continent.

Reactions to the Outbreak of the Great War

The Irish response that followed the outbreak of the Great War is a fairly paradoxical one. The beginning of the conflict on the Continent actually defused the highly critical situation in Ireland – the war was "greeted with a short sense of relief" (Pennell 2008, 39). The outbreak of the Great War also very quickly resulted in an unfolding of new opportunities for both nationalists and unionists to achieve their goals and reinforce their definitions of Irish and Ulster identities. By the contribution of both sides to the British war effort, existing aggressions were diverted, thereby also reformulating the military purpose of the Ulster Volunteer Force and the Irish Volunteers. It is actually quite astonishing how swiftly both groups managed to integrate the participation in the war into their political and military agendas. John Horne remarks, all of "[t]his was entirely compatible with the belief that the war embodied the values for which they stood. In both cases politics were underpinned by a 'self-mobilisation' that perhaps entitles one to talk of unionist and nationalist 'war cultures'" (Horne 2008a, 8). Both Redmond and Carson promised the support of their organisations for the British cause and encouraged volunteering among their groups – both combined their call for enlistment with political demands, jockeyed for position and attempted to extract every ounce of political advantage from the situation (cf. Pennell 2008, 45). Home Rule, the original matter of dispute of the two organisations, was granted at this point but its implementation was postponed until the end of the war.

For Carson and his unionists, the Great War offered an opportunity to highlight their allegiance to the British Empire, demonstrating their psychological integration into a fervent British patriotism (cf. Hennessey 1998, 123f.), despite the idleness and the lack of interest that the British government had displayed for their concerns in the years leading up to the conflict. Unionist opinion quickly and fully embraced the war effort, emphasising the common notion of imperial unity and of the shared sacrifice for the British Empire. For example, the *Belfast Evening Telegraph* gloried in the prospect that

> [t]he Empire is to be cemented anew by the hardest and longest lasting of cement, the blood of her sons spilt in the battlefield. From every corner of the world comes the

answer to the call, the rallying to the flag. War is a disastrous, a horrible thing; but it has its finer side, and the flame of the sacrifice that has swept the Empire end to end is something we shall remember to the end of our lives.

(*Belfast Evening Telegraph*, 13 August 1914, quoted in Hennessey 1998, 83)

Ulster's identification as an integral part of the Empire is crucial here, stressing its position in the imperial framework and its duty to play its part along with the other British "corners of the world", like Australia, South Africa or Canada. Even more important is the subtext of such attitudes as the one presented in the *Belfast Evening Telegraph*: In the eyes of the unionists, the ultimate sacrifice of Ulster's sons for the sake of Britain and the British Empire would make their call for the maintenance of the imperial status quo impossible to be ignored – the introduction of Home Rule in Ireland after such a costly demonstration of loyalty and patriotism would be an outrageous sacrilege.

It should be noted, however, that this ideology of sacrifice was not only aligned with the specific political objectives of unionism. It also belongs to a wider European context of glorified militarism, a widespread mentality at the time, based on the conviction that war would finally effect a much needed spiritual regeneration, rectifying a dangerous condition of decadence and dullness into which European societies had degenerated.[15] The sentiment expressed in a commentary by the Protestant Bishop[16] of Meath in the *Derry Standard* on 12 August 1914 is exemplary of this celebration of the cleansing effects of war:

War was a dark cloud, but it was a cloud with a silver lining, bringing out in glorious relief some of the noble points of the human character. The call for self-sacrifice was just what our nation wanted. It had been felt that as a nation we were rapidly drifting into a state of materialistic luxury and self-indulgence, which if unchecked, might be our undoing. What a wonderfully bracing effect the last fortnight had on every part of the Empire! – What unity there was in the face of the common enemy!

(*Derry Standard*, 12 August 1914, quoted in Hennessey 1998, 83)

Altogether, unionist support for the war, as it found public expression, followed the official lines of British war propaganda, completely subscribing to and reproducing what Thomas Hennessey calls "the British national myth, with its notions

---

15 See, for example, Mosse 1985, 116. See also the section on war and masculinity in chapter II. 1.

16 John Horne notes how "[c]hurchmen played a key role [in stirring up support for the war] as Presbyterian or Church of England clergy invoked British traditions of religious liberty while the Catholic clergy denounced the German oppression of Catholic Belgium and most (but not all) the bishops endorsed the nationalist crusade" (Horne 2008a, 8).

of freedom, liberty and fair play" (ibid.). This resulted in the image of the Great War as a British war of defence, motivated not by selfish interests but driven by a sense of honour and the duty to protect the weak and liberate the oppressed from Prussian militarism and aggression.

While the brazen support of the unionists for the war effort appears as a logical consequence of their allegiances, the decision of an overwhelming majority of nationalists to back Britain and take part in the war seems more surprising. This decision, however, was not only a strategic one, informed by the idea to gain Home Rule as a British reward for the Irish contribution to the war effort. It is also an expression, at least in the early stages of the conflict, of a genuine belief in the righteousness of the war against Germany. As in Britain, Germany was largely perceived as aggressive and tyrannical in Ireland; also, in Ireland's deeply Catholic society, Germany's Protestantism was resented, German bellicosity being perceived as an inevitable expression of godlessness. A spell of militant anti-German sentiment manifested itself also in Ireland, for example, in a series of attacks on German shops in Dublin during August 1914 – a violent eruption common across European towns and cities (cf. Pennell 2008, 41f.).

Redmond was certain that the war had been "undertaken in defence of the highest principles of religion and morality and right" (quoted in Denman 1992, 26). An important facet of the assumed righteousness of the war was the conviction that it was a war in defence of the rights and the freedom of small nations such as Belgium and Serbia. Particularly the German invasion of "gallant little Belgium", the reports of German atrocities against Belgian civilians, the destruction of the Catholic university library in Louvain, and the mass exodus of refugees, some also fleeing to Ireland, stirred Irish nationalists to support the war against Germany (cf. Horne 2008a, 7). The suffering of the Catholic "sister state" Belgium became a recurrent element in recruitment discourses. As John Horne summarises, the war was envisioned to be about "defending the same democratic values and self-determination that Home Rule was to bring to Ireland", ultimately "a democratic crusade" (ibid.), and a war to protect the Christian life of Europe from Prussian "Nietzschean" brutality (cf. Hennessey 1998, 95).

There was, however, a further facet to the Irish endorsement of the war, one of great significance for identity politics, both nationalist and unionist. Since the nineteenth century, the beginning of the age of mass armies, participation in war has had deeply political connotations and has been intricately connected to "the symbolic currency of nationhood" (Horne 2008a, 9f.): Military service and a shared experience of war constitute fundamental steps for the creation of national narratives and, thereby, national communities – a people's participation in war can be regarded as the expression of a claim of nationhood, including all the entailing rights, privileges and reforms (cf. ibid. and Larkin 2014, 213). In this sense, the Great War was understood by Redmond as a crucial rite of passage for Ireland, an opportunity to substantiate Ireland's assertion of nationhood before the eyes of the international community:

> No people can be said to have rightly proved their nationhood and their power to maintain it until they have demonstrated their military prowess; and though Irish blood has reddened the earth of every continent, never until now have we as a people set a national army in the field [...]. It is heroic deeds entering into their traditions that give life to nations – that is the recompense of those who die to perform them.
>
> (John Redmond, quoted in Denman 1992, 29)

> [I]t would be a disgrace for ever to our country, and a reproach to her manhood, and a denial of the lessons of history, if young Ireland confined her efforts to remain at home to defend the shores of Ireland from an unlikely invasion, and shrunk from the duty of proving on the field of battle that gallantry and courage which has distinguished our race through its history.
>
> (John Redmond, quoted in Denman 1992, 26)

The second quotation is taken from Redmond's famous Woodenbridge speech of 20 September 1914. In this speech, Redmond urged the Irish Volunteers to enlist, to "go on drilling and make yourself efficient for the Work, and then account yourselves as men, not only for Ireland itself, but wherever the firing line extends, in defence of right, of freedom, and religion in this war" (ibid.), wholly ignoring the reservations among the more radical circles of the nationalist movement. Apart from living up to Ireland's ambitions as a young nation and the moral obligation to fight for the rights of small nations, there is a further, less idealistic, nuance in Redmond's call to arms: Redmond also reckoned that a professionally trained and military fit Irish nationalist force would be of great importance in case the Home Rule settlement required a violent confrontation after the war (cf. Larkin 2014, 213).

Such considerations were of course not part of Redmond's official rhetoric throughout the war years. In fact, Redmond frequently pictured the Great War as a possible source of reconciliation of unionists and nationalists, amending the existing divisions of Irish society by means of a shared war experience, literally forging in blood a new collective national identity:

> [T]heir union in the field may lead to a union in their home; their blood may be the seal that will bring all Ireland together in one nation, and in liberties equal and common to all.
>
> (Redmond, quoted in McNulty 2010, 66)

For the first time in history, we have to-day a huge Irish army in the field. Its achievements have covered Ireland with glory before the world, and have thrilled our hearts with pride. North and South have vied with each other in springing to arms, and please God, the sacrifices they have made side by side on the field of battle will form the surest bond of a united Irish Nation in the future.

(Redmond pamphlet, reprinted in Johnson 2003, 30)

Diarmaid Ferriter notes that "Redmond was seen by many to be visionary because of his idea of inclusivity, of reconciling imperialism with nationalism" (Ferriter 2005, 125f.). Still, at the same time, Redmond undermined these unifying thoughts through his unbridled triumphalism about the granting of Home Rule (cf. ibid.), never leaving much doubt which Ireland was to emerge from the Great War – a state dominated by the nationalists with Redmond in an executive leadership role.

Of course, Redmond's attitudes and his energetic campaigning for recruitment did not appeal to all sections of the nationalist movement, the Irish Volunteers covering a wide spectrum from constitutional Redmondite "Home Rulers" to radical republicans who would rather fight the British than join their forces. The call for recruitment was also at odds with the previous position of Redmond's Home Rule party, having displayed a sceptical stance towards Irish enlistment in the British forces. As Stephen Gwynn, a nationalist MP and, later, an officer in the Great War, remarks about the years before 1914: "Enlistment had been discouraged, on the principle that from a military point of view Ireland was regarded as a conquered country" (quoted in Denman 1992, 30f.). Consequently, a split occurred in the Irish Volunteers in September 1914. About six per cent, between 8,000 and 11,000, of the more radical members broke away. Under the official leadership of Eoin MacNeill, Professor of Irish History and Early Irish Law at University College Dublin and a highly respected public figure, a new force was established, claiming the name Irish Volunteers, while the remaining part of the organisation led by Redmond was labelled "National Volunteers". The radical nationalist deserters may seem like a negligible splinter group for its size, yet, this group included many of the most energetic and vocal activists of the nationalist movement – from these circles, a revolutionary conspiracy began to take shape to which the whole concept of Home Rule was irrelevant, which clearly identified England and not Germany as Ireland's enemy, and which instantly turned to various forms of anti-war activities (cf. Pennell 2008, 45).

Going off to War

In the heated political climate in Ireland at the outset of the Great War, Britain did not dare to enforce conscription – still, thousands of new soldiers were needed. Accordingly, extensive campaigns for volunteering were organised, including, for example, large-scale postal campaigns, every Irishman between the age of 19 and 41 receiving a promotional recruitment letter, as well as recruitment tours featuring representative Irishmen from local Irish regiments who propagated enlistment (cf. Novick 2001, 20f.).[17] The number of Irish volunteers, particularly in the early stages of the war, is astonishing, considering the heated political situation. At the outbreak of the conflict, 58,000 Irish servicemen were mobilised, and by the end of the war, a total of 206,000 Irishmen had contributed to the British war effort (cf. Fitzpatrick 1995, 1017). Interestingly, the development of recruitment numbers in Ireland altogether followed the general patterns and fluctuations observed in Britain until the introduction of conscription in Britain in 1916 (cf. Fitzpatrick 1995, 1021); there was even a minor increase in Irish volunteering in the final months of the Great War, when it had long become obvious how mind-bogglingly brutal and costly the conflict really was and when Irish public opinion had already drastically turned against the war.

Recruitment in Ireland was crucially boosted by the pre-war development of nationalist and unionist militarism, supplying the British forces with both pre-trained Catholics and Protestants (cf. Fitzpatrick 1995, 1029). Recruitment strategies could also draw on the substantial military tradition of Irishmen serving in the British forces. In the 1830s, for example, Irish soldiers made up 40 per cent of the British army; in 1914, there were still 60,000 Irishmen serving in the regular British forces or in the reserves, stationed all across the British Empire. Furthermore, the strong officer tradition of the Anglo-Irish gentry showed in the fact that a considerable section of the leading ranks in the British army in 1914 came from this section of Irish society (cf. Orr 2008, 65).[18] Another resource for British recruitment propagandists was the military heritage of Irishmen who fought in other countries' armies in the sixteenth, seventeenth and eighteenth centuries, the "Wild Geese", who gained an almost mythical reputation for courage[19] and robustness (cf. ibid.).

---

17 The main protagonist of Shaw's *O'Flaherty V. C.* is such an Irish "war hero" made to advertise recruitment in Ireland. See chapter III.1.1.

18 For example, Lord Kitchener, one of the most prominent figures of the Great War, was born in Ballylongford, near Listowel in Co. Kerry (cf. Denman 1992, 21).

19 For example, Franz Stefan I., the Emperor of Austria, praised the qualities of the Irish in his army: "Je mehr Iren in österreichischen Diensten stehen, um so besser! So werden unsere Truppen immer gute Disziplin halten; ein irischer Feigling ist eine große Seltenheit, und wenn die Iren auch grundsätzlich eine Abneigung gegen etwas haben, tun sie es dennoch in ihrem Wunsche, Ruhm zu erwerben" (quoted in Orr 2008, 66).

Understandably, the appeal of Ireland's 'English' military legacy was a difficult one to convey to the nationalist Irish public – still, Redmond's Irish Party relied heavily upon it in its encouragement of recruiting instead of focusing on the mythology of the nationalist community (cf. Hennessey 1998, 99). The fundamental contradiction underlying the idea of Irishmen in the British army, and, simultaneously, the moral challenge inherent to this contradiction for Irish nationalists, becomes obvious in Stephen Gwynn's 1914 poem "The Irish Brigade 1914":

> From Fontenoy, from Lamden, the message runs again,
> Once more the fields of Flanders are strewn with Irish slain,
> And once again, oh! once again, the herald thrills to tell
> How gloriously an Irish charge avenged the brave who fell ...
>
> Must English fill the Rangers' ranks? Welsh pad the Munsters' line?
> Where stood the Dublin Fusiliers, Scots give the counter sign?
> Or when the Inniskilling faint, shall Sikhs the trench re-man?
> Pathan and Gurkha finish what the Irish Guards began? ...
> They fought for Louis, fought for James, for every despot's throne:
> Shall we not fight who may defend a freedom like our own? ...
>
> (Gwynn quoted in Hennessey 1998, 100)

The sentiment expressed here is indicative of a profound sense of doubt about the incongruous allegiances to be created for the war and the sacrifice to make, a thought that troubled even moderate Irish nationalists like Gwynn, who were convinced of the righteousness of the war, of the moral obligation to go out and "defend a freedom like our own", and of the war's purpose in the grand scheme of achieving Irish self-rule.

In this context, it is important to note that Irish and Ulster enlistment in the British forces did not mean a dissolution or, perhaps, a merging of political attitudes and identities within the framework of an apolitical military organisation. Both Redmond and Carson expected their movements to be incorporated as separate divisions of the new army recruited in Ireland (cf. Fitzpatrick 1995, 128). Nationalist army recruits, Redmond demanded, "should be kept together as a unit, officered as far as possible by Irishmen, composed, if possible, of country battalions, to form, in fact an Irish Brigade [...] so that Ireland may gain credit for their deeds, and feel, like other communities of the Empire, that she too has contributed to an army bearing her name in this historic struggle" (quoted in Denman 1992, 27). This demand was granted by the War Office in order to safeguard Irish recruitment – as Herbert Asquith announced in Dublin on 26 September 1914: "I should like to see, and we all want to see, an Irish Brigade"; Irishmen, Asquith declared, should not fear that by joining up "they will lose their identity and become absorbed in some invertebrate mass, or [...] be artificially distributed into units which have no national cohesion or character" (quoted in Denman 1992, 27f.). The War Office demonstrated even greater willingness to correspond to unionist demands and fully supported their efforts of recruitment, which becomes obvious, for example, in authorising the UVF to run its own recruitment offices and, in effect, to set up a division of their own (cf. ibid.).

Three divisions were raised in Ireland during the Great War: The 10th Division was the first to be formed right at the outset of war, followed by the 36th (Ulster) Division, which was created mostly in the north and became a stronghold of the Ulster Volunteer Force. Finally, the 16th (Irish) Division was raised, sponsored by the leadership of the Irish Parliamentary Party, becoming a home for the men of Redmond's National Volunteers. In this way the division of Ireland, the profound antagonism of social, religious and colonial attitudes and identities was relocated into a new arena – as John Horne writes, "different kinds of volunteer[s] expressed the competing versions of nationality that came to a head in the conflict" (Horne 2008a, 10).

The 36th (Ulster) Division mirrored the make-up of Protestant Ulster, attracting many radically unionist working-class men "often possessing little aptitude for discipline" (Orr 2008, 67), who frequently came under the command of young graduates of the Queen's University Officer's Training Corps (ibid.). The degree of political and religious exclusivity of this division was remarkable, many of its members having been directly transferred from the UVF to the division. In February 1915, there were merely fourteen Catholic soldiers in the division and even they, allegedly, had been required to sign the Ulster Solemn League and Covenant (cf. Denman 1992, 27).

The 16th (Irish) Division was structurally more heterogeneous. While the ranks were 98 per cent Catholic, the officer corps was 85 per cent Protestant. The division included Dublin working-class recruits, among them many former dockers who had lost their jobs in the labour disputes of 1913. It also featured members of prominent Dublin commercial families, well-known representatives of Dublin academia, Protestant aristocrats from the Irish countryside, and, famously, a group of rugby players[20] known as the "Dublin Pals". The nationalist profile of the division was also raised by the service of Stephen Gwynn, John Redmond's younger brother Willie, and another nationalist MP, the journalist, poet and leading intellectual Tom Kettle (cf. Orr 2008, 67f.).

---

20 Cf. Stephen Walker's *Ireland's Call: Irish Sporting Heroes Who Fell in The Great War*. Dublin: Merrion Press, 2015.

Considering this diversity of social, political and religious backgrounds of recruits from Ireland, it is necessary to shed some light on the question of how and why decisions to join up were formed. Thomas Dooley suggests that, in Ireland as in other nations, already "the lure of war's glamour" was frequently strong enough to inspire men to enlist, the "sight of uniforms, the pomp of military life and an infectious militarism [touching] the popular imagination and [making] a definite appeal" (Dooley 1995, 128). In his study of Ireland's "logic of collective sacrifice" during the Great War, David Fitzpatrick stresses the powerful influence of group loyalties that encourages men to enlist, "persuading [them] to subordinate individual gratification to the collective interest" (Fitzpatrick 1995, 1029), and he points out how belonging to militias, fraternities or sports clubs[21] made men particularly susceptible to collective psychological pressure. The decision to enlist was centrally determined by the attitudes and behaviours of peers – kinsmen, comrades, neighbours, fellow-members of political organisations. It was this context of self- and group-mobilisation, particularly in the early phases of the Great War, which helped to construct the act of volunteering not as an irrational but as a decent and 'manly' thing to do (cf. Horne 2008a, 10). The influence of the family worked in both directions, both promoting enlistment, sons having to follow the examples of fathers or brothers or even having to live up to their family's military tradition, and preventing enlistment, keeping sons and fathers at home to ensure the economic survival of family-owned businesses and farms (cf. Fitzpatrick 1995, 1030).

Economic considerations, and this was also noted by the recruitment strategists of the War Office, indeed played as much of a role for (or against) the decision to enlist as political convictions, the feeling of having to act on a moral or religious responsibility, or the desire for adventure and military excitement. Enlistment appeared to many Irishmen as an opportunity for a more financially secure life. Indeed, many urban working-class and lower-class Irishmen did join up out of economic necessity, "the king's shilling being preferable to starvation and disease in the tenements of Dublin, whatever the risks" (Brown 1993, 226f.). Recruitment in the Irish countryside, however, turned out to be a more difficult task. Still very much an agricultural society, the family farm remaining the most dominant form in the organisation of Irish labour (cf. Fitzpatrick 1995, 1018), a substantial section of the Irish population simply was unavailable for war service – official and contemporary reports throughout the war lament the reluctance of

---

21 The notion of fighting as a team sport was a very common theme in recruitment and propaganda, particularly the connection of football and war. See also chapter III.1.2 on Sean O'Casey's *The Silver Tassie*.

Irish farmers and farm workers to join the forces. Recruitment, consequently, was most intense in the industrialised north-east, both among Catholics and Protestants (cf. Fitzpatrick 2008, 133).

Considering the extent of volunteering and the origins of volunteers, Ulster nearly matched the level of British recruitment, while the Catholic south clearly fell short of the British rate and also lagged behind the level of volunteering reached in other Dominions of the Empire. Australia, for example, with a population of a similar size as Ireland and also exempt from conscription, sent 330,000 men overseas and had 85,000 men on home duties (cf. Fitzpatrick 2008, 135) – twice as many as Ireland. An explanation for this gap between the Irish and the Australian readiness to serve in an imperial conflict might be found in the issue of national identity – the different colonial status and the different degree of national consciousness of the two regions. As Keith Jeffery suggests, by the outbreak of the Great War, Australia had existed as a federal state for thirteen years and the war became "the first time that young men from the island continent went to war, and died, as Australians" (Jeffery 2008, 271). Redmond, as mentioned above, frequently imagined a similar effect of national recognition, identification and unification by Ireland's contribution to the Great War – however, these hopes were grounded on a much less consolidated basis, not one of national independence but of a postponed Home Rule act which had led Ireland dangerously close to civil war. The Great War simply had begun too early for an Irish nation still too polarised. Despite these limitations, it is vital to recognise that the military involvement of Ireland in the Great War has remained unmatched in Irish history up to this day. There was not a parish in Ireland unaffected by the war, no matter which political, religious or social make-up (cf. Fitzpatrick 2008, 133), and the death of approximately 30,000 soldiers from Ireland in the Great War exceeded anything in contemporary Irish experience (cf. Horne 2008a, 12).

In the winter of 1914, all three divisions underwent training in barracks across Ireland. In 1915, the 16th (Irish) Division and the 36th (Ulster) Division were relocated to England for further training before moving to France later that year (cf. Orr 2008, 68). The departure of the troops from Ireland was not accompanied by indifferent or hostile Irish reactions to the soldiers as professed in later nationalist myths. Catriona Pennell mentions the common sight of cheering crowds on the roads of Dublin and cites a soldier named Charles Arnold, who left Dublin with his regiment on 13 August 1914: "What crowds there were to see us off! The Dublin people went mad, flags were flying, bands playing, in fact we got a right Royal [sic] send off (including a packet of fruit, cakes and cigarettes for each man)" (Pennell 2008, 39f.). Altogether, Irish cities saw heartfelt public gestures of farewell in those days. As mentioned before, the (non-unionist) Irish public in general was not overly enthusiastic about the outbreak of the war, there was more of a humane sense of a moral obligation to give soldiers an appropriate send-off, anticipating the tough times that awaited them (cf. ibid.).

The Home Front

The outbreak of the Great War and the departure of a large number of Irishmen obviously transformed life in Ireland in various respects. According to David Fitzpatrick, the most visible impact of the war on Irish families was an almost complete stoppage of emigration to America by 1915 – apart from the option to enlist in the British army, other employment opportunities, such as working in the war industries or taking up jobs vacated by war volunteers, had opened up to potential emigrants (cf. Fitzpatrick 2008, 136). Also, the increased demand for food from Britain led to a new prosperity of the rural economy of Ireland (cf. Horne 2008a, 9).

The war also affected the lives of Irish women. Many Irish women could enjoy a more comfortable standard of living based on the compensation payments they received on behalf of their husbands' service in the war. Others became involved in the war effort and were confronted with the realities of warfare themselves, working as nurses, occasionally even as doctors, in Irish, British and French hospitals (cf. Fitzpatrick 2008, 139). Furthermore, a considerable number of Irish women, across the spectrum of political, religious and class affiliations, took part in voluntary work supporting Irish soldiers as well as war refugees. For example, Catriona Pennell mentions a charity programme for Belgian refugees at the Palace Theatre in Cork, the house being "specially decorated for the occasion, prominently displayed being the Irish and Belgian flags entwined, and surmounted by the Union Jack" (Pennell 2008, 41), symbolising a notion of a shared fate and moral duty to defend the rights of small nations that also called out to women.

Apart from such philanthropic efforts, large numbers of Irish working-class women, just as working-class women in Germany, France or England, entered the war industries, taking over the jobs of men who had enlisted. For many Irish women, this was the first experience of the "mainstream of economic life", a domain previously completely dominated by men (cf. Fitzgerald 2008, 139). Vigorous propaganda campaigns were launched, many specifically aiming at Irish single women, urging Irish daughters to take some financial strain off their families by taking up jobs in British munition factories and textile plants (cf. Culleton 1997, 157f.). The many Irish women who did so and became 'munition girls' frequently had to face not only a life determined by an exhausting, dangerous and strictly policed work environment, but also the hostilities of British co-workers and supervisors, who often mistrusted and mistreated them for being Irish (cf. ibid.).[22] Furthermore, they became a target of radical nationalist propaganda at home, which condemned their recruitment for the war effort as much as the recruitment of Irishmen for the British army.

Irish women were also affected by the war in another way. In the early phase of the war, the phenomenon of 'khaki fever' – young women all across Britain appearing to be 'dangerously' and 'immodestly' attracted to men in military uniform (Woollacott 1994, 325) – was detected also in Ireland by some contemporary observers. The concern and unease about women's social and sexual behaviour in this time of crisis and diminished male authority at home shows in the establishment of the Irishwomen's League of Honour[23] in November 1914, an organisation dedicated to upholding "the standard of women's duty and honour during the time of war [...] and to combat some of the social and moral dangers emphasised by the war; to deepen amongst women and girls a sense of their responsibility for the honour of the nation, and by their influence to uplift manhood" (quoted in Pennell 2008, 41). In the eyes of radical nationalists, the thought of amorous encounters between Irish women and soldiers of the British forces naturally acquired a further dimension of depravity – such forms of fraternisation were not only judged as morally indecent but also as treacherous and even as 'racially' unhealthy. This mind-set is exemplified in a 1914 handbill by

---

22 In her essay on the role of Irish working-class women in the Great War, Claire Culleton cites the diary of Gabrielle West, who patrolled several British war factories as a member of the British Women's Police Service. West depicts the Irishwomen she encountered as "the roughest of the rough [...]. They steal like magpies, fight, get up scandalous tales about each other, strike, and do their best to paint things red" (Culleton 1997, 161). In one entry, West describes the aggressions between Irish and English women workers in a Hereford shell-filling factory in 1917: "There has been a lot of bad blood between them & the English. The Irish sang Sinn Féin songs & made offensive remarks about the Tommies. The English replied in kind. Each side waxed very wroth. The Irish wore orange & green, & the English Red white and blue" (Culleton 1997, 162).

23 Similar organisations can be found in Britain. As Angela Woollacott notes, "[a]nxiety about wartime loss of social control crystallised in the formation of the middle-class Women Patrols Committee and Women Police Service, both of which found their patriotic calling in policing public places for young working-class women going astray" (Woollacott 1994, 327).

49

Inghinidhe na hÈireann,[24] reproduced in the 2008 collection *Our War*, edited by John Horne, which warns young Irish women of the dangers of fraternisation:

> [R]emember you are walking with traitors […] you are walking with your country's enemies, and with men who are unfit to be companions of any girl, for it is well known that the English army is the most degraded and immoral army in Europe, chiefly recruited in the slums of English cities, among men of the lowest and most depraved characters. You endanger your purity and honour by associating with such men and you insult your Motherland. Hearken to the words of Father Kavanagh, the Irish Franciscan Patriot Priest, who pronounces it a heinous crime against Ireland, for Irishmen to join the forces of robber England. Do you think it is less a crime for Irish girls to honour these men with their company? Remember the history of your country. Remember the women of Limerick and the glorious patriot women of the great rebellion of '98, and let us, who are their descendants try to be worthy of them.
>
> (1914 handbill by Inghinidhe na hÈireann, reproduced in Horne 2008, 153)

Irish women who mingle with members of the British forces, we learn here, willingly expose themselves to the threat of English contamination, endangering the purity and besmearing the patriotic legacy of Irish womanhood, and, consequently, they need to be controlled. That the assumed female frenzy about the public sight of soldiers can be attributed as much to mere visual attraction and youthful emotionality as to a concealed feeling of frustration of young women about their disqualification from participating directly in the war effort, is an insight only gained in retrospection – it is an explanation for 'khaki fever' based on the notion that at the time, as Angela Woollacott argues convincingly, the closest most young women "could come to war activity was to hang about on the fringes of the male domain of war preparation" (Woollacott 1994, 331f.).

As the war progressed, however, the potentially attractive sight of processions of soldiers proudly marching off into battle was increasingly countered by the return of thousands of injured, disfigured and disabled soldiers, the convalescents in their distinctive 'hospital blues' becoming familiar figures on Irish streets (cf. Leonard 2008, 212). During the worst periods of the war, Dublin hospitals admitted up to 500 new casualties a day (cf. Novick 2001, 17). As the horrible human cost of the war was becoming more and more obvious by 1915, public support for the war in Ireland – as in most other countries involved in the war – gradually began to shrink. A heavy blow to the status of the war were the Irish

---

24 Inghinidhe na hÈireann ("Daughters of Ireland") was a radical nationalist women's organisation led by Maud Gonne until the group was absorbed into Cumann na mBan, the women's branch of the Irish Volunteers.

casualties sustained in the blundered campaign of Gallipoli, in which the 10th Division lost almost half of its 17,000 men within two months, among them the 'Dublin Pals', who were shattered on an exposed mountain ridge overlooking Suvla Bay. As one commentator notes, "the graveyards in this part of Turkey are filled with tombstones that read like entries from an Irish street directory" (Orr 2008, 70). Before withdrawing at the end of 1915, 140,000 allied soldiers had been killed, injured or gone missing in this operation. In the aftermath of the catastrophe of Gallipoli, the impression grew across large sections of the Irish public that Irish troops were intentionally selected for risky operations, and also that the sacrifice and heroism of Irish regiments as well as the uncommon loyalty of the nationalist community were not sufficiently appreciated by England (cf. Hennessey 1998, 108f.).[25] Worries about the possible introduction of conscription in Ireland, fearing that even more Irish lives were to be wasted by incompetent British leaders, intensified (cf. ibid.). Still, despite this increasing uneasiness and the continuous anti-war work of radical nationalist groups, the home front was largely intact until the rise of Sinn Féin in the wake of the Easter Rising of 1916. A majority in Ireland held on to the consent to the war effort. The staunch unionist commitment in the north remained unchanged.

Radical Nationalist Opposition to the War

In the situation of 1914, the radical nationalists who rejected the Irish involvement in the Great War were well aware of their isolated position and the limited appeal of their dissent. As Desmond Fitzgerald, an Irish Volunteer, Easter rebel, and later a member of the first government of the Irish Free State, remembers, it had "immediately become apparent" at the beginning of the war that Redmond's views "really represented the views of the majority of the Irish people" (quoted in Denman 1992, 32). Fitzgerald lamented how at the time "the Irish people had recognised themselves as part of England", the Irish public being largely satisfied with an interrupted Home Rule settlement. "There was no evidence to lead one to expect that the people could do more than shrug their shoulders and say they expected as much", and, Fitzgerald continues, "those of us who thought of Home Rule as something utterly inadequate were a very small minority, without influence; impotent" (quoted in Ferriter 2005, 138). This general detachment of the public from anti-war concerns showed, for example, in the Dublin anti-recruitment meetings of the nationalist pacifist Francis Sheehy-Skeffington which only earned him the

---

25 For example, the Irish regiments involved were not mentioned by name in the reports of the failed Gallipoli campaign (cf. Hennessey 1998, 109).

scorn of the public and ended with Sheehy-Skeffington being "arrested for his own protection" (ibid.). Patrick Pearse, one of the most vocal and influential nationalist figures of the period and a leading member of the Irish Volunteers, had to realise that parents had started to withdraw their sons from his school, St. Enda's College. As Pearse notes on 26 September 1914, "we have fewer boys than last year. My political opinions are looked upon as too extreme and dangerous and parents are nervous" (quoted in Pennell 2008, 45).

The rejection of the British forces in Ireland, and, naturally, the rejection of the notion of Irishmen serving in the British forces, had been an integral part of nationalist ideology, including the pre-war attitudes of Redmond's Irish Parliamentary Party. In this vein, Arthur Griffith, the leader of Sinn Féin, pointed out in an article for the party paper on 15 August 1914 that the "Irishman who fights under the Union Jack fights for the Act of Union – fights for the evil work […] and the perpetuation of the evil work of the man who plotted and the man who carried the Union" (quoted in Hennessey 1998, 93). And Eoin MacNeill, the head of the Irish Volunteers, stressed how this Great War really was a "[w]ar of Empire, a war for Empire" (ibid.), underlining his view that the origin of this war actually lies in the very existence of the British Empire, and that the threat of Prussian militarism pales against the actual damages suffered in Ireland through British militarism – "[i]f it is Ireland's duty to fight against militarism […] we need not go to France" (ibid.).

Unsurprisingly, the war became the central theme in radical nationalist propaganda. During the war, there were twelve radical nationalist newspapers with a national circulation (cf. Ferriter 2005, 137), exploiting the topic in all its facets to reinforce public aggression against the age-old oppressor England. Propagandistic efforts always both influence and reflect public opinion and, consequently, as Ben Novick notes in his extensive study of the subject, Irish radical nationalist propagandists "were able and willing to change classic tenets of nationalist faith in order to match public opinion and win votes" (Novick 2001, 17). The increased attention to public sensibilities becomes visible in the development that radical nationalist propaganda soon began to avoid direct slurs and mockery against Irish recruits after the first months of the conflict, not repeating the affronting ideas of the Irish soldier in Britain's army as morally and physically degenerated, "a traitor to his country and a felon in his soul" (Denman 1992, 31), which had been a well-established image in pre-war discourses of Irish nationalism. As the numbers of Irish war casualties increased in 1915, nationalist anti-war propagandists concentrated on exposing what they saw as the lethal fraudulence at the heart of the recruitment efforts, accusing England and her Redmondite accomplices of luring impressionable young Irishmen into service and onto the blood-soaked killing fields, this war meaning nothing but certain death (cf. Novick 2001, 51f.). The article "The Typical Soldier", published in January 1916 in *The Gael*, exemplifies this notion, explaining to readers how ordinary Irish volunteers are "hectored, brow-beaten, repressed, sworn at, made into a machine to obey all orders". And the author warns his readers: "How would you like to be him. Do you not pity him" (quoted in Novick 2001, 59).

Nevertheless, a sentiment of pity and mourning did come to dominate much of nationalist anti-war and anti-recruitment writing, relentlessly documenting the Irish losses of the war. Importantly, the death of young Irishmen in European battlefields was not only seen as a human tragedy but also as a national one because it decimated Ireland's young male population, depriving Ireland of potential volunteers in the fight for Irish independence. This thought found expression, for example, in Alice Ffrench's poem "Too Many Irish Again": "But the statesmen of England are wiser to-day / They are killing two birds with one stone; / To death and to glory! for England – away! / And your place they'll fill up with one of their own" (quoted in Novick 2001, 57). Another poem, written by "The Wounded Irishman", published in *The Worker's Republic*, spells it out even more directly: "Full many a noble Irish lad had bravely fought and fell, chum: / And oh! It makes my heart feel sad, to think 'twas all for Belgium" (quoted in Novick 2001, 64). These lines again are exemplary of the aforementioned departure of propaganda from the stereotype of the treacherous Irishman in British uniform. In fact, despite the anger and disgust about recruitment, the sense of sympathy and respect, even pride for "noble Irish lads" obvious in the poem was not uncommon in radical nationalist circles – as Eoin MacNeill commented in February 1916, "if any Irishman is convinced that he will serve Ireland by becoming a British soldier, and if he acts on this conviction, he is a patriotic and brave man" (Novick 2001, 60). However, such attitudes soon were rendered obsolete. The violent eruption of Irish radical nationalism in the shape of the Easter Rising of April 1916 led to a brutalisation of anti-British discourses (cf. Novick 2001, 65) and, as will be shown, eventually resulted in a major turnaround of Irish attitudes towards the war and its Irish participants.

The Great War and the Easter Rising

In various ways, the Great War functioned as the essential backdrop to the 1916 Easter Rising, not only considering the commonly held notion of 'England's difficulty' being 'Ireland's opportunity', the English occupation with the war effort constituting a weak moment to be exploited by Irish nationalists for their revolution. There are further connections: For example, the plans of the insurgents heavily relied on German support for the revolt, including the arrangement of a landing of 20,000 German arms, assistance by German officers and military advisors, and at least one submarine in Dublin harbour (cf. Hennessey 1998, 130f.). Also, the ideology of sacrifice and of the glorification of bloodshed that notoriously underpinned the Easter Rising[26] actually very much belongs to the greater European context of war enthusiasm and eugenic militaristic obsessions that has been outlined before. This becomes obvious in a speech of the Irish Volunteer Sean MacDermott in the summer of 1914, mentioned by Thomas Hennessey. During a Volunteer meeting, MacDermott warned his companions, as Hennessey summarises, "that the separatist nationalism of Tone and Emmet was almost dead, that the generation now growing old was the most decadent generation nationally since the Norman invasion, and that the Irish patriotic spirit would die forever unless a blood sacrifice was made in the next few years" (Hennessey 1998, 128). Here, MacDermott exactly repeats the doctrine of eliminating degeneracy by bloodshed and of revitalising patriotism through warfare that was also a part of the discourses of Ulster unionists, German and English imperialists and others. Apart from these organisational and ideological considerations linking the Easter Rising and the Great War, the leaders of the Easter Rising were also informed by the hope to take Ireland out of the Great War altogether, in this way preventing further Irish bloodshed in a war perceived as without merits for Ireland by means of one short violent outburst (cf. Kiberd 1999, 21). As David Fitzpatrick summarises, "the Rising would have been inconceivable in the absence of war" (Fitzpatrick 2008, 141).

When it finally happened, the rebellion quickly turned out to be pathetically ill-planned, chaotic and locally isolated, ending in a complete defeat of the rebels. After a week of fighting in Dublin against British troops, including Irish soldiers standing up to their fellow countrymen, more than 500 people had lost their lives and roughly 2,500 had been wounded, among them many civilians. As Ben Novick notes, "the Rising brought home the war to Dubliners" (Novick 2001, 64), trenches running through St. Stephen's Green, the city centre destroyed by British artillery. However, military success had never been a prime objective of the rebellion. The symbolic value and the spectacle of the insurgence as an inspiring demonstration of resistance and of the willingness to die for an independent 'Irish' Ireland outweighed the profane question of the actual military outcome – it was to be a 'triumph of failure', heroic martyrdom for Ireland heralding salvation, spurring a dormant Irish public to finally wake up and shake off the shackles of British oppression. This notion also shows in a pronounced sense of theatricality evident in

---

26 See also chapter II.3.2.2 on Pearse and radical nationalist war writing.

various aspects of the proceedings, from selecting Easter with its connotations of messianic resurrection as a highly symbolic date for the rebellion, to the choice of the General Post Office as its main venue, which proved a bad decision from a military point of view but a good one considering publicity, taking the Irish revolution to the heart of the capital, centre stage for everyone to see (cf. Kiberd 1999, 29). In this sense, Declan Kiberd suggests that what the rebels, whose leaders were deeply involved in literary and artistic circles, really did was to stage their revolution as a street performance – they transferred their agenda of a cultural and political renewal of Ireland into real action, a claim to nationhood and independence underscored by bloody sacrifice: "'[T]o be fit to govern others we must be able to govern ourselves': and the rebels had done just that. During Easter Week's performance, they were enabled both to show feeling and to control it: and so, in the eyes of their audience, both Irish and international, they had literally governed themselves" (Kiberd 1999, 25).

The immediate reaction to the rebellion by the Irish public is difficult to gauge and very much determined by aspects of class[27] and political affiliation, yet, altogether, it certainly was not overly enthusiastic. The Irish media generally was horrified by the sight of the destructions at home (cf. Larkin 2014, 222). In the immediate aftermath of the event, for many in Ireland this shock and a sense of disloyalty apparently overshadowed possible sympathies for the cause of the rebels and their plight – as the author Frank O'Connor, then a 13-year-old in Cork, whose father was away at the front at the time, remembers:

> [T]he daily papers showed Dublin as they showed Belgian cities destroyed by the Germans, as smoking ruins inhabited by men with rifles and machine guns. At first, my only reaction was horror that Irishmen could commit such a crime against England. I was sure that phase had ended with the Boer War in which father had fought, because one of his favourite songs said so – "You used to call us traitors because of agitators but you can't call us traitors now."
>
> (O'Connor, quoted in Ferriter 2005, 150f.)

In the same week as Dublin was convulsed by the Rising, 570 soldiers of the 16th Irish Division died on the battlefields of the Great War and the front's focus was on the horrors of gas warfare (cf. Ferriter 2005, 147; Orr 2008, 70). When the news of the Dublin rebellion and its outcome reached Irish and Ulster troops in

---

27 Diarmaid Ferriter notes that the Dublin middle classes remained somewhat indifferent while Dublin's poor saw in the Rising an opportunity to loot (cf. Ferriter 2005, 151). Hilary Larkin summarises that "Dubliners were ill-at-ease, although there was some plain curiosity" (Larkin 2014, 222).

France and elsewhere, reactions of soldiers were mixed. While for many soldiers, both unionist and nationalist, the insurrection was a stab in the back,[28] some of them giving expression to their anger by hanging effigies of Sir Roger Casement above their trenches, others began to question their political allegiances or were worried about the disciplinary and political consequences of the failed rebellion for Ireland (cf. Orr 2008, 71).

Ironically, it would be this very aspect, the British reaction to the rebellion, which would come to transform the divided public opinion on the failed nationalist coup into a broad consensus about the heroism and righteousness of the Easter Rising. The measures taken by Westminster during and after the insurrection were harsh and based on a crude application of communal penalties, such as mass internment and the introduction of martial law, which included the suspension of common-law rights and banning of fairs and markets – a punitive strategy that was soon perceived as disproportionate and that profoundly damaged the progress in British-Irish relations made in the years before (cf. Fitzpatrick 2008, 141). The decision of the British government to execute the leaders of the Rising was even more fatal in the eyes of the public, causing indignation throughout Ireland. The executions completed the sacrificial agenda of the rebels, turning them into the martyrs as which they had envisioned themselves. The executions created among large sections of Irish society a "moment of synthesis between Catholicism and national struggle – all was swept up in an outpouring of national grief" (Larkin 2014, 224). This affected even traditional and conservative circles which previously had not approved of the rebellion, but then began to open up towards the radical nationalist position. Altogether, in its handling of the insurrection, "the British government had done an almost spectacularly good job in alienating moderate Irish people" (ibid.). The Rising and its aftermath brought the unresolved condition of the Irish Question back into the eye of the public, in a fiercer and more polarised manner than ever before. As Hugh Law, MP of Redmond's Irish Parliamentary Party for West Donegal, was to tell the House of Commons: "You raised the issue there after those men were shot, the definite issue of English versus Irish" (quoted in Hennessey 1998, 134). The events of this phase re-invigorated Irish separatism and helped to establish it as a mainstream attitude, breaking the dominance of Redmond's party over Irish nationalism. The Redmondite notion of an *entente cordiale* between nationalist

---

28 An item in a trench magazine of the 36th (Ulster) Division asked: "What kind of death do these insurgent dogs deserve? Those swine who seize upon the fact that the soldiery is away […] to murder a whole host of innocent people" (quoted in Orr 2008, 71).

Ireland and imperial Britain that had underpinned the consent to the war of many nationalists had become unsustainable by the summer of 1916 (cf. Hennessey 1998, 158).

The events in Dublin shifted the focus of the Irish public away from the Great War. The brutal sacrifice made by Irish and Ulster troops in the Battle of the Somme two months after the Easter Rising hence proved a complicated subject to integrate into changing political sensibilities. At the same time, an unfaltering Ulster unionism unreservedly celebrated its soldiers for, as Edward Carson hymned, "the glory and the honour [the dead] have won for the Imperial Province" (quoted in Longley 1994, 78). The Ulster Division's experience at the Somme in 1916 quickly attained the status of a sacred sacrifice and went on to become an integral source of Ulster identity (cf. Jeffery 2008, 267). In contrast to this, the notion that the significance of the haunting Irish experience at the Somme and elsewhere was likely to pale against the appeal of the mythical martyrdom of the Easter Rising was not lost on Irish soldiers. As Tom Kettle, who would be killed at the Somme in September 1916, bitterly predicted, the Easter rebels "will go down to history as heroes and martyrs, and I will go down – if I go down at all – as a bloody British officer" (quoted in Lyons 1983, 293), anticipating the fundamental change in the concept of Irish patriotism which was triggered by the Rising and which would leave no room for the thousands of men who had sought to enforce Irish independence by enlisting (cf. Grene 1999, 243). The demise of the nationalist ideals of soldiers like Kettle would be completed in the final years of the war.

Ireland until the End of the Great War – The Return of Irish Soldiers

As casualties mounted throughout 1916 and public opinion turned against the Great War, recruitment numbers in Ireland began to drop significantly. By 1917, many young Irishmen faced ridicule or even social ostracism if they dared to enlist (cf. Fitzpatrick 2008, 135). All three divisions recruited from Ireland encountered great difficulties in replacing the men who had fallen – their ranks had to be filled up with conscripts from Britain, weakening the Irish character of those troops.[29] Although not as purely Irish as before, the 16th (Irish) Division and the 36th (Ulster) Division fought side by side for the first time in the Battle of Messines of 1917, the two opposing traditions directly cooperating in a common cause. The political and symbolical significance of this bilateral effort did not go

---

29 This development continued, which shows, for example, in the "Indianised" condition of the 10th Division by 1918, when most remaining Irishmen had been substituted by colonial troops (cf. Orr 2008, 74).

unnoticed in Ireland – yet, the event was partly overshadowed by the war death of Willie Redmond, John Redmond's brother, diverting public attention from the potentially unifying story of Messines. The aftermath of Willie Redmond's death is a striking example of how circumstances at home had changed since 1916: The following by-election in Willie Redmond's East Clare constituency was not won by a Redmondite but by a Sinn Féin candidate – with Éamon de Valera, a senior commander of the Easter Rising took Redmond's position.

The local victory of de Valera is part of a series of successes Sinn Féin enjoyed in elections during the final two years of the war, culminating in the triumph over the Irish Parliamentary Party in the general election of December 1918. Before the election, Sinn Féin had continuously stressed its rootedness in an Irish history of resistance to British rule, underlining the party's insistence on "our un-broken tradition of nationhood, on a unity in a national name which has never been challenged, on our possession of a distinctive national culture and social order, on the moral courage and dignity of our people in the face of alien aggression" (quoted in Ferriter 2005, 183). This includes, of course, the rejection of 'England's' Great War, in particular the rejection of conscription in Ireland. This issue was perceived as a great threat among almost all sections of Irish society. Consequently, the introduction of the Military Service Bill by the British government in April 1918, extending British conscription to Ireland, could not have come at a better time for Sinn Féin, causing widespread outrage, even among some commentators in England. For example, G. K. Chesterton called the decision to enforce conscription in Ireland "a piece of rank raving madness", leading to the manufacturing of German sympathisers "steadily and systematically as if from a factory" (quoted in Ferriter 2005, 181). W. B. Yeats gave expression to his worries about the consequences of forcing Irishmen into the war in a letter to the senior Liberal politician Lord Haldane:

> [I]t seems to me a strangely wanton thing that England, for the sake of fifty thousand Irish soldiers, is prepared to hollow another trench between the countries and fill it with blood. If that is done England will only suffer in reputation, but Ireland will suffer in her character, and all the work of my life-time and that of my fellow-workers, all our effort to clarify and sweeten the popular mind, will be destroyed and Ireland, for another hundred years, will live in the sterility of that bitterness.
>
> (Yeats, quoted in Ferriter 2005, 183)

To Yeats, the introduction of conscription would mean not only a costly and pointless prolonging of the war but also a subsequent devastating and irrevocable embitterment and radicalisation of Irish society. Even the Catholic Church, which had previously been rather silent about the issue, officially opposed the plans, the

Bishop of Down and Connor professing that "no power has any moral right to coerce young Irishmen to fight in the alleged interests of freedom until they have been allowed to enjoy freedom for themselves" (quoted in Ferriter 2005, 182).

As the resistance against Irish conscription grew and more and more Irishmen became involved with the Irish Volunteers and other radical nationalist organisations precisely because of the threat of conscription, the British government decided to postpone its plans and instead focused on the containment of Sinn Féin by arresting 73 prominent party members for their alleged involvement in pro-German conspiracies (cf. ibid.). Still, these measures did not stop the rise of Sinn Féin. The party emerged as the clear winner from the general election of December 1918, securing 73 of Ireland's 105 seats, while the moderate Irish Parliamentary Party suffered a crushing defeat. In the south, Sinn Féin had profited from an electorate profoundly weary of the Great War and radicalised by the experiences of the Easter Rising and the threat of conscription. Demographic and legal changes further contributed to the landslide victory of Sinn Féin, for example, the virtual stoppage of emigration during the war had created a larger and younger electorate without existing ties to the dominant Irish Parliamentary Party. To a majority of voters in 1918, the party's aim of Home Rule must have appeared outdated, unrealistic or even foolish, even more so its endorsement of the war effort. As Diarmaid Ferriter summarises, in fact "[t]he mandate Sinn Féin received in 1918 was not a mandate for war, but for peace" – yet, it must be mentioned, it was not necessarily a clear mandate for Irish separatism, "many supporters at this time having little interest in the republic or the constitutional status of Ireland" (Ferriter 2005, 184). The election of 1918 can be judged as a key moment in twentieth-century Irish history, foreshadowing the cementation of political divisions in Ireland as much as prefiguring the incompatibility of the legacy of Ireland's Great War with the Irish state to emerge from this situation.

After the end of the Great War, a substantial number of Irish soldiers chose not to go back to Ireland, most of them staying in Britain as civilians or becoming professional soldiers. About 100,000 demobilised veterans of the war returned to Ireland until May 1920. Their homecoming naturally "was different from that in Britain and had more in common with other parts of Europe where borders were being redrawn and political identities remoulded" (Leonard 2008, 211). They found themselves, as Jane Leonard aptly labels it, in an "uneasy no man's land of post-war Ireland" (Leonard 2008, 218), in a country transformed and further radicalised since their departure, caught up in new violent conflicts about Ireland's future which would turn into the War of Independence and the Irish Civil War. Some ex-soldiers rejoined paramilitary movements on returning home, while a considerable number of Irish veterans continued their military careers by re-enlisting in the new armies and armed police forces.

The public solidarity with Sinn Féin since 1916 had exacerbated Irish attitudes to those who had served in the British army, returning soldiers frequently encountering resentment (cf. Leonard 1997, 62), being reminded of how the allegiances they embodied when they left for the Continent had become obsolete. This hostility found expression in various forms of intimidation and aggression, including many cases of physical violence against ex-soldiers – beatings, mutilations, kidnappings, expulsions from Ireland, even murders. Between 1919 and 1924, more than 120 veterans of the Great War were killed by the IRA[30] or other republican forces and the vast majority of those men seem to have lost their lives in retribution for their part in the war (cf. Leonard 2008, 218; Leonard 1997, 63). Hostilities also extended to Irish veterans' organisations such as the Comrades of the Great War and the Federation of Discharged and Demobilised Soldiers and Sailors, whose premises and staff came under attack.

The reintegration of Irish ex-soldiers into civilian society was obstructed in various ways. For example, the refusal to let former hurlers and Gaelic football players re-join the Gaelic Football Association if they had served in the war is indicative of the cultural dimension of the rejection Irish ex-soldiers had to face (cf. Leonard 1997, 63). Moreover, offices of local War Pensions Committees were attacked, homes and smallholdings provided for veterans under the 1919 Irish Land (Soldiers and Sailors) Act were threatened and boycotted, sometimes vandalised or even burned down (cf. ibid.), and councils dominated by Sinn Féin frequently denied veterans access to local welfare, medical services and vocational colleges, also barring them from applying for jobs reserved for former IRA members (cf. Kelly 2012, 18). Consequently, Irish veterans often faced unemployment,[31] poverty and homelessness (cf. Kelly 2012, 14–22), which further aggravated their peripheral position in Irish society and seemingly confirmed the stereotypes of the moral and

---

30 After the victory of Sinn Féin, the Irish Volunteers understood themselves as the army of the new Irish state to be formed, becoming the Irish Republican Army (IRA).

31 The large-scale problem of unwanted, unemployed and impoverished veterans also occurred in other nations after the Great War, including Britain. However, as Jane Leonard argues, "[u]nemployment was far higher among veterans in Ireland than in Britain, where only 10 per cent were out of work by the autumn of 1919. In Ireland, where 76,000 veterans had returned by that stage, 46 per cent were receiving out of work donation of 29s per week (ex-servicewomen only qualified if disabled). One in two Irish veterans remained unemployed a year later. […] The situation in Ulster was less severe than in the west and south" (Leonard 2008, 216).

physical degeneration brought about by collaborating with the British that radical nationalist propaganda had promoted before and, to a smaller extent, during the war (cf. Decker 2015, 83).

The grim situation of veterans and their families in the 1920s and afterwards is impressively illustrated by letters reproduced in John Horne's collection *Our War*. For example, in a 1926 letter to King George V., a former army nurse from Dublin complains about the "stigma" of war service, the abuse and the social downfall she has experienced since the end of the Great War:

> Sunrise and sunset saw Your Majesty's devoted subject at her post holding Florence Nightingale's lamp, without weariness, continuing without a falter during the subsequent civil strife and all the bitter antagonism which fell upon the faithfull's [sic] head. And for the reason, Your Majesty's loyal subject was not a hired servant, I do dutifully, respectfully and humbly, beg your Gracious Majesty's protection from the stigma now vouchsafed those loyal women who served also. That they may not be demoralized by been [sic] thrown by the Sherriff's men on the roadside [...]. In grief and sorrow, my lovely Home, the trophies of my profession, has been sold by public auction. The presents from grateful patients, each household god fraught with fragrant memories of triumph and success. And Your Majesty's loyal subject's heart is broken, having returned the Royal Red Cross bestowed by Your Gracious Majesty, in order to obtain justice by been [sic] relieved of the onus of my service to my beloved King in Ireland.
>
> (Emily K. Harris to George V., 10 November 1926, repr. in Horne 2008, 254)

The hardship faced by ex-soldiers also shows in a 1928 petition of Irish veterans, reporting how there "has been no employment here for Ex-Service men for the past 2 or 3 years, and there is no scheme whatever around here to provide work for them. In fact 90% of them are out of work and no prospect of getting any in the near future" (petition of the Bagenalstown branch of the British Legion of Ex-Servicemen, 28 August 1928, reproduced in Horne 2008, 255).

That the difficult social and economic condition of veterans did not greatly improve as time passed becomes visible in a 1957 letter of a veteran's wife to Éamon de Valera, then Taoiseach of the Republic of Ireland, in which she explains that without a pension "leaving our home is the spectre looking into our faces" (letter of Margaret Freeman to Éamon de Valera, 17 July 1957, reproduced in Horne 2008, 256) – in his curt reply, de Valera's secretary makes it abundantly clear that he was instructed to tell her that "the question of an award of pension in respect of service in the World War of 1914–1918 would not be a matter of the Government of Ireland" (ibid.). Whether or not the rejection of the veteran's wife's demand was justified, the answer to her letter epitomises the official attitudes of Ireland towards the Great War that had developed since the achievement of Irish independence: This war was "not a matter of the Government of Ireland". Despite the direct involvement of hundreds of thousands of Irishmen, the wide-ranging Irish support for the war until 1916 and the manifold connections between the war and the achievement of Irish independence, Ireland's Great War experience was shunned and re-constructed as an entirely foreign affair, a misguided or even embarrassing episode of no relevance for the discourses of Irish political, social and cultural identity circulating in the new republican state.

The Problematic Legacy of Ireland's Great War

In Britain, Germany, France, Australia, Canada and, of course, unionist Northern Ireland, the significance of the Great War found expression in extensive cultures of public and private war commemoration. The Protestant north embraced its war experience as a powerful confirmation of its status as a British province within the union. This view becomes manifest, for examples, by the 'Ulster Tower' at Thiepval, completed already in 1921, near the heart of the battlefield, confidently lined up with the national memorials built by Australia, Canada, New Zealand and South Africa. Also, Armistice Day ceremonies in Northern Ireland came to be dominated by unionists and were endorsed by the province's new elites, particularly celebrating the sacrificial myth of Protestant unionist heroism at the Somme, turning it into a major source of identification (cf. Horne 2008, 13), albeit including a note of bitterness at the split of Ireland and the establishment of an independent south. The complex and subtle ranges of meanings which could have been drawn from the common tragic experience of the war were overwhelmed by a simple patriotic and predominantly Protestant type of commemoration in Northern Ireland (cf. Jeffery 1993, 153).

In contrast to this, the intense domestic upheavals of the War of Independence and the Civil War as well as the legacy of Sinn Féin radicalism profoundly complicated the attitudes and the public treatment of the Great War in Ireland in the following decades. As Keith Jeffery summarises, "the post-war conflict and partition undermined the political integrity of the war as it was remembered and commemorated" (Jeffery 1993, 148). The result was a marked distancing of the Irish Free State and, later, the Republic of Ireland from the Great War and its Irish heritage that would last until the 1980s (cf. Fitzpatrick 2001, 191; Jeffery 1993, 152). Among the revolutionary republican generation that had come into power in Ireland in the 1920s, the participation of Irishmen in the Great War largely came to be perceived as a case of treason against the Irish nation, no matter which good intentions and excusable conditions – the freedom of small nations, Home Rule, the fight against Prussian militarism and godlessness, an escape from poverty – had spurred them to join the British forces (cf. Fitzpatrick 2001, 191). This view became ingrained in the ideology of the new Irish state, surviving the fragmentation of Sinn Féin and being transmitted to Cumman na nGaedheal as well as Fianna Fáil and its rival parties. The animosity towards the Great War and its veterans was a common and persisting one and also made an official endorsement of the commemoration of Ireland's Great War difficult and implausible (cf. ibid.).

Instead, the leaders of the new Irish state heavily relied on the commemoration of the 1916 Easter Rising, appropriating the Rising's myth of individual heroism and martyrdom to mobilise support for them, selecting the Rising as the foundation stone of the new state and as a major source for the republican state identity (cf. Fitzpatrick 2001, 186). As Terence Brown suggests, the state ideology of Ireland since independence was dominated by the notion that "the ancient Gaelic nation had finally thrown off the thrall of foreign subjugation and that her true destiny lay in cultivating her national distinctiveness as assiduously as possible" (Brown 2004, 134). Thus, unsurprisingly, the reconciling potential of the experience and memory of the shared sacrifice made by Catholics and Protestants, nationalists and unionists as members of the British forces on European battlefields remained unrecognised (cf. Fitzpatrick 2001, 191). The "international story" of Ireland's Great War, to return to Hilary Larkin's concept mentioned at the beginning of this chapter, was at odds with a new Irish state that was decidedly inward-looking and "un-international".

The sweeping fixation in republican discourses on the Easter Rising and other nationalist traditions as well as the parochial attitudes to the Great War, are strikingly illustrated, for example, by popular songs and poems of the post-war period. The 1919 rebel song "The Foggy Dew" suggests how the only war that matters and deserves commemoration was the one declared against Britain in April 1916 in the General Post Office, not the one that led Irishmen astray to the killing fields on the Continent:

> Right proudly high over Dublin town they hung out the flag of war.
> 'Twas better to die 'neath an Irish sky than at Suvla or Sed el bar.
> 'Twas England bade our Wild Geese go that small nations might be free.
> But their lonely graves are by Suvla's waves
> and the fringe of the grey North Sea.
> O, had they died by Pearse's side or had fought with Cathal Brugha,
> Their names we'd keep where the Fenians sleep,
> 'neath the shroud of the Foggy Dew.
> (Charles O'Neill, "The Foggy Dew", quoted in Grene 1999, 243)

"The Foggy Dew" is permeated by the notion of a regrettable and illicit abandonment of Ireland by those who fought in the Great War, a notion that is exemplary of the insularity and isolationism of Irish republicanism that would shape the new independent Ireland. This sentiment is even more prominent in another popular poem, written still during the war by the passionate republican Dora Sigerson Shorter, in which the perfidious "foreignness" of the Great War is stressed:

Ah, Grannia Wael, thy stricken head
Is bowed o'er thy dead,
Thy dead who died for love of thee,
Not for some foreign liberty.
Shall we betray when hope is near,
Our Motherland whom we hold dear,
To go to fight on foreign strand,
For foreign rights and foreign land?

(quoted in Jeffery 2008, 270)

Looking at popular texts such as these, it seems as if the harsh sense of rejection that underpins Maud Gonne's 1900 statement about Irishmen in the British forces had become an accepted view some twenty years later: "If they die, if they live, it matters not to me, they are no longer Irishmen" (Gonne 2004, 185). In the eyes of the republican mainstream, it seems, Irish recruits have forfeited their right to a place in the national community by committing to a "foreign" cause, having taken "a historical wrong turning" (Brown 1993, 229) away from the true concerns of Ireland which effectively leaves them "tainted with the stain of collaboration" (Gregory and Paseta 2002, 5). The narrative of Irishmen risking their lives for the cause of the former oppressor was incompatible with the values of the new independent nation. The identity project of independent Ireland relied on a construction of a collective identity based on nationalist myths like the Easter Rising and on a deeply Catholic anti-modernism, creating a sense of Irish insularity that shunned any foreign influences (cf. O'Mahony and Delanty 2001, 156f., 184f.) – a denunciation of "a modern world closely identified with Anglicisation and England itself" (Brown 2004, 203). This is also reflected in the 1937 constitution of Ireland, another monumental step towards independence, which embodied a definite narrative of Irish identity, constructing an exclusive version of Irishness, "an essentialised Irish type, a *fior Gael*, who was Catholic and a nationalist, [...] the dominant subject of Irish law" (Patrick Hanafin in Brown 2004, 397).

However, this does not mean that without substantial official endorsement and in the face of public rejection there was a complete absence of efforts of Great War commemoration in Ireland. Commemorative meetings as well as memorial plaques, rolls of honour and other monuments were privately organised by companies, clubs, educational institutions and veterans' organisations. For nearly two decades after the war, for example, Dublin still saw public demonstrations on Armistice Day, the most impressive one taking place in 1924, when 20,000 veterans paraded through Dublin in front of 50,000 spectators – a display indicative of the social magnitude of the Irish involvement in the Great War, no matter how strongly it may have been rejected by the republican mainstream and restricted[32] by the government. In the immediate post-war phase, such commemorative events frequently included conciliatory attempts on behalf of veterans to link the war with the Irish national cause and to integrate the service of Irishmen into contemporary Irish historical and political consciousness. For example, at the unveiling of a memorial in Virginia, Co. Cavan, in August 1923, Major-General Sir Oliver Nugent expressed his hope that "[t]he day [...] is not [...] far distant when the memory of all those of our country who gave their lives for civilisation as we interpret it and in obedience to what they believed to be their duty will be honoured and perpetuated in every town and village in Ireland" (quoted in Jeffery 1993, 149).

Of course, ceremonies such as those on Armistice Days also were bitterly contested events, frequently becoming sites of conflict and violent confrontation, including republican assaults on parading veterans and their families as well as bomb and arson attacks on war memorials and British Legion halls (cf. Leonard 1997, 66f.). In this context of public conflict, a particularly telling practice developed among participants of Armistice Day events: They would hide razor blades in the poppies they wore in order to fend off republicans who wanted to rip them off (cf. Brown 1993, 228) – a striking image in which the complicated and divided legacy of the war and its fraught entanglement in Irish issues becomes obvious. Animosities grew continuously and by the late 1960s and early 1970s, as the Northern Irish conflict intensified, attacks and threats by radical republicans against commemorative events would eventually lead to a large-scale abandonment of those practices.

Considering official discourses and policies, the sense of embarrassment and detachment from Ireland's part in the Great War displayed by the new Irish state is probably most exemplarily visible in the development of Ireland's National War Memorial. In the mid-1920s, plans to build a war memorial park in the centre of Dublin were rejected because, as W. T. Cosgrave, head of government of the Irish Free State, reminded a unionist senator, among the population "there is a certain hostility to the idea of any form of War Memorial" (quoted in Fitzpatrick

---

32 The restrictions placed on veterans' ceremonies by Cumann na nGaedheal included, for example, a ban on the use of military commands and the flying of British flags. They were largely upheld until the end of the Second World War (Kelly 2012, 3).

2001, 192).[33] Furthermore, the suggested location, directly opposite the seat of the government, would, in the words of Kevin O'Higgins, then Minister for Justice, "give a wrong twist, as it were, a wrong suggestion, to the origins of this state", visitors possibly concluding that the origins of this state [...] were connected with the lives that were lost in the Great War in France, Belgium, Gallipoli and so on. That is not the position" (quoted in Wills 2009, 139). After years of negotiations, postponements and changes of plans, the project was completed shortly before the outbreak of the Second World War – however, not in the city centre but in Islandsbridge, on the outskirts of Dublin. A landscaped park was built with a towering cross, a "Stone of Remembrance", rose gardens, fountains and stone pavilions. Tellingly, right after completion, the monument fell into a state of neglect that lasted for almost fifty years. It remained formally unopened until as late as 1988 (cf. Jeffery 1994, 89).

During the Second World War, in which Ireland remained neutral, commonly referring to the conflict as 'The Emergency', the official silence and deliberate forgetfulness about the Great War intensified. It was this period in which the self-imposed isolation of Ireland became painfully obvious to many,[34] and in which the much-cited sense of a national amnesia of Ireland's Great War was cemented. As Keith Jeffery summarises, in this period "any commemoration of the Great War could become identified with the support of the British war effort", so much that, eventually, Armistice Day parades in Dublin were banned (cf. Jeffery 2008, 272). Anti-British sentiments, even in this situation,[35] remained strong, some sources suggesting that sixty per cent of the Irish population expected or even hoped for a German victory (cf. Waite 2011). Only a minority openly backed Britain's war effort this time – still, it should be mentioned, several thousands of Irish civilians left their home country enlist. The state's unchanging unwillingness to accept Irish

---

33 This debate about the war memorial has been addressed by the Anglo-Irish (war) poet Lord Dunsany in his defiant poem "To the Fallen Irish Soldiers": "Since they have grudged you space in Merrion Square, / and any monument of stone or brass, / And you yourself are powerless, alas, / And your own countrymen seem not to care; / Let then these words of mine drift down the air, / [...]Sleep on, forgot a few more years, and then / The ages that I prophesy, shall see / Due honours paid to you by juster men, / You standing foremost in our history, / Your story filling all our land with wonder, / Your names, and regiments' names, like distant thunder." (Dunsany 2008, 38).

34 For example, the writer Sean O'Faolain regretted how life in wartime Ireland "is so isolated now that it is no longer being pollinated by germinating ideas windborne from anywhere" (quoted in Brown 2004, 163).

35 The IRA even attempted to establish contacts with German intelligence services during the war (Brown 2004, 160).

contributions to another British war effort becomes obvious in the fate of the roughly 5,000 Irish professional soldiers who switched uniforms and joined the British forces in the fight against Nazi Germany. Like the Irish veterans of the Great War, they faced not only public resentment[36] but also severe retributions by the state upon return, falling victim to a "starvation order", which included the loss of all pay and pension rights as well as a scheme to prevent them from finding work by banning them for seven years from any state-funded employment (cf. ibid).

In the decades after the Second World War, the official disinterest in the Irish legacy of the Great War and the exclusive preoccupation with Ireland's "national" story were upheld. This shows most strikingly in the unbridled triumphalism exposed during the extensive state-sponsored celebrations of the fiftieth anniversary of the Easter Rising in 1966. The revolutionary events in Dublin predominated the festivities to the exclusion of almost everything else, the Great War, if mentioned at all, only serving as a mere tragic backdrop to the "main action" of the Rising (cf. Jeffery 2008, 273; Ferriter 2005, 147). The simultaneous fiftieth anniversary of the Battle of the Somme went by unmentioned in the Republic of Ireland (cf. Boyce 2002, 191).

The Recovery of Ireland's Great War since the 1980s

In the late 1960s, the notion of the Great War as being consciously written out of Irish history, the Irish contribution to the war being 'extirpated' from political and historical consciousness, began to be recognised and criticised for the first time. In a ground-breaking 1967 article, the Irish historian F. X. Martin publicly addressed the "Great Oblivion", the "collective amnesia" about the Great War that had befallen the Irish public, pointing out how for every Irishman taking part in the Easter Rising, there were actually sixteen Irish volunteers in the British forces, and how the history of non-republican Ireland had been marginalised for the sake of an inflated and distorted narrative of Ireland's fight for independence: "[T]he GPO would need to be four times its size in order to hold all who claimed to have fought there during Easter Week" (quoted in Bowman 2014; cf. Ferriter 2005, 132). In 1971, the Great War made a comeback in Irish historiography with the publication of F. S. L. Lyons's *Ireland since the Famine*, but it was not until

---

36 In a 2011 documentary feature for the BBC, John Waite interviewed Irish veterans of the Second World War. One of them, John Stout, remembers how he was treated as a pariah after his return to Cork: "What they did to us was wrong. I know that in my heart. They cold-shouldered you. They didn't speak to you. They didn't understand why we did what we did. A lot of Irish people wanted Germany to win the war – they were dead up against the British" (Waite 2011).

the 1980s[37] that detailed studies of the Irish participation in the Great War were undertaken (cf. Novick 2001, 16).

The decisive context to encourage such efforts of rediscovery[38] and, to some degree, rehabilitation, was the development of the Northern Ireland conflict, in which the unresolved political and religious divisions of Ireland and within Northern Ireland painfully and glaringly resurfaced. For example, the IRA bombing of the Enniskillen war memorial on Remembrance Sunday 1987, killing eleven people, proved how powerful and bitterly contested the symbolic legacy of the Great War still was, seventy years later and at a time when first steps of reconciliation in the Northern Irish conflict had already been made (cf. Jeffery 2008, 272). The Troubles and the peace process provoked a new questioning of Irish and Northern Irish identities and their foundation in nationalist or unionist versions of an Irish past, inviting new explorations of Irishness in which the Great War was not blanked out in embarrassment or disappointment, at last beginning to recognise the significance of the war (cf. Boyce 2002, 207). It was increasingly comprehended, in the words of Terence Brown, that "the nasty little Northern Irish war which began in 1968, [...] had its roots in the soil of 1912 and 1916 as well as that of the Great War" (Brown 1993, 232).

As the Northern Irish peace process as well as the modernisation and globalisation of Irish society progressed and as the temporal distance to the events of the 1910s increased, attitudes to the Great War in Ireland and Northern Ireland began to ease. Since the 1990s, the conciliatory potential of the war experience and the importance of the Great War for Ireland and the achievement of Irish independence have been recognised in Irish politics and public discourses,[39] while in Northern Ireland the contribution of Catholics and nationalists to the war effort has increasingly been acknowledged. The south has become more comfortable with the Irish legacy of the Great War. A considerable number of

---

37 The essay collection *Ireland and the First World War*, edited by David Fitzpatrick (Dublin: Trinity History Workshop, 1986), is one of the earliest works focussing on the subject.

38 This also happened within a wider European context of a reawakened public interest and cultural engagement with the Great War in the 1970s, as the war generation was dying out (cf. Jeffery 2011, 257).

39 These changed attitudes to the Irish past also include the Irish contribution to the Second World War. This shows, for example, in calls by Irish parliamentarians for the rehabilitation of those who deserted the Irish army to fight against Nazi Germany. In the words of TD Gerald Nash, "[w]hat happened to them was vindictive and not only a stain on their honour but on the honour of Ireland" (quoted in Waite 2011).

68

communities throughout the Republic of Ireland have begun to erect or restore war memorials and to explore the histories of the war's local impact (cf. Leonard 1997, 60f.). A landmark in Ireland's official recognition of the Great War in the 1990s was the dedication of the Irish Peace Tower in Messines on Armistice Day 1998 to all Irish and Ulster soldiers of the Great War by Queen Elizabeth II and the Irish President Mary MacAleese, a ceremony that underlined an understanding of the war as a historical point of unity for both traditions, both "nations" on the island (cf. Larkin 2014, 212). Furthermore, the honouring of the participation of Irish soldiers in the Battle of the Somme, that complemented the official celebration of the 90th anniversary of the Easter Rising in 2006, underlines a newly found public acknowledgement of the interdependencies of Ireland's Great War and Ireland's revolution. As mentioned earlier, the aspiration to do justice to the historical significance of the Great War was also a central concern in the commemorative efforts surrounding the centenary of the outbreak of the war. In response to his 2014 commemorative speech in Glasnevin, the Irish President Michael D. Higgins commented that

> a real republicanism has a glowing centre of egalitarianism and how could it be very republican to ignore the deaths, the injuries and the families of the working people of Ireland and Britain who were sucked into a war that was not a war of their making or did not advance their welfare in any significant way. [...] I said in my Glasnevin speech there are a whole series of different motivations that you must try and understand before you rush to judgment on their actions. [...] A hundred years on from World War One we should be inclusive, and that does not require any amnesia.
>
> (quoted in Collins 2014)

A century later, it seems like the complex, ambiguous and conflicted chapter that the Great War constitutes in Irish history has legitimately entered mainstream Irish political consciousness and has become part of official discourses of a new and more integrative form of Irish identity.

Summary

The history and the legacy of Ireland and the Great War is closely connected to the Irish struggle for independence and the competing versions of Irish and Ulster identities engaged in this struggle. The outbreak of the Great War interrupted a fierce militarised domestic conflict about Irish independence between nationalists and unionists. Until 1916, an overwhelming majority supported Ireland's participation in the war for a variety of reasons – political, moral, emotional, familial, or economic. Both nationalists and unionists interpreted their part in the war as a claim to separateness, nationalists in the sense of a demonstration of the nationhood of Ireland which justifies independence, unionists in the sense of a separateness from the nationalist majority, insisting on the imperial integrity of Ireland instead. This pre-existing clash of political and national self-conceptions was also transferred to the Great War by the establishment of Irish (largely nationalist) and Ulster (almost exclusively unionist) divisions, which were entered by more than 200,000 recruits.

Life at the home front in Ireland brought with it social transformations visible in all countries affected by the war, most notably in the lives of Irish women, some of whom discovered new and more independent lifestyles. The home front also saw activities of a small but vocal minority of radical nationalist organisations such as the Irish Volunteers and Sinn Féin that campaigned against the war. These groups eventually succeeded in turning public opinion against the Great War as the number of war casualties, doubts about British leadership and fears about the introduction of conscription in Ireland increased, and, most importantly, as the harsh policies of Westminster in the aftermath of the failed Easter Rising of 1916 caused major outrage throughout Ireland.

By 1918, the values and aims for which constitutional nationalist Ireland had entered the war had become obsolete. Irish soldiers returned to a profoundly changed country shaken by the turmoil of new domestic conflicts at the beginning of the 1920s. After achieving independence, the new republican leaders constructed a vision of Ireland and Irish identity exclusively based on anti-British nationalist traditions and myths such as the Easter Rising, and on a Catholic conservatism and anti-modernism. For both the society and the ideology of independent Ireland the Irish veterans of the Great War had become irrelevant and were frequently openly resented, despite the lasting social magnitude and consequences of the war. The new Irish state and society was clearly uncomfortable with the legacy of the Great War which shows not only in the large-scale absence of an official culture of war commemoration but also in the marginalisation and the manifold hostilities veterans and their families encountered. From the late 1930s to the late 1960s, a collective amnesia about the Great War was cemented. In stark contrast to this, the Great War, particularly the narrative of the sacrifice made by the Ulster Division in the Battle of the Somme, became a cornerstone of Protestant unionist identity in Northern Ireland and was integrated into the history of unionist patriotism.

A change to the polarised legacy of the Great War was only brought about by the experiences of the Troubles and of the eventual modernisation of Ireland since the 1970s and 1980s. The violent conflict and the peace process as well as the obvious changes within Irish society invited a reconsideration of Irish and Northern Irish identities and their rootedness in the conflicts of the past, resulting in a re-evaluation of the importance of the Great War and the rehabilitation of those Irishmen who had taken part in it, underlining their importance in a new and more inclusive notion of what it means to be Irish.

II.3 Literary Context

In the following section, some basic ideas about the processes and implications of writing, communicating and re-imagining the Great War and its legacy will be outlined, altogether embracing a comprehensive and inclusive notion of 'war literature', arguing for an expansion of the traditional notion of the genre as combatant or battlefront literature, and also addressing aspects of literary form. Against the backdrop of the English tradition of Great War literature, an overview of the Irish literary response to the Great War, from the outbreak of the conflict to the present, will be provided, investigating the historical, political, social and cultural conditions, as well as their relatedness to issues of identity, that led to the comparative scarcity of Irish war writing. The section will be concluded by a brief examination of Irish nationalist writing and Easter Rising literature, which, in its militancy, mythology, and sense of a sacrificial 'lost generation' of 1916 might be viewed as a parallel or even rival discourse to the depiction of Ireland's Great War.

II.3.1 Writing and Re-Writing the Great War

The notion of the First World War as the 'Great War' is justified not only considering its political magnitude and the unprecedented scale of mobilisation, territorial expansion, destruction and intensity of warfare. It was also a 'great' war in the sense of the abundance and diversity of cultural responses and transformations it provoked, both as it took place and in the decades to follow, up to the present day. Samuel Hynes, in his seminal study *A War Imagined: The First World War and English Culture*, stresses the overwhelming importance of the war as a transformative force and as a source of (frequently traumatic) inspiration and imagination, both for those directly involved in it as for later generations affected by its long-term repercussions, including the complex and persisting myths and narratives of the war. The Great War, Hynes argues, was "the great military and political event of its time; but it was also the great *imaginative* event" (Hynes 1990, 1). Its dimension effectively "changed reality" and thereby "altered the ways in which men and women thought not only about war but about the world, and about culture and its expression" (ibid.). The Great War famously also was an "artists' war", both in the sense of the enormous number of sensitive and articulate participants who would record their experiences using various kinds of artistic expression, and in the sense of having become a persistent creative and imaginative resource.

In this manner, the war has been read by Hynes and others as a vital creative context, even as a watershed in twentieth-century literary history. With regard to English literature, the war has been seen as a crucial step towards Modernism, as the beginning of a fundamental break with existing literary conventions – essentially, a farewell to Victorian and Edwardian forms of literary expression (cf. Hynes 1990, 30), introducing "a new way of seeing" (Ouditt 2005, 253). Still, in this respect, it must be noted that this view has also been challenged, for example, by Jay Winter who observed a continuity of conservatism and traditional forms of expression also in the post-war period (cf. Winter 1995). Also, the type of writing most famously associated with the Great War, the frontline poetry of soldier-poets like Wilfred Owen, Isaac Rosenberg, Siegfried Sassoon, or, to add a less prominent but Irish note, Francis Ledwidge, still very much followed well-established conventions. These poets widely eschewed the stylistic and conceptual radicalism, the complexity and experimental spirit of early Modernism in favour of more conventional but gruesomely realistic protest poetry. Nonetheless, modernists such as Virginia Woolf were from the beginning interested in the writings of those who served, in the suffering endured in the war and in the moral as well as aesthetic implications of witnessing, describing and narrating suffering (cf. Tate 2009, 160f.), and the modernist reactions to the Great War have proven to be enlightening and insightful contributions to the understanding of the conflict. Considering the influence of the Great War on Irish Modernism, it has been argued, for example, that the Great War represents an essential background to Joyce's *Ulysses* – as Jacques Darras remarks, "[y]ou cannot have James Joyce or *Ulysses* without a European war roaring in the background or across the Swiss border [...]. You may ignore it. You may pretend that it did not exist or that it were not worth mentioning. But facts are hard to beat" (quoted in Jeffery 1999, 3).

Altogether, it was the above-mentioned type of poetry that would dominate the production of war literature during the conflict.[40] English Prose writing about the war reached its peak in the late 1920s, after a decade marked by a large-scale literary silence about the Great War (cf. Erll 2003, 125), in the shape of a veritable boom of war-related works – novels, memoirs, diaries, biographies and histories. Compared to this, the treatment of the Great War in English drama represents the least successful of the main literary genres and only plays a minor

---

40 Hynes mentions a bibliography of English Great War poetry that lists over 3,000 works by 2,225 poets (cf. Hynes 1990, 29).

role. After being overshadowed by the Second World War in the 1940s and 1950s, a major revival of the Great War occurred in the 1960s, frequently including a re-contextualisation, re-imagination and re-evaluation of established narratives and themes, shedding light on facets of the conflict and its implications previously neglected or concealed, for example, the complex nexus of death and sex, and of masculinity and heroism (cf. Ouditt 2005, 250).

As the Great War has provoked cultural reactions and eventually helped to re-shape literature, literary representations and reworkings of the war have massively shaped contemporary and retrospective conceptions of the conflict. As Trudi Tate remarks, "it was in literature that readers at the time could learn something of what was really happening" (Tate 2009, 160) and, regarding readers after 1918, the Great War has been, in effect, "a war remembered through the way in which it had been imagined" (Brearton 2000, 116). Consequently, cultural and historical commentators like Hynes, or the equally influential Paul Fussell in his 1975 work *The Great War and Modern Memory*, have drawn heavily on literary responses to the Great War, particularly focusing on war poetry, in order to make sense of how it was perceived at the time of the conflict and how it was mythologised and re-constructed in its aftermath.

A key result of their research is the identification of an overly negative but powerful myth of the Great War that would prove instrumental in determining attitudes to the conflict and that has been re-produced in literature and other forms of artistic expression to this day: the disillusioning collective narrative of an idealistic young 'lost generation' pointlessly sacrificed by incompetent military leaders for the sake of cynical politicians and pitiless war profiteers. However, more recent research[41] has challenged the validity and exclusivity of this narrative. Critics have pointed out that it is the outcome of a disproportionate and thus distorting concentration on the largely unrepresentative war experiences of prominent soldier-writers, who were mostly well-educated middle-class officers, while the experiences of common soldiers, for whom the war actually was by no means exclusively meaningless and futile, have been neglected (cf. Taylor 2013,

---

41 See, for example, Gary Sheffield's *Forgotten Victory: The First World War: Myths and Realities*. London: Review, 2002. Randall Stevenson also emphasises that the resistance against the negative myth of the Great War is not exclusively a phenomenon of the late twentieth century but has its origins in the 1930s. Douglas Jerrold's *The Lie about the War: A Note on Some Contemporary War Books* (1930) is a major example (cf. Stevenson 2013, 196).

25ff.; Stevenson 2013, 193ff.). Against this misrepresentation, revisionist[42] critics have been calling for a more comprehensive and complex approach to war experiences and their narration, including a greater awareness of aspects of class, nation and gender. The investigation of the long-neglected Irish war experiences and their literary representations undertaken in this study is very much in line with this re-defined approach.

The traditional and, as outlined above, somewhat problematic dominance of the 'myth' of the Great War is also closely connected to the question of authorship and genre, i. e. the question of how to categorise texts and discourses as war works. Definitions of what makes a text 'war literature', who qualifies in which way as a 'war writer' and which subjects, attitudes and modes of expression are adequate for war writing, vary. A focal point in this debate is the historically dominant status of the soldier-poets in the perception of the cultural responses to the war, a status which they share with the canonical and immensely successful war works by combatant novelists such as Henri Barbusse, Robert Graves, Ernst Jünger and Erich Maria Remarque – as Kathleen Devine observes, a selection of texts and authors that has "tended to set the critical agenda for consideration of war literature" (Devine 1999, ix; cf. Brearton 2000, 39), and that was instrumental in perpetuating the narrative of purposeless sacrifice. This status has enforced the notion that the literary treatment of the Great War primarily is reserved for combatants, an attitude that also underpins, for example, the notorious rejection[43] of Sean O'Casey's 1928 war play *The Silver Tassie* by W. B. Yeats. Such attitudes effectively boil down the task of writing and communicating the Great War to an autobiographical issue, to an exclusive matter of first-hand experience and by that also to a quite narrowly male affair, "making it difficult for those traditionally denied access to the war zone to claim validity for their accounts" (McLoughlin 2009, 16) – apparently, only those who have experienced the war, such attitudes suggest, have gained the authority to narrate or re-imagine it.

The assumed gulf between combatant and non-combatant perspectives and identities that informs this definition of war writing is fundamentally connected to questions of authenticity and to the perceived issue of the difficulty of actually giving expression to the experience of war. The frequently lamented problem of the incommunicability of the Great War has been seen as the result of the new quality of destruction and misery that combatants were exposed to on

---

42 The different implications of revisionism, specifically considering the use of the term in an Irish context, are explained in chapters II.1.2 and in the introductory part of chapter III.3.

43 See also chapter III.2.3.

the battlefield and that was perceived to have traumatised and alienated soldiers from the civilian societies they fought for, creating an insurmountable gap in experience: "the collision between events and the language available – or thought appropriate – to describe them" (Fussell 2009, 212). Richard Aldington, for example, notes how writing the war "was a question of trying to communicate the incommunicable. There was no ratio between the two races of men – those, I mean, in the line and those who had never touched it" (quoted in Bonikowski 2013, 3). The German writer and soldier Rudolf Binding radicalises this thought in *Aus dem Kriege* (1925), when he judges that the "history of this war will never be written. Those who can write it will remain silent. Those who write have not experienced it" (ibid.).

This is why, Kate McLoughlin summarises, we should be aware of the idea that war writing structurally "constantly advertises its own inadequacy" (McLoughlin 2009, 15), and we should also keep in mind that this inadequacy of communicating war in a satisfactorily 'authentic' way is not an issue recognised only since the Great War. The persistent problem of the 'reality' of war and the imaginative limitations of literary expression are addressed, for example, also in the prologue to Shakespeare's *Henry V* (1600):

> [...] But pardon, gentles all,
> The flat unraised spirits, that hath dared
> On this unworthy scaffold, to bring forth
> So great an object. Can this cockpit hold
> The vasty fields of France? Or may we cram
> Within this wooden O the very casques
> That did affright the air at Agincourt?
>
> (Shakespeare 2005, 78f; cf. McLoughlin 2009, 15)

McLoughlin points out how this acknowledgment of the impossibility of re-enacting full-scale military conflict on stage is countered by Shakespeare's subsequent call for the audience to activate their imagination ("And let us, ciphers to this great account, / On our imaginary forces work" (Shakespeare 2005, 79)), establishing a link between the imperatives of realism and imaginative freedom – a key technique in conveying war (cf. ibid). The act of communicating war, Trudi Tate similarly argues, principally is concerned with sharing something of that experience, explaining it to others and eventually creating a shared memory of war, a cultural imagining that extends beyond those originally involved (cf. Tate 2009, 165). In the case of the Great War, the sentiment of being unable to describe the unfamiliar intensity of warfare can also be explained, Fussell suggests, by combatants only having access to familiar literary idioms – modernist innovations of expression which could have been perceived to do greater justice to the new reality of war were still largely unavailable (cf. Fussell 2009, 218). In the light of these considerations, the exclusive claim to authenticity of one group of course does not automatically disqualify other imaginative efforts of dealing with the war, particularly, since those other writers might be able to employ more powerful modes of presentation, and also, as will be shown shortly, since the experience of the Great War in all of its facets is not necessarily as exclusive, and the divisions as clear-cut, as assumed.

The traditional but limited concept of war literature which, more or less, entails a ruling-out of non-combatant writings as adequate representations of the conflict has been problematised extensively,[44] critics addressing the issue of subjectivity, authenticity and the general problem of 'reality' – did not the Great War effect a shift of perception and unsettle established perspectives in the first place? As a consequence, a more comprehensive and integrative idea of war writing has been suggested, an idea based on the expansion of the concept beyond the notion of frontline literature – an expansion that is both spatial and temporal, covering not just the (immediate, remembered or reconstructed) experience of the battlefield and the trenches but also the ambiguity of the so-called 'home front', as well as the Great War's echo, its persisting effects on identities, ideologies, society and history in the decades to follow. In the face of the expansion of the concept of 'war' that the conflict of 1914–1918 entailed, this opening up of the understanding of war writing to include non-combatant (particularly women's) writing, the depiction of the home front, pacifist as well as propagandistic writing, memoirs, biographies, letters and retrospective re-contextualisations and re-imaginations of the Great War (cf. Kosok 2007, 1ff.), appears to be more than justified. The conventional approach that envisions and imagines the war only on the level of military experience simply cannot be sufficient considering the hitherto unparalleled social, political, geographical and economic scope of the Great War – the first fully industrialised and total war, completely involving the entire social and economic fabric of the warring nations. This war did affect combatant *and* non-combatant lives, identities and allegiances deeply and persistently in so many ways that a restriction of 'true' war experience and war writing to events in trenches and barracks must mean to cut short and distort the realities of the Great War and its repercussions. The war happened just as much at iconic and mythologised locations associated with mud, blood and butchery, such as Ypres,

---

44 See, for example, Hynes 1990, Devine 1999, Tate 2009, Bonikowski 2013.

Gallipoli or Verdun, as it happened on the home front, a very telling term in itself, touching both soldiers and the civilian populations at home.

In the light of the factual blurring and complication of civilian and military spheres and identities that the Great War entailed (cf. Cole 2009, 31), the clear-cut separation into military and civilian realms of identity and experience that underlies the traditional notion of war writing as combatant writing also appears as untenable, the war being not majorly fought by professional soldiers but by volunteers and conscripts. Participants of the war did not simply block out or dispose of their civilian identities and mind-sets upon entering the army. This is noted, for example, by Ford Madox Ford in 1924, who recounts how

> apart from the occasional, petulant question, "When the deuce will our fellows get going and shut 'em up?" your thoughts were really concentrated on something quite distant: on your daughter Millicent's hair, on the fall of the Asquith Ministry, on your financial predicament, on why your regimental ferrets kept on dying, on whether Latin is really necessary to an education.... You were there, but great shafts of thought from the outside, distant and unattainable world infinitely for the greater part occupied your mind.
>
> (Ford 1924, 205)

The notion of a split between combatant and non-combatant, military and civilian, is further destabilised, for example, when we take into account phenomena such as the establishment of so-called "Pals battalions" (cf. Petter 1994, 136) within the British army, in which recruits who had enlisted together, belonging to the same town, village, university, sports club or workplace, were also kept together as a military unit, enabling them to fight alongside their peacetime peers, effectively transferring the social make-up of civilian spaces into the military environment.

Altogether, considering the high degree of interdependence between war and civilian spheres, and taking into account the embeddedness of the Great War in Irish domestic contexts and the variety of Irish responses to the war outlined earlier, it seems advisable to appropriate the spirit of Julian Symons's comprehensive notion of war writing formulated in 1942: "[W]ar poetry is not a specialised department of poetry: it is [...] quite simply the poetry [...] of people affected by the reality of war" (quoted in Devine 1999, xviii). Of course, this is also applicable to prose and dramatic writing. Along with Symons, the notion of "the reality of war" is understood in this study to encompass a wide range of experiences and perspectives that are not limited to the wartime period and to military locations – from 'going over the top' into no man's land to women entering the war industries, from flying over devastated landscapes to attending a memorial service on Armistice Day, from training with the 36th (Ulster) Division in England to listening to the stories of veterans decades after the outbreak of the war. Only such an extended and flexible sense of war writing can do justice to the scope of the conflict and its influential legacy and, as will be shown in the following section, of covering the extensively heterogeneous Irish literary responses to the Great War in a workable manner.

Consequently, this study, analogous to Heinz Kosok's general definition of war plays (cf. Kosok 2007, 3), understands Irish Great War literature in the sense of texts (1) that present actual events of the Great War from an Irish, Anglo-Irish and Northern Irish perspective, both in the actual war zones and at the home front; (2) which deal with the Great War's consequences, either for their central characters or for society at large and also beyond the actual time of the Great War itself; (3) that use the experience of the Great War as a starting point for the exploration of related conflicts; and (4) that focus on theoretical issues raised by wartime events. Furthermore, analogous to the theoretical background outlined in chapter II.1, this project is underpinned by the notion of war writing defined by Bernard Taithe and Tim Thornton, who stress the inextricable connection between the individual, identity politics and war, arguing that "[a] war narrative is fundamentally a narrative of identity, which seeks a rationale to the war itself and mostly finds it in identity" (Taithe and Thornton 1998, 12), often in retrospective constructions of war and soldier identities, including the paradoxes inherent in this understanding with regard to the condition of the incommunicability of war and its ambiguous but powerful survival as myth.

II.3.2 Writing Ireland's Great War

As outlined in the chapter on the historical context, the position of the Great War in Irish history and memory is ambiguous and problematic, and until the 1980s it was difficult to adequately integrate this event into the official and collective narratives of Irish history. The official silence about the Great War was paralleled by a cultural and literary silence. As Terence Brown notes, for decades after the war "[i]t was as if the Irish had agreed collectively, if for widely differing reasons, to dismiss from consciousness their own involvement in the greatest cataclysm ever to have befallen European civilization. And the silence of the country's writers speaks volumes" (Brown 1993, 229). There is a general consensus about the marginal status of the Great War in Irish literature as well as in Northern Irish literature, which is fairly surprising considering the much more accepted status of the war in Northern Ireland. There is no substantial Irish tradition of writing the Great War that could be compared to the English literary output, both with regard to quality and quantity. The Great War in England, Fran Brearton summarises, "has a tragic status and imaginative impact it has never attained in Ireland"

(Brearton 2000, 37), and, taking into account the size and international role of Ireland, this also applies to more balanced comparisons of Irish war literature to the respective conditions in Australia or Canada.[45]

The commonly attested lack of Irish imaginative engagement with the topic is astonishing, considering, on the one hand, the scale and complexity of the Irish involvement in the conflict and the importance of the Great War as a context for the achievement of Irish independence, and, on the other hand, the profound interest in national self-inspection that has been a persistent concern of Irish literature. The latter issue, the re-formulation of a national identity for a colonised nation, was the central motivation that drove the Irish Literary Revival in the early decades of the twentieth century and this issue has remained a main interest of much Irish literature until the present day (cf. Middeke and Schnierer 2010 viii f.). In this continuous search for identity, which has been seen as the symptom of a profound (post-)colonial national insecurity (cf. Lonergan 2008, vii), the re-imagination and appropriation of the Irish past, both in politics and in literature, has been instrumental. As Ian McBride argues, in "Ireland, as is well known, the interpretation of the past has always been at the heart of national conflict", noting even how "the time-warped character of Irish mind-sets has become a cliché of scholarly and unscholarly writing" (McBride 2001, 1). Why, then, within a literary tradition almost stereotypically bent on exploring the past, has Ireland's Great War history played only a marginal part for such a long time? And which ideological, cultural and literary factors contributed to cast it as such an undesirable part of Irish history, resulting in a large-scale literary silence?

The central reason for the Irish literary silence about the Great War lies in Irish politics of memory and state ideology that effectively led to a blanket marginalisation of the Great War as a part of Irish history, some commentators even going so far as to speak of the war as having been "officially extirpated from the record"[46]

---

45 For Australia and, to an even stronger degree, for Canada, the Great War has played a crucial role as a source of national identity, which is also reflected in the literary output concerning the war. Vance, for example, remarks how in Canada the war's legacy for writers, artists and intellectuals is not one "of despair, aimlessness, and futility, but of promise, [and] certainty [...] that the war had been a just one, fought to defend Christianity and Western civilisation" (Vance 1997, 266f., cf. Thompson 2008, 97). See also Laird 1971, Vance 1997 and Meyer 2001.

46 Keith Jeffery sees this notion of a radical and complete historical erasure of Ireland's Great War as an inexact simplification, claiming instead that the phenomenon of the conscious "forgetting" of the Great War was much less uniform, reaching its greatest intensity between the 1940s and the 1960s (cf. Jeffery 2011, 256).

(Kiberd 1996, 239). As outlined in chapter II.2, the history and memory of the Great War indeed was seen as incompatible with the identity project of an independent and nationalist-republican Ireland that insisted on the myth of the Easter Rising and other revolutionary nationalist feats as its central source of origin and as the sole historical narrative at its foundation. The domestic upheavals of the early 1920s and the resulting need to re-organise and stabilise an unsettled and polarised nation also did not invite a balanced engagement with the recent involvement in the Great War and a possible integration of this contested episode into the new state identity. The experience of revolutionary struggle and civil war apparently were more immediate concerns for many than the suffering of Irishmen who had left to fight in a war re-defined as a foreign affair (cf. Brown 1993, 229), regardless of the scale of Irish casualties and the manifold personal and historical connections to the event. As Nuala Johnson remarks, during the war and in the following years, the "neat binaries of victor and vanquished, enemy and friend, Christian and heathen, public and private, individual and collective collapsed" (Johnson 2003, 13), the war turning into a highly ambiguous event. In England, the Great War was perceived as a major threshold – an event essentially burying an Edwardian age nostalgically remembered as peaceful, pastoral and complacent, and inaugurating a much rougher age of modernity. In Ireland, such a nostalgic sense of a pre-war idyll could not be entertained and processed by literature as the pre-war period was dominated by harsh political dispute, the Great War only displacing an ongoing conflict-laden domestic situation verging on civil war (cf. Haughy 2002, 16). As Fran Brearton aptly summarises, the "Great War in Ireland cannot be separated in memory from the violence that preceded and followed it" (Brearton 2000, 41).

The ideological and cultural climate of the Irish Free State and the Republic of Ireland generally was not conducive to the re-imagination of the Great War. Keith Jeffery mentions an episode that strikingly exposes the cultural dimension of the common unwillingness not only to acknowledge the Irish part in the war, but even to shun the Great War in its entirety: In 1920, the annual Royal Dublin Society Taylor Art Prize was won by Mainie Jellett, a young painter from a prominent Protestant family and later a pioneering Irish modernist, for a painting showing a serene scene of her sisters and other girls on a sunny beach. The title of the work, "Peace", was a direct reaction of relief by Jellett to the end of the Great War, yet, the painting subsequently and persistently became known not as "Peace" but as "The Bathers' Pool", completely neutralising its original context (cf. Jeffery 2000, 71ff.). In a similar way, the War Memorial Library at Trinity College Dublin became known as the "1937 Reading Room", as if the war that occasioned it had never taken place (cf. Horne 2008a, 13f.). The marginalisation of the war as a relevant Irish event was also advanced by the mainstream of Irish historians who neglected the topic for decades, with the exception of a few rather journalistic pieces hastily written during the conflict and in its immediate aftermath by loyalist or Anglo-Irish authors (cf. Haughey 2002, 18f.). This historiographic ignorance is also at the roots of the large-scale absence of the Great War in Irish school curricula for the greater part of the twentieth century (cf. Leonard 1997, 68), another decisive step towards the amnesia concerning the Irish part in the conflict and certainly specifically detrimental to the entering of the narrative and imagery of the Great War into common Irish imagination.[47]

The image of Ireland and the concept of Irish identity which was to be promoted by the state from independence well up to the 1960s was one of a distinctly un-English, hermetic, archaic, rural and Catholic nation. This was formulated most resonantly by Éamon de Valera, then in his second term as Taoiseach, in a 1943 radio speech, who propagated his vision of Ireland as "a land whose countryside would be bright with cosy homesteads, whose fields and villages would be joyous with the sound of industry, with the romping of sturdy children, the contests of athletic youths, the laughter of comely maidens; whose firesides would be forums for the wisdom of old age" (quoted in Middeke and Schnierer 2010, xi). This quaint construction of a state identity was accompanied by a strict cultural and religious protectionism, reinforced through draconic censorship. Cultural policies after independence were characterised by what Brown calls an official "almost Stalinist antagonism to modernism [...] combined with prudery [...] and a deep reverence for the Irish past" (Brown 2004, 135) – that is, an Irish largely consisting of the Gaelic civilisation and seven hundred years of struggle against Britain (cf. Ferriter 2005, 22). All of this was programmatically geared towards safeguarding Irish independence – practically, it meant isolation and stagnation, maintaining the old social structure of an essentially rural Ireland "dominated by

---

47 Interestingly, the Great War was also not too prominently featured in school curricula in Northern Ireland and when it was taught, the role of soldiers from the Catholic south of course was left out. For example, Jim Haughey remembers how "the only book about the war that I read in high school was Robert Graves's *Good-bye to All That* (1929), while the period between 1914 and 1918 was largely reviewed as a minicourse in Easter Rebellion studies" (Haughey 2002, 18). This is a result of the urgent need of Northern Ireland to consolidate the state by a strict insistence on separation, something that becomes apparent, for example, in the memories of the poet Michael Longley of his early education, who notes how "there was little on the curriculum to suggest that we were living in Ireland; no Irish history except when it impinged on the grand parade of English monarchs; no Irish literature; no Irish art; no Irish music" (ibid.).

the social, cultural, and political will of the farmers and their offspring" (Brown 2004, 139). After achieving Irish independence, Declan Kiberd argues, "[i]nstead of a liberating leap into the future, all movement ceased" (Kiberd 1988, 49), social, cultural and historical heterogeneity was almost openly suppressed (cf. Peach 2004, 5). Many intellectuals, artists and writers, among them Liam O'Flaherty, Frank O'Connor and Sean O'Faoláin, expressed a deep disillusionment about the paralysis independence had inaugurated (cf. Brown 2004, 142).

In such a cultural climate, literary excursions into a contested episode such as the Great War almost naturally seem improbable and beyond the ideological and imaginative capacities of mainstream Ireland – as Bernard Taithe and Tim Thornton argue, "historical identities and identifications can misfire when they appear too removed from the identity lived and practised" (Taithe and Thornton 1998, 10). The war represented an event of an politically inconvenient and un-ambiguously international scope that was perceived largely as a British matter, and that was altogether more an affair of the obsolete Anglo-Irish class and the urban Irish working class than of the peasantry and rural Catholic bourgeoisie (cf. Fitzpatrick 1995, 1018). It was a topic at odds with an obsessively inward-looking, anti-modern and aseptic post-independent culture. In the decades after 1922, as Terence Brown observes,

> the abstractions of international relations […] could scarcely stir the popular imagina-tion. Conservative ideology and the social fabric were bound up with one another, both expressive of the atavistic and widespread conviction that the essential Irish reality was the uniquely desirable, unchanging life of small farm and country town in the Irish-speaking west. There was neither competition nor pressure for ideological innovation in the dynamics of social complexities or large-scale rapid change.
>
> (Brown 2004, 170)

And Hugh Leonard, describing the cultural climate from the perspective of an Irish dramatist, tellingly comments how

> [w]ith the coming of the Irish Free State our drama became even more parochial. We had a peasant government and a reactionary clergy, both of which were intensely anglo-phobic. What passed for Irish culture was imposed on artists and audiences alike: not for intrinsic values but as a deliberate negation of all things English. […] For more than thirty years – from the 1920s until the mid-1950s – Irish theatre has concerned itself with Irishmen first and men later.
>
> (Leonard 1978, 78)

How could a play, novel or poem about Irishmen in British uniform, fighting in an industrialised and inconceivably horrific war on the Continent, or, to acknowledge the expanded sense of war writing outlined earlier, a work about the Irish home front or about the Irish aftermath of the Great War, emerge in such circumstances? Terry Phillips summarises, "Ireland's literature is constructed by the codes of identity and difference as a coherent and distinctive entity. Such a construction, with its identitarian impulse, inevitably produces a master narrative that excludes minor and not so minor traditions" (Phillips 2010a, 50) – and the writing of the Great War from an Irish perspective obviously did not belong to this master narrative but to excluded traditions and excluded identities.

One of the most influential critical Irish voices of the 1920s and 1930s, Daniel Corkery, declares in an elitist definition of Irish literature in the opening chapter of *Synge and Anglo-Irish Literature* (1931) that an authentic Irish writer should be Catholic and concerned with the land and the nationalist movement (cf. Phillips 2010a, 45). According to Corkery, insisting on a principle of radical decolonisation, every Irish writer is faced with the decision "whether to express Ireland and the life of the nation or to exploit her" (cf. Kiberd 2005a, 50), and the episode of the Great War and the Irish part played in it was not seen as belonging to the life of the nation. In this respect, it is unsurprising that the few prose works to address the topic of Ireland and the Great War in the first couple of decades after independence were mostly written by authors who already occupied a position on the fringes of Irish society and cultural life themselves as members of the declining Anglo-Irish class and as female writers – writers such as Pamela Hinkson or Margaret Barrington.

Only by the late 1950s and early 1960s, the insular condition of Irish society, perceived as "lying in the stagnant sidestreams of history" (Brown 2004, 200), having eventually led to a widespread rejection of rural life and to waves of emigration that almost amounted to an Irish exodus (cf. Brown 2004, 174f.), was beginning to break up. Ireland experienced a much needed social, economic and cultural transformation. This enabled new challenges to the existing paradigms of Irish culture and memory and made possible attempts at the re-imagination of the Irish past. Social commentators at the time very much speculated about how much of what was taken to be Ireland's "traditional" identity could be preserved in these new circumstances (cf. Brown 2004, 297). Yet, it would take another twenty years and the development of a revisionist school of historiography and literature to establish the Great War both as a pertinent part of Irish history and as a relevant literary topic.

There were also other related literary factors that thwarted the development of an extensive Irish tradition of Great War literature and that hindered the reception and critical appreciation of the existing Irish war works. For example, the genre of the realist war novel which yielded some of the most influential and resonant accounts of the Great War and which, as mentioned earlier, experienced a veritable boom in Britain and Germany in the late 1920s, likely did not find many practitioners in Ireland because the realist novel in general did not have a tradition in Ireland and Northern Ireland that was as substantial as the one in English culture (cf. Peach 2004, 1f.). The Irish cultural nationalist mainstream at the beginning of the century tended to discard the novel as an adequate medium for the representation of Ireland, locating its roots in British cultural traditions and British middle-class concerns, also perceiving Irish society as too thin and homogenous to sustain a novelistic tradition (cf. ibid). These attitudes were also transferred into independent Ireland and seem to have lasted well up to the middle of the century, which becomes visible, for example, in Sean O'Faoláin's assessment that in the twenty-five years since the establishment of the Irish Free State in 1922, a meagre total of four realistic Irish novels had been written (cf. Foster 2006, 16).

Much of the indifference towards the Irish poetry of the Great War has been linked to the general perception of Great War Poetry as Anglocentric (cf. Haughey 2002, 16). The genre has been majorly, and possibly justifiably so, associated with the figure of the middle-class and upper-middle-class English officer, those works typically emphasising Englishness, this "Anglo ethnocentrism [...seemingly] overshadow[ing] the rest of the British archipelago's literary response to the war" (ibid.), as Jim Haughey observes – another problem of identification and also one of style and aesthetics, given "the extent to which the Irish imagination was subjugated by a British imperial idiom" (Haughey 2002, 99), Irish poetry of the war hardly ever finding ways of expression beyond the aesthetic standards of English war writing. That this condition of aesthetic as well as thematic dependence, ironically, also applies to a large section of the poetry of the Easter Rising will be shown at the end of this chapter.

Haughey further relates the historical lack of attention to the narrow field of Irish war poetry to the dominance of "the Yeats and Joyce industries" (ibid.), the bias of Irish literary studies and criticism towards Irish modernism. War poetry, including the Irish kind, has been usually "closeted with Georgian forms and themes, romantic obsessions and a sense of rural escapism" (Haughey 2002, 16f.) – for critics preoccupied with Irish modernism's theoretical and aesthetic complexities and experiments, this kind of writing must appear unattractive as an object of investigation. In this context, it is important to add that the notion of stylistic conventionality and conformity is not restricted only to the Irish poetry of the Great War but characterises much of the Irish prose and dramatic efforts concerning the war. Up to Frank McGuinness's *Observe the Sons of Ulster Marching Towards the Somme* (1985), Irish literary excursions into the topic had been largely relying upon naturalistic modes of presentation. The only major exception to this is Sean O'Casey's war play *The Silver Tassie* (1928), the play's second act offering a stylistically experimental and highly ritualistic depiction of the horrors of the battlefield, frequently regarded as expressionist or post-expressionist. However, O'Casey's aesthetic and imaginative leap, his "passion play" (cf. Jeffery 2011, 254), was not particularly well-received either by Irish audiences or critics (cf. Welch 1999, 120; Brown 1993, 228).

Finally, the most prominent critic of O'Casey and at the time the central and most influential cultural figure in Ireland, W. B. Yeats, has also been identified as a central influence on the rejection of the Great War as a subject for Irish literature (cf. Devine 1999, xii; Haughey 2002, 17; Brown 2008, 244). As Brearton argues, Yeats helped to "consolidate the view that the tragedy of the Great War was primarily an English not an Irish tragedy, and, as such, [...] it was remote from cultural life" (Brearton 2000, 44). Yeats's aversion towards the literary treatment of the war becomes apparent most blatantly in his poem "On Being Asked for a War Poem"[48] (1915), as well as in his harsh rejection of *The Silver Tassie*, and in his exclusion of the Georgian war poets from his *Oxford Book of Modern Verse* (1936), reasoning that "passive suffering" (Yeats 1936, xxxiv) has no place in poetry. Brown even speaks of the sense of "a Yeatsian interdiction" concerning (not only) Irish literary approaches to the war, "their unearthing of the experience of the Great War" amounting to nothing but the rejection of "a set of allied cultural and social conventions" (Brown 2008, 244). Paradoxically, Yeats himself actually did address the war several times in his works beyond the issue of (not) writing the war itself.[49] Personally affected by the war death of Lady Gregory's son Robert Gregory, Yeats wrote "An Irish Airman Foresees His Death" (1919) which sheds light on the contradictory colonial identity politics connected to the situation of Irishmen serving in the British forces:

> Those that I fight I do not hate,
> Those that I guard I do not love;
> My country is Kiltartan Cross,
> My countrymen Kiltartan's poor,
> No likely end could bring them loss
> Or leave them happier than before.

(Yeats 2008, 8, ll. 3–8)

---

48 "I think it better that in times like these / A poet keep his mouth shut [...]" (Yeats 2008, 9, ll. 1–2).

49 In fact, more than forty of Yeats's poems have been identified as engaging with the Great War in some manner (cf. Kosok 2008, 154).

Two years later, under the impression of the atrocities of the Anglo-Irish War,[50] Yeats returned to this very topic once more in a poem entitled "Reprisals", imagining the ghost of Robert Gregory as a revenant, categorising him as one of the "other cheated dead" (Yeats 2008, 14, l. 24) of the war. Yeats here very much follows the pattern of the contextualisation of the Great War within other Irish domestic affairs that characterises so much of Irish war writing. Tellingly, "Reprisals" was not published in Yeats's lifetime, only appearing in print in 1948 in an Ulster journal of poetry (cf. Brown 1993, 227), confirming the impression that in many ways "Ireland's Great War literature is a diffuse set of writings" (Brearton 2000, 39) with an awkward history.

The Great War in Irish Literature – An Overview

Considering the adverse ideological and cultural conditions in Ireland that instigated the comparative scarcity and heterogeneity of this field of writing, it is, as mentioned earlier, not entirely unproblematic to speak of 'war literature' in the context of Ireland, effectively requiring an extensive notion of war writing. In this manner, a considerable number of the works discussed in this study under the umbrella term of 'war literature' does not focus on the direct experience or the legacy of the Great War as their only concern, and only a fraction of the authors participated in the war themselves. Instead, in works such as Lennox Robinson's *The Big House* (1926) or Nicola McCartney's *Heritage* (1998), the Great War is a crucial context in which related conflicts and histories, both personal and political, are embedded. Only very few works by Irish authors conform to the classic conventions of the genre of war literature, most notably, the altogether rather formulaic war novels of Liam O'Flaherty and Patrick MacGill.[51]

As Keith Jeffery notes, "over the years there has been a simmering of interest on the part of Irish writers in the First World War" (Jeffery 1994, 93) – the Irish reaction to the conflict is not at all limited only to the war years. An attempt to chronicle the Irish literary output relating to the Great War might result in three major segments of Irish war writing, strongly determined by the amnesiac tendencies concerning the war and the eventual overcoming of this condition. The first period could be identified to cover the war years and the decade following

---

50 "Half-drunk or whole-mad soldiery / Are murdering your tenants there. / Men that revere your father yet / Are shot at on the open plain" (Yeats 2008, 14, ll. 15–18).

51 Yet, as will be shown later, these two authors hardly ever problematise the subject of Irishness or Irish identity in their war works – which is an interesting aspect in itself but rules them out as major objects of investigation in this study.

the war, characterised most notably by war poetry by Irish writers from a variety of backgrounds and by few Irish war novels. Additionally, there are works in this period centring on the Easter Rising, relating in various degrees of directness to the Great War as a backdrop for Irish revolutionary struggle. The second period, from the 1930s to the 1970s, is the most heterogeneous one in which the insular nature of the Great War as an Irish literary topic becomes very obvious, as the war, if re-imagined at all, is most frequently employed as an evocative context in works by Anglo-Irish authors following the Big House theme. The third period, which could be seen as something like a Great War revival, taking place almost thirty years after the one in England, is dominated by drama and arguably has its principal starting point in Frank McGuinness's 1985 play *Observe the Sons of Ulster Marching Towards the Somme*. This phase is characterised by a pronounced sense of a conscious political re-envisioning of Ireland's Great War in the light of contemporary Irish political and social conditions and questions of identity.

Despite their diversity in origin, form, theme, setting and outlook, Irish literary representations of the Great War and its legacy share several central elements. As in other traditions of Great War writing, there is a tendency towards the autobiographical (cf. Johnson 2003, 126), this also includes writers of the post-war generations, who frequently process family memories or histories in their works. Furthermore, there is a general tendency of perpetuating the highly influential narrative of the Great War as constructed in the English tradition outlined earlier – the war as a futile, meaningless and almost incommunicable cycle of slaughter, injury and disease. As Keith Jeffery comments, in almost all Irish war works, "the whole affair [is] desperately serious; only Protestants and Unionists fought at the Somme; and the violence of the war appeared to have had no moral justification" (Jeffery 2011, 261f.). Yet, Irish literary representations of the Great War also frequently introduce a sense of distance, disengagement or detachment from the war (cf. Jeffery 2000, 79) that is more unique. This is the result of the complicated and frequently contradictory combination of Irish allegiances and identities with the service in the British forces – "Those that I fight I do not hate, / Those that I guard I do not love" – creating a predicament for many that culminated in the moral and political challenge posed by the Easter Rising.

The comparative prominence of this predicament, however, also directs us to a discrepancy within the Irish literary responses to the Great War. What about the war experiences of the large number of Irishmen and Ulstermen who did not specifically integrate their war service into a certain political identity or agenda – Redmondite, Carsonite, internationalist – but who went to war to escape poverty and confinement at home? In fact, apart from the works of MacGill and two plays by the socialists Shaw and O'Casey, the war experiences of the Irish working class are rarely a feature in Irish war writing (cf. Jeffery 1999, 17). Considering the general disregard of the world of the urban proletariat as a literary subject evident in much of twentieth-century Irish writing (cf. Brown 2004, 94),[52] this is not too surprising, however, taking into account the impact of the war on those classes, this condition definitely constitutes an imbalance.

An even greater imbalance is the pronounced absence of the Great War in Northern Irish writing, particularly in Ulster unionist writing. As mentioned earlier, the Ulster contribution to the war effort, most emblematically the fight of the Ulster Division at the Somme in 1916, was quickly and persistently embraced in the north, turning into the "mytho-poetic core" of Ulster communal identity and of the new Northern Irish province that emerged in the post-war period (McNulty 2010, 64), paralleling the mythological nation-building role of the Easter Rising in the south. The Somme and the Rising became events which were "held to encapsulate the inherent qualities of the true Ulster Protestant (proud, reticent, unimaginative) or true Irish Catholic (spiritual, voluble, imaginative), oppositional stereotypes used and abused on both sides" (Brearton 2000, 37), both grounded on simplified and biased historical narratives. The sacrifice made by Ulstermen at the Somme entered unionist political discourses as a sacred and eternal seal of Ireland's union with Britain; yet, this was also accompanied by a sense of disillusionment and betrayal caused by the suspicion of Ulster soldiers' lives being wasted too easily by British military command and, more critically, by Britain's readiness to make concessions to Irish republicans since 1916 which worked against the fundamental concerns of unionism and eventually led to partition.

In the early post-war years, there was indeed a wave of war works about the feats of the Ulster Division, however, they were authored by unionist historians and politicians mostly in a dogmatic attempt at prescribing how to remember the Somme rather than engaging with the actual experience (cf. Brearton 2000, 30). Apart from a small amount of propagandistic and triumphalist popular ephemeral verse, there is no substantial tradition of Ulster war poetry from this time (cf. ibid), also, there

---

52 The overwhelming disregard of class issues and social conditions was a common feature of Irish political consciousness and discourse. Generally, unlike much of modern Europe, socialist ideas had little currency in an Ireland long dominated by the Catholic Church, the rural bourgeoisie and endless debates about the national question (cf. Brown 2004, 94). Taoiseach Charles J. Haughey professed in 1987 how "[s]ocialism, an alien gospel of class warfare, envy and strife, is also inherently un-Irish and therefore unworthy of a serious place in the language of Irish political debate" (quoted in Foster 2004).

are hardly any Northern Irish prose or dramatic works[53] that deal with the experience of Ulstermen at the front or the home front (cf. Jeffery 1999, 17). This can be seen as related to the very nature of Ulster unionist culture (cf. McMinn 1992, 48), a tradition – as opposed to the Catholic nationalist one – frequently not associated with imaginative literary expression (Brearton 2000, 35). Fran Brearton provides a further angle on the absence of Ulster war writing, based on the notion of the incommunicability of the war, suggesting that the "Somme was beyond literal or imaginative control: if it had been incorporated into literature with any fidelity to the original experience, it would potentially have lost whatever value it might have had politically in Ulster" (Brearton 2000, 34f.). Consequently, the war experiences of Ulstermen and the memory of those experiences were mostly absorbed by official political discourses and became the subject of an extensive tradition of ceremonial remembrance, rather than being expressed in literature.

A substantial rediscovery of the topic in Northern Irish writing only happened after the beginning of the Northern Irish conflict, particularly in poetry. For the authors of that generation, the Great War already was something "tangential, something overheard or witnessed from afar" (Dawe 2008, xviii). In several works by poets like Derek Mahon, John Hewitt or Michael Longley, frequently taking the form of "act[s] of familial archaeology" (Brown 1993, 231), the sectarian violence of the second half of the twentieth century in Northern Ireland is linked back also to the embittering experience of the Great War, uncovering the muddled past of fathers and grandfathers. For example, Michael Longley's elegiac 1973 poem "Wounds", one of the earliest poems to re-imagine the Ulster experience of the Great War, lays bare the toxic militancy and radicalism with which many unionist Ulstermen went off to fight and which would persist to fuel the flames of Irish conflicts in the decades to follow:

> Here are two pictures from my father's head –
> I have kept them like secrets until now:
> First, the Ulster Division at the Somme
> Going over the top with 'Fuck the Pope!'
> 'No surrender!': a boy about to die,
> Screaming 'Give 'em one for the Shankill!'
> 'Wilder than Gurkhas' were my father's words
> Of admiration and bewilderment.
> Next comes the London-Scottish padre
> Resettling kilts with his swagger-stick,

---

53 Frank McGuinness, author of *Observe the Sons of Ulster Marching Towards the Somme*, is a writer from Donegal, a part of Ulster that belongs to the Republic of Ireland.

With a stylish backhand and a prayer.
Over a landscape of dead buttocks
My father followed him for fifty years.
At last, a belated casualty,
He said – lead traces flaring till they hurt –
'I am dying for King and Country, slowly.'
I touched his hand, his thin head I touched.

(Longley 2008, 334, ll. 1–17)

The violence and extremism that misled the generation of the fathers, Longley suggests in the poem, is both inherited and hereditary, received and passed on to the next generation, when, in the second stanza, he extends the sympathy for his dead father to the perpetrators and victims of contemporary conflicts – three "teenage soldiers, bellies full of / Bullets and Irish beer" (ibid., ll. 21f.) and a bus conductor murdered in his home by a "shivering boy who wandered in / Before they could turn the television down / Or tidy away the supper dishes" (ibid. ll. 30–32) (cf. Brearton 2000, 257f.). Longley here also stresses the fluidity of concepts of military and civilian spaces next to the fluidity of militant mind-sets.

Poetry

In the following, the existing body of Irish war writing will be outlined and characterised, beginning with poetry. There are a number of Irish representatives of the combatant poetry of 1914 to 1918 that proved so dominant and influential in the English cultural legacy of the Great War. These Irish soldier-poets came from a variety of different political, social and cultural backgrounds, some of them, like the constitutional nationalist MPs Thomas Kettle and Stephen Gwynn, indeed operating at the intersection of Irish and British politics and literature, exemplified, for example, in their collection *Battle Songs for the Irish Brigades* (1915) which they published during a recruiting tour. Patrick MacGill was the only working-class voice in Irish war poetry to achieve greater popularity, expressing the experiences of ordinary soldiers in works such as "The London Lads" or "The Dug-Out". The poet and novelist Winifred M. Letts was born in England, raised and educated in Dublin and worked as a nurse during the war, publishing her collection *Hallowe'en and Poems of the War* in 1916. Lord Dunsany (Edward Plunkett) belonged to the Protestant Anglo-Irish aristocracy, had fought in the Boer War and had been a well-known figure of the Irish Literary Revival before enlisting, fully supporting the war effort and Ireland's part in it, as expressed, for example in the post-war sonnet "To the Fallen Irish Soldiers", where, in a Brookean eulogy, he honours "[t] he soil that wraps her [Ireland's] heroes slumbering there" (Dunsany 2008, 38, l. 8).

Francis Ledwidge, Lord Dunsany's somewhat unlikely protégé, considering their difference in class and political outlook, is possibly the most important and popular Irish poet of the trenches. Ledwidge epitomises the complexities of identity and allegiances produced by the Irish involvement in the Great War. Coming from an impoverished rural Catholic background, Ledwidge became a poet and a nationalist activist with socialist leanings, joining the 10th (Irish) Division despite being a member of the anti-Redmondite Irish Volunteers.

The strong pastoral element in Ledwidge's works has been frequently emphasised (cf. Jeffery 2000, 105), Ledwidge positing his careful evocations of Irish landscapes and nature against hints of the destruction and violence of his war experience, frequently in an escapist gesture. As already mentioned, aesthetically, much of the writing of the Irish soldier-poets relied on well-established Victorian and Edwardian techniques, themes and idioms (cf. Haughey 2002, 70f.), characterised by a sense of pastoralism, ruralism and romantic escapism. Outspoken anti-war attitudes as popularised by the protest poetry of authors like Owen or Sassoon can hardly be found in their works; tensions, doubts or criticism are frequently only addressed indirectly (cf. Haughey 2002, 70f., 73).

A more unique feature of Irish war poetry that distinguishes it from the English tradition is the literary treatment of the question of enlistment and allegiance, which frequently boils down to the question of identity. While it seems that for most ordinary Irish recruits their sense of "Britishness in [...] the Empire was flexible enough to accommodate other identities within it" (Hennessey 1998, xxi), many Irish war poets recognised the ambiguous nature of their service and struggled to integrate their involvement in the British forces with their nationalist convictions and self-image (Haughey 2002, 73).[54] The greatest strain on the loyalties of those Irish soldiers came in the event of the 1916 Easter Rising, forcing nationalist poets like Kettle and Ledwidge to re-examine their positions, resulting in disappointment and the indistinct feeling of being on the wrong side of history. Ledwidge fully identified with the rebels, which becomes obvious in elegiac poems such as "Thomas MacDonagh" or "To Mrs Joseph Plunkett", written while away at the front.

---

54 For example, in his poem "To My Daughter Betty, The Gift of God", Thomas Kettle explains to his daughter his motivation for enlisting, assuring her and himself that his war service is dedicated to the common people of Ireland: "[...] they'll give you rhyme / And reason: some will call the thing sublime, / And some decry it in a knowing tone. / So here, while the mad guns course overhead, / And tired men sigh, with mud for couch and floor, / Know that we fools, now with the foolish dead, / Died not for flag, nor King, nor Emperor, / But for a dream, born in a herdsman's shed / And for the secret Scripture of the poor" (Kettle 2008, 55, ll. 6–14).

At the Irish home front, Katherine Tynan produced elegiac pro-war poetry that was immensely popular in Britain (cf. Wills 2009, 125). Yet, the most prominent non-combatant Irish poets to address the war and its political and cultural implications during the conflict and in its immediate aftermath, were, ironically, the reluctant W. B. Yeats and Yeats's lifelong friend Æ (George Russell). A particularly striking poem by Æ, "Salutation: To the Memory of Some I Knew who are Dead and who Loved Ireland" (1917), encapsulates both the problematic image and heritage of the Great War in Ireland and its entanglement with the context of revolutionary struggle, effectively anticipating the integrative attitudes towards this marginalised section of Irish history that developed in the final decades of the twentieth century. In the poem, Æ interweaves the fates of the leaders of the Easter Rising with those of prominent nationalist figures of the Great War like Kettle and Willie Redmond, paying respect to their opposing commitments which Æ identifies as united in their love for Ireland, even if he himself cannot subscribe to all of them:

> I listened to high talk from you,
>> Thomas McDonagh, and it seemed
> The words were idle, but they grew
>> To nobleness by death redeemed.
> Life cannot utter words more great
>> Than life may meet by sacrifice,
> High words were equaled by high fate,
>> You paid the price. You paid the price.
>
> *You who have fought on fields afar,*
>> *That other Ireland did you wrong*
> *Who said you shadowed Ireland's star,*
>> *Nor gave you laurel wreath nor song.*
> *You proved by death as true as they,*
>> *In mightier conflicts played your part,*
> *Equal your sacrifice may weigh,*
>> *Dear Kettle, of the generous heart.*

(Æ 2008, 20, ll. 17–32. Italics in the original)

Yet, such integrative notions were rare and at odds with the political and cultural climate of the 1920s. Poets like Stephen Gwynn, Lord Dunsany or Samuel McCurry, who insisted on the virtue and integrity of their service and who embodied in their poetry a diversity of views about Irish identity in the decade after the war, soon found themselves alienated in the new independent state.

Irish poetry about the war published in the 1930s and 1940s is characterised by an "absence of a coherent and unified statement about the First World War"

(Haughey 2002, 233). There is no homogenous narrative of the conflict, some Irish poets instead employing the war memory for specific political ends. Still, Jim Haughey argues, in the decades to follow, the Great War would "[provide] modern Irish writers with a range of archetypes, symbols, and metaphors that continue to function as interpretive signs in Ireland's ongoing political and cultural wars" (ibid.), making it almost impossible also for Irish poets to circumvent the war as an (albeit frequently indirect) imaginative source.

The revival of the Great War in connection with the Troubles did not only occur in Northern Irish poetry, as visible in the works of Longley, Mahon or Hewitt. Eavan Boland and Eiléan Ní Chuilleanáin, to name two contemporary poets from the south, have also employed the iconography and imaginative resources of the Great War in their examination of contemporary Irish conflicts and their rootedness in the past, both poets being outspoken critics of Ireland's fatal attraction to myths of violence (cf. Haughey 2002, 263). Boland's "A Soldier's Son" from her 1975 collection *The War Horse*, for example, establishes a similar sense of inherited violence as Longley's "Wounds":

> A young man's war it is, a young man's war,
> Or so they say and so they go to wage
> This struggle where, armoured only in nightmare,
> Every warrior is under age –
> A son seeing each night leave, as father,
> A man who may become the ancestor
> [...]
> Son of a soldier who saw war on the ground
> Now cross the peace lines I have made for you
> To find on this side if not peace then honour,
> Your heritage, knowing as I do
>
> That in the cross-fire of his gun he found
> You his only son [...]
>
> (Boland 2008, 372, ll. 1–6, 9–14)

Nevertheless, it should be noted, today the Great War in Irish poetry also functions beyond its relevance as a context for contemporary Irish political issues, being envisioned, as in English culture, in a more general way as a monumental process of transformation that continues to affect and inspire contemporary thought and the global landscape. "Even when the Great War is not directly addressed in their work", Jim Haughey summarises, "a number of Irish poets call upon powerful images from the Great War to serve as catechistic texts on modern man's alleged sociocultural decline" (Haughey 2002, 258).

Prose

As opposed to the English tradition, Irish prose writing of the battle front is rather sparse. While there is a more considerable body of Irish home front novels, the depiction of the war zone itself is more or less limited to two authors, Patrick MacGill and Liam O'Flaherty, who fictionalise in their works their own war experiences on the Continent. However, as mentioned earlier, both authors, hardly ever tackle the issue of Irish identity, the ambiguous implications of fighting the war as Irishmen – a condition that will be examined in slightly greater detail in the following.

Patrick MacGill (1890–1963) is a writer of the war who enjoyed significant popularity in the 1910s and 1920s before being largely forgotten, attracting greater critical attraction only in recent years.[55] His minor status as a writer can mainly be traced to his distinct non-affiliation with the dominant cultural and political discourses of the Ireland of his time. Known as a working-class writer, the 'navvy poet' MacGill was not associated with the Irish Literary Revival, Gaelic nationalism, or Irish Modernism, embracing instead an anti-clerical, personal, and altogether simplistic version of socialism very much inspired by his own austere upbringing. A simple farmer's son from Donegal, MacGill had to leave his impoverished home for Scotland at the age of fourteen to work as an unskilled farm labourer and later in construction and on the railways. Consequently, it is the Irish and British working-class and migrant milieu on which MacGill concentrates in his works, including his war writings, which were understood by the British reading audience "as exemplars of 'Irish' writing and in Ireland as the worst exemplars of anti-Irish writing" (Johnson 2003, 137). In this manner, the 'Irishness' of MacGill appeared to be questionable to many, particularly in post-war Ireland where he was seen as an increasingly anglicized figure (cf. Taylor 2013, 6), as well as from the point of view of literary critics, who have found it difficult to classify MacGill within the existing categories of Irish, Ulster and British writing.[56]

MacGill decided to join the London Irish Rifles in 1915 and spent the war as a stretcher-bearer in France, where he was also wounded. Between 1915 and 1921, he produced a series of popular autobiographical frontline novels, among them *The*

---

55 The modest re-discovery of MacGill is related to the increased interest in Ireland's role in the Great War. David Taylor's *Memory, Narrative and the Great War. Rifleman Patrick MacGill and the Construction of Wartime Experience* (2013) is the first full-length study dedicated to MacGill.

56 MacGill has been categorised as an "Ulster novelist", "British working-class writer" and, more recently, as an "Irish war novelist" (cf. Johnson 2003, 137).

Amateur Army (1915), *The Great Push* (1916), *The Red Horizon* (1916) and the more pessimistic *Fear!* (1921). Furthermore, there is a later melodramatic war play by MacGill entitled *Suspense*, published in 1930. As a soldier and writer of the war, like many others, MacGill faced certain pressures and restrictions. On the one hand, his London publisher Herbert Jenkins, who also published Francis Ledwidge's poetry, very likely influenced MacGill to conform to the well-selling formulae of war fiction, encouraging a somewhat simplifying propagandistic heroic spirit in his works. On the other hand, MacGill's works were subjected to censorship, MacGill even being threatened with court-martial in case he disclosed any sensitive details of warfare in his works (cf. Taylor 1998, 240). These conditions might be part of the reason why the tenor of MacGill's war works, despite their scathing documentation of the horrors of the battlefield, has been assessed as not very sophisticated and "not in any fundamental way subversive" (Jeffery 1999, 10).

MacGill approaches the war in his works pragmatically, focusing on the day-to-day experiences of British trench communities (cf. Devine 1999, xi) rather than contextualising and theorising war service and soldier identities within a greater psychological, philosophical or ideological framework. This pragmatism is encapsulated, for example, in *The Red Horizon*, when a discussion about reasons for enlistment during battle ends on the conventional note of 'having to do one's bit':

> Bill cowered down as the shell burst, then sat upright again.
>
> "I'm gettin' more afraid of these things every hour," he said, "what is the war about?"
> "I don't know," I answered.
> "I'm sick of it," Bill muttered.
> "Why did you join?"
> "To save myself the trouble of telling people why I didn't," he answered with a laugh. "Flat on yer tummy, Rifleman Teake, there's another shell."
>
> About noon the shelling ceased; we breathed freely again and discovered we were very hungry.
>
> (MacGill 1916, 199)

In scenes such as this, it becomes apparent that MacGill's soldiers obviously did not go to war specifically to enforce or prevent Home Rule, nor in a crusade against godless Prussian militarism or to transcend degenerative civilian complacency. The question of enlistment is also addressed in *The Amateur Army* in similar terms, the protagonist beginning his account with the announcement that "the psychological processes [...] that led to my enlisting in 'Kitchener's Army' need not be inquired into" (MacGill 1915, 13); also, as the scene continues, after his comrades have presented their reasons for joining up, none of them related to Ireland or Ulster, and all of them "unilluminating" for the protagonist, he contents himself without further inquiry "remembering that the Germans despise us because we are devoid of military enthusiasm" (MacGill 1915, 14f.). Here, "us" clearly means "British soldiers", not "Irishmen".

For MacGill's working-class soldiers, the war in *The Red Horizon* and his other works constitutes simply "an immutable fact of life" (Jeffery 1999, 10), which they handle much in the same way as they confront and accept the defining hardships of their pre-war civilian working-class lives. In this manner, the war experience in MacGill's works is essentially reduced to a corporeal dimension and not connected to any more sophisticated discourses. This pragmatic view of the experience of the Great War, however, could also be appreciated for its clarity and as a sobering counterweight to the overwhelming middle- and upper-class Great War myth of sacrifice, futility, corruption and despair. As, for example, Joana Bourke emphasises in her study of British working-class soldiers:

> [W]orking-class values produced an army that was comfortable with hierarchy, formal and informal, and one which understood authority and its limits. In war, as in peace, men learned to make the best of things, to make do and mend, to grasp any opportunity to improve living conditions, to stick by their pals, to establish and maintain social norms, to draw lines of demarcation and acceptable behaviour, to find distraction in entertainment, gambling and drink. It was an army with a remarkable degree of social cohesion, built to resist and endure.
>
> (Bourke 2003, 249f., cf. Taylor 2013, 34)

In this manner, instead of a shared overarching national, political or, perhaps, philosophical context, MacGill's soldiers are determined by the sense of their literally self-serving community, built on unwavering loyalty, comradeship and principles of sharing (cf. Phillips 2010a, 33) and by the perceived stability and reliability of military hierarchies and authority. They successfully manage to transfer and adapt their civilian identities to the system of the army and military conflict.

Irishness never predominates in MacGill's war narratives (Phillips 2010a, 35). When Ireland is evoked in *The Red Horizon* or *The Great Push*, it only takes the form of a pastoral and romanticised escapist space, and the Irishness of the soldiers depicted is more or less irrelevant, functioning only as a politically neutral, even somewhat decorative marker alongside the non-Irish, majorly Cockney, soldiers. The sense of Irishness attributed to MacGill's soldiers even verges on the folkloristic at times, for example, when the protagonist of *The Red Horizon* happens to meet a group of fellow countrymen belonging to the Scots Guards: "In the traverse where I was planted I dropped into Ireland; heaps of it. There was the brogue that could be cut with a knife, and the humour that survived Mons and the Marne, and the kindliness that sprang from the cabins of Corrymeela and the moors of Derrynane". And the scene goes on: "'Irish?' I asked. 'Sure,' was the answer. 'We're everywhere. Ye'll find us in a Gurkha regiment if you scratch the beggars' skins" (MacGill 1916, 82f.). In such moments, it becomes obvious how in MacGill's war works the British regiments are portrayed as hybrid communities which enable a co-existence of Irishness within Britishness (cf. Taylor 2013, 240f.). In this respect, it is striking how MacGill's concerns are "markedly different from writers such as Kettle and Ledwidge who constantly seek to reconcile nationalist sympathies and engagement in Britain's war" (Phillips 2010a, 51) – MacGill simply seems to be uninterested in such sympathies. The position of national belonging, or, rather, disengagement, from which he writes the war is the one exemplified in his self-characterisation provided in the preface to *The Amateur Army*: "I am one of the million or more male residents of the United Kingdom, who a year ago had no special yearning towards military life, but who joined the army after war was declared" (MacGill 1915) – a universal statement, in essence more geographical than identitarian.[57] In this respect, MacGill could be said to rather belong to a more universalist tradition than that of the Irish war writer; or, as Nuala Johnson suggests, he could be seen as a "migrant writer" as "the spaces of trench warfare transform all men into migrants as they experienced the alien landscape of war" (Johnson 2003, 138). It is this unity in experience and the shared, sometimes even romanticised, acceptance and enduring of the war's horrors in MacGill's writing that trumps any previous or persisting Irish affiliations – a theme that reappears also in other Irish war works.

The presentation of the Great War in two works of Liam O'Flaherty (1896–1984), also is not very much determined by Irish perspectives; yet, O'Flaherty's outlook is much grimmer than MacGill's universalist working-class bonhomie. Like MacGill, O'Flaherty participated in the war, though his reasons for enlisting were far more ambiguous and his going off to war seems to belong to a series of seemingly impulsive contradictory turns. In the years before the war, O'Flaherty had been on his way to become a Catholic priest, then he joined the republican Irish Volunteers.

---

57 MacGill's steering clear of addressing Irishness is also apparent in his pre-war works. For example, David Taylor observes in MacGill's popular 1914 semi-autobiographical novel *Children of the Dead End* how "there is [...] no indication of any awareness of specifically Irish issues, nor are there many explicit references to Irish identity. If anything, there is a suspicion that there is an element of deliberate stereotyping to present an English audience with a familiar and picaresque figure – the hard-talking, hard-drinking, hard-fighting Irishman – but one who from the very marginality of his existence is relatively unthreatening" (Taylor 1998, 239).

Abandoning the seminary and attending lectures at University College Dublin, he became interested in Marxism – a theme that would dominate his works in the decades to come. Finally, abandoning the anti-war Irish Volunteers, he enlisted in the Irish Guards in 1915 as "Bill Ganly", in a spirit of seeking adventure, wanting to "take part in a world drama" (quoted in Johnson 2003, 134). O'Flaherty was severely wounded in 1917 and returned from the war shell-shocked, suffering from depression and a profound insecurity about his future. In the early 1920s, after a period of travelling, O'Flaherty began his impressive and influential career as a writer. While in some way all of O'Flaherty's fictional and autobiographical writing could be seen as influenced by his war experiences, he only addresses the Great War directly in two works, a short story entitled "The Alien Skull" (1928) and in the novel *The Return of the Brute* (1929).

The Return of the Brute belongs to the general flurry of gruesomely realistic war novels of the late 1920s, writers no longer having to fear military censorship, as in the case of MacGill, and working for a newly receptive and frequently decidedly pacifist British readership. However, as Jeffery notes, O'Flaherty's novel was not a great success and was "decently forgotten" until being reprinted in a facsimile edition in 1998 (cf. Jeffery 2000, 99). In the oeuvre of O'Flaherty it represents a low point, some critics describing it as "*All Quiet [on the Western Front]* without the sensitivity" or even as "one of the worst [novels] ever published" (quoted in ibid.). In contrast to this, "The Alien Skull", very similar in theme, was more positively received, earning, for example, the praise of T. S. Eliot (cf. Eliot 2012, 144).

Despite the fact that O'Flaherty was an Irishman once clearly affiliated with Irish political movements directed against the Great War, in both of his war works there is no trace of any doubts about the potentially troublesome reconciliation of Irishness and war service. In fact, apart from O'Flaherty's choice of names for his characters, both works do not make any references to Irish contexts at all, also the question of motivations for enlistment is not specifically addressed. What the two texts are centrally concerned with is the shocking dehumanising force of the war that turns men into animals. The main protagonist of *The Return of the Brute*, a soldier named Bill Gunn, is relentlessly exposed to the chaos, brutality and deprivation of trench warfare in its most extreme forms and gradually slips into homicidal insanity, culminating in the attack of a hallucinating and feral Gunn on Corporal Williams, his cold-hearted superior:

> "Now," cried Gunn, and again the words appeared before his eyes in letters of fire. Then with his chest pressed against the Corporal's writhing body, he slowly sought the throat, found it and enlaced it with his fingers and pressed fiercely. The Corporal began to go limp.

Then he lay still. Gunn clutched the throat for a long time after the Corporal had become still. Then, uttering queer sounds, he began to mangle the body with his bare hands. Now he was really an animal, brutish, with dilated eyes, with his face bloody. [...] A bullet struck him. He waved his arms about his head and ran on, bellowing. He was running around in a circle. Then they turned a machine-gun on him and brought him down.

(O'Flaherty 1929, 185f.)

The horrors of the war have dehumanised Gunn and unleashed animalistic instincts, underlining the notion of war as transcending the limits of human civilisation, laying bare man's crude inherent brutality.

The same thematic pattern is evoked in "The Alien Skull", however, in a manner more narratively refined and convincing. The main character, war-hardened and abused Private Mulhall, is sent out into No Man's Land to capture an enemy soldier. When Mulhall ambushes his lone target, the enemy does not attack Mulhall but smiles at him and offers him a piece of bread. This gesture of kindness, so unexpected and inappropriate for this situation, puzzles Mulhall deeply and triggers an almost unreal interruption of warfare as well as a temporary dissolution of the two opponents' warrior identities:

Then Mulhall surrendered completely to this extraordinary new feeling of human love and kindness. Were it not for his native sense of reserve, he would return the enemy's kiss. Instead of that he smiled like a happy child and his head swam. He took the enemy's hand and pressed it three times, mumbling something inaudible. They sat in silence for a whole minute, looking at one another in a state of ecstasy. They loved one another for that minute. [...] They were carried up from the silent and frightful corpse-strewn battlefield into some God-filled place [...].

(O'Flaherty 1999, 53)

This illusion of peace is ended by the sound of firing guns. The enemy soldier prepares to leave and, briefly exposing his skull, triggers in Mulhall savage instincts underneath the war-torn veneer of humanity that also made Bill Gunn murder his Corporal: "As soon as he saw it the lust of blood overwhelmed him, as if he were a beast of prey in sight of his quarry. The enemy's bare skull acted on his senses like a maddening drug" (ibid.). Mulhall shoots the enemy soldier as he is walking back towards the German lines, only to be shot himself seconds later.

In this manner, both O'Flaherty and MacGill suggest in their frontline works a notion of the Great War as a conflict in which national or ethnic differences as well as the intricacies of Irish domestic politics become irrelevant in the face of more pressing universal concerns – in the case of O'Flaherty, the dehumanising effect of warfare and the uncovering of the inherent bestiality of man, and in the case of MacGill an empowering and resilient sense of unity among the working

99

classes, Irish or not. Perhaps, the pronounced absence of Irish issues in their writing could also be seen as an indication of the sense of disruption and rejection that characterised the Irish home front after 1916, in some way foreshadowing the unwelcome status of the Great War in independent Ireland.

In the Irish novels of the home front, such considerations are rare, which is the result of their essentially non-combatant outlook as well as their overwhelming rootedness within Anglo-Irish concerns and milieus. The attitudes towards the war present in these works are more strongly determined by the contemporary political circumstances in which they were written; also, as mentioned before, the war frequently is recognised as an important but not the only context within which the action takes place. An example for this condition would be the novel *Gossamer* (1915) by George A. Birmingham (pseudonym of James Owen Hannay), a unionist Protestant clergyman from Belfast, who became an army chaplain in 1916, and who was known as a prolific writer of light-hearted comedies. *Gossamer*, set majorly in London in the years leading up to the outbreak of the war in 1914, was published early in the war and thus, while concentrating, oddly, on international banking as its main theme, could reflect rather uninhibitedly the rushing to arms of Redmondite nationalists (cf. Jeffery 1999, 4f.). In the novel, the character of Michael Gorman, an idealistic Irish nationalist MP, declares how the war is "a vast struggle, an Armageddon in which the forces of reaction, absolutism, tyranny, a military caste are ranged against democracy. It is their last appearance upon the stage of history" (Birmingham 1915). Yet, this notion is countered by the novel's main protagonist, Sir James Digby, a member of the Anglo-Irish gentry who had to sell his estate, and who goes off to war for fairly indistinct reasons: "I don't know what my real reason is. It's not patriotism. I have not got any country to be patriotic about. It's not any silly belief in liberty and democracy. I don't know why I'm doing it. I just have to. That's all" (ibid.) – a profound sense of Anglo-Irish dislocation also found in other war works.

St. John Ervine's *Changing Winds* (1917) is exemplary of the historical and literary embeddedness of the Great War, and with it, the depiction of the home front, in the context of the Irish revolutionary struggles at home. Ervine himself embodies the ideological transformations and radicalisations concomitant with the turbulences of this period of Irish history. Born in Belfast, Ervine moved to London, joined the intellectual circles of the Fabian Society and became involved in theatre, befriending W. B. Yeats and eventually becoming manager of the Abbey Theatre in Dublin for some time. A determined advocate of Home Rule, dreaming of an Ireland where "Protestants and Catholics, Orangemen and Ancient Hibernians put their hands together, and the four beautiful fields of Cathleen ni Houlihan become one pasture" (quoted in Sullivan n. d.), Ervine enlisted in October 1917. Yet, when Ervine returned, he had not only lost a leg at the Western Front but also his belief in Home Rule, and went on to become a radical supporter of Ulster unionism, rejecting Catholic Ireland and especially Irish nationalism (cf. Jeffery 1999, 7f.).

Changing Winds, dedicated to the memory of Rupert Brooke, was written partly in response to the Easter Rising. Set in Dublin and London, the novel focuses again on an Anglo-Irish main character, a young man named Henry Quinn, from a landowning Protestant family in County Antrim, and his three English friends from the English public school they attended together. As his English companions decide to enlist at the outbreak of the Great War, Quinn is held back from following their example by fear, a profound aversion to violence and jingoism, and by an affiliation to his country too weak and undefined to convince him of sacrificing himself in the war:

> And just as Mary, moving through the Devonshire lanes, had felt that everything proclaimed its Englishness and hers, making them and her part of each other, so he, looking out of the window across the fields, felt something inside him insisting, "You're Irish. You must be proud! You're Irish! You must be proud! ..." [...] There seemed to Henry to be in that, all that there was in patriotism. Irrationally, impulsively, unaccountably one loved one's country. [...] But if this stirring in one's nature made a man both a sacrament and a partaker of a sacrament, was there not yet something horrible in this spilling of blood, this breaking of bodies? Was this sacrament only to be consummated by the butcher? [...] Was there not an honourable rivalry among nations, each to be better than the other, to replace this brawling about boundaries, this pettifogging with frontiers? Was there to be no end to this killing and preparing for killing?
>
> (Ervine 1917, 525f.)

The final part of the novel depicts Dublin during the Easter Rising and it is Quinn's puzzled witnessing of the violent chaos, the disastrous sacrifice of the rebels, and the sense of duty of the English soldiers who put down the rebellion, that eventually overpowers his doubts about war service (cf. Jeffery 1999, 7f.):

> There was a strange quietness in his heart. He had lived through a terror and had not been afraid. He had seen men immolating themselves gladly because they had believed that by so doing they would make their country a finer one to live in. "It was the wrong way," he said to himself, "but in the end, nothing matters but that a man shall offer his life for his belief." [...]
>
> He would not see Dublin again. Firmly fixed in his mind, was that belief. He would serve ...and he would die. Foolish, he told himself, to think like that, but, even while he was rebuking himself, the thought thrust itself into his mind again.
>
> (Ervine 1917, 569–71)

In this manner, Ervine's work eventually unites the Great War and the Irish republican struggle through the universal value of the 'purity' and 'honesty' of sacrifice and an inescapable, almost natural, sense of masculine determination, or even self-destruction.

Ervine, like Birmingham and several of the other Anglo-Irish prose authors writing about the war, crucially employs a main character who already consciously inhabits a liminal social and ideological position before the war, finding it hard to subscribe, or be subscribed, to either tradition – Anglo-Irish, English, or Irish – and this displacement of identities complicates attitudes to the Great War, as will also be shown in the chapter dedicated to Anglo-Irish war writing. On the whole, the thought of the validity of a position in-between the established demarcation lines of identity and predetermined political and social affiliations eventually seems impossible in Irish war works, and not only in those of this early period.

A female view of the Irish home front is provided in the 1918 novel *The Fire of Green Boughs* by Mrs Victor Rickard (Jessie Louisa Rickard). Born in Dublin into a Protestant nationalist family, Rickard, initially loosely related to the Irish Literary Revival, became a very prolific and moderately successful writer of popular novels, particularly of detective novels. Her second husband, Lieutenant Colonel Victor Rickard, was a professional officer in the British army; he was killed during the Battle of Aubers Ridge in 1915. The war death of her husband spurred Rickard to write, producing a series of journalistic pieces and stories about the Royal Munster Fusiliers before turning to the writing of novels. Rickard's *The Fire of Green Boughs* can be seen as a precursor to the works of Hinkson and Barrington that will be discussed in chapter III.2. She shares with them the combination of Irish, Anglo-Irish and English characters and settings of the war period and the focus on a fairly explorative female protagonist – in the case of Rickard a young Englishwoman named Sylvia Tracy – who struggles with the gulf between combatants and non-combatants (Phillips 2009, 271), a highly gendered dichotomy.

Ireland is for Sylvia, as for her cousin Dominic Roydon, a Church of England minister returned disabled from the war, first and foremost an attractively remote refuge from the discomforts of wartime London – "the cleaner, greener land [...] England is no place at all for a person who is over-sensitive" (Rickards 1919, 114). Yet, moving to Ireland, Sylvia is confronted with the actual tensions and polarisations of the Irish situation. As the housekeeper Mrs Casey laments: "What with the wars and the Sinn Féin, and all, I've lived to see queer changes, Miss Tracy. Once it was the gentry against the Nationalists, and the man with a gun behind the hedge, and now seemingly, all the gentry is Nationalists, and it's the boys are lepping to be fighting the troops. Changes, love, changes; ever and always changes" (Rickards

1919, 128). It is at the lonely western coast of Ireland where Sylvia eventually overcomes her wartime ennui and performs her "life-transforming action, which is both futile and heroic" (Phillips 2009, 272). In a spirit of protest at the suffering of her generation, Sylvia hides a dying German naval officer in her home whose submarine had sunk near the coast. She is assisted by the Irishwoman Mrs Casey, who justifies the illegal harbouring of the German by her own experiences of English brutality: "Just as von Rudendorf stood to Sylvia as the momentary embodiment of all the inarticulate masses of young men, who relinquished life and hope and the fair promise of their days, so he stood to [Mrs Casey] for the memory of an unforgotten past" (Rickards 1919, 178). In this manner, Rickard establishes across the English-Irish divide "a common ground of resistance" (Phillips 2009, 274) of women both against war and political violence.

As Eugene McNulty remarks, in most Irish war works of the home front, the Great War frequently functions as a "contextual 'sounding-board', uniformed bodies appear back from the war and head off towards it, but its function is really to reveal the internal dynamics of Irish history at this moment of crisis" (McNulty 2010, 69), and this is particularly true considering the prose works addressing the topic written during the most intense phase of the Irish amnesia about the war, the period spanning the 1930s up to the late 1960s. The almost exclusive dominance of female Anglo-Irish writers – Pamela Hinkson, Margaret Barrington, Iris Murdoch, Jennifer Johnston – in this section of (Anglo-)Irish war writing is striking and can be taken as an indication of the marginal nature of the topic. Of course, a major concern in those works is the complicated role of women at the Irish (and English) home front during the Great War and the recurring motif of an enforced, and sometimes unbearable, feminine passivity and alienation – an alienation from husbands, sons and lovers who have seemingly entered a different and inaccessible world by going off to war, and from other women at the Irish home front whose families are unaffected by the war. For example, Stella Mannering, one of the central characters of Pamela Hinkson's *The Ladies' Road* (1932), muses how "if she had been a boy, she could have given a false age.... in a year or so, with her hair up – she had tried it today in the dormitory when there was no one there – she might look eighteen" (Hinkson 1946, 75). She envies an older schoolmate, Muriel, who "had gone to France to drive an ambulance. She might with luck get almost up to the line" (ibid.), Stella hating the thought of being cut off from the reality of war her male relatives and peers experience.

Another prominent theme in those works, which frequently take the form of family portraits, is the demise of the Anglo-Irish as a relevant social class in Ireland, specifically the theme of the downfall of the Anglo-Irish 'Big House'.

Elizabeth Bowen's *The Last September* (1929) depicts the troublesome demise of an Anglo-Irish estate in County Cork during the War of Independence, the shadow of the Great War still looming in the background. Margaret Barrington's *My Cousin Justin* (1939) engages with the sense of the continuity of violence more directly and emphasises the social divisions and imbalances between the Catholic Irish and the Anglo-Irish that crystallise in the Great War and erupt in the domestic Irish conflicts to follow in the immediate post-war phase.

Jennifer Johnston's *How Many Miles to Babylon* (1974) also belongs to the Big House genre, however, unlike the other works just mentioned, her novel does not only re-imagine the home front but actually enters the realm of the war zones on the Continent. Also, unlike Hinkson and Barrington, Johnston does not focus on the female experience of the era but rather on Irish class issues which crystallise vividly against and within the hierarchical structures of the army. In the greater context of Irish war writing, Johnston's novel could be seen as transitional as her work was written in a proto-revisionist spirit foreshadowing contemporary reformed attitudes to writing the war – Johnston clearly identified the Great War "[i]n Ireland [... as] the beginning of the Troubles we are now in" (quoted in Ferriter 2005, 757).

After Johnston, the latest novels to substantially re-imagine the Great War from an Irish angle are Tom Phelan's *The Canal Bridge* and Sebastian Barry's *A Long Long Way*, both published in 2005. Barry moves away from Anglo-Irish contexts, tracing the emblematic war experience of Willie Dunne, a young recruit from a Dublin Catholic loyalist family. The novel belongs within a larger agenda of Barry, consciously aiming at a re-envisioning and re-evaluation of sections of twentieth-century Irish history obscured by the dominance of the nationalist narrative, which includes, in the case of *A Long Long Way*, a re-imagination of the Easter Rising from the perspective of an Irish soldier in British uniform, and a resonant depiction of the sense of displacement and homelessness Irish veterans experienced as their identity and loyalties were rendered obsolete in the new Irish state. Phelan's novel works along similar lines. Through a series of personal reminiscences, *The Canal Bridge* presents the story of two young peasants from the Irish Midlands who join the British forces in 1913 mostly to satisfy their *wanderlust* and end up in the Great War. Phelan's depiction of the gruesome war experience and the difficult homecoming of Irish soldiers is embedded, as in the case of Barry, in a revisionist project. The novel represents a direct assault on the ideology and identity concepts of radical Irish nationalism and is clearly positioned against the nationalist views of the war period.

Drama

Surveys of English and Irish Great War literature have varied greatly in the number of works identified as war plays, ranging from a mere dozen to more than 200 (cf. Kosok 2007, 1f.), which also is the outcome of varying definitions of the genre and differing critical outlooks. A generally observable trend in the development of war plays in English literature is that after a series of realistic war plays written until the late 1920s, the Great War as a dramatic topic largely fell out of fashion in the 1930s and disappeared completely from the stage in the era and aftermath of World War II. Only since the 1960s, particularly since the 1963 production of the stage musical *Oh! What a Lovely War*, has dramatic interest in the war been reawakened; since then the Great War has remained a frequently revisited topic (cf. Kosok 2007, 4).

This pattern also roughly matches the situation in Irish dramatic writing, although the revival of Irish dramatic interest in the war began twenty years after the one in Britain. Heinz Kosok suggests that until the 1980s there "were only two World War I plays set in Ireland, with theme and subject matter essentially Irish" (Kosok 2007, 56), G. B. Shaw's *O'Flaherty V. C.* (1915) and Sean O'Casey's *The Silver Tassie* (1929), both of which were prevented from being premiered in Ireland, revealing how "the War was a taboo subject for Irish playwrights as well as for Irish society in general" (ibid.). The two plays represent key texts for the understanding of Ireland's Great War experience and the concomitant interplay of Irish identities and will be studied in detail in chapter III.1.

As already mentioned, the cultural and ideological conditions in independent Ireland were generally not conducive to a re-imagination of the Great War, and in the case of Irish war drama, the circumstances seem to have been particularly unfavourable, playwrights depending more intensely on the public and institutional literary infrastructure than writers of poetry or prose. As Middekke and Schnierer argue, Irish drama in "its constitutive categories of dialogue, interaction and immediacy in performance [...] by definition always had a close affinity to the structures of the particular society they reflect" (Middekke and Schnierer 2010, vii) – and Irish society, almost exclusively following nationalist discourses after independence, had largely turned its back on the Great War and the Irishmen who fought in it. Drama in Ireland was more politicised and more intensely claimed by cultural nationalism than any other literary form, nationalists valuing the theatre as the most important tool in forging and popularising a new identity for the new independent Irish nation. Therefore, an essentially sympathetic portrayal of Irishmen in British uniforms on the Irish stage was problematic in the eyes of leading cultural figures such as W. B. Yeats and others – it was too much of a risk in the 1920s, considering also how audiences were still very much directly aware of the activities of British soldiers in Ireland during the Easter Rising and the War of Independence (cf. McNulty 2010, 68), and it disappeared as a potential topic for later generations as Irish drama developed towards an introspective fixation on the rural play in the following decades.

As a consequence, the body of war plays by Irish writers is a mixed bag. The war works of G. B. Shaw, except for *O'Flaherty V. C.* (1915), do not address issues of Irishness – tellingly, Jay Winter calls Shaw an "Irish-born English playwright" (Winter 1995, 191). Patrick MacGill's *Suspense* (1929) is the only war play written by an Irish soldier, yet, it works completely within a British context,[58] showing a group of British soldiers who have to deal with enemy miners digging underneath their trench. Similarly, there are several other dramatic works by Irish and Ulster authors such as St. John Ervine, Monckton Hoffe or C. K. Munro, who picture the conflict and its effects entirely from a British point of view, eschewing the specific conditions created by the war in Ireland (cf. Jeffery 2000, 95; Kosok 2007, 55f.).

Percy French's *The Letter from the Front* (n. d.)[59] and Flann O'Brien's *Thirst* (1942) are two short works hardly ever mentioned in the context of Irish war drama. They were written by Irishmen and address the war in Irish contexts, yet, they work on the level of music hall sketches and, considering their explicit stage Irishness, they seem more geared towards British audiences than Irish ones. In French's short skit, a young girl named Eileen O'Connor brings a letter from her lover Andra, who has enlisted in the British forces, to Matthew Kavanagh, her former schoolmaster, who is busy writing exercises for his students that include lines such as "The Hun saw my son with a gun – he run!" (French 1959, 157). Eileen recounts the letter, telling Kavanagh how Andra went straight "in[to] the thick of it" (French 1959, 158) since he joined up only four weeks ago, and she wants Kavanagh to help her write an answer. When it is revealed that Eileen's reply to Andra will actually not go to Flanders but to a training camp in Aldershot, "a town he tuk from the Germans the first week he joined" (French 1959, 162), Eileen angrily recognises the joke Andra played on her. Yet, Kavanagh reminds her of Anda's exemplary courage, being the first of his village to enlist at the outbreak of the Great War: "Let him have his joke! – he's not fightin' yet, but he's learnin' to fight, an' where he's goin' is no joke! God help you girl, you don't know a hero when you see one" (French 1959, 163). And Eileen recognises the error of her ways: "Fightin' or no fightin', he's the boy I love, and he IS a haro [sic]!"

---

58 The single, very faintly, Irish aspect of this play is that one of the miners was played as an Irishman in the first London production (cf. Jeffery 2000, 95).

59 Taking into account its spirit of encouraging Irish recruitment and French's life dates (1854–1920), this sketch very much seems to belong to an early phase of the Great War.

(ibid.). Obviously, *The Letter from the Front* was designed as a propagandistic effort to encourage (not only) Irish recruitment. The skit advertises the conflict as a war against "them Germans" (French 1959, 157) and paints it as an arena with a potential for masculine heroism and glory, not touching on any of the expressly Irish implications and motivations for enlistment. Along these lines, French could have chosen any other part of the British Empire that is stereotypically associated with backward rural life as the setting for his work.

In its handling of the war theme, O'Brien's *Thirst* is only slightly more specifically Irish than French's sketch. Set in a pub somewhere in Ireland, it features the publican and two customers who are having drinks after the official curfew. When a policeman enters to have the pub shut for the night, the publican begins to tell anecdotes from his time as a soldier in the Great War, when he was "out beyond in Messpott" (O'Brien 1977, 107), vividly describing the inconceivable heat and dryness that the soldiers were exposed to in order to make the policeman thirsty himself and persuade him to keep the pub open: "We know you're only doin' your duty. Just the same as we were when we were servin' in the King's uniform out in Messiopotamia [sic] before it was burnt off our back with the heat" (O'Brien 1977, 109). Impressed by the publican's spectacular stories of his melting rubber boots, the boiling water in his field bottle and the hallucinations induced by his brain drying up, the policeman comes to the counter and gets three drinks for himself, and the night continues with singing and drinking. Here, the war only serves as part of a comical music hall ploy, yet, there are at least hints, for example, at the unfamiliar exoticism the war experience offered to some Irishmen;[60] to read the publican's notion of Irishmen "doing their duty" connected to his image of the King's uniform being "burnt off our back" in the context of the unfavourable turn against the war and its veterans in post-war Ireland would be an over-interpretation in the context of the light-hearted nature of the text.

Apart from those works, the Great War in Irish drama makes reappearances, as in fiction, in the context of Big House works, most prominently in two plays separated not only by decades but also by attitude – Lennox Robinson's sympathetic *The Big House* (1926) and the work of a minor playwright, Sean Dowling's *The Bird in the Net* (1960), the latter connecting the theme of the Big House and the Great War with the Easter Rising, giving testimony to the ideologically hardened perspectives on both the Great War and Anglo-Irish identity that came to dominate historical consciousness in republican Ireland by that time.

---

60 In this context, Patrick MacGill ironically speaks in *The Red Horizon* of the Great War as "the poor man [...] having his first holiday on the Continent" (MacGill 1916, 25).

As in poetry and prose, the massive outbreak of sectarian violence in Northern Ireland starting in the late 1960s also eventually led to a rediscovery of the Great War in Irish and Northern Irish drama. The works of the period beginning in the 1980s generally operate from revisionist perspectives on Irish and Northern Irish history and memory, re-evaluating the relevance of the Great War as a source for contemporary conflicts. In a much applauded effort of cross-cultural understanding, the republican playwright Frank McGuinness re-imagines the harrowing experiences of Ulstermen at the Somme in *Observe the Sons of Ulster Marching Towards the Somme* (1985), challenging identity constructions shaped by Orange radicalism and an Ulster cult of death, questioning, as several other texts of this section, the destructive power of memories and politicised versions of the past. Christina Reid's *My Name, Shall I Tell You My Name?* (1987) does not take audiences to the Somme but to 1980s' Derry, presenting an investigation of the power of established narratives in forming identities and the clash of conflicting memories of the past from a female Northern Irish perspective, exposing, in a similar way as the Northern Irish poets mentioned earlier, how the militancy and the masculinist attitudes inherited from the Great War were still at work in Northern Ireland in the late 1980s. *The Steward of Christendom* (1995) is another chapter in Sebastian Barry's "extraordinary theatrical history of anomalous people" (O'Toole 1996, v), its main protagonist Thomas Dunne in 1932 reliving scenes from his then inglorious career as an officer of the Dublin Metropolitan Police and memories of his family, including a stirring visit by the ghost of his soldier son Willie who was killed in the Great War. Nicola McCartney's *Heritage* (1998) has a more indirect war resonance and has been characterised as a Troubles play. It is set in the milieu of Irish immigrants in Canada during the Great War which adds another dimension to the political and social complexity of Irish experience in those tumultuous years, continuing and varying the motif of the burden of history, or, "heritage", that runs through the other texts of this section and that has complicated and aggravated Irish relations. Finally, Dermot Bolger's *Walking the Road* (2007) represents the most sustained revisionist dramatic approach to the war, taking the form of an experimental re-imagination of the life of Francis Ledwidge, underlining the ghostly position of Irish veterans, stranded in the limbo of Irish historical consciousness.

Writing the Easter Rising – Ireland's Actual Great War Literature?

As outlined in the previous chapters, there is a variety of vital connections and interrelations between the Great War and the 1916 Easter Rising, yet, in Irish historical consciousness, the suffering of Irish soldiers at the battlefront and the sacrifice of the Easter rebels came to be regarded as belonging to separate universes of discourse – in the words of Edna Longley, "the Somme, 1 July 1916, complicated the politics produced by the Rising on 24 April: two sacrificial shrines – the people crucified, a chosen people massacred – demanded their incompatible due" (Longley 1994, 78). For much of the twentieth century it seemed impossible to integrate these two violent episodes into the narrative of Irish history and conceptions of Irish identity.

The cultural legacy of the Easter Rising clearly overpowered the cultural legacy of Ireland's Great War – as Fran Brearton summarises, "Ireland does not have an anthologised or canonised tradition of Great War literature; but it does have an anthologised canon of Easter Rising literature. The aesthetic canon is closely allied with the victorious political canon" (Brearton 2000, 15). Apart from being directly associated with the achievement of Irish independence, the overwhelming appeal of the Rising, as opposed to the Great War, for Irish literary imagination is grounded in several aspects. The directness of the experience – the insurrection taking place in the centre of Dublin, not in some remote Flanders field – certainly played a role, just as the event's clarity about the acting rebels themselves and their aims and enemy, epitomised in their proclamation of independence – the participation of Irishmen in the Great War required much more ambiguous reasoning. The attractive deliberate theatricality, iconography and symbolic power of the whole event and its calculated memorability (cf. Longley 1994, 72) have already been mentioned in chapter II.2. Also, the short-lived nature of the insurrection, its relatively small number of casualties and its relevance as a catalyst for subsequent Irish developments did not provoke much of a critical reflection on the grim reality of blood-sacrifice as in the case of the years of brutal stalemate that characterised the Great War (cf. Dawe 2009, xiii; Brearton 2000, 18; Kiberd 1999, 29), inviting uninhibited glorification. Facing these conditions, Fran Brearton, among others, has cautiously suggested the possibility that the literature of the Easter Rising might actually be seen as Ireland's Great War literature (Brearton 2000, 15) – that the real war of the 1910s to be narrated, dramatized and re-imagined by Irish authors simply was the brief one waged in April 1916 around Dublin's General Post Office, not the years of mass slaughter on the Continent in the backdrop of which the Rising took place.

In the following, the combative ideology and identity concepts integral to Irish nationalist writing of the 1900s and 1910s will be addressed in the sense of their assumed position as a rival discourse to the writing of the Great War, shedding light on the aesthetic and thematic parallels between the seemingly opposed traditions of writing the Easter Rising and the Great War. The section will be concluded with a brief look at the transformation of perspectives on the Rising and Rising literature in the light of the changing attitudes to traditional concepts of Irish history and identity.

Irish nationalism, in contrast to Ulster unionism, very much was determined by cultural and literary discourses. The 'literary' character of the Easter Rising was unmistakable, all of its leaders belonging to literary or journalistic circles, and very much characterised by a sense of romantic idealism. Patrick Pearse, Thomas MacDonagh and Joseph Plunkett were "poets who spoke politics in that very idiom[,…] all of them self-dramatists who couched the struggle in epic terms" (Larkin 2014, 216) and who would see themselves and their struggle as a continuation of the cultural project begun by the dead revolutionary leaders of the past, trying to wake Ireland to embrace a new and liberated national consciousness and identity (cf. Wills 2009, 130). A central concern of their romantic idealism was the concept of patriotic martyrdom, the enthusiastic dedication of one's life and death to the greater good of an independent Celtic and Catholic Ireland. This was expressed most vigorously by Pearse, who had been fascinated by the idea of self-sacrifice for Ireland from an early age and who cultivated an exceptionally morbid literary imagination, combining nationalism and Catholic iconography, which was channelled into his fervent campaigning for Irish liberation. This sacrificial fervour also extended to Pearse's pedagogical concepts, introducing a belligerent note to his teachings of Irish myth and legend as revealed, for example, by an anecdote from St. Enda's College, his school in Rathfarnham, about the winner of a students' poetry competition being presented not with a book, money or sweets but with a rifle (cf. Ferriter 2005, 146).

As Ian McBride notes, it was Pearse who "defined the ideal of sacrificial martyrdom for future generations" (McBride 2011, 35). One of the most notorious of Pearse's formulations of the necessity of sacrifice and revolutionary violence can be found in his political essay *The Coming Revolution*, where he announces that "bloodshed is a cleansing and sanctifying thing, and the nation which regards it as the final horror has lost its manhood. There are many things more horrible than bloodshed; and slavery is one of them" (Pearse 1913, 99). Significantly, Pearse's idea of violent patriotic struggle as "cleansing" and "sanctifying" is connected to nationalist fears of degeneration[61] and emasculation which were seen as the result of the foreign English influence on Ireland that were particularly strong in the 1910s. As a commentator in the August 1911 issue of *Irish Freedom*,

---

61 See also the section on nationalist fears about the illicit fraternisation between Irish-women and English soldiers at the Irish home front in chapter II.2.

an Irish Volunteer newspaper, warns, "England is an unclean nation. She is one of the most diseased nations in the world – socially, physically and mentally. It is to this leper among the nations that our country is wed [...]" (quoted in Harris 2002, 130); and a piece in the subsequent issue goes straight for the ultimate remedy: "Give us war, say we. War in our time, O Lord. Send the lightening of thy thunderbolts through the tyrant nations of Europe; let them rend and tear each other; to the end that the crucified nations shall have freedom and nobility at the last; and that the earth may purge itself from its sins in good red blood" (quoted in Harris 2002, 128). The contiguity of such attitudes with the overarching cult of militarism that gripped Europe in the years leading up to the war is obvious. As Keith Jeffery notes, Pearse and the Irish nationalists, along with the "Ulster Volunteer Force, [...] the Vorticists, Rupert Brooke and those who flirted with the cleansing power of violence are all part, perhaps, of a seamless European robe" (Jeffery 1994, 93), they all belong to the same European generation of 1914 that rejected the pre-war status quo as dull, degenerate and decadent and enthusiastically embraced war and its promise of heroism and a eugenic purification of the *Volkskörper* – only Pearse's glorious 1914 was delayed by little less than two years. In this manner, the thought of Pearse and his companions as some sort of 'soldier-poets' does not seem an assessment too far-fetched.

Irish nationalist writing in the years leading up to and during the war unsurprisingly constructed the Irish Volunteer as the ideal embodiment of male Irish identity and masculinity, being pictured as a symbol of health, boldness, strength and determination, willing to fight and sacrifice his body for Ireland.[62] Violence, in such discourses, becomes the natural expression of a healthy and virile Irish subject who has recognised the dangers of the "British disease" (Harris 2002, 138). This is exemplified, for example, in Seamus O hEaluigh's "Ode to a Rifle", a typical *The Irish Volunteer* poem, in which a nationalist's veneration of

---

62 An archetype of this concept of masculinity can be found, for example, on the cover sheet of *The Irish Volunteer*, the official newspaper of the movement and successor to *Irish Freedom*. The ideal Irish Volunteer depicted there is a young, strong, clean-shaven, broad-shouldered man, pictured at the top of a mountain, on which he is planting a flag. The image is not only symbolic of patriotic pride, struggle and success – it is also an image of sexual potency and eroticism. At first glance, this Volunteer even appears to be topless, wearing only boots, very tight breeches and a bandoleer. And of course his rifle, sticking out from between his legs and held at the level of his crotch, is charged with phallic significance. The rifle here is introduced not only as part of the true Irishman's identity, but even somehow as a natural part of his body – to use Pearse's vocabulary again, bloodshed is an integral part of Irish manhood. (cf. Harris 2002, 130f.).

revolutionary violence even reaches erotic dimensions: "A rifle! at that very word / My blood boils up anew; / And every vein within me's stirred / As I the barrel view" (quoted in Harris 2002, 136).

In contrast to this, the ideal Irishwoman must remain outside the martial realm occupied by nationalist men. The part of women is mainly envisioned as restricted to that of the passive, asexual, spiritual mother or, less frequently, wife, enduring willingly the sacrificing of her sons (or husband) for Ireland, in this sense fulfilling the classical role of exemplifying virtue and selflessly negotiating between the public and private order for the greater nationalist good (cf. Mosse 1985, 17). This concept becomes obvious, for example, in several of Pearse's poems, works like "A Mother Speaks" (1916) or "The Mother" (1916):

> I do not grudge them: Lord, I do not grudge
> My two strong sons that I have seen go out
> To break their strength and die, they and a few,
> In bloody protest for a glorious thing,
> They shall be spoken of among their people,
> The generations shall remember them,
> And call them blessed;
> But I will speak their names to my own heart
> In the long nights;
> The little names that were familiar once
> Round my dead hearth.
> Lord, thou art hard on mothers:
> We suffer in their coming and their going;
> And tho' I grudge them not, I weary, weary
> Of the long sorrow – And yet I have my joy:
> My sons were faithful, and they fought.

(Pearse 1979, 27)

In this manner, the ideal Irishwoman is depicted as a combination of Cathleen ni Houlihan and the Virgin Mary. The similarity in theme and combative attitude of such works to the poetry of English poets of the Great War like Rupert Brooke or Henry Asquith is striking. Edna Longley has identified in the sacrificial patriotic poetry of Pearse and Brooke a shared notion of "an inversion – some might say perversion – of normative values. Words and images, more usually mustered for poetic celebrations of life, are turned to the service of death," Brooke and Pearse in their works presenting "renunciation – of all things earthly, bodily, sensory, human – as fulfilment" (Longley 1994, 78). Along these lines, despite diametrically opposed political outlooks, Irish nationalist writing actually appears to be close to the traditions against which it is directed. The shared pre-occupation with Christian sacrifice frequently is recast analogously either in an imperial or nationalist version. Also, in the light of these similarities, the aforementioned Irish rejection of Great War verse for its Anglocentric nature appears somewhat unwarranted.

Parallels between patriotic Great War poetry and Irish works with a nationalist sensibility are also visible in the most famous literary reaction to the Easter Rising, W. B. Yeats's commemorative poem "Easter 1916", which represents a more sophisticated and critical engagement with the event and the subject of revolutionary violence than the works of most other nationalist authors, also reflecting on the contradictory implications of commemoration itself. Yeats both celebrates and problematises the heroism of the rebels and recognises the tragic nature of their sacrifice.[63] Yet, Yeats also uses established patterns: the speaker describes his acquaintance with the leaders of the rebellion before their revolutionary act, "[c]oming with vivid faces / From counter or desk among grey / Eighteenth-century houses" (Yeats 2001, 85, ll. 2–4), exchanging merely "polite meaningless words" (Yeats 2001, 85, l. 6). The "terrible beauty" of their sacrifice in the rebellion means the end of the "casual comedy" (Yeats 2001, 86, l. 37) of complacent civilian life and they enter an iconic realm in Irish memory: "MacDonagh and MacBride / And Connolly and Pearse / Now and in time to be, / Wherever green is worn, / Are changed, changed utterly: / A terrible beauty is born" (Yeats 2001, 87, ll. 75–80). This pattern of a transformation of men (and women, in the case of Yeats's poem) from pale civilian life to eternal patriotic icons also is a common theme in the poetry of the Great War, ranging in outlook from the glorification of Herbert Asquith's "The Volunteer" to the bitter irony of Siegfried Sassoon's "They".[64] And, to add another

---

63 Yeats was unsettled by his own role as a spiritual or ideological resource for the rebellion, particularly considering the impact and legacy of his 1902 play *Cathleen Ni Houlihan* that celebrates Ireland's history of national struggle and encourages self-sacrifice for the liberation of Ireland – "Did that play of mine send out / Certain men the English shot?" (quoted in Kiberd 1999, 18), Yeats wondered years later. The force of the play also troubled the Irish nationalist MP and war poet Stephen Gwynn, who remarks after seeing the play how he "went home asking myself if such plays should be produced unless one was prepared to go out and shoot and be shot. Miss Gonne's impersonation had stirred the audience as I have never seen an audience stirred" (quoted in Ferriter 2005, 113).

64 In his elegy, Asquith describes the glorious transformation by war of a simple "clerk who half his life had spent / Toiling at ledgers in a city grey" with "no lance broken in life's tournament" into a soldier who finds fulfilment in death on the battlefield, joining "the men of Agincourt" (Asquith 2008, 163). In Sassoon's poem, the transformation of men into warrior icons is suggested in the speech of a bishop directed to a group of soldiers: "'When the boys come back / 'They will not be the same; for they'll have fought / 'In a just cause: they lead the last attack / 'On Anti-Christ; their comrades' blood has bought /

facet to this parallelism, what Yeats and others created with their commemorative and glorifying works effectively amounted to an Easter Rising version of the English myth of a lost generation of brilliant young officers cut down in their prime in the trenches of the Great War (cf. Kiberd 1999, 49) – a myth that, by the way, has been seen as an explanation for the spiritual poverty of independent Ireland, the nation having lost its spiritual leaders on the way to independence.

Beyond the age of Pearse and Yeats, the Easter Rising has remained a powerful and continuously revisited subject in Irish writing to this day, appearing across genres and the spectrum of aesthetic conventions, and being re-imagined from divergent ideological standpoints – Heinz Kosok, for example, has identified at least fourteen Irish Easter Rising plays (cf. Kosok 2007, 60). The development of Easter Rising literature mirrors the status of the event in Irish collective consciousness. For example, the first plays addressing the Rising appeared as early as 1918, when the greater outcome of the rebellion was still unclear and official attitudes towards the Rising had not yet consolidated – consequently, a work like Maurice Dalton's *Sable and Gold* (1918), which depicts the effects of the Rising on a Cork family, was anxious not to make too bold a statement about the events in Dublin; as Kosok remarks about its sense of remoteness from the action, "today [it] reads not unlike a home-front play written under Irish conditions" (Kosok 2007, 60) – which again hints at the notion of Easter Rising literature as Ireland's Great War literature. By the 1920s and 30s, the sacrosanct status of the Rising had been established as a significant part of state identity and, accordingly, the literary treatment of the Rising was increasingly dominated by a sense of glorification. Unsurprisingly, in such a cultural climate, Sean O'Casey's satire *The Plough and the Stars* (1926) caused public outrage, also because it was staged at the nationalist institution of the Abbey Theatre. Generally, more critical works such as Ervine's aforementioned *Changing Winds* (1917) or Eimar O'Duffy's novel *The Wasted Island* (1919) only found tiny audiences in Ireland (cf. Wells 2009, 147).

This condition remained essentially unchanged until the mid-1960s. Sean Dowling's aforementioned play *The Bird in the Net* (1960), connects the theme of the Easter Rising prominently with the Great War, however, it largely repeats

---

'New right to breed an honourable race [...]" (Sassoon 2008, 176, ll. 1–5). Yet, the soldiers point out in their reply how their transformation really is much less spiritual but physical, having been disfigured and maimed by the war: 'We're none of us the same!' the boys reply. / 'For George lost both his legs; and Bill's stone blind; / 'Poor Jim's shot through the lungs and like to die; / 'And Bert's gone syphilitic: you'll not find / 'A chap who's served that hasn't found *some* change' (Sassoon 2008, 176, ll. 7–11) – in an altogether different way, it could be argued, this poem shares Yeats's notion of the "terrible beauty" of sacrifice.

established stereotypes of idealistic but failing rebels, misguided and exploited Irish soldiers and cruel Anglo-Irish landowners. Intriguingly, the fiftieth anniversary of the Rising in 1966 saw not only lavish festivities that included Bryan MacMahon's propagandistic *Seven Men: Seven Days*, but also a new production of *The Plough and the Stars* at the Abbey Theatre and the premiere of Eugene McCabe's short play *Pull Down a Horseman*, which pictures confrontational negotiations between the Catholic nationalist Pearse and the socialist Connolly, planning their revolution. Kosok specifically notes how *Pull Down a Horseman* dares to portray the Rising's leaders unfavourably in several moments (cf. Kosok 2007, 64f.); yet, considering the Great War, which serves as an important backdrop to the play's debate, McCabe lets his two protagonists reiterate established positions and reactions:

> CONNOLLY: A speaker at a recent recruitment meeting in Dublin declared that death in Flanders was more unlikely than death in a Dublin slum. […] *(Pause).* […] These patriots met daily and pledged themselves to smash trade unionism, to bring hunger and misery into the poorest of our Dublin homes, and every man or boy who joins the British army gives these craw filled cocks another crow.
> CHORUS [*of middle to upper-class Mothers, Wives and Sisters*): Shame, Shame, Shame, Shame.
> CONNOLLY: Aye, deeply shameful.
> CHORUS (*of women*): Our sons and husbands / Our lovers and our brothers / Lie in Flanders' mud unburied / With maggots in their mouths / Shame. Shame.
> CONNOLLY: They've sold you, Redmond and his men, no by God, given you away as cannon fodder, in the cause of liberty!
> CHORUS (*of women*): Shame / Shame!
> PEARSE: Those Irish men who promise Irish loyalty to England are wrong. I believe them honest, but they have sat so long at English feasts, that they have lost communion with the ancient unpurchasable faith of Ireland, that ancient stubborn thing that forbids any loyalty from Ireland to England, any union, any surrender of one jot of our claim to freedom.
>
> (McCabe 1979, 16f.)

Those who joined up, the play echoes fifty years later, have been misled, are even guilty of playing into the hands of capitalist oppressors or of betraying Ireland and its "unpurchasable" spirit. Yet, possibly, the minimalistic and unornamented mode of presentation of the play, reducing Connolly and Pearse to their key positions, might also invite audiences to a renewed confrontation of the attitudes presented.

With later works such as *Gale Day* (1979) McCabe would introduce a new phase of dealing with the Rising in Irish writing (cf. Kosok 2007, 65), re-contextualising the event, essentially humanising its leaders, stripping them of the cult of sacrifice and hero worship that had determined perspectives on the Rising for decades. This re-evaluation is part of the revisionist tendencies that had begun to enter Irish culture by this time and that eventually resulted in the loss of the unique position of the Rising in Irish communal consciousness by the end of the twentieth century – for example, the celebrations of the seventy-fifth anniversary of the Rising in 1991 already were markedly subdued compared to the triumphalism of 1966. By 1979, commentators like Conor Cruise O'Brien – of course not without meeting considerable opposition – could call Pearse "a maniac, mystic nationalist with a cult of blood sacrifice and a strong personal motivation towards death" and explain how a "nation which takes a personality of that type as its mentor is headed towards disaster" (quoted in Ferriter 2005, 748). Edna Longley, in a less scandalised manner, suggested in 1994 how "it is no apostasy to treat Pearse and Co. as historical figures rather than as saints; to set the Rising in its early twentieth-century contexts; to demystify its transcendental permanence [...]. The spirits of 1912 and 1916 froze all kinds of energy, diversity and possibility. [...] The de-consecration of Irish memory is overdue – and underway" (Longley 1994, 85).

As the construction of the singular significance of the Rising was reassessed and toned down, new Irish perspectives on the Great War emerged. A central writer to engage with these conditions is Sebastian Barry. An interesting and telling conflation of themes of Irish history and the re-adjustment of perspectives can be found in his 1992 play *White Woman Street* (cf. Kosok 2007, 67), which is set in Ohio around Easter 1916 and focuses on an ageing gang of cowboys led by Trooper O'Hara, an Irish expatriate:

> CLARKE: [...] Where you from, mister?
> TROOPER: Where from? Ireland.
> CLARKE: I knew. We get plenty Irish in here. Place there burning like Richmond, I hear. Some big mail depot or someplace. Fire and ruin in Dublin. Fellas put in jail and likely to be shot. Fighting the English.
> TROOPER: (*not listening, fixed on the door*) That right?
> CLARKE: So I hear. I sure like to get the news. Fighting the English. My grandpa fighting the English too. English won.
>
> (Barry 1996, 175)

O'Hara is ostentatiously unaware of and uninterested in the events shaking his home country; in the explicitly wide-ranging scope of the play, combining Irish and American history, the Rising is reduced to a mere distant incidental remark (cf. ibid.). Significantly, instead of engaging with the news of revolutionary violence at home, Barry has his protagonist demonstrate a striking sense of self-critical colonial reflection in an earlier moment of the play, when O'Hara, thinking about the treatment of Native Americans, states how the sight of the rough "Indian" tent towns reminded him "of certain Sligo hills, and certain men in certain Sligo hills. The English had done for us, and I was thinking, and now we're doing for the Indians" (Barry 1996, 158). This is an inversion and an unfavourable self-reflection which becomes possible through the separateness of the protagonist from his original Irish contexts, challenging the narrative of Irish victimhood that underpinned the Rising. Barry radicalises this sense of an inversion and re-contextualisation, of seeing the tables turned, in his 2005 war novel *A Long Long Way*, which, as will be shown later, includes a de-mystification of the Rising by picturing it from the perspective of an Irish soldier ordered to take part in its suppression.

Summary

The Irish literary response to the monumental event of the Great War can be described as an altogether heterogeneous and patchy phenomenon. This centrally is the outcome of the politics of collective memory and identity in independent Ireland, exclusively focusing on a narrow nationalist understanding of Irishness, Irish history and culture into which the Great War could not be easily integrated. Also, in Northern Ireland, the Great War was largely absorbed by an official ceremonial culture of commemoration rather than being processed in literature. The number of Irish war works which follow the classic conventions of battlefront writing is comparatively small – except for Irish war poetry – and frequently completely embedded within British perspectives. Instead, there is a more substantial body of Irish texts, written in the course of a century and widely diverging in attitudes and aesthetics, that focus on the Irish home front or that employ the Great War as a context in other ways, specifically addressing the predicament of Anglo-Irish identities or connecting the militancy of the period of the Great War to the sectarian violence of the Northern Irish conflict of the last third of the twentieth century. Irish war works since the 1980s have recurrently embraced revisionist approaches, consciously setting out to reassess and reposition the narrative of Ireland's Great War within the national narrative. This is also accompanied by a re-evaluation and de-consecration of the Easter Rising, the central source of state identity and identification, which has been more strongly repositioned in the context of the Great War, also pointing out the manifold similarities and parallels between the discourses of writing the Easter Rising and the Great War. Altogether, the war literature of and about the 1910s and 1920s reflects the combination of "voices of ethnic subcategories of Irishness […] with those affiliated to various political and cultural versions of Irish and British nationalism" (Phillips 2009, 266), the period and its depiction becoming a site of complexity and fluidity of Irish identities.

III. Readings

In this section, aspects of identity in Irish and Northern Irish dramatic and prose representations of the Great War will be investigated based on the theoretical framework outlined earlier and against the historical and cultural backdrop defined in the preceding chapters. The readings are arranged roughly chronologically, tracing the development and transformation of the subject of Irish identities and the Great War and its literary treatment.

I will begin with two plays by two prominent but – considering their ideological orientation as socialists – fairly atypical Irish writers, G. B. Shaw's *O'Flaherty V. C.* (1915) and Sean O'Casey's *The Silver Tassie* (1928), which are essential for the understanding of Ireland's Great War experience and of the conflicting discourses and identity politics that have characterised the event and its aftermath. Although very different in form, mood and style, and although the two plays were created in different historical situations, they share much in themes and authorial outlook (cf. Kosok 2008, 165). Both works centrally focus on the Irish home front during the war, introducing key themes of the subject: class contradictions magnified by the war, the complications and ambiguity of male heroism and the sense of female wartime domestic disorder. By means of the Great War, both plays challenge, in different degrees of directness, the identity constructions of Irish nationalism and the respective conditions of Irish society in the 1910s and 1920s that have been outlined in the contextual sections.

III.1 Socialist Perspectives – Shaw and O'Casey

III.1.1 George Bernard Shaw's *O'Flaherty V. C.* (1915)

As a prominent and provocative writer and vocal political activist, G. B. Shaw (1856–1950) could not leave the subject of the Great War untouched. A notorious critic of the war, Shaw visited the front himself in 1917 and was both fascinated and appalled by what he saw. His wide interest in examining and discussing the Great War is reflected substantially both in his dramatic works and in his political prose writing. The treatment of war and military issues and the study of military characters is a persistent element in Shaw's oeuvre, from early plays such as *Arms and the Man* (1894), which concentrates on the Serbo-Bulgarian War of the 1880s, to late works like the collection *Farfetched Fables* (1948), where new uses of the atomic bomb become a subject. The Great War is addressed directly and indirectly in over a dozen of Shaw's plays (cf. Wisenthal and O'Leary 2006, 1ff.), probably most resonantly in *Heartbreak House* (1919), where Shaw gives expression to his despair about the war in a series of disjointed apocalyptic and surrealistic sketches (cf. Winter 1995, 192). Another of Shaw's most central works, *Saint Joan* (1923), has been described as "more directly concerned with war than any of his other plays" (Wisenthal and O'Leary 2006, 1). Yet, despite this wealth of Shaw's war-related writing, a distinctly Irish perspective on the Great War by the Irishman Shaw – even if the centre of his activities was England – can only be found in *O'Flaherty V. C.: A Recruiting Pamphlet* (1915), a not very well-known short play that has also been mostly overlooked or discounted by scholarly criticism (cf. Kosok 2008, 169).

Throughout his life as a writer, the Fabian socialist and pacifist Shaw was determined to expose and attack the inequality and hypocrisy of English society, advocating an evolutionary socialism to be reached by conveying the "the simple truth that poverty was vice and its elimination virtue" (Winter 1995, 192) to the English public, particularly addressing the English leading classes. Unsurprisingly, Shaw also understood the Great War within the context of such class issues and disparities and he rejected the militaristic spirit and patriotic propaganda of the age. As he writes in *Common Sense about the War* (1914), an 80-page supplement to his political journal *The New Statesman*, he opposes "the nauseous mixture of schoolmaster's twaddle, parish magazine cant, and cinematograph melodrama with which we were deluged" (Shaw 1915, 22). Shaw deliberately affronted British patriots, for example, when he pointed out the hypocritical nature of the common indignation about the sinking of the Lusitania, considering the much less outraged reactions to the much costlier British disasters at Gallipoli and elsewhere (cf. Winter 1995, 192). Furthermore, he refused to join in the popular anti-German tendencies of the time that propagated the notion of an intrinsic barbarity of the German people, Shaw insisting instead on the distinction between the Germany of much treasured high culture and the Germany marked by destructive Prussian militarism and *Junkertum* – political and social phenomena that Shaw saw at work just as much in Britain as in Germany,[65] both countries being seen as trapped by the hold of a 'squirearchy', the rule of the class of the landed gentry (cf. Wisenthal and O'Leary 2006, 9f.).

---

65 "Militarism must not be treated as a disease peculiar to Prussia. It is rampant in England; and in France it has led to the assassination of her greatest statesman. If the upshot of the war is to be regarded and acted upon simply as a defeat of German Militarism by Anglo-French militarism, then the war will not only have wrought its own immediate evils of destruction and demoralisation, but will extinguish the last hope that we have risen above the 'dragons of the prime that tear each other in their slime'" (Shaw 1915, 59).

Such attitudes earned Shaw the reputation of being a notorious pacifist, or, even worse, of being a public enemy gone pro-Kaiser – a view which is unwarranted: Shaw indeed was convinced of the fundamental righteousness of Britain's standing up to Germany's aggression, yet, he soon came to view the moral purpose of the intervention as flawed and as overshadowed by a sense of selfish imperial rivalry and by the notion of the conflict essentially being a waste of lives of the common people of Britain and Germany on behalf of their respective *Junker* rulers (cf. Wisenthal and O'Leary 2006, 11). Also, Shaw was not fundamentally opposed to the military as such. Contrasting it ironically with the brutality and arbitrariness inherent to capitalist civilian life, he envisioned the army as a realm of sanity and order. In his commentaries collected in *What I Really Wrote about the War* (1930), Shaw notes, for example, how "[o]ur industrial system, or rather chaos, murders more souls in a year than any military system murders bodies" (Shaw 1930, 12), and he relishes the thought of compulsory military service as a collective contribution to the state – "if only it would be taken out of the hands of the upper soldiery" (Shaw 1930, 13). Finally, in the preface to *Heartbreak House*, Shaw recounts how during the war "[t]o pass from the newspaper offices and political platforms and club fenders and suburban drawing-rooms to the Army and the munition factories was to pass from Bedlam to the busiest and sanest of workaday worlds" (quoted in Wisenthal and O'Leary 2006, 6). Such ironies are also manifest in Shaw's recruitment satire *O'Flaherty V. C.*

Shaw tackles the subject of the Irish involvement in Britain's war effort in *Common Sense about the War*, highlighting the underlying problem of identification and conflicting national affiliation: "Lord Kitchener made a mistake the other day in rebuking the Irish volunteers for not rallying faster to the defence of 'their country.' They do not regard it as their country yet" (Shaw 1915, 11). This thought also dominates the acerbic preface to *O'Flaherty V. C.*, which was added to the play in 1919. Here, Shaw addresses the English recruitment campaigns in Ireland during the Great War and points out their supposedly misguided and absurd premise. As Shaw recounts, the young male population of Ireland, specifically needed for "those military operations which require for their spirited execution more devilment than prudence" (Shaw 1972, 985), in fact consisted for the most part of "Roman Catholics and loyal Irishmen, which means that from the English point of view they were heretics and rebels" (ibid.). The military advertising strategies that concentrated on agitating Irishmen to remember the German atrocities committed in Catholic Belgium were foolish since, according to Shaw, any act of Irish remembrance inevitably also must bring up Ireland's long history as a victim of British tyranny. Finally, after 1916, Shaw explains, the appeal to recall Belgium and the destruction of Louvain had become an even bitterer farce to Irishmen since Dublin's centre had been reduced to ruins itself by British artillery during the Easter Rising. Nonetheless, the internationalist and socialist Shaw, who did not identify with the concerns of Irish cultural nationalism at all, does not end his observations on such an entirely anti-English note that seems for itself to be close to the anti-war attitudes of Irish radical nationalists. Going to the Continent to fight for the English, even if falsely and clumsily advertised, Shaw argues, still is preferable to the prospect of having to stay in dull and parochial Ireland. Instead of hypocritical talk of Belgium, English recruitment strategists simply should have appealed to the Irishman's "discontent, his deadly boredom, his thwarted curiosity and desire for change and adventure, […] to escape from Ireland, [the Irishman] will go abroad to risk his life for France, for the Papal States, for secession in America, and even, if no better may be, for England" (Shaw 1972, 986). As Ireland truly is inhabited by "tyrants and taskmasters, termagants and shrews" (Shaw 1972, 987), escaping their reach by enlisting is sarcastically suggested by Shaw as a sensible and eye-opening solution. This is why Shaw decided to "advance" recruitment through his play, "[k]nowing that the ignorance and insularity of the Irishman is a danger to himself and to his neighbours" (Shaw 1972, 986).

In this vein, Shaw ironically calls his play "a recruiting poster in disguise" (Shaw 1972, 985), and, unsurprisingly, both the British authorities and censors as well as the Abbey Theatre, for which the play had been commissioned and scheduled to be premiered on 23 November 1915, had great doubts about putting it on stage. Apart from concerns about the play's possible adverse effects on the war effort, authorities were worried by the possibility of Shaw's play inciting riots within the nationalist community akin to the ones caused by Synge's *Playboy of the Western World* in 1907 (cf. Phillips 2010, 136). In a 1915 letter to Lady Gregory, Shaw himself acknowledged the disruptive potential of his play: "The picture of the Irish character will make the *Playboy* seem a patriotic rhapsody by comparison. The ending is cynical to the last possible degree. The idea is that O'Flaherty's experience in the trenches has induced in him a terrible realism and an unbearable candour" (quoted in O'Flaherty 2004, 131). Shaw's protagonist, after leaving Ireland for the trenches, can see his nation for what it really is and the view provided is anything but flattering. Consequently, and ironically, the first performance of *O'Flaherty V. C.* was not carried out at the Abbey,[66] but by a group of English officers at the Western Front at Treizennes, Belgium, on 17 February 1917.

---

66 In a statement entitled "Censorship and Recruiting" in the *Manchester Guardian* on 17 November 1915, Shaw emphasises that there was no official decision against the

The play's main character was modelled by Shaw on Sergeant Michael O'Leary, V. C., perhaps the first Irish 'hero' of the Great War, who became the face of a recruitment campaign of the Central Council for the Organisation of Recruiting in Ireland in early 1915.[67] Interestingly, O'Leary's warring exploits were also acknowledged with pride by Irish radical nationalist propaganda, while at the same time his participation in recruitment drives made him the target of nationalist mockery and scorn (cf. Novick 2001, 59). It is this area of conflict, in which contradictory national identities, political affiliations, concepts and narratives of heroism and individual experiences ambiguously clash, which Shaw sarcastically documents in his play.

The play is set outside the country house of the Anglo-Irish General Sir Pearce Madigan in Ireland in the summer of 1915. Private Dennis O'Flaherty, who was recently awarded the Victoria Cross for outstanding courage, returns from a tour of public appearances, advertising recruitment in Ireland, to have tea at the home of Sir Pearce, on whose estate O'Flaherty grew up. A debate between O'Flaherty and the general evolves, in the course of which both the naïve imperialistic ideas of Sir Pearce about the war as well as fundamental concepts of Irish nationalism are ridiculed and deconstructed, and it turns out that O'Flaherty is not the hero Sir Pearce thought him to be. When O'Flaherty's mother and later his sweetheart Teresa Driscoll, a maid in the home of the general, enter the scene, a shrill and abusive argument ensues, at the end of which O'Flaherty expresses his wish of being back "in the quiet of the country out at the front" (Shaw 1972, 1013).

From the beginning of the play, Private Dennis O'Flaherty, V. C., makes sure to undermine the air of respectability and honour that his new status as a decorated hero of the Great War seems to have given him. O'Flaherty cannot subscribe to the English sense of heroism which he has come to embody and which he has to promote exhaustingly, "saluting the flag til I'm stiff with it" (Shaw 1972, 989). He is quick to convey to Sir Pearce the artificial and ambiguous nature of the supposed social advancement the Victoria Cross effected for him, for example, when he recounts to Sir Pearce his meeting with the English monarchs:

---

staging of the play in order to counteract accusations of being pro-German: "The Castle authorities have not intervened, and neither I nor the Abbey Street Theatre would think for a moment of producing a play if the military authorities felt that it could do the slightest harm to recruiting or anything else" (Shaw 1972, 1015). Eventually, it was the Abbey's management that was responsible for suppressing the play (cf. Innes 2010, 43).

67 For example, O'Leary was featured on a prominent recruitment poster with the heading "An Irish Hero", showing a picture of O'Leary framed by his Victoria Cross, including the subheading "1 Irishman defeats 10 Germans" (cf. Phillips 2010, 135).

All the quality shakes hands with me and says they're proud to know me, just the way the king said when he pinned the Cross on me. And it's as true as I'm standing here, sir, the queen said to me: "I hear you were born on the estate of General Madigan," she says; "and the General himself tells me you were always a fine young fellow." "Bedad, Mam," I says to her, "if the General knew all the rabbits I snared on him, and all the salmon I snatched on him, and all the cows I milked on him, he'd think me the finest ornament for the county jail he ever sent there for poaching."

(Shaw 1972, 989)

Despite the honours received and the invitation to the home of his landlord, O'Flaherty's transformation to official heroism does not overpower his original social status as a poor rural Catholic Irishman, who, it turns out, has to steal from his landlord to survive, even if this is presented as a bittersweet anecdote. The essential condition of class disparity remains untouched despite Sir Pearce's flattering admission that "that little Cross of yours gives you a higher rank in the roll of glory than I can pretend to" (Shaw 1972, 988). O'Flaherty's highly decorated body is still the body of an Irish peasant, even if it has been recruited as a signifier of compliant 'imperial' Irishness and a tool for propaganda.

Thus, Sir Pearce and O'Flaherty obviously still live in different spheres, yet, O'Flaherty's war experiences seem to have endowed him with a sense of fearlessness and audacity that allows him to affront Sir Pearce and to disturb both his contrived colonial self-image as an Anglo-Irish baronet and the uniform sense of patriotism that determines his understanding of the war and that he assumes to be shared by the Irish community of his estate:

SIR PEARCE: [...] After all, he is our king; and it's our own country, isn't it?
O'FLAHERTY: Well, sir, to you that have an estate in it, it would feel like your country. But the divil a perch of it ever I owned. And as to the king, God help him, my mother would have taken the skin off my back if I'd ever let on to have any other king than Parnell.

(Shaw 1972, 990)

The central vehicle for O'Flaherty's sweeping critical revelations and uncomfortable truths about the allegiances of the Irish is his mother, a character Shaw describes in his preface as "a Volumnia of the potato patch" (Shaw 1972, 987). In the course of the conversation, Sir Pearce is shocked to hear that O'Flaherty's mother, of whom he previously thought as a deferential and "most loyal woman" (Shaw 1972, 990), is revealed to be actually a rampant nationalist who taught her son to pray to "St Patrick to clear the English out of Ireland the same as he cleared the snakes" (ibid.). Also, to go to war, O'Flaherty had to deceive his mother, making her believe that he actually went out to fight not for but against the English. Finally, Sir Pearce has to learn that it was not an exalted sense of selfless duty and patriotic courage that made possible the feats for which O'Flaherty was awarded the Victoria Cross but the years of violent bullying by his mother, which fostered in O'Flaherty the brutality and tenacity needed to survive on the battlefield:

> O'FLAHERTY: She mustn't find out [*that O'Flaherty is in the British Army*]. [… I] can't bring myself to break the heart in her. […] Besides, didn't she win the Cross for me?
> SIR PEARCE: Your mother! How?
> O'FLAHERTY: By bringing me up to be more afraid of running away than of fighting. I was timid by nature; and when the other boys hurted me, I'd want to run away and cry. But she whaled me for disgracing the blood of the O'Flahertys until I'd have fought the devil himself sooner than face her after funking a fight. […] That's the way I came to be so courageous. I tell you, Sir Pearce, if the German army had been brought up by my mother, the Kaiser would be dining in the banqueting hall at Buckingham Palace this day […].
>
> (Shaw 1972, 991f.)

In this manner, O'Flaherty fully demystifies his status of a daring warrior for King and Country signified by his medal and originally ascribed to him by an increasingly puzzled Sir Pearce. The scene is typical of the parody of racial constructions of seemingly innate Irish bellicosity and rowdiness in the play (cf. Luckhurst 2006, 305), Shaw dabbling with the stereotype of bloodthirsty Irishmen and Irishwomen against which Irish cultural nationalists struggled.

Crucially, the first-hand experience of the horrors of the Great War, from which General Madigan is detached, has transformed the Irish peasant O'Flaherty in a way that makes it impossible for him to subscribe to any of the available politicised collective soldier identities informed by English patriotism or, possibly, by Redmondite Irish nationalism. O'Flaherty does not understand the war and his own part in it within the official ideological frameworks dominant in Ireland and Britain. Instead, he argues from a fairly diffuse neutral or even internationalist stance, addressing the collective suffering and the general dehumanisation that the war produces (cf. Shaw 1972, 996), a reality that cannot be justified by the, in the words of Sir Pearce, "simple question of patriotism" (Shaw 1972, 994), and that is at odds with the empty and misguided sense of heroism and national sacrifice promoted by the authorities at the home front:

> O'FLAHERTY: Arra, sir, how the divil do I know what the war is about?
> SIR PEARCE: [*rising again and standing over him*] What! O'Flaherty, do you know what you are saying? You sit there wearing the Victoria Cross for having killed God knows how many Germans; and you tell me you don't know why you did it!
> O'FLAHERTY: Asking your pardon, Sir Pearce, I tell you no such thing. I know quite well why I kilt them, because I was afeard that, if I didn't, they'd kill me.
>
> (Shaw 1972, 994)

SIR PEARCE: Really, O'Flaherty, the war seems to have upset you a little.

O'FLAHERTY: It's set me thinking, sir; and I'm not used to it. It's like the patriotism of the English. They never thought of being patriotic until the war broke out; and now the patriotism has taken them so sudden and come so strange to them that they run about like frightened chickens, uttering all manner of nonsense.

(Shaw 1972, 998f.)

O'FLAHERTY: [...] [T]he English: they think there's no one like themselves. It's the same with the Germans, though they're educated and ought to know better. You'll never have a quiet world til you knock the patriotism out of the human race.

(Shaw 1972, 1000)

In this manner, O'Flaherty is straightforwardly employed as a vehicle for the anti-militarist and anti-patriotic attitudes of Shaw. The reason O'Flaherty eventually gives for volunteering, apart from the economic one, is vaguely connected to a sentiment of an obligation to share in the collective suffering of ordinary men like himself who have been sent out to fight – "I'd be ashamed to stay at home and not fight when everybody else is fighting" (Shaw 1972, 1003).

Yet, the deprecation of English wartime patriotism and pathos is not the only concern in Shaw's unlikely recruiting play. O'Flaherty's disaffection with the public absorption of his persona by English official discourses of war does not mean that he is drawn towards the other side, the anti-English self-images provided by Irish nationalism. In fact, O'Flaherty's war experience and, specifically, the concomitant experience of leaving Ireland, has expanded and liberated his mental scope and clarified his view on his home. O'Flaherty arrives at the recognition that "I've been made a fool of and imposed upon all my life" (Shaw 1972, 1008) – the nationalism of his community being perceived by O'Flaherty as just as stifling and repressive as the English rule against which it is directed. Mindless Irish patriotism, O'Flaherty deplores, again in a Shavian tone demanding internationalist solidarity, has "kept Ireland poor, because instead of trying to better ourselves we thought we was the fine fellows of patriots when we were speaking evil of Englishmen that was as poor or good as ourselves" (Shaw 1972, 994).

The markedly female sphere of the home front to which O'Flaherty returns, consisting of his mother and his sweetheart Teresa, exemplifies the destructive and inhibiting effects of Irish nationalism. They are coarse and obstinate specimens of Irish peasant femininity marked by spiritual and material poverty – a condition magnified by the context of the war. O'Flaherty's mother is labelled "the wildest Fenian and rebel" (Shaw 1972, 990), characterised by the display of a frenetic and ridiculously misinformed fixation on Irishness: "She says all the English generals is Irish. She says all the English poets and great men was Irish.

[…] She says we're the lost tribes of the house of Israel and the chosen people of God. […] She says that Moses built the seven churches and that Lazarus was buried in Glasnevin" (Shaw 1972, 1000). Mrs O'Flaherty is a vicious parody of Cathleen Ni Houlihan, the mythological prototype of nationalist motherhood who encourages young Irishmen to sacrifice themselves for Ireland. From the first reference to Mrs O'Flaherty, she is associated with violence and brutality. O'Flaherty recounts how cheerfully she celebrated his departure, as she thought, to fight the English, and she is scandalised when she finds out about O'Flaherty having lied to her, seeing her son in the papers shaking hands with the English king at Buckingham Palace. However, the way in which O'Flaherty defuses his mother's rage about her son's betrayal of Ireland tellingly reveals an entirely unpatriotic trait of greed in her:

> MRS O'FLAHERTY: If you wanted to fight, why couldn't you fight in the German army?
> O'FLAHERTY: Because they only get a penny a day.
> MRS O'FLAHERTY: Well, and if they do itself, isn't there the French army?
> O'FLAHERTY: They only get a hapenny a day.
> MRS O'FLAHERTY: [*much dashed*] Oh murder! They must be a mean lot, Dinny.
> O'FLAHERTY: […] I went where I could get the biggest allowance for you; and little thanks I get for it!
>
> (Shaw 1972, 1003f.)

The money earned by O'Flaherty eventually outweighs his mother's concerns of ideological allegiances and national belonging. Similarly, O'Flaherty's girlfriend Teresa Driscoll, a servant of Sir Pearce, is characterised by materialistic interests and opportunism. O'Flaherty's present of a golden necklace, taken illegally from a German prisoner of war, only incites Teresa to ask whether it was real gold and if she could have it assessed by a jeweller. Her main concern is O'Flaherty's money, his veteran's pension that she expects to live off in the future and that might be bigger if her lover returned from the war as a cripple – "You'll have a pension anyhow, Denny, won't you, whether you are wounded or not?" (Shaw 1972, 1007). In this manner, also Teresa becomes a tarnished Cathleen Ni Houlihan, demanding the sacrifice of her lover, not for Ireland but for her own well-being. O'Flaherty is disgusted by the attitudes of his mother and his girlfriend – "it's nothing but milch [sic] cows men are for the women" (1010) – realising the corrupted condition of his home. Yet, the women remain unimpressed by his outburst and instead engage in a foul-mouthed and violent argument over his earnings until they have to be separated by force and are pushed off the stage with the help of Sir Pearce.

Importantly, the behaviour of the Irishwomen of Shaw's play is not the outcome of a war-induced lack of male authority or of an innate Irish aggressiveness and depravity; it is also not driven by a frustrated female desire for glory and second-hand thrills, a common theme of the home front during the Great War (cf. Phillips 2010, 137). It is poverty, the play suggests, that dominates Irish domestic life and produces devious women like Mrs O'Flaherty and Teresa Driscoll, and it is the archaic and inhibiting culture of Irish nationalism that keeps Ireland poor (cf. Shaw 1972, 994) and keeps them from recognising and changing the oppressive conditions in which they live. Only O'Flaherty, who has managed to gain a sobering outside perspective by going away to war, can penetrate the predominant orthodoxies of Irish and English nationalism – still, his insight leaves him disillusioned. At the end of the play, O'Flaherty expresses an almost surreal desire to be back in the homosocial realm of the war zone, undisturbed by domestic disorder:

> Only a month ago, I was in the quiet of the front, with not a sound except the birds and the bellow of a cow in the distance as it might be, and the shrapnel making little clouds in the heavens and the shells whistling, and may be a yell or two when one of us was hit; and would you believe it, sir, I complained of the noise and wanted to have a peaceful hour at home. Well: them two has taught me a lesson. This morning, Sir, when I was telling the boys here now I was longing to be back taking my part for king and country with the others, I was lying, as you well knew, Sir. Now I can go and say it with a clear conscience. Some likes war's alarums; and some likes home life. I've tried both, sir; and I'm all for war's alarums now.
>
> (Shaw 1972, 1013)

This is the cynical conclusion that Shaw announced in his aforementioned letter: Compared to the shrill turmoil and disorder at home, the mayhem of the Western Front appears pastoral and serene to O'Flaherty.

To sum up, *O'Flaherty V. C.* reflects Shaw's rejection of *Junkertum*, of the misguided sense of upper-class militarism and patriotism that underpinned the Great War. Even more evocatively, Shaw parodies and deconstructs central identity concepts of Irish nationalism in the play – the image of the spiritual, Marian, sacrificial Irish mother, just as the heroic image of the cunning Irish warrior. While satirising the naivety and aloofness of the Anglo-Irish gentry, embodied by Sir Pearce, Shaw also undermines Irish Anglophobia and exposes the self-destructive militancy of Irish nationalism (cf. O'Flaherty 2004, 131). Through the lens of the Great War, *O'Flaherty V. C.* exposes how the grip of Irish nationalism creates myopic Irish selves at odds with the actual political and economic realities – an Irish society dominated by figures like Mrs O'Flaherty cannot progress and is to a certain degree complicit in its own oppression. Through his protagonist, for whom the Great War is a brutal but eye-opening experience considering the question of national belonging, Shaw discards the relevance of 'nation' for identification, suggesting instead a vision of a more open-minded Irish identity, characterised by an awareness of internationalist solidarities.

The next work to be analysed is one of the most prominent Irish war plays, Sean O'Casey's *The Silver Tassie*. As mentioned earlier, O'Casey shares various themes with Shaw's play and also touches on socialist and internationalist sensibilities. Centrally, there is the shared notion of a fundamental clash between a disorderly Irish home front and Irish soldiers transformed by the war – however, this time, the transformation does not as much affect nationalist self-images and perceptions but the physical integrity of fighting Irishmen and with it their place in a pitiless civilian world.

III.1.2 Sean O'Casey's *The Silver Tassie* (1928)

Written almost ten years after the end of the Great War, *The Silver Tassie* was created in a situation very different from the immediacy of war concerns and pressing Irish disputes that characterises Shaw's play. Within the oeuvre of Sean O'Casey (1880–1964), the play represents a significant shift of perspective and of the overall direction of his career as a dramatist. O'Casey, who was strongly influenced by Shaw and a lifelong admirer of both his plays and politics (cf. Kosok 2008, 165f.), began to work on what was to become *The Silver Tassie* in London in 1926, having chosen exile over staying in a post-independence Ireland with which he was deeply dissatisfied. O'Casey was disgusted by the continuous and unquestioning subservience of his compatriots to the Catholic clergy, by the new dominance of the Irish middle classes and by the intellectual snobbery of Dublin's "gods and half-gods" (Malone 1969, 40), W. B. Yeats and Æ. Most of all, O'Casey was tired of the narrow-mindedness of the Irish public that characterised these conditions and that had led to common outrage about *The Plough and the Stars*, in which O'Casey had dared to doubt the all-around sacredness of the Easter Rising (cf. Malone 1969, 40f.).[68] The subject matter of *The Silver Tassie*, the Great War and the Irish home front, represents another choice at odds with the concerns of the nationalist Irish cultural mainstream of the 1920s and afterwards – the involvement of Irish soldiers in the British army being a part of Irish history "which the new state most emphatically did not wish to commemorate" (Phillips 2010, 115).

---

68 The vital context of the Great War is also mentioned several times in O'Casey's Easter Rising play (cf. Brown 2011, 82f.).

Interestingly, before the decade of violent turmoil in Ireland that began in the mid-1910s, O'Casey himself had been a committed nationalist, supporting the militant aims of the Irish Republican Brotherhood. It was only the Dublin lock-out of 1913 that turned O'Casey towards socialist concerns; finally, the 1916 Rising, which he saw as a tragic error, made O'Casey condemn aggressive Irish republicanism (cf. Murray 1999, 81). Against nationalist political and cultural doctrines, O'Casey set out to demythologise lofty ideals of national spirit, patriotic heroism and blood sacrifice, contrasting them with the much less glamorous and less metaphysical issues of urban poverty and class disparity, counteracting W. B. Yeats who previously had massively contributed to the romantic image of the Irish commitment to rebellion, of a war for Ireland. For O'Casey, the Irish needed to be liberated from nationalist myths and discourses that prevented a much needed social revolution in Ireland (cf. Stubbings 2000, 119).

In this respect, *The Silver Tassie* represents a shift in perspective for O'Casey since, up to this play, his focus had been on the nationalist consciousness and identity of the emerging Irish state and its conflict with O'Casey's socialist visions for Ireland (cf. Murray 1999, 90). In *The Silver Tassie*, O'Casey for the first time makes an international context the subject of his work: the Great War and its repercussions for a Dublin working-class community. Interestingly, the play does not include direct references to Irish nationalism or to related issues such as Home Rule; also, there is no explicit political discussion about why Irishmen go to war beyond the money that can be earned and the compensation their families receive. Instead, O'Casey emphasises the dehumanisation and de-individualisation that the experience of war entails, and he also exposes the cruelty and coldness inherent to materialist Irish urban social dynamics. In this manner, the play transcends the more obvious nationalist-unionist-imperialist concerns.

The Silver Tassie was also breaking new ground regarding the aesthetic conventions of O'Casey's oeuvre. Departing from the naturalism of his Dublin trilogy, O'Casey includes in *The Silver Tassie* an experimental and highly symbolical second act, moving the setting to a devastated war zone in France. Here, O'Casey appropriates techniques of post-war expressionism, expressing bitterness, disillusion and despair through fragmentation, raw emotion and lurid universal symbolism – this part has been likened to the dream play in Ernst Toller's *Masses and Men* (cf. Starkie 1939, 167; McAteer 2010, 70). The famous and much-cited controversy[69] about the *The Silver Tassie* between W. B. Yeats and O'Casey, which

---

69   Walter Starkie notes in 1939 how "[n]ot only the Irish and English but also the American newspapers devoted long columns to the contest, and dramatic critics had their

would complete O'Casey's alienation from Irish culture, and which has been interpreted as one of the most telling episodes concerning Ireland's fraught relation to the Great War, was also related to this impression of aesthetic deviation. Yeats, then one of the directors of the Abbey Theatre for which the play was written, rejected O'Casey's play also because he felt it was dramaturgically flawed, the play not obeying the unifying principles of Aristotle's *Poetics* – apparently, Christopher Murray quips, Yeats simply "had not the faintest idea what expressionism was" (Murray 1999, 92).

More importantly, Yeats rejected the play because he generally discounted the Great War as a literary subject, the technologized mass conflict reducing its countless participants to helpless victims, denying any potential for individual agency, heroism and catharsis (cf. Grene 1999, 244; McDonald 2002, 116f.) – the Great War was seen by Yeats as nothing but a "bloody frivolity" (Yeats in a 1915 letter to Henry James; Yeats 1954, 600). For Yeats, *The Silver Tassie* merely served as a vehicle for O'Casey's socialist beliefs with which he could not identify at all. In a letter to Olivia Shakespear, Yeats renounces the play as "all anti-war propaganda to the exclusion of plot and character" (quoted in Murray 1999, 91), unsuitable for the Abbey stage. Furthermore, in a condescending gesture of "imaginative isolationism" (Grene 1999, 244), Yeats suggests in a letter to O'Casey that O'Casey had been thwarted by the "mere greatness of the world war" (Yeats 1954, 741). He accuses him of not actually being "interested in the great war; you never stood on the battlefields or walked its hospitals, and so write out of your opinions" (Yeats 1954, 741), O'Casey supposedly choosing ideology over fact and experience. O'Casey, whose Dublin trilogy, despite the public controversies that accompanied the plays, had previously ensured the Abbey Theatre's financial as well as artistic survival, reacted vigorously:

> I am afraid your statement […] is not only an ignorant one, but it is a silly statement too. […] Do you really mean that no one should or could write or speak about a war because one has not stood on the battlefields? Was Shakespeare at Actium or Phillippi? Was G. B. Shaw in the boats with the French, or in the forts with the English when St Joan and Dunois made the attack that relieved Orleans? […]
> But I have walked some of the hospital wards. I have talked and walked and smoked and sung with the blue-suited, wounded men, fresh from the front. I've been with the legless, the armless, the blind, the gassed and the shell-shocked; one with a head bored

---

field-day. Some even rumoured that O'Casey had challenged Yeats to a duel; others that the Abbey directors suffered from internal combustion […].Then suddenly the air was cleared by the publication of the entire correspondence between the Abbey directors and O'Casey" (Starkie 1939, 168f.).

by shrapnel who had to tack east and tack west when before he could reach the point he wished to get to; with one whose head rocked like a frantic moving pendulum. Did you know "Pantosser," and did you ever speak to him? Or watch his funny, terrible antics, or listen to the gurgle of his foolish thoughts? [...] And does war consist only of hospital wards and battlefields?

(O'Casey 1975, 271–2)

O'Casey refutes Yeats's criticism as fundamentally misguided and illicit, stressing his awareness of the horrific realities of the Great War, pointing to his intimate knowledge of and relation to those who have "stood on the battlefield" and left it disfigured, disabled or traumatised. Also, O'Casey stresses the all-encompassing scope of the Great War that Yeats, despite speaking of its "greatness", does not seem to see: "[D]oes war consist only of hospital wards and battlefields?" – it would be foolish, O'Casey suggests, to blank out the war's relevance for and effect on those who witnessed it at the home front. Indeed, as will be shown shortly, O'Casey's play suggests that, possibly, war is just a displaced expression of the grim conditions at home, not vice versa.

The Silver Tassie premiered in London's Apollo Theatre in October 1929. While it was not a big commercial success, it was favourably reviewed by critics. For example, one English reviewer particularly lauded O'Casey's choice of moving the play to an actual battlefield in the second act, thereby addressing the difficult status of the war in Ireland: O'Casey "has followed Heegan to the guns in Flanders, justly remembering that countless Irishmen did make that journey" (quoted in Jeffery 2011, 254). Another enthusiastic reaction came from St. John Ervine, as mentioned earlier, a writer and Ulsterman crippled in the war himself, who sees in the "intensely human" play "a cry of pain wrung from the lips of an onlooker at the war who has been deeply moved by the spectacle of human suffering" (quoted in ibid.).

At last, in 1935, O'Casey and Yeats made peace and *The Silver Tassie* was staged at the Abbey Theatre, the new board of the Abbey trying to make amends for the earlier affront against O'Casey. In Ireland, the play caused a public outcry – however, it was not extensively attacked for the uneasy subject matter of the Great War, this aspect largely remained in the subtext. Some took issue with the play's unfavourable depiction of Dublin working-class women as greedy, selfish and calculating (Welch 1999, 120). Furthermore, the Catholic Church was appalled by the use of liturgical and religious iconography and symbolism in the second act; also, the overtly sexual nature of the final act and the religious hypocrisy of the character Susie Monican caused offense (cf. Phillips 2010, 120). *The Irish Catholic* of 7 September 1935 demanded a ban of O'Casey's plays altogether and P. T. McGinley, president of the Gaelic League, wanted to see the Abbey Theatre closed down (cf. Welch 1999, 121f.). The play clearly was at odds with the ideals and concepts of Irishness defined in dominant nationalist discourses. O'Casey's brutal, fatalistic and sexualised Dubliners, some of them wearing British uniforms and being portrayed sympathetically for the injuries suffered on the battlefield, were deemed inappropriate for the stage of the national theatre.

Surprisingly, *The Silver Tassie* appears to be the only Irish war work to feature more prominently the motif of the permanently shell-shocked, disfigured or disabled veteran returned home – one of the most emblematic characters in Great War writing.[70] The general prevalence of this type of character in war literature of course is the outcome of the unprecedented destructive capacity of the Great War, the conflict producing an entire generation of physically and mentally traumatised men. During and after the war, mutilated and disabled men became a common public sight, a mass phenomenon. As Joana Bourke observes, the Great War "magnified the experience of deformity" (Bourke 1996, 31) and in this manner, it brought about a fundamental change of the common perception of the disabled, which previously had been one characterised by uneasiness, disgust or curiosity, disability being seen by the public as divine punishment, bad luck or monstrosity. At least until the end of the 1920s in Britain, disfigured and disabled veterans were largely encountered in a spirit of empathy and gratitude, the public acknowledging a national responsibility to care for them (Bourke 1996, 31). In fact, the British public even came to idolise veterans who 'triumphed' over their disability by embracing new careers or activities in spite of or even integrating their handicaps (cf. Leonard 2008, 212f.).[71] These altered sentiments, as well as the economic need to restore the employability of the disabled, contributed to the post-war period becoming the starting point of modern concepts of rehabilitation and prosthetic technology (Dederich 2007, 103f.).

However, we must keep in mind that these developments and attitudes were common in Britain and that Ireland was a different case. In Ireland, specifically after the transformations of 1916, the war disabled, just as the war itself, hardly

---

70 I have addressed the subject of war, disability and gender in *The Silver Tassie* also in an earlier essay entitled "'You half-baked Lazarus' – Masculinity and the Maimed Body in Sean O'Casey's *The Silver Tassie*" (cf. Decker 2014). Several of the ideas to be outlined in the following can also be found in this essay, however, with a stronger emphasis on the dimension of disability.

71 An example of this is Belfast-born Captain Gerard Lowry, who was blinded at the Western Front in October 1914. Lowry retrained to be a masseur and osteopath and then became a sporting legend as a boxer, celebrated in the 1927 film *Victory over Blindness* (cf. Leonard 2008, 212f.).

were seen as a national cause. During the war, David Fitzpatrick notes, "injured and disabled soldiers were to be seen in every Irish town, mutely or loudly reproaching those who had stayed out of the conflict" (Fitzpatrick 2008, 135). As outlined in the chapter on the historical context, returning Irish servicemen generally encountered severe difficulties in re-adapting to an uncaring or even hostile home community. They returned to an utterly changed country that did not specifically value their sacrifice – for wounded and disabled Irish veterans, the situation was even harder. For example, in her interviews with Irish Great War veterans, Jane Leonard mentions the case of Sam Hutchinson, who spent most of 1918 as a patient in a Ministry of Pensions hospital in Dublin. Hutchinson remembers how invalided soldiers of the British forces like him, identifiable for the public by their distinctive blue uniforms, fell victim to verbal and physical abuse on their walks around an increasingly nationalist Dublin: "[T]he finger of scorn was pointed at us" (quoted in Leonard 2008, 212). Similarly, a 1919 report of the City of Dublin War Pensions Committee notes that when Irish servicemen "came back disabled and broken down in some cases they found that their own relatives had changed their views on public affairs and matters were extremely uncomfortable for the unfortunate man [...] the public in its resentment is inclined to threaten the disabled man" (quoted in Bourke 1996, 70).

It is such a sentiment of wilful ignorance or even aggression towards disabled Irish soldiers that takes centre-stage in the two closing acts of *The Silver Tassie*. However, as I will show in the following, the play relates this rejection not explicitly to nationalist fervour and ignorance but to a discriminative and materialist ideology of masculine strength and fitness, an unforgiving socio-economy of bodies determined by an almost pathologic idolisation of male physical force, health and beauty. These are the foundations upon which the identity constructions of the characters are grounded. The Great War serves as the catalyst through which these conditions and their extremism are exposed in all their harshness.

The Silver Tassie is set, apart from the second act, in O'Casey's trademark dramatic situation of working-class Dublin, in 1916. In the first act, the main protagonist Harry Heegan, an Irish soldier in the British forces and local football star, returns home from a match, having won for his team a much desired trophy, the "Silver Tassie". However, Harry's triumph is only very brief, since he and his comrades Teddy Foran and Barney Bagnal are rushed by their mothers and wives to the ship which takes them back to the Western Front. The second act is formally and narratively detached from the rest of the play, consisting of a surreal and expressionistic depiction of the delusional war experiences of a group of anonymous soldiers (except for Barney) and their absurdly nonsensical superiors. Harry Heegan and the other characters reappear in the third act, which is set in a Dublin hospital. Shot in the spine, Harry now is a paraplegic in a wheelchair, disillusioned, most painfully by the rejection of Jessie Taite, the girl who had once been obsessed with him in his glorious days as a football hero. The fourth and final act shows crippled Harry and blinded Teddy Foran at a party at Harry's former football club. There, the two victims of the war are not only pushed aside but treated as disruptive factors, particularly by Jessie Taite and her new lover Barney, who was awarded the Victoria Cross for saving Harry's life. After a helpless violent outburst in which Harry smashes the "Silver Tassie", the fallen hero resigns. While the revellers keep dancing to the music of the orchestra, Harry and his blinded friend Teddy admit defeat and abandon their former companions.

From the start, O'Casey depicts the Dublin working-class environment of *The Silver Tassie* as a world governed and fascinated by men's bodies and male strength, yet, as already mentioned, this fascination is not linked to nationalist ideals of Irish masculinity. O'Casey supports this physical fascination also in his stage directions which include detailed and colourful descriptions of the bodily appearance and integrity of his characters. Sylvester Heegan, Harry's father, for example, is "a stockily built man of sixty-five; he has been a docker all his life since first the muscles of his arms could safely grip a truck, and even at sixty-five the steel in them is only beginning to stiffen" (O'Casey 1964, 5); contrastingly, Mrs Heegan, Harry's mother, is "stiffened with age and rheumatism; the end of her life is unknowingly lumbering towards a rest: [...] everything she has to do is done with a quiet mechanical persistence. Her inner ear cannot hear even a faint echo of a younger day" (O'Casey 1964, 6f.).

The image of violent heroism and fame attributed to Harry is powerfully established already at the outset of the play. Waiting for the return of the victorious footballer, Sylvester Heegan and his friend Simon Norton revel in anecdotes of Harry, thereby revealing their obsession with the physical, with violence and masculinity. Their praise of Harry's body, his power and aggression is euphoric, Sylvester recounting how he has watched his son "do it, mind you. I seen him do it. Break a chain across his bisseps!" (O'Casey 1964, 7). Another anecdote even verges on the homoerotic, Sylvester recounting an altercation of Harry with a policeman which rather evokes the image of a romantic mating ritual than a street brawl:

> An' the hedges by the road-side standin' stiff in the silent cold of the air, the frost beads on the branches glistenin' like toss'd-down diamonds from the breasts of the stars, the quietness of the night stimulated to a fuller stillness by the mockin' breathin' of Harry, an' the heavy, ragin' pantin' of the Bobby, an' the quickenin' beats of our own hearts [...].
> (O'Casey 1964, 8)

In this manner, Harry's powerful position in his community is introduced, a high rank based on an extraordinary capacity for violent self-assertion. This is a condition frequently described in Irish drama, the absence or inefficiency of authorities like fathers or the law leading to a degeneration of the sons or even of Irish social life at large (cf. Kiberd 1992, 129ff.). Masculinity in the social environment of *The Silver Tassie* is defined only by strength and health, and the strict hierarchies deriving from this condition are established through violent contests – as a consequence, the strongest and most reckless men epitomise what Connell has defined as "hegemonic masculinity".

These conditions correlate to Joanna Bourke's observations of civilian disablement in Britain in the first decades of the twentieth century. Bourke stresses how the "deliberate injuring of another man was part of growing up. [...] To be 'decorated' or 'well-painted' with blood was a manly accomplishment. It trained men for war, and could sometimes be as damaging to the male body" (Bourke 1996, 35f.). This concept also applies to the Irish setting of the play. Football, the sport that cements Harry Heegan's dominance among his working-class peers in the first act, functions as a peacetime arena for such feats. It belongs to the same category of violent contests between men as the war for which Harry enlisted. Thus, O'Casey reflects the conflation of sports, athleticism and warfare that was firmly established in the discourses of the Great War. British recruiting strategists of the 1910s were aware of the power of the sporting motif and employed it in their campaigns, associating warfare with glamour, masculine team spirit and the illusion of fair play, also providing "potential recruits with reassurance of continuity between civilian and military life" (Fitzpatrick 1995, 1030). This conflation of football and domestic and wartime violence is played out repeatedly in *The Silver Tassie*. Harry embodies the contiguity of these spheres of corporeal violent experience when he enters the stage for the first time, wearing "khaki trousers, a military cap stained with trench mud" and his football shirt, "a vivid orange-coloured jersey with black collar and cuffs" (O'Casey 1964, 25). Similarly, Harry's later recounting of the match is characterised by aggressive and martial imagery, his description of his decisive goal resembling an attack on the battlefield: "[S]eeing in a *flash* the goalie's hands sent with a *shock to his chest* by the *force* of the *shot*, his *half-stunned* motion to clear, a *charge*, and then carrying him, the ball and all with a *rush* into the centre of the net!" (O'Casey 1964, 28, my emphasis).

In this manner, the Great War in the play becomes an extension of the culture of violence at home, a bitter form of the aforementioned continuity between civilian and military life. The farewell scene at the end of the first act underlines this notion impressively. Harry and his fellow Dublin comrades are swiftly and happily sent off to the front, accompanied by the collective shout "They must go back!" (O'Casey 1964, 31). There is no expression of fear or grief on behalf of the soldiers' parents and wives. Parading the football trophy in front of the soldier's triumphal march to the ship, going to war is obviously understood by the depicted community as another tournament in the violent competition of male bodies started at home. Tellingly, in the second act at the front, the soldiers receive parcels from home, one containing a football and a note saying "To play your way to the enemies' trenches when you go all over the top" (O'Casey 1964, 51) – in *The Silver Tassie* "athletics are warlike, war is athletic" (Harkness 1978, 134). Along these lines, the soldier identities of Harry, Teddy and Barney can easily be integrated with an already belligerent public and private self. It is not the Great War that carries violence and disharmony into a peaceful civilian community – violence and disharmony are there from the start. As Ronan McDonald remarks, in some way the play suggests that "the war is a result of the prevailing social structure, rather than vice versa" (McDonald 2002, 120).

Within this structure, women play a very unfavourable part, recalling the negative images of women common in some examples of Great War poetry like Sassoon's "The Glory of Women" (cf. Johnson 2003, 119). Using the context of the Great War, O'Casey, like Shaw, deconstructs ideals of Irish femininity and motherhood, Pearse's suffering sacrificing mothers and the comely maidens of de Valera. Through characters like Mrs Heegan, O'Casey reflects the stereotype of the 'separation women', for whom the service of their husbands and sons was a welcome source of income, enabling them to enjoy a higher standard of living and a greater degree of independence than before the war. During the war, such women were frequently pictured as violent and offensive in their protests against the nationalist rejection of the war service of Irishmen (cf. Ferriter 2005, 136).[72] In *The Silver Tassie*, such forms of materialistic motherly and wifely degeneration

---

72 For example, a Sinn Fein activist noted the anti-nationalist sentiment of local "separation women" during the 1917 East Clare by-election: "The women were kept well plied with drink by a number of publicans who were supporters of the Irish party and in their drunken condition they were a frenzied and ferocious crowd to deal with. On a couple of occasions the volunteers were obliged to use the ash plant in order to protect Sinn Fein supporters to be mauled by these infuriated females" (Ferriter 2005, 136). Similarly, after a parade of the radical nationalist Irish Volunteers in Limerick, Ernest Blythe, later a Free State government minister, recalled how "the rabble of the city, particularly the 'separation women', got into the mood to make trouble and a large crowd of them gathered near the station to attack the Volunteers as they moved to the train. There was a certain amount of stone throwing and blows were struck at Volunteers as they passed by" (ibid.).

are acute. For example, Mrs Heegan's greatest worry in the first act is not the danger of losing her son but losing the compensation payment she receives, O'Casey repeating the model established by the mother in Shaw's satirical play:

> MRS HEEGAN: [...] He's overstayed his leave a lot, an' if he misses now the tide that's waitin', he skulks behind desertion from the colours.
> SUSIE: On Active Service that means death at dawn.
> MRS HEEGAN: An' my governmental money grant would stop at once.
>
> (O'Casey 1964, 18)

Mrs Foran sends her husband Teddy to the front and uninhibitedly breaks into cheerful song at the thought of being on her own again: "I'll be single again, yes, single again; / An I goes where I likes, an' I does what I likes, / An' I likes what I likes now I'm single again!" (O'Casey 1964, 11). This desire to escape male authority and supervision could also be seen as a parallel to the ending of *O'Flaherty V. C.*, an escape from, in this case, male-induced domestic disorder and violence into an entirely female homosocial community. Mrs Foran's desire for autonomy, for an existence beyond her prescribed identity as a subservient wife and homemaker, of course cannot go unpunished: Outraged, Teddy ravages the couple's flat before leaving for the front again, which includes the smashing of the couple's much-loved wedding-bowl, foreshadowing Harry's later smashing of the "Tassie", and, to some degree, reproducing the chaos and destruction of the front at home. Teddy's fury exemplifies the gap in experience between men at war and women at home and suggests the notion of the home front as the venue for a "festival of female misrule" (Leed 1979, 49), a condition proclaimed by various observers during the war.

Another example of uneasy and contradictory femininity is Susie Monican. Throughout the first act, Susie appears as a fanatic Catholic, who annoys her environment by chanting biblical platitudes. The reason for the "peculiar bend in Susie's nature" (O'Casey 1964, 16), as which her religious fervour is perceived, is her frustration about Harry's lack of interest in her and, possibly, her detachment from the realm of power and agency reserved for the men. Susie's anger and sexual frustration are channelled into a strange religiously charged fascination with the Great War (cf. Doyle 1978, 30). For the greater part of the first act, Susie, the "gospel-gunner" (O'Casey 1964, 17), is occupied with the ambiguous activity of polishing Harry's rifle, also announcing with great determination that "the men that go with the guns go with God" (O'Casey 1964, 29). In such moments, the parallels between war propaganda and nationalist ideas of male martyrdom for Ireland become obvious – Susie Monican is a parody of both ideas. In the third act, Susie re-appears transformed: She is a nurse in a hospital, taking care of the war-wounded, including Harry, obviously having traded her contradictory obsession with God, guns and the mortification of the flesh for the joys of professional life, indulging both in her newly gained authority and the proximity to the realities of the war.

The most negative example of Irish womanhood transformed and liberated by the war in the play is the figure of Jessie Taite – a young, opportunistic and thoroughly sexualised woman, constantly in search of fame and adventure which she attains by bluntly offering herself to the popular and heroic. Jessie's provocative behaviour, however, is not just the result of a disinterest in respectability – her liberty of selecting and enjoying whoever she's temporarily interested in is also made possible by her financial independence brought about by the war. Working in an ammunitions factory, Jessie, unlike Mrs Heegan and Mrs Foran, has an income and even a bank account of her own. The character of Jessie Taite confirms Susan Gilbert's observation of "a release of female libidinal energies" (Gilbert 1983, 436) connected to the socio-economic transformations of the war, and Jessie's crucial part in the eventual downfall of Harry Heegan is exemplary of the notion of the harmful "deviant non-domestic woman" (Pierson 2000, 47) produced by the war.

As opposed to Shaw's play, female domestic disorder is not sarcastically eased by a sense of order and certainty at the front. The second act of *The Silver Tassie* is set in the war zone of the Battle of the Marne, showing a field hospital next to the ruins of a monastery. Apart from Barney Bagnal, tied to a gun wheel for disciplinary reasons, there remain no recognisable characters from the first act. The previous heroism and the masculinist hierarchy are dissolved into a collective identity characterised by shared suffering, also uniting English and Irish soldiers in deprivation and pain – an image identified by Terry Phillips as provocative for Irish audiences of the 1930s (cf. Phillips 2010, 116). Instead of the voices of Harry Heegan and Teddy Foran, O'Casey presents a bitter rhythmical incantation about the torment of warfare by four anonymous soldiers, underlining the notion of military service as effecting a de-individualising transformation and as a profoundly dehumanising and irrational experience (O'Riordan 1978, 26). As "crucified" Barney sings to the chorus of "Auld Lang Syne": "We're here because we're here, because we're here, because we're here!" (O'Casey 1964, 39).

Despite its setting, the second act does not feature any actual fighting, instead, it stresses the complete loss of any sense of individual agency of the men and the complete surrendering of their selves to a military system of authority, run by the higher classes, that wants to make sure that its subjects "eat well [...] sleep well [...] whore well [...] fight well" (O'Casey 1964, 49), but does not adequately explain for which end. It also underlines Eric Leed's observation of trench warfare eroding "officially sponsored conceptions of the soldierly self as an agent of aggression" (Leed

1979, 106). It is this scenery in which the crucial theme of mutilation enters the play, bringing the traumatised and wounded bodies of the war on stage (McDonald 2002, 120). The set description mentions "heaps of rubbish, lean, dead hands are protruding" (O'Casey 1964, 35), and the wounded on the stretchers sadly chant "Carry on, carry on to the place of pain, / Where the surgeon spreads his aid, aid, aid" (O'Casey 1964, 48). In the final moment of the act, the Staff-Wallah, completing his meaningless patter of commands and militaristic jargon, orders all who "can run, or can walk, even *crawl*" (O'Casey 1964, 56, my emphasis) to the guns.

The third act is set in a Dublin hospital and heralds the rapid downfall of the former hero Harry Heegan. Harry was severely wounded on the battlefield and has lost the ability to move his legs. Both his self-perception and the way he is perceived and treated by his environment have been altered radically by the loss of his physical integrity – this new otherness is manifest throughout the entire rest of the play. Sylvester and Simon, once his most passionate admirers, seem embarrassed and unsure about how to approach a brooding and frustrated Harry. For Susie Monican, who once begged for Harry's affection and is now his nurse, Harry is nothing but another damage case to be handled professionally, reducing him to patient "Twenty-Eight", thus continuing the theme of de-individualisation of the second act. Harry has turned from an object of admiration and desire to a "shrivell'd thing" (O'Casey 1964, 76), an object of pity, charity and medical inspection. This transformation from power to weakness is a sudden and overwhelming process. His confrontation with the new reality of disability is abrupt, which, according to Russell Shuttleworth, typically leads affected men into a shocked state of frustration, fatalism and a sentiment of embodying defeated masculinity (cf. Shuttleworth et al. 2012: 184) – "Life came and took away the half of life" (O'Casey 1964, 95). Harry must recognise that his former identity and status have become matters of the past – an agonising situation he deeply detests: "It's a miracle I want – not an operation. The last operation was to give life to my limbs, but no life came, and again I felt the horrible sickness of life only from the waist up. [*Raising his voice*] Don't stand there gaping at me, man" (O'Casey 1964, 64).

The mutilation of Harry's body is immediately presented as a mutilation of his masculinity. Right at the start of the third act, Sylvester and Simon watch Harry in his wheelchair:

SYLVESTER: Trying to hold on to the little finger of life.
SIMON: Half-way up to heaven.
SYLVESTER: And him always thinking of Jessie.
SIMON: And Jessie never thinking of him.

(O'Casey 1964, 59)

The figure of Jessie Taite is instrumental in determining Harry's masculine status. Through her, O'Casey demonstrates the selective mechanisms that govern the hierarchical relations between the rivalling male bodies in the world of the play. The play's celebration of masculinity, Terry Phillips argues, "goes hand in hand with a crudely exploitative sexuality" (Phillips 2010, 118), and possessing Jessie is the most explicit indicator of social and sexual power – Jessie is a trophy much more significant than the silver cup that Harry brought home earlier. Replacing a degraded Harry, Barney Bagnal wins the suggestive affection of Jessie, returning from the war 'decorated', in the aforementioned sense of Bourke, with his left arm in a sling and the Victoria Cross. Contrastingly, Harry's impairment and the accompanying lack of independence have relegated him to an asexual, quasi-infantile status, which, for example, becomes apparent when Mrs Foran reminds Nurse Monican of the importance of hospital visits by relatives and the harm that might be done "by keeping a wife from her husband and a mother from her son" (O'Casey 1964, 71) – she is unaware of the bitter irony that the functions of wife and mother for Harry have in fact become identical. Harry, just like his comrade Teddy, who returned home blind and now is at the mercy of his wife, has become solely an object of pity and care.

While the hospital setting of the third act at least permits emotions of pity and care, the final act, set at a festive gathering in the hall of Avondale FC, puts the transformation of Harry, as well as blind Teddy, in a much harsher and less understanding social context. The presence of the paraplegic at the party is perceived as uncanny and disturbing, it is obvious that he has become an alien body:

> JESSIE. [*Hot, excited, and uneasy, as with a rapid glance back she sees the curtains parted by Harry*] Here he comes prowling after us again! His watching of us is pulling all the enjoyment out of the night. It makes me shiver to feel him wheeling after us.
> BARNEY. We'll watch for a chance to shake him off, an' if he starts again we'll make him take his tangled body somewhere else.
>
> (O'Casey 1964, 81)

Harry's desperate attempts to challenge his degradation, calling out Jessie for her disloyalty and confronting Barney, his successor in the role of the principal male, are unsuccessful. Harry is left with no option but to give in to the principle of segregation that his able-bodied environment sees as natural and self-evident: "Cram pain with pain, and pleasure cram with pleasure" (O'Casey 1964, 82), "[t]o carry the sick and helpless to where there's nothing but life and colour is wrong" (O'Casey 1964, 83). The war apparently has not changed the ableist and masculinist regime at home, the community remains strangely unfazed by the casualties it suffered.

The closing moments of the play complete Harry's and Teddy's alienation and expulsion from their community. After a violent row between Harry and Barney,

Barney savagely confirming the primacy of masculine strength over emasculated weakness, threatening to "tilt the leaking life out of" Harry, the "half-baked Lazarus" (O'Casey 1964, 99f.), the disabled veterans resign to a world of their own. They resort to the conflicted memory of their soldier identities, the cordial bonds of fate and the homosocial realm of the trenches. This (re-)departure is also illustrated stylistically by Harry picking up the incantatory mode of the second act (cf. McDonald 2002, 124): "For a spell here I will stay / Then pack up my body and go – / For mine is a life on the ebb, / Yours a full life on the flow!" (O'Casey 1964, 93). Teddy announces that "what's in front we'll face like men, dear comrade of the blood fight and the battlefront!" (O'Casey 1964, 102), holding on to Harry's shoulder while being led out of the dance hall along with the elderly – a bitter and futile gesture of defiance. Harry and Teddy have left their pre-war identities on the battlefield, "[b]ehind the trenches", "[i]n the Rest Camps", "[o]ut in France" (O'Casey 1964, 94), as their mantra goes. Fixed forever in powerless, marginalised positions, they are excluded from communal life, the defining contests of masculinity, symbolised most drastically by Harry's destruction of the "Silver Tassie", making it "[m]angled and bruised as I am bruised and mangled" (O'Casey 1964, 102).

The ruthlessness of the social environment from which Harry and Teddy have been dismissed is exposed in the final declaration of a newly empowered Susie Monican, speaking on behalf of her community:

> Teddy Foran and Harry Heegan have gone to live in their own world. Neither I nor you can lift them out of it. No longer can they do the things we do. We can't give sight to the blind or make the lame walk. We would if we could. It is the misfortune of war. As long as wars are waged, we shall be vexed by woe; strong legs shall be made useless and bright eyes made dark. But we, who have come through the fire unharmed, must go on living. [*Pulling Jessie from the chair*] Come along, and take your part in life! [*To Barney*] Come along, Barney, and take your partner into the dance!
>
> (O'Casey 1964, 103)

Without any sense of empathy, Susie stresses the dichotomy of 'us' and 'them', coldly insisting on the irreconcilability of the disabled and the able-bodied, defining "life" as reserved for the strong. In this manner, Susie reflects an attitude observed by Tobin Siebers: The feelings of the able-bodied towards the disabled frequently "expose the idea that they are dead – even though they may insist that they are not dead yet" (Siebers 2009, 161). The relation to the war revealed in her declaration is a fatalistic one of passive acceptance; it is not in any way connected to a specific political or national context. War seems to be an inescapable part of life, a standard bodily practice, albeit a distressing one; those who experience the "misfortune" of falling victim to war must not encumber those who survived it unscathed. As Surgeon Maxwell, Susie's suitor, concludes, "[h]e to whom joy is a foe, / Let him wrap himself up in his woe" (O'Casey 1964, 103) – the disturbing realities of the war are unwelcome and irrelevant.

Summing up, in *The Silver Tassie*, O'Casey eschews an explicit discussion of the specific conflicted Irish political contexts of the Great War in favour of more universal observations of social mechanisms within the Irish urban working class. Still, against the backdrop of the period in which the play was created and eventually staged in Ireland, the play's sympathetic and humanising representation of Irishmen in the service of the British army represents a challenge to the identity politics of the emerging independent Irish state (cf. Phillips 2010, 121). O'Casey, like Shaw, discards patriotism as a motivation to enlist – it is not the identification with any nation that leads Harry Heegan into the British army, but the conditions at home. As in Shaw's play, this Irish 'home' is not a peaceful haven – it is marked by a conflicted and contiguous but essentially apolitical interrelation between civilian and soldier identities. O'Casey depicts a Dublin community devoid of solidarity and empathy, its members being characterised by a hedonistic and materialist striving for social as well as sexual prestige, participating in and perpetuating an unforgiving socio-economy of bodies. Similar to Shaw's *O'Flaherty V. C.*, O'Casey presents Irishmen and Irishwomen as too self-absorbed and misguided to rationally grasp the true nature of their situation, the brutality integral to their environment. The Great War, being perceived as part of the sequence of violent contests that determines the milieu's sexual and social hierarchies, magnifies these conditions. Those who return from the 'contest' of the war (cf. Scarry 1985, 84ff.) permanently damaged experience a merciless erasure of their previous identity and the collapse of their social relevance.

The play does not offer a solution. Its hints at the integrative potential of shared suffering do little to alleviate the bleakness of the wartime civilian world depicted. The soothing but remote alternative of a solidary and collective soldier identity that is embraced by Dennis O'Flaherty in Shaw's play is radicalised by O'Casey in the second act of *The Silver Tassie*, depicting de-individualised and de-nationalised soldiers united in pain – however, this unity cannot be transferred effectively to the Dublin home front. Furthermore, in *The Silver Tassie* there is no trace of the benevolent and level-headed female characters of O'Casey's earlier works like *Juno and the Paycock* or *The Plough and the Stars*, who insist on sanity and decency (cf. Harkness 1978, 132) – in fact, O'Casey de-mystifies his earlier concept of female integrity in the play (cf. Stubbings 2000, 136), making women part of the milieu's discriminative system, either as conscious actors as in the case of Susie Monican, or as signifiers of hegemonic masculinity as in the case of Jessie Taite.

Through the figures of the second act – the Corporal, the Staff-Wallah and the Visitor, an opportunistic politician touring the war zone – O'Casey's play links militarism particularly to the middle and upper-middle classes, at the cost of the ordinary soldiers (cf. Phillips 2010, 116), a central tenet of socialist and internationalist views of the war. Similarly, in Shaw's *O'Flaherty V. C.* it is the baronet Sir Pearce who spouts militarist and patriotic propaganda. In the context of Ireland's Great War, these class connections lead us to another arena of war experience to be covered in this study, the massive contribution to the war made by members of the leading Anglo-Irish class. In the following section, literary representations of the complexity of Anglo-Irish war experiences and their relatedness to issues of identity will be examined, the Anglo-Irish representing a part of Irish society already in decline before the beginning of the conflict.

III.2 Anglo-Irish Perspectives

The Great War experience of the Anglo-Irish is illustrated in a comparatively substantial number of literary works. For this distinctive section of Irish society, the conflict and its harrowing outcome represent the beginning of its final crisis and its ultimate social demise. In fact, the Great War, Peter Martin summarises, was for the Anglo-Irish leading classes "their last chance to play their traditional role of defenders of the empire and leaders in their local communities" (Martin 2000, 44). In the following, the Great War's relevance in literary representations of the transformation and obliteration of Anglo-Irish identities during the tumultuous 1910s and 1920s, "a precariously transitional and therefore liminal phase" (Phillips 2007, 76), will be elucidated. The texts to be analysed in this section largely belong to what has been called the 'Big House' genre, literary works focusing on the upper-class Anglo-Irish country mansion and its inhabitants. Consequently, the discrepancy of different class identities and national affiliations (Irish – English – Anglo-Irish) – both complicated and magnified by the Great War – is at the centre of those works. Compared to the war works of Shaw and O'Casey, most of the selected texts are much less prominent considering the status of their authors and their reception both by readers and theatre audiences and by scholarly criticism. Also, unlike the public political figures of Shaw and O'Casey, the attitudes of their authors to war in general and the Great War in particular are much less extensively documented. After a brief introduction to the historical context of the Big House, Anglo-Irish identity and the significance of the Great War for this, as Terry Phillips notes, "historically anomalous" (Phillips 2007, 70) part of Irish society, I will focus on two dramatic texts from different periods in twentieth-century Irish and Anglo-Irish history: Lennox Robinson's

The Big House (1926) and Sean Dowling's *The Bird in the Net* (1960), two plays that address the final collapse of the social and political integration of Irishness and Anglo-Irishness in Ireland, boosted by the Great War. After that, I will turn to novels of the home front by Anglo-Irish writers who provide intriguing female perspectives on the ambiguous interplay of war, challenging national affiliations and self-perceptions, in particular Pamela Hinkson's *The Ladies Road* (1932) and Margaret Barrington's *My Cousin Justin* (1939). The section will be concluded by an analysis of Jennifer Johnston's novel *How Many Miles to Babylon* (1974), a work that problematises the intersection of Irish and Anglo-Irish identities in the Great War and that can be seen as exemplary of the transformation of Irish attitudes to the Great War in the later twentieth century.

III.2.1 Context: The Anglo-Irish, the Big House and the Great War

At the outset of George A. Birmingham's novel *Gossamer* (1915), the main protagonist Sir James Digby introduces himself as a (former) member of the Anglo-Irish gentry, expressing a sense of profound dislocation:

> I happen to belong to that unfortunate class of Irishmen whom neither Gorman nor any one else will recognise as being Irish at all. I owned, at one time, a small estate in Co. Cork. I sold it to my tenants and became a man of moderate income, encumbered with a baronetcy of respectable antiquity and occupied chiefly in finding profitable investments for my capital. [...] No definition of the Irish people has yet been framed which would include me, though I am indubitably a person – I take "person" to be the singular of people which is a noun of multitude – and come of a family which held on to an Irish property for 300 years. My religion consists chiefly of a dislike of the Roman Catholic Church and an instinctive distrust of the priests of all churches. My father was an active Unionist, and I have no political opinions of any sort. I am therefore cut off, both by religion and politics, from any chance of taking part in Irish affairs. On the other hand I cannot manage to feel myself an Englishman. Even now, though I have fought in their army without incurring the reproach of cowardice, I cannot get out of the habit of looking at Englishmen from a distance. This convinces me that I am not one of them.
>
> (Birmingham 1915, n. p.)

Birmingham here reflects the liminality inherent to Anglo-Irish identity: not truly belonging to either tradition, dominated by a sense of displacement that had become blatant and increasingly difficult to handle in the face of political and ideological developments in Ireland since the late nineteenth century. Also, Birmingham hints at the benchmark for 'Irish' Englishness that the Great War represented. The Anglo-Irish, Terry Phillips notes, had been occupying a shifting liminal space, "continuously negotiating and renegotiating the boundaries which divide them from the Irish and the English, and crossing and re-crossing the thresholds which link them" (Phillips 2007, 76). For centuries, the Anglo-Irish had represented the wealthiest and most privileged class in Irish society. Descendants and successors of the Ascendancy, essentially Protestant, unionist and generally tending to follow English customs considering politics, culture, law and economics, the Anglo-Irish traditionally occupied the central positions in Irish economy, professional life and administration. Also, they were disproportionally represented in the British army and in British colonial administration.[73] However, by the time of Birmingham's novel, they were feeling the stress under which their status and identity had come, a class clearly in decline.

The beginnings of this class can be traced back as far as the twelfth century, when the Anglo-Normans invaded Ireland and established a permanent stronghold. To assert and ensure 'English' military power as well as administrative and political domination, the concept of the Big House was introduced, importing a social order to Ireland following the principles of contemporary English aristocracy – a far-reaching feat of identity politics. The land, seized by conquest from Gaelic tribes, was leased by Anglo-Irish landlords to tenant farmers, who sub-let the leased land or employed landless labourers to work it (cf. Rudd 1991, 32). English and Scottish tenants and servants were introduced as a kind of shield against the native population and to spread English culture and values among the Irish peasantry (cf. MacAodha 1991, 46). The landlord's usually fortified home, the Big House, came to constitute the centre of local power, economy and various forms of patronage – functioning both as "a landmark of English domination and a protection of English identity" (Feltmann 1991, 15), asserting the "political and economic ascendancy of a remote colonial power structure" (Kreilkamp 2006, 60).

The high walls of the Big Houses were designed to separate the Gaelic population from the class of the landowners, a partition that "gave birth to two separate worlds, both perfectly alien and yet close to and intertwined with each other" (ibid.). This partition ran along the lines of class, religion, culture and privilege, however, it must be noted, not as rigidly along the lines of national identity. The roots of the Anglo-Irish Ascendancy truly are not exclusively English but also include Scottish, Welsh, Norman, Huguenot and, of course, Gaelic Irish influences, and generally, despite the religious, cultural and economic gulf between them and the Catholic majority, the Protestant landowning class saw itself as Irish, frequently seeking to distance itself from an English aristocracy which belittled their lifestyle

---

73 My use of the term "Anglo-Irish" in the following might be understood as a simplification at times – I am aware of the fact that not all Anglo-Irish were wealthy landowners and not all were Protestant unionists.

and manners. From the eighteenth century onwards, the Anglo-Irish gentry ruled Ireland in its own interests, wanting the Kingdom of Ireland to outshine the Kingdom of England (cf. Rudd 1991, 32f.), which found expression, for example, in the many elegant Georgian or mock-Gothic versions of the Big House, bearing witness to the optimism and confidence of their owners.

The nineteenth century marks a turning point in the fate of the Anglo-Irish. The Act of Union in 1800 devalued Dublin's political and social relevance and promoted the malpractice of absenteeism, some Anglo-Irish landowners choosing to spend most of their time in London while their Irish estates fell victim to neglect and mismanagement (cf. Vormann 2001, 174). Catholic Emancipation, achieved in 1829, weakened the Anglo-Irish monopoly on power, Catholic families being absorbed into the Ascendancy. The catastrophe of the Great Famine of 1845–48 put the landlord-tenant system under severe stress, leaving many landowners so heavily in debt that they were forced to sell their estates (cf. Rudd 1991, 34). The Land Acts of 1870 and 1881 strengthened the rights of tenants and further contributed to the disintegration of large estates. Altogether, by the end of the nineteenth century, it was obvious that the economic and political position of the Anglo-Irish gentry was no longer secure.

Furthermore, their naturally ambiguous claim of being Irish came under attack through the growth of new and more radical kinds of Irish nationalism in this period. As Terence Brown comments on the increasingly nationalist political climate, even those Anglo-Irish who "had sought to sympathize with Irish needs and aspirations […] found themselves denied a secure hold on their own Irish identity in these years by the propagandist outspokenness of the Irish Irelanders" (Brown 2004, 95f.). The co-existence of the Irish and the Anglo-Irish had never been unproblematic, but at the turn of the nineteenth century nationalist resentment rigidly focused on the Big House and its inhabitants, arriving at a view of the Big House as an icon of ruthless English imperialism and exploitation, as a symbol of a divided society. This view ignored that the Big House had also been a valuable part of Ireland's cultural heritage for centuries and that almost all great nationalist leaders as well as cultural and political spokesmen for Ireland, from Wolfe Tone to W. B. Yeats, had actually been Anglo-Irish, the latter, Yeats, even an outspoken supporter of the Big House as a symbol of a tradition of cultured leadership (cf. Owens and Radner 1990, 286; Phillips 2007, 71f.).[74] Sean O'Faoláin resonantly summarises the general attitudes concerning the Anglo-Irish that had

---

74 For example, Yeats protests against the loss of Lady Gregory's family home in the poem "Coole Park, 1929". In his 1938 play *Purgatory*, he celebrates the Big House as the place where "great men grew up, married, died" (quoted in Owens and Radner 1990, 286).

evolved by the early decades of the twentieth century: "Ireland was their country, Ireland was never their nation" (quoted in Mortimer 1991, 209).

The final collapse of the Big House and Anglo-Irish identity took place in the first two decades of the twentieth century in a series of violent events: the Home Rule crisis, the Great War, the Easter Rising, the War of Independence and the Irish Civil War. While the Rising drastically turned around public opinion in Ireland against England and facilitated the rise of Sinn Féin, the two domestic wars of the 1919–1923 period brought with them evictions of Anglo-Irish families and even full-blown attacks on Big Houses, radical republicans burning down an estimated five to ten percent of the Ascendancy mansions, also forcing many Anglo-Irish families out of the country (cf. Rudd 1991, 39). Finally, as outlined earlier, the independent Irish state that evolved from the nationalist struggle of these years embraced an ethos which was decidedly Catholic and anti-English – a state in which the Anglo-Irish, as much as the 'English' affair of the Great War, had no place. As Terence Brown observes, "[t]he Celt and the Irish language were the new orthodoxies comprising an ethnic dogmatism that cast Anglo-Ireland in the role of alien persecutor of the one true faith" (Brown 2004, 96). At this point, the years of fighting for economic and actual survival had left the Anglo-Irish without the ideological resources to counter their degradation (cf. ibid.).

The carnage of the Great War represents a particularly severe blow to the class of the Anglo-Irish before they were rendered irrelevant by the state doctrines of independent Ireland. For many Anglo-Irish, the war was a matter of utmost seriousness and their contribution to the war effort an indisputable duty and consequence of their self-image, resulting in large-scale volunteering. In his study of Anglo-Irish aristocracy during the Great War, Peter Martin mentions an enlistment ratio as high as 59 percent among the peerage (Martin 2002, 40). Similarly, Lennox Robinson observes in his 1931 biography of the Anglo-Irish politician and writer Bryan Cooper how during the Great War "[a]lmost without exception […] the big houses were emptied of all men of a fighting age" (quoted in Jeffery 2000, 70). The war was of such importance for this part of Irish society because it represented an opportunity for the Anglo-Irish to reinforce their connection to the British Empire in the face of increasingly unfavourable conditions in Ireland, depending on the success of the Empire for their survival as a class, also frequently reckoning that the war might subdue the heated nationalist-unionist antagonism in Ireland (cf. Martin 2002, 28).

The price they paid was high. The sons and husbands of the Anglo-Irish gentry, who almost exclusively served in the officer ranks, suffered disproportionally heavy casualties in comparison to the losses of any other Irish social group involved in the war. Investigating military participation and class aspects in the Great War, Jay Winter observes that "the higher up in the social scale a man was, the greater were the chances he would serve from early on in the war and that he would do so in a combat unit. [...] The most dangerous rank in the army – the subaltern – was recruited from [...] the finishing schools of the propertied classes" (Winter 1986, 65f.). In total, about thirteen percent of all men mobilized in Britain were killed in the Great War, in some Anglo-Irish circles, however, the fatality rate was more than twice as high (cf. Phillips 2007, 75). Anticipating this enormous scale of bloodshed, *The Irish Times* had warned already in October 1914 that "before the war is over many old and respected families will have come to an end so far as their male line is concerned" (quoted in Martin 2002, 38). Similarly, Robinson's aforementioned biography of Cooper notes how "[the war] was to be the last chapter in the history of many families" (quoted in Vormann 2001, 175). In this manner, the famous British notion of a lost generation, Keith Jeffery suggests, "applies most forcefully to this single segment of Irish society" (Jeffery 2000, 70) – the suddenness and scale of deaths was a great shock to the already declining fortunes of the Anglo-Irish.

The losses of the Great War, along with the withdrawal of British forces from Ireland and increasing emigration, caused the overall proportion of Protestants in the Irish Free State, an indicator of the Anglo-Irish presence, to reduce to eight percent already by 1926 – they were not actively prosecuted in the new state by any means, it was demography that worked against the Anglo-Irish (cf. Rudd 1991, 39f.). The remaining members of the Anglo-Irish Ascendancy carried on, often with great difficulty, impoverished older generations staying on their feudal estates which – stripped of their economic and social base – rapidly deteriorated. Robinson's biography of Cooper offers an evocative description of these conditions:

> Behind the high stone walls, at the end of the long avenue, in the Georgian house or sham-Gothic castle, there remained now only an old father and a couple of ageing daughters. [...] When they died it would pass to some distant English relation who would never dream of living in Ireland and who would sell it at once. Meanwhile the house was too full of memories of past greatness, too full of memories of boys who had shot rabbits in the long summer evenings and fished for trout in the river, of summer parties for cub-hunting and of shoots; it seemed better to sell out now and finish life in some English watering-place or some London suburb.
>
> (quoted in Vormann 2001, 175)

Since the 1960s, a considerable number of the remaining Big Houses in Ireland has come into state ownership and was opened to the public as museums or parks. While the former political and social significance of the Big House unsurprisingly is still not particularly cherished in modern Ireland, its legacy is at least no longer completely discarded as an entirely regrettable episode in Ireland's history, which is also an outcome of the revisionist tendencies in Irish culture (cf. Feltmann 1991, 17). The disappearance of the Big House, Christopher Murray argues accordingly, "cannot be seen simply as a victory for democracy or as a symbol of the achievement of national independence, for there was loss as well as gain in the event" (Murray 1982, 16).

The Big House in Irish literature has a very substantial tradition, beginning in the early nineteenth century. The topic has attracted the interest of numerous writers with differing approaches, from Maria Edgeworth, whose 1800 novel *Castle Rackrent* initiated many conventions of Big House literature, to Somerville and Ross, the most prolific chroniclers of the Big House, to Elizabeth Bowen, Brendan Behan, Brian Friel, Jennifer Johnston, John Banville and Aidan Higgins. In critical discourses of the 1970s and 1980s, the Big House as a literary topic has been seen unfavourably, modern Irish writers being accused by critics of perpetuating the romanticising Yeatsian myth of a cultured and refined Protestant Ascendancy, the nobleman set against the 'natural' Catholic Irish, supposedly living in paternalistic agreement.[75] Seamus Deane, one of the central voices of these discourses, argued in 1977 that Irish novelists have prevented the Irish novel from engaging with "wider questions about fiction, its nature and status, its methods and its philosophy" (quoted in Weekes 1990, 191) by resorting either to the worn out image of the Big House or that of the alienated artist (cf. ibid.). Such views are legitimate, yet, in some cases they also represent a debatable generalisation – for example, as will be shown later, a Big House work like *How Many Miles to Babylon?* by Jennifer Johnston, a writer formerly dismissed for the domesticity and narrowness of her works (cf. Backus 1994, 57), in fact operates from a similar stance of a re-consideration and re-interpretation of the Irish past that characterises revisionist discourses (cf. Weekes 1990, 192).

Altogether, Big House literature remains an intriguing object of study, typically employing a double vision that represents two spheres of an identity and relationship, English and Irish, which can never be fully reconciled, frequently resulting in a sense of confusion and displacement (cf. Carpenter 1977, 180; Backus 1994, 49). It reflects the seemingly fixed material identity of the Anglo-Irish, carrying within

---

75 Generally, the Irish Literary Revival's and, particularly, Yeats's myth-making was perceived as problematic and in urgent need of deconstruction by revisionist critics as it was seen as contributing to the ideological resources upon which the sectarian violence in Northern Ireland of the 1970s was founded (cf. Allison 2006, 240f.).

it fundamental contradictions which undermine that very identity (Phillips 2007, 77). As Terry Phillips observes, the

> writers of the Big House create a nation within a nation as a reaction against liminality. If the liminal is by definition fluid and hybrid, the house has clearly marked boundaries. Yet of course the boundaries are a response to liminality and inextricably bound up with it, [...] and that evidence of liminality endures within Big House literature.
>
> (ibid.)

The decline and fall of the Big House and, consequently, of a central part of Anglo-Irish identity, has been a persistent theme in the genre from the start (cf. Berge 1994, 11) – the part that the Great War plays in this demise will be addressed in the following.

III.2.2 Lennox Robinson's *The Big House* (1926)

Lennox Robinson (1886–1958) was born in Douglas, Co. Cork, as the son of a Protestant clergyman. In spite of his conservative and decidedly unionist upbringing, Robinson became passionately involved with Irish nationalism and its cultural dimension of the Irish Literary Revival – his interest in drama was sparked by a visit of the Abbey players in Cork for a performance of Yeats's *Cathleen Ni Houlihan*. After a brief period in London under the patronage of G. B. Shaw and Granville Barker, Robinson joined the Abbey Theatre as a manager, producer and director in 1909 and remained there, apart from a short interruption,[76] in various positions until his death, playing an important role[77] in the central cultural Irish institution to determine and debate questions of national identity in the formative period of independent Ireland. Robinson wrote more than twenty plays for the Abbey during his career and also worked as a novelist, essayist and theatre historian. In his dramatic works, mostly well-made tragicomedies focusing on middle-class and small-town Irish life, Robinson provocatively confronts a great variety of social and political ideologies prevalent in Ireland before World War II, against Yeats's vision of the Abbey as a "temple of modern poetic drama" (Eisen 1997, 315).

Coming from the fringes of the Anglo-Irish gentry himself, Robinson was aware of the looming downfall of his class and of its twofold alienation from

---

76 Robinson resigned from his position at the Abbey in 1914 after a dispute about offending an English benefactress of the theatre by refusing to close the Abbey in mourning for the death of Edward VII. He returned to the Abbey in 1919 and became a member of the Board of Directors (cf. Owens and Radner 1990, 285).

77 Robinson has been called "the major minor figure of the Anglo-Irish theatre in the first half of the century" (Eisen 1997, 316).

England and the Catholic Irish majority (cf. Murray 1986, 122). For Robinson, it was characteristic of his class that "though they were of Ireland – their families having been in Ireland for very many generations – they were slightly *déraciné*, they didn't quite belong, yet they belonged to no other country in the world, certainly not to England though they were firm loyalists. Maybe, even forty years ago, they felt their class defeated" (quoted in Murray 1992, 109). This liminality and ambiguity is also evident in Robinson's attitudes to the Great War. For example, when Robinson, whose brother Arthur had been killed in France, reconsidered enlistment in the British army as late as in June 1918 (an earlier attempt to join up had failed), he states in a letter to Sir Horace Plunkett that he actually does not "want to go (who except fools do?)" but believes he "ought to if only to show that one can be anti-English without being pro-German" (quoted in Murray 1992, 110) – a complicated setup of identification and allegiances.

The sense of uniqueness, hybridity, isolation and defeat of the Anglo-Irish that characterises such views is also at the heart of *The Big House*. The play investigates the implications of what it means to live with the 'hyphen' in troubled times, portraying sympathetically a feudal society and its disintegration during the years of crisis of the late 1910s and early 1920s, formulating most resonantly the notion of the gulf between the two traditions in Ireland. The play premiered at the Abbey Theatre on 6 September 1926 and turned out a success. Some conservative nationalist commentators criticised the play's bold case for Anglo-Irish distinctiveness, one critic even referring to the alleged physical degeneration of the Anglo-Irish as an outcome of the separateness of their class, the Ascendancy barring "its windows against the native vitality" (quoted in Brown 2004, 108f.). However, the play also found a prominent and enthusiastic supporter in Æ, who celebrated Robinson's work in *The Irish Statesman* as a vital contribution against the ideological constrictions of Irish nationalism and its fixation on Gaelic culture.[78] Referring to *The Big House*, Æ underlines his vision of an Ireland

---

78 "Those who inherit the national tradition should not be so scared at the suggestion that Irish people lately of another tradition might take an active part in the building up of the new self-governing Ireland. Man for man they are just as good human beings as any of their nationalist fellow-countrymen. It is their misfortune to be on the losing side in the political struggle" (quoted in Brown 2004, 111). According to Æ, it would be wrong and harmful for the new Irish state to exclude the Anglo-Irish also from a cultural point of view. Without the Anglo-Irish cultural contributions of authors like O'Grady, Yeats, Hyde, Synge, Lady Gregory or O'Flaherty "the country would be almost intellectually non-existent as far as the rest of the world was concerned" (quoted in Brown 2004, 112).

of diversity, of a harmonious national synthesis for Ireland in which no ethnic group is predominant, seeing Ireland as "a fertile creation of the historic fusion of races, culture, and language" (Brown 2004, 110):

> We do not want uniformity in our culture or our ideals, but the balancing of our diversities in a wide tolerance. The moment we had complete uniformity, our national life would be stagnant. We are glad to think we shall never achieve that uniformity which is the dream of commonplace minds and we imagine that many who saw *The Big House* felt a liberating thrill [...].
>
> (quoted in Brown 2004, 109)

In *The Big House*, Robinson looks back to Irish political events still recent at the time, the years of the Great War, the War of Independence and the Civil War, confronting "the shifting ground on which Anglo-Irish identity found itself" (Phillips 2007, 85) during this period. The play's four scenes are set in Ballydonal House, the country mansion of the Alcock family in Co. Cork. It begins on the last day of the Great War, Armistice Day, in 1918. The Alcocks, an un-stereotypically decent and honourable Anglo-Irish family, generally well-liked by the Catholic Irish community over which they preside, await the return of their son Ulick from the battlefields of France. Ulick is supposed to inherit and run the Alcock's estate after his older brother Reginald had been killed earlier in the war. While the bell in the garden is rung to celebrate peace, a telegram arrives reporting the death of Ulick, which particularly shocks and infuriates his sister Kate, the play's central character. Kate – young, confident and working hard to bond with the locals – had dreamed of taking over and revitalising the family's estate together with Ulick. The following scenes show the Alcocks during the War of Independence and the Civil War. Facing increasingly impoverished and threatening circumstances, the family fears to be "burned out" of their home by radical republicans like many other Ascendancy families. The Alcocks discuss their feelings of foreignness and the gulf between them and the Irish. Kate is sent away to a safer life in London, however, her stay there irreversibly confirms her belonging to Ireland and Ballydonal and she returns home soon: "[In London,] I was behaving like any Irish girl in a tenth-rate novelette written by some horrible Colonial [...] I knew that for my soul's salvation the sooner I left the better" (Robinson 1982, 181) – Kate cannot simply dispose of her Irishness at will (cf. Vormann 2001, 179).

Eventually, the house is raided by republican extremists and burned down. In a passionate final performance amidst the motley heap of furniture saved from the fire, Kate fully embraces the uniqueness of her origins and announces that she will rebuild the estate against all odds, insisting on the continuation of the Anglo-Irish tradition and its place in Irish society: "We are formidable if we care to make ourselves so, if we give up the poor attempt to pretend we're not different. We must glory in our difference, be as proud of it as they are of theirs. [...] [W]e're what we are. Ireland is no more theirs than ours" (Robinson 1982, 196). This provocative gesture of defiance and the drama's extensive investigation of class differences are at the centre of the, in total, limited critical attention to Robinson's play. In the following, the focus will be on another aspect, one previously hardly discussed beyond its alleged unimportance (cf. Jeffery 2011, 255): the role of the Great War in the play, specifically, the significance of the (semi-)absent figures of Reginald and Ulick, the dead soldiers, who exemplify oppositional concepts and prospects of Anglo-Irish identity.

Robinson's work offers a large variety of "positions along the spectrum of racial and political identity" (Phillips 2007, 85). Kate and Ulick embody a reformed Anglo-Irishness; their father, St. Leger Alcock, is a benevolent but reluctant and tired administrator of his estate without a special connection to the place, while Mrs Alcock, "a respectable Hampshire woman [...] in exile" (Robinson 1982, 149), is completely alienated from her Irish surroundings and wishes to abandon Ballydonal altogether. The Alcock's Irish butler, Atkins, fully identifies himself with his masters, while the Alcock's maid, Annie, eventually conspires with the radicals who burn down the house. This diversity of affiliations is also reflected in an interesting interplay of different attitudes to the Great War, which is strikingly illustrated in a conversation in the first scene between Alcock, the visiting English soldier Despard and the Alcock's neighbour, Vandaleur O'Neill, another Anglo-Irish landlord, who, however, seems to have completely adopted the lifestyle and manners of the Irish peasants:

ALCOCK: Well, this is a great day, Vandaleur.
VANDALEUR: Indeed, 'tis wonderful weather for this time of year.
ALCOCK: I wasn't thinking of the weather. [...] I meant the war – the Armistice.
VANDALEUR: Oh, to be sure. Is it today or tomorrow?
ALCOCK: Within an hour.
VANDALEUR: Fancy that now. I suppose they'll fire off a big gun like or ring a bell.
DESPARD: Were you fighting?
VANDALEUR: I was not. [*To Alcock*] I met Michael Dempsey on the avenue and he was telling me that you have some sheep sick. [...]
ALCOCK: [*To Despard*] Do you feel up to a stroll?
DESPARD: I'm afraid not. I've got to rest my foot as much as possible.
VANDALEUR: Are you after hurting your foot? [...]
ALCOCK: He got a nasty knock in France.
VANDALEUR: France?
DESPARD: There happens to be a war on there.
VANDALEUR: Sure I know ...Jerry Mangan's not the better of the fall he got. [...] Sure he's the rottenest rider in the country.

(Robinson 1982, 145–47)

In such moments, the play reveals manifold and contradictory gradations of interest, motivation and compassion concerning the war. For the level-headed Alcock, the conflict mostly means a threat to the fortunes of his family that has to be endured passively and gracefully. His announcement of a toast to "the King and Victory" (Robinson 1982, 144) in the evening is not a triumphalist gesture but instantly connected to the memory of the fallen son Reginald. In contrast to this, the rugged Englishman Despard has found fulfilment in risking his life for King and Country in the war – "[i]t's taught me what living is" (Robinson 1982, 152), however, in the course of the play, Despard's brutalisation becomes obvious, his earlier display of patriotic boldness turning into violent despair. For Vandaleur, on the contrary, despite being Anglo-Irish, even belonging to a very distinguished aristocratic family, and being of fighting age, the war is spectacularly irrelevant, it is just another nation's affair that does not evoke any feelings of sympathy – a mind-set widespread among the rural Catholic Irish majority. Like his peasants, Vandaleur is ostentatiously occupied with local countryside matters like the weather or his sheep. For him, the war takes place in another world, his perspective remains firmly within his rootedness in the local surroundings.

This dissonance of attitudes and affiliations also runs within the Alcock family. In Kate's description of her brother Reginald, she notes how Reginald "went straight from school into the army" (Robinson 1982, 153), escaping from the responsibilities and the rural confinedness of Anglo-Irish landlord life into the adventure of war. Kate coolly remarks how Reginald's death on the battlefield actually represents an appropriate end for him: "I'm glad Reggie's dead, glad he died like that, honourably, with letters after his name and mentioned in despatches and all that sort of thing" (Robinson 1982, 154) – his death corresponds to his official class identity. The war service of the other brother, Ulick, on the contrary, means for Kate "four years stolen out of life" (Robinson 1982, 152) – like Kate (and Vandaleur), Ulick's place is Ballydonal, not the battlefields of Europe. The soldier death of Ulick does not only mean a tragic and heart-breaking personal loss, it is also presented as a catastrophe because it is equivalent to the demise of the Alcock's estate. Aware of the growing social, political and economic pressure on the Alcock's Big House, the original plan of installing Ulick, "a born farmer" (Robinson 1982, 153), fluent in Irish, who will "fit perfectly into the Ballydonal picture" (Robinson 1982, 155) as the head of the estate, might have secured its existence – but this plan has become obsolete and there is no third male heir. In the moment of the news of Ulick's death, the downturn of the family's fortune unfolding, the bell of peace resounding in the background, St. Ledger Alcock helplessly reminds his daughter of the greater good, King and Country, for which

Ulick has fallen – a point of view furiously rejected by Kate, who insists that "Ulick's life was here, here. All he loved, all he worked for" (Robinson 1982, 158). The Great War, the play suggests in this moment, brought about a wrongful and ultimately purposeless termination of life in the case of Ulick, the promising 'Irish' Anglo-Irishman whose atypical integrative hybridity could have introduced an era of harmony in the play's endangered community, but who fell victim to the traditional values and social mechanisms of his class – mandatory service in the King's army – with which he actually could not identify.

Robinson underlines this notion of an untimely death and an interrupted and unfinished existence by means of a melodramatic effect at odds with the realist tone of *The Big House* (also frequently pointed out as a dramaturgical flaw of the play): the apparition of Ulick as a ghost at the end of the second and fourth scene. The image of the revenant, dead soldiers returning home in a dream, hallucination or as a supernatural apparition, is a concept frequently used in Great War writing and film, including several Irish works dealing with the Great War.[79] Usually, the motif is used for a shocking bridging of and moral confrontation between the spheres of the front and the home. One of the earliest and most powerful examples of this device is Abel Gance's 1919 silent film *J'accuse*, introducing a typical pattern (cf. Winter 1995, 15f.). In *J'accuse*, hundreds of fallen French soldiers rise from the battlefield and stumble home to their villages to see if their sacrifices are honoured, yet, they only encounter immorality and opportunism, unfaithful wives and wartime profiteers. The shocking sight of the dead soldiers eventually makes the ungrateful villagers change their ways and the dead return to their graves. Importantly, in Robinson's *The Big House* the revenant does not appear to frightfully question the integrity and idealism of those for whom he went to war and gave his life. The return of Ulick is much more related to a persisting longing and loyalty to his place (cf. Welch 1999, 101) than to his role in the Great War – his personal Ballydonal identity clearly outweighs his official affiliation to the Empire. Ulick cannot leave behind his earlier existence; his pre-war personality and outlook have not been transformed by the war. However, at the same time, the transcendent presence of dead Ulick, Christopher Murray adds, also gives rise to an anxiety – it foreshadows the destruction of the Alcock's Big House (cf. Murray 1992, 113) and,

---

79　See chapter III.3.1 on Frank McGuinness's *Observe the Sons of Ulster Marching Towards the Somme* and, even more prominently, chapter III.3.5 on Dermot Bolger's *Walking the Road*, where the undead Ulster and Irish soldier symbolises his problematic and liminal position in Irish historical consciousness, pictured as trapped in a historical no-place, a world between memory and forgetting, life and death.

on a grander scale, the social demise of the Ascendancy, the impending ghostliness of the Anglo-Irish in the Ireland to come.

As outlined earlier, despite the destruction of the Alcocks' Big House, a striking symbol of how the tides have turned against their class, the play does not end on a note of complete despair. Through her passionate announcement of resistance, of rebuilding the estate no matter what and upholding her freedom, her reformulated identity and the cultural legacy of her class, Kate offers rest to Ulick's spirit (cf. ibid.). There is the prospect of a home for Ulick to return to after his life was wasted in a war irrelevant to the Irish-Anglo-Irish outlook of Ulick and Kate:

> ATKINS: [*He is lifting a chair into the summerhouse, he drops it and starts back in terror.*] Miss Kate! Miss Kate! Miss Kate!
> KATE: [*coming back quickly*] What is it, Atkins? What's the matter?
> ATKINS: [*babbling*] I seen him there – in the summerhouse – as clear as the day – Master Ulick –
> KATE: Ulick? Go away, Atkins, go away. [*She pushes him out. She turns to the summerhouse and speaks softly.*] Ulick! Are you there? [*Her face lights up.*] Oh, my dear, you've come to me again, after all those years ...And you're smiling, so I'm right. It's what you'd have done ...[*A pause, she seems to listen to someone talking.*] Yes ...Yes ...So – kiss me, my dear ...[*She raises her face as if she were being kissed, she closes her eyes.*]
> (Robinson 1982, 198)

In this manner, Ulick's ghostly presence effects an empowerment of his sister, even if, at the same time, the image of the romantic union of Kate and her undead brother amidst the rubble of their former home also introduces uneasy overtones. Jacques Derrida has addressed the act of communing with 'ghosts' in *Spectres of Marx*, formulating his concept of "hauntology". For Derrida, the figure of the ghost represents a blurring of presence and absence, of past and present, of self and other – consequently, "to commune with ghosts is to be open to a world that respects otherness and difference, even the otherness that resides within oneself" (Price 2015, 38), it represents an engagement with the "Other" (cf. McKean 2011). This is exactly the positively liminal condition exemplified and embraced by Kate Alcock.

To audiences of the 1920s, the glimpse of hope for the Anglo-Irish gentry that the play offers at its conclusion already must have seemed unrealistic – Robinson himself directly contradicted the final sentiment of his play some years later in his other Big House drama, *Killycregs in Twilight* (1937), when one of his characters comments how she wishes she "had been burned out in the Troubles ... I wouldn't have behaved liked that fool-girl in the play, *The Big House*. I would never have rebuilt Killycregs, I'd have thanked God to be quit of it" (quoted in Murray 1982: 17). Still, writing in the mid-1920s, Robinson obviously was much more optimistic and at least could imagine a scenario in which the endangered Big House can somehow overcome the harrowing effects of the Great War and the other turbulences of the period, suggesting a form of Anglo-Irish identity that can become a part of the new Irish state. With *The Big House*, Robinson sympathetically illustrates the strain of the Great War on Anglo-Irish families and their fortunes. Also by means of differing attitudes to the Great War, Robinson constructs facets of Anglo-Irish identity beyond the clichés of bellicose unionism, imperialism and feudal snobbery. Even if he does not fundamentally touch upon the issue of class privileges, Robinson diversifies and humanises prevalent nationalist stereotypes of the Anglo-Irish.

Robinson's play, Colin Owens and Joan Radner argue, "is the most [...] balanced dramatization of the dilemma facing the Ascendancy" (Owens and Radner 1992, 286) during the troublesome years of national struggle. For Christopher Murray, however, this sense of balance is the play's weak spot, Robinson's work collapsing under its "determination to be fair to both sides" (Murray 1986, 122). The next work to be analysed, Sean Dowling's *The Bird in the Net*, written almost 35 years later in an Ireland that had internalised a widespread negative consensus about both the Great War and the Anglo-Irish, re-creates a situation of Anglo-Irish crisis similar to the one of Robinson's play but is not at all "burdened" by an excess of balance and fairness between the two traditions.

III.2.3 Sean Dowling's *The Bird in the Net* (1960)

Of all the authors covered in this study, Sean Dowling (1897–1977) probably is the least prominent one. The amount of available information and academic criticism on this Dublin-born dental surgeon and author of two history plays, *The Bird in the Net* (1960) and *The Best of Motives* (1965), both produced by the Abbey, is minimal. *The Bird in the Net*, which shows the Irish home front during the Easter Rising, rarely ever appears in the few existing surveys of Irish Great War literature and when it is mentioned at all, it is usually not more than namechecked.[80] This is somewhat surprising considering the exemplary fashion in which *The Bird in the Net*, admittedly a fairly clichéd work by a minor playwright, reflects the complicated issues of conflicting affiliations and identities within the context of the Great War and the nationalist struggle of the period, and, also, how it reveals an ideologically hardened and unforgiving attitude to this issue forty years later.

---

80 The only exception to this is Heinz Kosok, who at least dedicates a paragraph to the play (cf. Kosok 2007, 63f.).

The Bird in the Net was first performed on 28 March 1960 at the Queen's Theatre in Dublin where it enjoyed a brief but moderately successful run. Later, Dowling also sent the script of *The Bird in the Net* to Sean O'Casey, who replied cordially to the aspiring elderly playwright. O'Casey points out several flaws but also calls it "a very sincere play" that at least kept him "interested to the end", even if it clearly "isn't a masterpiece, but you have no reason to be ashamed of it" (O'Casey 1992, 275). The play's major legacy seems to be the minor controversy it provoked, some contemporary critics suggesting that the play hints at a homosexual relationship between the main characters who were taken by Dublin audiences to represent the Irish war poet Francis Ledwidge and his aristocratic sponsor Lord Dunsany (cf. Jeffery 1994, 93; Curtayne 1972, 195) – an interpretation that seems far-fetched and that is also rejected by Ledwidge's biographer Alice Curtayne (ibid.).

Recreating a dramatic situation similar to the ones in *O'Flaherty V. C.* and *The Big House*, the three acts of Dowling's play are set in the Co. Galway Big House of Sir William D'Arcy, an Anglo-Irish landowner, in the days immediately after the 1916 Easter Rising. Sir William has invited his protégé to his mansion, Michael Tyrrell, a Catholic Irish officer in the British army and soldier-poet of some fame, recently decorated with the Military Cross. Unaware of the failure of the rebellion in Dublin, a small group of radical Irish Volunteers take the D'Arcy's Big House by force, arrest the aristocrats and their visitor Tyrrell, and declare the house their headquarters. Confronted by the rebels, Tyrrell, the Irishman in British uniform, reconsiders his position and eventually switches sides the following day. However, as the Irish revolution turns out to be short-lived and limited to Dublin, the rebels must flee and Tyrell has to return to the army. Tyrell is killed soon after in France, leaving behind a new poem, which his mother gives to Sir William. Recognising its rebellious nationalist spirit, Sir William burns it.

The theme of class disparity and class conflict dominates *The Bird in the Net* and its investigation of the meanings and effects of the Great War and the Easter Rising for Irish society. Right at the beginning of the play, in an intriguing display of Shavian *Junker* paternalism, it becomes obvious that the pitiless militarist Sir William expects his Irish subordinates to enlist, insisting on his position as the natural leader of his community. In the expositional dialogue with Tyrrell, Sir William's butler, who has only recently replaced his predecessor who had gone off to the war, ironically laments how he is "of military age and should be at the front with the Connaught Rangers" (Dowling 1961, 4) but could not pass the medical examination – "Sir William knows […] that I wanted to join up […]. Very sad. And I leppin to spill my blood for Belgium, or Montenegro, or some other small nationality" (ibid.).

Also, very early on, the play establishes the same problematic situation that Robinson's Alcock family faces – the only son of the Big House was killed in the Great War and the family line is in danger of going extinct. However, in Dowling's work, the issue is contrastingly presented from the point of view of the common Irish:

> TYRRELL: It's over a year now since he was killed.
> BUTLER: Himself hasn't got over it – if he ever will. That's the worst of these pigeon's clutch families with only two chicks in the nest …Lose one, and where are you! That wasn't the way with your family or mine. Mick …eh?
> TYRRELL: No, we could spare some.
> BUTLER: "Easy got, easy gone," was the motto in our circles. Of course the title dies now with Sir William and that's a bitter blow to him too.
>
> (Dowling 1961, 5)

Here, the play emphasises not the tragedy that has befallen the D'Arcy family but the class differences between the privileged Anglo-Irish Ascendancy and the poor Irish peasants – a disparity later exposed in an even harsher light, when Tyrrell mentions in conversation with an oblivious Sir William how all but one of his siblings died from malnutrition, and Sir William, only seconds later, bluntly reveals his crude feudal self-image and hatred of the common Irish in front of Tyrrell: "I do represent a class. And this riff-raff are bound against us" (Dowling 1961, 15).

The death of his only son obviously has not marred Sir William's fervent support of the Great War. The butler mentions to Tyrrell how the war even enabled a bittersweet posthumous reconciliation of Sir William and his son: "His father forgets what a heart-scald he was to him all his life. The only thing he remembers is the Military Cross won at Mons" (Dowling 1961, 6). Considering Sir William's relationship with the lower-class Irishman Tyrrell, accordingly, it is not only Tyrrell's poetry but his military service and the honours he received in France which make him an acceptable part of the refined circle of the D'Arcys: "[T]he army has made a gentleman of you" (Dowling 1961, 7), Sir William rejoices, paralleling the faux emancipation and re-identification that Private Dennis O'Flaherty V. C. experiences in Shaw's play. Even Tyrrell's nationalist sympathies, having joined up as a supporter of Home Rule, are redeemed by his war service in the eyes of the D'Arcys – "all the Nationalists are loyalists now" (Dowling 1961, 14). Yet, throughout their conversation, Sir William fails to recognise the sense of pessimism about the war that is evident in Tyrrell's words. Tyrrell's doubts and fears are brushed aside by Sir William with high talk of the nearing victory and "the high price of freedom" (Dowling 1961, 8), underlining Sir William's militancy, cold-heartedness and his detachment from the grim realities of the war.

The arrival of the republican rebels leads to an unmistakable disclosure of the contradictions of class and identity inherent in Tyrrell's condition in the play and it initiates his conversion. The rebels' abrasive confidence and their invigorating idealism incite Tyrrell to confront the D'Arcys and, more importantly, himself with the fact that he really is only a "temporary gentlem[a]n"[81] (Dowling 1961, 34), who has entered an upper-class world in which he does not belong:

SIR WILLIAM: You were […] fighting for these scum here, while they were skulking at home. […]
TYRRELL: If you spoke to that wounded boy, Burke, he looks about 18 years old – you'd know that he has a pure, an almost poetical ideal for which he is quite ready to die. He had the strangest effect on me. […] He made me realize how far I had got from his world, the world I was born in. I had forgotten it really.
FELICITY: Keep on forgetting it is my advice. There's a better world than theirs.
TYRRELL: There's another world, of course, and once I thought I might reach it, but it was a dream.

(Dowling 1961, 22)

SIR WILLIAM: […] These rebels have broken in here bent on robbery and murder. […]
TYRRELL: They probably think you're the burglar – in their house.
SIR WILLIAM: What! We are robbing them?
TYRRELL: Well, that you represent England, and that England is a robber and a murderer in Ireland. Or has been anyway.
SIR WILLIAM: Where do you stand in this Tyrrell?
TYRRELL: Where do I stand. I wish I knew. I stand between two worlds and belong to neither as far as I can see.

(Dowling 1961, 35f.)

It was the Great War and a false promise of fame to be won as a war hero and war poet, the play seems to suggest, that produced in Tyrrell a misleading and pointless

---

81 Actually, the majority of the British officers of the Great War came from outside the traditional officer class of professional soldiery and the elevation in rank and social status that these 'temporary gentlemen' experienced due the war frequently turned out problematic, specifically in the post-war period when many of them had to cope with their social decline. As Martin Petter argues, it was "the contrast between the value placed on his role at the front, and the depreciation of his talents in the struggles of the post-war world, that produced the greatest sense of dislocation and bitterness" (Petter 1994, 152). The image of the troubled ex-officer became part of the popular imagination in the post-war years and was widely featured in the literature of the period. Pamela Hinkson (using the pseudonym 'Peter Deane'), for example, focuses on the fate of an English ex-officer in her 1925 novel *The Victors* (cf. Petter 1994, 128ff.).

mingling of identities; two worlds, two classes, which truly are antagonists and meant to stay separate. The presence of the rebels means for Tyrrell a confrontation with a newly configured social landscape, to quote Stuart Hall, "not of a single, but several, sometimes contradictory or unresolved identities" (Hall 1995, 598), that stirs in Tyrrell a rediscovery of what he perceives as his 'true' origins. Tyrrell recognises in the ideas of the rebels a sense of vitality and purity somehow dormant in his self, which overpowers his own doubtful convictions and established self-image, and against which also the poetry that pleases people like Sir William seems pretentious and pallid – "And an hour ago I was proud of it. 'Pale vaporous trees.' Bah! Pale vaporous thoughts that never got beneath the surface of life at all" (Dowling 1961, 23).

In a later confrontation, Regan, one of the commanders of the rebel group, spells out how Tyrrell supposedly has been deceived into enlisting, how he has become a tool of the Protestant Ascendancy and the Empire:

> TYRRELL: I did what I thought was right for Ireland.
> SIR WILLIAM: And so it was right.
> MULVEY: You thought it was. Like thousands of other Irishmen who were tricked or bullied into putting on that uniform. You should know better now. [...]
> SIR WILLIAM: He put on that uniform like many other gallant Irishmen to fight for his own people, to fight for you.
> REGAN: [...] No matter whether Germany or England wins this war, Michael Tyrrell's poor old father and mother will go on starving in the same thatched cabin for the rest of their [lives], neither better off nor worse. What you were fighting for was Sir William D'Arcy [...]. You were fighting to secure for him his fine house and broad acres, his servants and horses, and all his privileges, like the bloody fool you are.
>
> (Dowling 1961, 26)

The Great War, Regan argues, is a war not fought for 'the people', for the rights and freedom of small nations like Catholic Belgium or against the evil imperialist ambitions of the Kaiser – it is a war fought for the Big Houses and, consequently, for English imperialism and exploitation. Regan's attitude is a reminder of the socialist tendencies of Irish nationalism exemplified by James Connolly (cf. Maurer 1998, 2667), and of the Shavian charge against international *Junkertum* and militarism – the Great War as a tragic and murderous confrontation of innocent and oppressed workers and peasants for the profit of the manipulative imperialist upper classes. Accordingly, the new state envisioned by the rebels in the play leaves no room for the destructive hierarchies and inequality that is seen as integral to Anglo-Irish identity – as Regan smugly announces to his upperclass prisoners: "The Republic guarantees equal rights and opportunities to all citizens, and you'll be citizens of the Republic soon – if you're not dead before it comes" (Dowling 1961, 20).

Through the figure of Tyrrell and his reasoning, the harsh edge of such comments and the extremism of the rebels are channelled into a more understandable and acceptable form. Yet, the rebellion against the Big House and the Great War is over before Tyrrell can play any part in it. The rebels must disband and Tyrrell must go back to France. At this point, Sir William has finally become fully aware of the threatening situation of his estate and his class. His response to the obvious turning of the tides unsurprisingly is not, as in the case of Robinson's Kate Alcock, the idea of an arrangement of co-existence, but a fierce reaction of mistrust, hate and a relentless wish for punishment:

> SIR WILLIAM: Of course shooting these fellows in Dublin was a fatal mistake. […] Giving that scum a soldier's death was criminal folly. Should have hanged every man jack of them. […] It's the greatest betrayal in history. People like us are being thrown to the wolves. […]
> HARMSWORTH: [But] the country never was so loyal. How many thousands are there fighting in France at the moment?
> SIR WILLIAM: Take it from me, those fellow's loyalty is less than skin deep. Look at Tyrrell, for instance.
>
> (Dowling 1961, 59f.)

The gist of this tirade of Sir William actually was not uncommon among the Anglo-Irish leading classes. As Peter Martin remarks, the "Rising was a shock to most nobles when it came. Most nobles […] blamed the government for being too soft on separatist nationalism from 1914 on" (Martin 2002, 43).

The poem Tyrrell leaves behind after his death is the most striking symbol of his futile conversion from what is presented as false Redmondite loyalism to republicanism. In the poem, which indeed recalls the pastoral tones of Francis Ledwidge's Easter Rising works, Tyrrell recognises the error of his soldiering ways and celebrates the dead leaders of the rebellion and their bold struggle for freedom:

> My feet are tangled in the net
> And now I strive to see it clear.
> Why did I walk where traps were set?
> What pleasant voices lured me here?
> I could have climbed the air like they
> And sung to greet the ring of day.
> And when the volley stopped our breath
> Together we'd have welcomed death.
>
> (Dowling 1961, 55)

The poem is also instrumental in completing the image of depravity and selfishness constructed around Sir William in the closing moments of the play. Tyrrell's grieving mother reveals to Sir William that her son's final wish was to have the poem included in the upcoming edition of his poetry. Appalled by the subject matter of the poem, Sir William tells her it is not good enough and sends her away. After discussing with his daughter how the publication of the poem might harm the sales of Tyrrell's books in England and "wouldn't enhance his reputation, either as a poet or a man, with the people who matter" (Dowling 1961, 65), Sir William sets fire to it – "in this life, there can be no divided loyalties" (ibid.). In this manner, Sir William tries to veil the conflicted case of Tyrrell, concealing an uncomfortable aspect of his life to maintain the myth of Tyrrell as a soldier-poet – considering the conflicted Irish history of the Great War, it is difficult to assess whether this highly ironic reversal was intended by Dowling.

Through the character of Sir William D'Arcy, Dowling's play repeats nationalist stereotypes of the cruel, arrogant and inhumane Anglo-Irish landlord who ultimately deserves the downfall of his class and traditions – stereotypes with which Dowling's audiences of the early 1960s were well-acquainted. The Great War in Dowling's work solely functions as a negative expression of Anglo-Irish identity, being pictured as a colonial and class war – an extension of the social question and the Irish question. Contrasting the almost pathological colonial militarism of Sir William and the essentially good-natured idealism of the nationalist Irish freedom fighters, the play reflects ideologically hardened attitudes both to the Great War and to the historical role of the Anglo-Irish that were only slowly beginning to ease in the Republic of Ireland of the 1960s.

The only female Anglo-Irish character in *The Bird in the Net*, Sir William's daughter Felicity, demonstrates the feminine conformity expected of her. Of course, she cannot agree to the offer of Tyrrell, at that point already a "fallen" temporary gentleman, to elope with him after they confess their love to each other. Also, Felicity represents a clichéd feminine detachment from the war and its political implications. For example, when Tyrrell tries to explain to her his Redmondite motives for joining up, she just replies how it is all too confusing for her – "I'm just a simple country girl" (Dowling 1961, 14). The two works to be analysed in the following, Pamela Hinkson's *The Ladies' Road* and Margaret Barrington's *My Cousin Justin*, offer a different and much more complex perspective both on the implications of the Great War for male and female Anglo-Irish identities and on the female experience of the home front, also centrally addressing the notion of a feminine separateness.

III.2.4 Pamela Hinkson's *The Ladies' Road* (1932)

Traditionally, war has been seen as constructed almost exclusively from male perspectives – as Claire Tylee summarises, "[c]lassic war texts primarily address men and all perpetuate the idea that 'war is men's business'" (Tylee 2004, 304f.) – this is also the case considering the Great War and its narratives. Only since the early 1990s a more substantial interest in women's war writing has emerged in British and Irish criticism, critics moving away from entirely male-centred perspectives by focusing, initially, on women's poetry addressing the Great War but also on drama, biographical writing and 'home front' novels by female authors (cf. Phillips 2009, 265).[82] The Great War has since been re-envisioned as representing an arena characterised by an intriguing intersection of gender, violence, the nation and national belonging – this understanding is also apt in the case of works like *The Ladies' Road* or *My Cousin Justin*, which provide female Anglo-Irish perspectives on the Great War and the home front, a specifically complex interplay of national and gender identities.

Pamela Hinkson (1900–1982), like Lennox Robinson, belonged to the fringes of the Anglo-Irish Ascendancy. Born in London as the daughter of the Catholic Irish poet, novelist and journalist Katharine Tynan and a Protestant barrister, Hinkson moved to Ireland when her father was appointed magistrate in Co. Mayo. Hinkson spent much of her childhood and adolescence, including the years of the Great War, at Brookhill House, near Claremorris, Co. Mayo, which greatly influenced her writing. After her father's death in 1919, Hinkson and her mother led a nomadic life in England, France and Germany, Hinkson also working as a journalist for a variety of newspapers and periodicals. Considering her attitudes to the Great War, Hinkson seems to embrace the constitutional nationalist attitudes held by her parents, who supported the Irish participation in the war effort; also, Hinkson's two older brothers enlisted and fought in the war. In a 1936 letter to *The English Review*, somewhat oblivious to the much more unfavourable Irish conditions of the time, Hinkson stresses her impression of how the Great War actually united those who had to suffer through it regardless of class or political identity, the Hinkson's Big House playing a specific role as a safe and compassionate refuge for all kinds of soldiers of the British forces:

> War-time conditions, so far from accentuating political differences in the War, threw a
> bridge over that gulf, made of common pain and pity, and sympathy and loyalties – a

---

82 See, for example, Dorothy Goldman's *Women and World War I*. Basingstoke: Palgrave Macmillan, 1993 or Sharon Ouditt's *Fighting Forces, Fighting Women*. London: Routledge, 1994.

bridge that remains, as it remains between the men of the opposing armies who now meet each other as old comrades. I may perhaps be forgiven a personal memory. It is of an Irish country-house in which the empty room of an absent son was often occupied by some young soldier; ill and removed from the Camp for better care [...]. [A]ny soldier who remembers Brookhill in those days will bear testimony that no country ever showed a more smiling and kindly face than that which Ireland turned to them in the summer of 1918.

(Hinkson 1936, 279)

This personal notion of the Big House as harmonious and secure, even escapist, during the Great War is also reflected in *The Ladies' Road*.

Although now almost completely forgotten, Hinkson had been a popular and widely published novelist and travel writer for many years. Among her oeuvre, *The Ladies' Road* is not the only work to address the Great War. In the 1920s, Hinkson, using the pseudonym "Peter Deane", wrote two grim formulaic novels dealing with the war's effects and aftermath (cf. Ouditt 2002, 20): *The Victors* (1925) deals with the fate of an alienated English ex-officer of the Great War who commits suicide because he cannot see a future for himself in the post-war world. *Harvest* (1927) is set in post-war Germany and presents the suffering of German women and children and the hopeless love of a French soldier and a German girl – "He and she, children of today, were just pawns, helpless things against the will of nations" (quoted in Ouditt 2002, 20). As one reviewer notes about *Harvest*, "[i]t is the harvest of despair that was reaped by men and women – so often by women – when peace came after war" (Novel Notes 1927, 224), a notion also prominent in Hinkson's 1932 novel to be discussed in the following.

The Ladies' Road, the second novel published under her real name, represents Hinkson's greatest success, the 1946 Penguin edition of the novel selling more than 100,000 copies, contemporary critics praising it for its "restrained sense of beauty" and "acceptance of life's trouble", "a story of England and Ireland during the war, in which beauty is made out of bitterness and agony, in which all the great issues of those tremendous years are seen, as most of us remember them, as they affected the private lives of men and women" (R. Ellis Roberts in *The New Statesman and Nation*, quoted in Hinkson 1946, 2). It was possibly the novel's sensitive and melancholic focus on "private lives" that made it such a success, almost completely steering clear of the conflict-laden political implications of the topic. Its setting switching between two country mansions in Ireland and England, as well as London, it represents a combination of the Big House novel and the home front novels written by British women writers who frequently recount a female experience of dreariness and monotony at home while husbands, sons, brothers and lovers are away at the front (cf. Phillips 2009, 267). This aspect, the separation of men and women in times of war, is the central theme of *The Ladies' Road* which is also expressed in the title – it refers to the Chemin des Dames, a ridge in northern France and site of a series of battles of the Great War including the Third Battle of the Aisne, in which the brother of one of the main characters dies in May 1918. The phrase also signifies the different paths of life and experience men and women have to take in war, a separateness that is presented in the novel as painful and evoking a powerful sense of loss – "the role of woman as bystander and as grieving mother, sister, lover" (ibid.).

The novel's focalisation is variable, its narration being shared by several characters. Hinkson panoramically presents the wartime ordeals of two related families, the Anglo-Irish Creaghs and the English Mannerings. Cappagh is the Big House of the Creaghs in Ireland, a place frequently described as mysterious, natural and beautiful, and much cherished by both families. Hubert Creagh is the head of this estate and the Creagh family. His wife Nancy, née Mannering, is an Englishwoman, whose side of the family resides at Winds, an estate in Kent. At the outbreak of the Great War all of the male family members of fighting age enlist without further ado: Hubert and his two sons, Guy and Philip, just as Nancy's nephews, Godfrey and David Mannering, and the family friends Edmund Urquhart and George Marsham. The women remain at home and take up different jobs contributing to the war effort, working as nurses or in canteens. The novel's major character, Nancy's adolescent niece Stella Mannering, suffers greatly from being too young to do her bit, longing to be part of the war effort, dreaming of becoming an ambulance driver at the front. Crucially, Stella is not an outright militarist or naively hungry for adventure – she is tormented by being separated from her favourite brother David and wants to be with him at the front. Eventually, Hubert, Philip and Edmund are killed in the war, as is Stella's other brother Godfrey, while George is severely wounded and Guy badly gassed. For the women of the novel, coping with the deaths and injuries of their beloved and their own position of helplessness and detachment proves extremely difficult. The men who return home on leave or invalided to Cappagh and Winds have been radically transformed and are disconnected from their earlier lives and their partners. The news that David is missing and probably dead deeply upsets Stella, who feels that her own life and future has come to an end. An overwhelming sense of loss dominates the end of the novel, set during the War of Independence in the summer of 1919. The remaining Creaghs have become suspicious of their Irish neighbours and eventually the Creaghs' Big House is burned down by radical nationalists.

Until the crisis of the War of Independence at the end of the novel, the Creaghs' Irish estate of Cappagh functions as a symbol of safety and happy memories, of stability and tradition, of innocence and of a life less burdened by conventions and worries than the one at Winds in England – Cappagh stands for an Ireland that almost seems to be cut off from the harsh realities of the period. Throughout the novel, almost all characters long to be back at Cappagh or indulge in memories of it – as Mo Moulton notes, to Hinkson "homesickness was constitutive to the Irish abroad" (Moulton 2014, 226). However, as the Great War progresses and the death toll among the two families rises, the notion of the happiness and beauty of Cappagh temporarily becomes problematic, appearing incompatible with the transformative experience of loss with which both the serving men and the women at home are confronted – it turns into a painful reminder of a life gone by. This becomes most obvious through the character of Philip and his death in war. Philip, a professional soldier educated at Sandhurst, is presented as the future of the family and their estate, similar to Ulick Alcock in *The Big House*: "Philip had belonged to Cappagh and Cappagh to him. […] They would wonder, the people about Cappagh, the woods and the lake too, old Dora the spaniel, everything what happened to Philip" (Hinkson 1946, 181f.). Nancy is traumatised by the death of Philip and she "shie[s] away in her thoughts from Cappagh" (Hinkson 1946, 67). For Guy, "Cappagh was too full of memories of his childhood and of Philip and Hubert" (Hinkson 1946, 182). Similarly, Stella lies awake one night, thinking of Philip and Cappagh, musing how "[t]here had been a life before the War. The War coming so soon after had blotted it out" (Hinkson 1946, 72f.). This elegiac nostalgia for an idyllic, orderly and secure pre-war life prevalent in Hinkson's novel is one of the central traits of much Great War writing, an influential myth in the war's legacy. The war is presented as a shocking loss of innocence or fall from grace, authors ignoring that pre-war Britain and Ireland in fact were by no means realms of peace and harmony but marked by serious social unrest and poverty (cf. Tylee 1990, 245). In Hinkson's novel, this loss of innocence, embodied by pre-war life at Cappagh, is linked with the irrevocable loss of Anglo-Ireland; along these lines, Claire Tylee argues, the novel's "[g]rief for the past is also part of the romanticisation of Empire" (Tylee 1990, 245).

The processes of identification of the Creaghs and their relatives as Anglo-Irish, particularly considering the female figures, are somewhat contradictory. On the one hand, clear boundaries to the Irish population are established, "masking cross-cultural exchange" (Phillips 2007, 80). Edmund Urquhart, a visitor to Cappagh, stresses the ambiguous nature of Anglo-Irish identity exemplified by Cappagh and how the Creaghs represent a history of conquest – a view that Terry Phillips describes as a "purely Cromwellian" (ibid.) construction of Anglo-Irishness:

He had come to Ireland and this wasn't Ireland, and yet it had the indefinable magic of the country about it. No one had told him about the life inside these houses, built so much of a pattern, big and grey with a suggestion of a fortress against their background of woods. They had been thrown down, he supposed, by the English as they passed through, coming as conquerors and colonists, and the English influence went just as far as the sunlight went into the woods and no further. Beyond that the country lay, unaffected.

(Hinkson 1946, 32)

On the other hand, the novel's sense of Anglo-Irishness becomes increasingly permeable as the novel progresses and the tragedy of the war deaths unfolds. Stella begins to feel strongly drawn back to Cappagh, leaving behind her Englishness: "The longer you stayed, the harder it was to move. Even if one didn't really belong to it. But Stella half-belonged really" (Hinkson 1946, 301). Also, Nancy comes to identify herself as "Irish", expressing her hope that her son Guy "will marry an Irish girl. Anglo-Irish marriages are a risk. [...] And English people don't understand our ways" (Hinkson 1946, 183f.). The painful effects of the Great War play a central role for this re-identification. Irishness, as it is understood in the upper-class perspective of the two Englishwomen Nancy and Stella, seems to suggest a rural soothing remoteness from the Great War and from the worrisome complexity and 'rationality' of life in England. Yet, withdrawing to a superficially unchanged Ireland, burdened by memory as mentioned above, eventually cannot make up for the losses suffered: "[I]n comparative security and quietness [Nancy] was able to think for the first time ever since the War began. And life stretched before her, long and desolate and empty; and even her garden at Cappagh might not fill it" (Hinkson 1946, 188). As mentioned earlier, the novel closes with the destruction of Cappagh and the concomitant end of Anglo-Irish Ireland. The resulting sense of displacement and identity confusion, which the female characters of the novel recognise by the end of the novel, is strikingly expressed by Stella, who now sees herself "always in a No Man's Land left by the War with a country on either side that was not hers" (Hinkson 1946, 313).

The Anglo-Irish identity of the male Creaghs is less changeable. Hubert and Philip unquestioningly act upon the privileges and paternalistic power their status gives them over the local community. The war service of Hubert, Philip and Guy seems to represent an unchangeable consequence of their identity as members of the Anglo-Irish gentry, fighting for the Empire and their class. It is part of the family tradition and apart from a single early interruption by Edmund Urquhart, who confronts Philip about his war service, foreshadowing his loss for the local community, it is never critically examined or questioned: "I think it's a pity [...]. Your being a soldier and all that. [...] You should be a landlord. [...] You'd make a good seigneur, Phil. And go into politics perhaps and atone for the sins of your ancestors" (Hinkson 1946, 25). However, Edmund, who is initially introduced as fairly rebellious and a pacifist, also eventually follows his friend Philip into the war and is killed alongside him.

The war experience of women is the central concern of the novel. Crucially, the war creates an enormous gulf between men and women. As the male characters are naturally sent off to the front to fight, the female characters remain relegated to a detached existence at the home front, forming homosocial communities of their own characterised by the fear for their husbands, sons, lovers and brothers – a fate presented as shared across the boundaries of nation and class, however, in an ambiguous and resentful way. Nancy observes how she "lived with other women, as women were living all over Europe in that strange isolation" (Hinkson 1946, 71), however, "[t]hey loved each other, these women, and hated each other at once, were in sympathy because they knew, and separated. Each one's safety menaced the other's safety. They, all of them, lived alone, touching each other and going back to that small world where they were shut in with some man who belonged to them" (ibid.). In this manner, the novel suggests, the Great War exposes a total dependence of women on the men in their lives. The war seems to overwhelm any sense of female individuality as, eventually, the fate of the soldiers determines the fate of 'their' women at home. The war work some of the female characters take up does little to alleviate their sense of isolation and passivity. Stella, who appeared to be the least uniform female figure for most of the novel, at last also arrives at the recognition of the inescapability of female dependency: "Stella thought that when one was married, one was married and quite different, even if one's husband had been killed. Cynthia was married and Mary was still married to Godfrey although he had been killed so long ago. If she had been old enough to marry during the War, Stella thought, she would have been a widow too probably" (Hinkson 1946, 301). This determination by a war from whose immediate realities women frequently feel detached is strikingly addressed also by Stella, when she thinks about "the names of towns she had never seen, which were yet more familiar than any towns she knew. Bapaume, Ypres, Menin, Loos. [...] They stamped themselves on her childhood, being part of it, to be remembered afterwards when many closer memories would be forgotten" (Hinkson 1946, 126).

The sense of female isolation in war is most vividly presented through Stella, who is so deeply distressed by the separation from her brother David and her own position of helplessness and passivity that she develops an almost obsessive interest in the war – "how intolerable monotony and safety were" (Hinkson 1946, 80), Stella living "on the excitement that came in from outside with the post and letters from the Front" (Hinkson 1946, 82). The female detachment from war even reaches a transformative physical dimension in the case of Stella. In a series of performative acts, she symbolically tries to transgress the gender limitations that separate her as a woman from David, attempting to enter the unreachable masculine realm of experience of the army: She considers dressing up as a boy and attempting to enlist, mortifies her body by swimming in the icy water of the school pool in a sleepless autumn night, openly proclaims her self-perception as a "useless mouth" (Hinkson 1946, 80) and tries to approach and understand David's war experiences through his letters, not only by reading but also by smelling them: "Holding it against her face she tried to define the smell. It was tobacco she supposed, and leather and uniform. It was the smell of David who had only learned to smoke, and of Godfrey and Francis. It filled all her thin, overgrown body with a curious pain …the smell of the War in this cold piece of paper against her face" (Hinkson 1946, 108). Yet, neither do her efforts lead to a satisfactory quasi-'masculinisation' that would enable her to be closer to David, nor are they interpreted by others as subversive gestures against unbearable female passivity enforced by existing gender norms. After David's war death, Stella is driven by the desire to reconstruct her brother's life in the army, even considering searching for David's body herself on the Chemin Des Dames – a powerful symbol of her desperation and loneliness. At this point, Stella is "staring at a road before her that seemed to lead nowhere – the Ladies' Road" (Hinkson 1946, 217), having lost any sense of direction in her life (cf. Tylee 1990, 247), remaining practically unable to exist on her own and beyond her dominant problematic female war identity.

However, disorientation also befalls those women who are reunited with their men (ibid.). The returning soldiers have been transformed by the war; they find themselves disconnected from their pre-war lives and identities and are also perceived as such. George's wife Irene must recognise that a stranger has returned to her: "Someone else, not George. She saw George sometimes looking at her as though over someone else's shoulder, from an immense distance. She could not reach him" (Hinkson 1946, 296f.). Similarly, Guy, recovering at home from a severe gas attack, comes to think of Cappagh and his childhood as "something belonging to someone else, seeing it clearly as another person's story and possession" (Hinkson 1946, 178). His mother Nancy also feels their alienation: "Guy moved about and talked to himself unintelligibly. She listened, holding her breath for a word, a clue that must help her. But she was shut outside as though he was a stranger speaking a strange tongue" (Hinkson 1946, 186).

At the end of the novel, Cappagh finally and completely loses its dated and exhausted nimbus of safety and stability as the tides turn against the Anglo-Irish in the War of Independence. Unlike in *The Big House* and *The Bird in the Net*, there is no extensive discussion of the political and social implications of the threatening conditions in Ireland, as none of the remaining inhabitants of Cappagh address the War of Independence beyond the immediate indispositions it entails. Still, the disposal of Hubert's and Philip's service weapons and other personal war memorabilia by Nancy, who dumps them in the estate's lake for her own safety, is a powerful image that can be read in multiple ways. It is not just indicative of the imminent threat she is facing, but symbolical of the downfall of her entire class, disposing of once powerful imperial insignia. The scene could also be interpreted as symbolical of the burying of the episode of the Great War in Ireland's national narrative after independence. Finally, it is a striking female gesture of protest against the patriarchal tradition of militarism and its fatal local and global consequences, from the destruction of Cappagh to the monumental event of the Great War itself.

Interestingly, when Cappagh eventually is burned down, the loss of the Big House and the imminent end of the Anglo-Irish tradition in Ireland does not come as a shocking defeat for the Creaghs. The loss of their specific liminal place in Ireland is recognised – "There would be [...] for the next generation, no world between two worlds, but only Ireland" (Hinkson 1946, 319) – however, their fall had already happened in the form of the Great War which is why the latest catastrophe is merely taken in a spirit of fatalistic indifference: "[N]one of this really concerned them, because they had spent everything in the War and so for all their lives afterwards must lie on the bank watching the stream of life go by unable to go with it or to discover clearly where it went" (Hinkson 1946, 319f.).

Altogether, in its depiction of the personal dimension of the harrowing losses of the Great War, as well as through the *petits récits* of the war experiences of the female Creaghs and Mannerings, Hinkson's novel perpetuates the famous myth of a lost generation, however, also constructing the image of a lost generation of women affected by the war, just as stranded in a No Man's Land as their alienated or dead husbands, sons and brothers. Ireland, which is only envisioned through the rural Big House, for the greatest part of the novel is perceived as an almost timeless place of refuge detached from the realities of wartime life. Anglo-Irishness is presented both in its conventional liminality and, considering the central female characters, as fairly flexible, Nancy and Stella embracing what they understand as 'Irishness' in an escapist gesture. Yet, the effects of the war, which exposes a dichotomy of simultaneous separateness and dependence between men and women, eventually prove too destructive to be compensated by a moribund Anglo-Irish culture.

The Ladies' Road, Terry Phillips summarises, "may be seen as its title suggests as a distinctly female rather than a pacifist voice" (Phillips 2009, 271). Hinkson's approach to the Great War, focusing on passive personal suffering, appears almost apolitical. In contrast to this, the next Anglo-Irish home front novel to be analysed, Margaret Barrington's *My Cousin Justin*, operates on a more complex and pronouncedly politicised level, "an interesting case study of the interaction of feminism, socialism, pacifism and nationalism" (Phillips 2009, 274), and features a female protagonist more insightful and critical than the women of *The Ladies' Road*.

III.2.5 Margaret Barrington's *My Cousin Justin* (1939)

Just like the other works covered in this section so far, Margaret Barrington's *My Cousin Justin* connects the Great War with the subsequent related conflicts in Ireland, presenting Anglo-Irish identities in the maelstrom of political and social pressure and violence. *My Cousin Justin* has a strong autobiographical touch and is the only major work of Barrington (1896–1982) apart from her journalistic writing and a number of short stories. Born as the daughter of a district inspector in the Royal Irish Constabulary, Barrington was brought up, like the heroine of her novel, by her grandfather on the north coast of Donegal. Despite her Anglo-Irish origins, Barrington turned to Irish republicanism and also became a lifelong socialist and pacifist. From 1926 to 1932, she was married to Liam O'Flaherty, who had previously returned from calamitous adventures in the IRA and, before that, the Great War, which he left shell-shocked, his mental health permanently impaired – certainly a tangible influence on Barrington's novel. Like many writers from Ireland, Barrington left Ireland for London in the 1930s. She became the editor of the woman's page in the *Tribune* and dedicated herself to various left-wing causes, actively supporting the Republicans in the Spanish Civil War and helping refugees from Nazi Germany. She returned to Ireland at the outbreak of World War II and continued to write occasional articles and short stories.

My Cousin Justin, published in 1939, was received by contemporary critics with enthusiasm (cf. Caherty 1985, 11). The novel's subject matter of the tumultuous years of the Great War and, much more importantly, the Easter Rising and the subsequent Irish conflicts, was still of great interest in Ireland twenty years later. However, as the novel appeared right on the eve of World War II, it was soon buried as public attention turned to more pressing concerns (cf. Campbell 1991, 117). The reissue of the novel in 1990 can be seen in the context of the revisionist tendencies of the era, representing a rediscovery of Barrington as an "interesting voice from the past" (ibid.) and as part of a rich and varied heritage of female Irish and Anglo-Irish writing that deserves greater attention – still, apart from an essay by Terry Phillips (cf. Phillips 2009) and a short reference in one of Keith Jeffery's surveys (cf. Jeffery 1999), *My Cousin Justin* has not attracted any further scholarly attention to this day.

The novel's plot is fairly complex. The main character and narrator, Anna-Louise "Loulie" Delahaie, an Anglo-Irish girl with Huguenot roots, is brought up in the Donegal Big House of her educated and benevolent grandfather, along with her cousin Justin Thorauld with whom she is deeply connected, a relationship "curiously balanced between the platonic and the sexual" (Phillips 2009, 275). After a violent row in which Justin almost kills Egan O'Doherty, one of the Irish boys of the local village, Justin is sent away to a public school in England. Also, Loulie is sent back to her parents in the Lagan valley, near Belfast. The Great War comes abruptly and Justin reluctantly enlists. When the cousins meet again at the Big House, Justin seemingly has been broken by his war experiences. It also turns out that, right before leaving for war, Justin had married a somewhat vulgar London girl, Nell, out of a fear of loneliness. Furthermore, Justin's teenage enemy Egan O'Doherty reappears at the Big House, now a soldier as well, and tries to make an approach to Loulie.

Loulie moves to Dublin to study at Trinity College. She begins to work for a Dublin newspaper and becomes the protégé of the editor Tom Hennessey, who plays an important part in radical socialist and republican circles. Tom furthers Loulie's political education and turns her Dublin flat into a hideout for republican fighters. One of the activists secretly harboured by Loulie turns out to be Egan O'Doherty and Loulie eventually falls in love with him. In the precarious years of the War of Independence and the Civil War, Loulie has to cope with the murder of Nell, who is killed by Egan along with Nell's new husband, a government agent, and with the death of her mentor Tom, who dies fighting for the IRA. Tired of the violence around her, Loulie eventually gives in to Egan's marriage proposal, leaving Dublin for London at once.

In London, Loulie and Justin are accidently reunited and return to the Big House together as Egan has disappeared yet again without notice. Justin bitterly looks back at his youth wasted in the war and expresses a deeply felt estrangement from the post-war world as a veteran and as a member of the defeated Anglo-Irish class. When he confesses his love to Loulie, Egan re-appears. Egan and Justin begin to spend the nights at the Big House together drinking; one night they crudely confront Loulie with their experiences of brutality, death and moral depravity in the war. The next morning Egan is gone again. Justin demands Loulie's love once more but is rejected. Back in London, Loulie and Egan eventually separate. She returns to the Big House for a last visit in preparation of a new life in Dublin, however, she quickly recognises that she cannot leave and stays with her cousin Justin.

The image of the Big House constructed in Barrington's novel is similar to the one in *The Ladies' Road*. Again, its location in rural Ireland and its (fading) legacy of Anglo-Irish local leadership and tradition is perceived by its Anglo-Irish inhabitants as producing a soothing sense of detachment from the bleaker realities of the unionist North-East, rebellious Dublin, busy imperial London and, of course, the harsh sphere of the battlefields on the Continent. The insularity and datedness of the Big House is most pointedly described by the outsider Nell: "To look at this place, you'd never think there was a war on. The last great adventure must have been the Flood" (Barrington 1990, 99). In this manner, the Big House again serves as a refuge and aim of escapist fantasies; however, even if it is not destroyed as in the other works discussed, the Big House of the Thoraulds also eventually becomes endangered as the political and economic fortunes of the Anglo-Irish are deteriorating and as its former inhabitants are transformed by age, life and war – as Loulie remarks upon returning home, "[o]ld books, old loves, dead as autumn leaves. I shivered. The old house was full of ghosts" (Barrington 1990, 223).

The self-identification of the novel's principal Anglo-Irish characters Loulie and Justin undergoes a series of changes and crises and is centrally influenced by their experiences of war, violence and political and social discord. At the outset of the novel, the sense of the traditional distinctiveness of their social position is established. The difference between Loulie, Justin and the Irish community bound to their estate is clear-cut even though Loulie's grandfather is a compassionate and well-liked landlord. The socialist Barrington makes sure to point out the crass material imbalance between the peasants and the landed gentry, for example, when she confronts Loulie and Justin with a group of starving harvesters about to emigrate to Scotland (cf. Barrington 1990, 45) – yet, at this point, her protagonists are still too young and inexperienced to fully grasp and react to the implications of inequality of such scenes.

When Loulie and Justin are taken out of the traditional and hermetic world of their Donegal Big House and their bond – which, in its almost claustrophobic intensity, proves the most durable source of identification for them throughout the novel – is temporarily broken up, their outlooks and the sense of their position in the world come under stress and they undergo a series of changes. Back at their Lagan home after years in Donegal, Loulie is disparagingly perceived by her estranged parents as "Irish" and her cold-hearted mother wishes to re-anglicise her. Loulie in turn increasingly becomes unsure of her position and detests the militancy and radical antagonism that characterises her new Ulster unionist environment – "I don't belong to them. I belong to you and want to be with people like you. I hate their black self-righteous Protestant God" (Barrington 1990, 87), she complains to her grandfather. Loulie leaves for Dublin and, shaken and impressed by the aftermath of the Easter Rising – "[t]he war had caught us up" (Barrington 1990, 133) – Loulie begins to identify with and work for the cause of Irish republicanism and socialism, diametrically opposed to the ideological foundations of her class. Yet, at the end of the novel, back at the Big House, disillusioned by political violence, Loulie must realise how her origins are inescapable and she somewhat naïvely pictures herself and Justin as part of a peaceful and equal co-existence of the Anglo-Irish and the Irish that again recalls Robinson's Kate Alcock: "We can take our place with the others, Justin, work with them, live with them" (Barrington 1990, 234).

The departure of Justin from the Big House "out into the world" (Barrington 1990, 69) proves traumatic. As in the case of the Anglo-Irishmen in *The Ladies' Road*, Justin's pre-war self is destroyed by the experiences of the Great War. The loss of control and the futility of individual agency in the war that, as Eric Leed notes, produces "a defensive personality" (Leed 1979, 106), as well as the war's uncovering of man's savagery shatter Justin's belief in a meaningful human existence and destroy any sense of optimism. As Loulie notes, "[i]t was a strange Justin who had arrived at the old house [...]. He wandered from one room to another like an uneasy spirit" (Barrington 1990, 88f.). A war-torn Justin laments that life "will do what it likes with us" (Barrington 1990, 90) and breaks down in Loulie's arms: "The world, Lou, the world, it's a loathsome place" (Barrington 1990, 94). His post-war career as a successful London lawyer cannot alleviate the sense of emptiness and alienation instilled by the war and his eventual retreat from "the world", going back to Donegal with Loulie, again underlining the remoteness of Ireland, seems to be his last resort. Back at the Big House, Justin takes over the position of his deceased grandfather, which puzzles and disturbs Loulie and which is portrayed as destined to fail:

> He possessed nothing of grandfather's kindly tolerance, none of his urbane goodwill towards men. There was in Justin's soul a dislike of his fellows which grandfather had never known, an inverted idealism which grew not from his reason, but from his emotional nature. Yet in every outward seeming he had become our grandfather. [...] The old house creaked like a ship at sea.
>
> (Barrington 1990, 231)

Justin's withdrawal is accompanied by a fatalist adoption of Anglo-Irishness, fully conscious of the liminality and the ongoing demise of his class – also an expression of his war-induced despair and resignation: "We are thrown out by both sides. We no longer have any power. We no longer serve any purpose. We are an unhappy race, nothing is left us but our personal life and our emotions" (Barrington 1990, 233f.) – and it is this personal dimension where Justin relocates himself, effectively planning to go extinct as a member of his class, together with Loulie.

Egan's war service is equally transformative. Like Justin, the Catholic Irish country boy Egan is devastated by the war and experiences an erasure of his pre-war identity: "I am an old soldier, now. When I see a fight I must get into it. I don't feel safe otherwise" (Barrington 1990, 154) – and indeed, after the Great War, Egan cannot but continue to fight in the subsequent Irish conflicts. He has entered an irreversible state of complete alienation from civilian life and cannot re-integrate into peace-time society: "[T]he day I got my discharge, I stood on the pavement and looked around me and I was terrified. I felt like a child who has lost his mother" (Barrington 1990, 263). Egan also lacks the capacity to maintain his relationship with Loulie which cannot compensate for the intense rootlessness he feels – a condition exposed in his habit of disappearing without notice, willingly disconnecting from the few personal ties left to him.

Unlike Justin, Egan does not attempt to find refuge in embracing his origins and returning to Ireland. During the war, his decision to become a soldier in the British army was met with scorn by his peers. On the one hand, his parents are dismayed as his volunteering means the end of his hard-earned studies at university, "an untold sacrifice in a family like this" (Barrington 1990, 118). On the other hand, his war service is also understood as treacherous to Ireland and inappropriate for his class, as expressed, ironically, by the Thorauld's main maid Bella:

"Egan O'Doherty it is. And more shame to him to be seen in that coat."
"It is the same coat as my cousin wears," [Loulie] answered sharply.
"It's one thing for the young master til wear it, but it's a mortal disgrace til see it on the back of his father's son."

(Barrington 1990, 115)

In this moment, Bella displays an intriguingly contradictory sense of liminality herself, based on an acceptance of the traditional hierarchies between the Irish and Anglo-Irish, integrating herself in two worlds. The ambiguous split inherent in her position is magnified by the topic of the Great War, the Catholic Irishwoman Bella rejecting the war service of the Catholic Irishman Egan while simultaneously condoning the war service of the Anglo-Irish family she works for and to which she belongs like a family member, practically replacing Loulie's unloving mother.

As in *The Ladies' Road*, the individual motivations of the male characters to enlist at the outbreak of the war remain largely unexplained. Both Justin and Egan never really clarify how they understand their position within the network of affiliations and ideologies that the war represents. In the case of Justin, going to war again seems to be an unquestioned consequence of belonging to the class of the Anglo-Irish, although Justin soon voices his lack of enthusiasm – "[h]ere I am in this goddamned camp learning to hunt the Hun" (Barrington 1990, 82), he once writes to Loulie. The outbreak of the Great War itself is introduced fairly casually and concisely by Loulie, reflecting her detachment: "It fell on us out of a clear summer sky. Before we realised what had happened, the boys who had played at being soldiers were soldiers in earnest" (Barrington 1990, 82). Unlike the women of *The Ladies' Road*, Loulie herself is not overwhelmed and determined by fear for her male relatives and tormented by enforced female wartime passivity. Yet, this condition is also reflected in Barrington's novel, Loulie recording how the bereaved wives and mothers of soldiers in Ulster are caught in a frenzy of anxiety, the "strange isolation" that Hinkson describes: "They hated those women whose sons had escaped or were safe in hospital, perhaps crippled for life, and most of all they hated those women who had no sons. They began to shout for conscription. They sent white feathers, wrote letters and talked hysterically. Let every man be taken" (Barrington 1990, 122) – in this manner, fear, danger and loss are fiercely collectivised by Barrington's Ulsterwomen.

Through Loulie's observations of her environment, Barrington offers a panoramic view of Ulster home front phenomena, such as a bout of spy mania and anti-German aggression, and of divided attitudes to the Great War, from nationalism ("This is England's war, not ours", Barrington 1990, 122) to disillusioned Ulster unionism ("[I]f all our lads are killed who will defend us from the Catholics?", ibid.), British patriotism ("This is a just war, a holy war, a war against aggression", Barrington 190, 124) and disillusioned internationalist solidarity ("If ever a son of mine says, 'What did you do in the Great War, Daddy?' I'll squirm, because I'll have to say, 'I did what the others did, son, I murdered my fellowmen", Barrington 1990, 125). In these debates, witnessed by Loulie in Ulster, she maintains her feminine passivity and remains uninvolved, also being only addressed once by one of the quarrelling men who feels sorry for her as "[a]ll your young men have been taken away" (Barrington 1990, 126).

However, Loulie's silence changes as her subsequent unorthodox political education in Dublin progresses, Loulie gaining both the confidence and the ideological resources to give expression to her position and to a new and theoretically well-defined political identity. Importantly, even before Loulie's political awakening, Barrington's socialist perspectives dominate the novel's approach to the Great War. For example, when the rushing to arms at the outbreak of the Great War is recounted earlier in the novel, it is described how men left "the plough, the mills, the shipyards" (Barrington 1990, 82) to enlist, not mentioning the Anglo-Irish realms of the Big Houses, banks, universities or government agencies. In this manner, the war again is majorly presented as an exploitative workers' war, the lower classes being pointlessly sacrificed on behalf of the upper classes. The socialist, international-ist and pacifist ideas fostered in Loulie are also extended to the post-war situation. Confidently discussing the impending Civil War in Ireland with Tom Hennessey, whose socialist principles have been defeated by his republicanism by this time, his "old hatred of England" having "eaten into [his] bones" (Barrington 1990, 175), Loulie assertively contradicts her political mentor:

> We hoped that out of this struggle the working class would seize power. It was a smoke dream. Free State or Republic, what does it matter? The little tradesman will have his day, and the big industrialist will have his, and the worker will go to the wall. [...]. The Irish Capitalist when he comes is no more our friend than the English Capitalist, but the English worker could be our brother. In reality he is fighting for the same ideal.
>
> (Barrington 1990, 174f.)

Towards the end of the novel, however, Loulie's new found political emancipation and confidence are overpowered – as Terry Phillips observes, Loulie's "socialism and her republicanism do not have a developed feminist dimension" (Phillips 2009, 277), Loulie eventually faltering under the pressure of her male peers. She cannot escape the forces of established class and gender norms, ultimately prov-ing unable to resist both the call of home of the Big House and the male authority of Egan, whom she marries despite his capriciousness and unfaithfulness, and Justin, to whom she returns at the end of the novel despite resenting his negativ-ity and his manipulative influence on her:

> "Why should you assume this right over me? I give my loyalty and my love where I wish and not where you wish."
> "You came back to me. I know now that no matter how often you turn away from me, you will always come back. [...] The love we have for one another must endure; it is of our bones and our blood. We might as well fight against the rising of the sun as fight against it."
>
> (Barrington 1990, 273)

Furthermore, Loulie eventually must recognise her essential detachment from the realities of war – and thereby from the realities of Egan and Justin. The novel ultimately suggests a view of the world as dominated by male aggression (cf. Phillips 2009, 276), relegating women to the role of ignorant carers or by-standers, or, at worst, to that of sources of corruption. This becomes most obvi-ous in the climactic scene of the novel when drunk Egan and Justin, temporarily united by shared wartime suffering across the class divide and personal aversion ("No matter what they talked of, in the end they came round to the same subject, the war. It lay always at the back of their minds, a dark dream, only released when the fumes of alcohol rose to their heads", Barrington 1990, 244), antagonise a terrified Loulie. They ruthlessly confront her with brutal and sordid episodes from their time in the Great War. Significantly, apart from death and destruction, their anecdotes centre on female and sexual depravity: licentious nurses, exhibitionist Frenchwomen, industrious prostitutes at the front (cf. Phillips 2009, 276). Thus, Loulie finally becomes fully aware of the gulf between her and the men, recognising their excruciating transformation:

> As I watched my husband and my cousin, I realised for the first time that though they had all their limbs intact, though the only sign of war on Egan's body was a scar on the leg and here and there blue marks, each was a badly mutilated as if he had lost an arm or leg. What they had lost was more because one could not see it. The scars of war lay on their souls, and old wounds ache. [...] I listened as they continued their meandering conversation. When they laughed, I shuddered, for those things which excited laughter in their minds filled me with horror. God forgive me, I was frightened.
>
> (Barrington 1990, 263f.)

This confrontation and Loulie's unsettling realisation come to underpin the end of her relationship with Egan and might even be read as something akin to a war trauma suffered by Loulie.

Its effect is the same as in the case of the war trauma of Justin – at the very end of the novel, Loulie's earlier socialist persona has vanished, she swiftly gives up her plan of living in Dublin on her own and returns to her familial Anglo-Irish origins, essentially abandoning "the world" along with her cousin Justin, the Donegal Big House becoming a comforting, if moribund, haven: "With one bright eye it leered to me and seemed to say: I am the womb to which you would return. [...] The house itself gathered me close to it, a warm, safe place. [...] This house did not belong to me but I to it. I yielded as a woman yields to her lover, knowing at the same time that she is the victor" (Barrington 1990, 287f.). This conclusion of the novel might also be read, Terry Phillips suggests, as "a retreat from the monstrosity of the new Ireland which Egan and his like have created" (Phillips 2009, 277), Loulie and Justin withdrawing from a society which was born out of violence and extremism and in which their original identities have been rendered irrelevant – however, this reading ignores that the waning world of the Big House to which they retreat was just as much founded upon inequality, hierarchy and exploitation, a point of view that Barrington establishes early in the novel.

Summing up, Barrington connects in her novel the effects of the ravaging experience of the Great War from a female perspective with ambiguous, changeable and ultimately inescapable forms of Anglo-Irishness, positioned in-between privilege, isolation and social decay. The Big House, a central marker of Anglo-Irish identity, is again envisioned as an escapist realm, not only representing a separate sphere considering aspects of class. It is also detached from the greater course of history; already a relic, its dilapidated condition and inherent aloofness mirrors the damages suffered by its returning inhabitants. Through the dysfunctional love triangle of Loulie, Justin and Egan, Barrington also shows and problematises the fraught interplay of Irish and Anglo-Irish identities centrally enabled and formed by the effects of the Great War.

This problematic combination of war and inter-class relationships is also the focal point of the final text to be covered in this section, Jennifer Johnston's *How Many Miles to Babylon* (1974). A novel from a different period in Irish writing, it still follows the, by that time, somewhat dated Big House pattern, but represents an important shift in literary representations of the Great War, the Big House and Irish and Anglo-Irish lives, considering its sense of conscious retrospection, its panoramic presentation of attitudes to the war, and its unveiled featuring of homosexuality.

III.2.6 Jennifer Johnston's *How Many Miles to Babylon?* (1974)

Jennifer Johnston is the first author covered in this project who did not experience the period of the Great War and its immediate aftermath herself. This sense of temporal distance, of a retrospective construction and of an increased reliance on the shifting realm of memory and pre-existing narratives when evoking the period of the 1910s clearly distinguishes her from the previous writers discussed. This condition is also directly reflected in *How Many Miles to Babylon?* when Johnston's main protagonist and narrator Alexander Moore declares right at the outset of his retrospective report how he has "only the past to play about with. I can juggle with a series of possibly inaccurate memories, my own interpretation, for what is worth, of events" (Johnston 2010, 1), essentially destabilising his own narrative. This notion of variability and constructedness is central to Johnston, who has been outspoken about her impression of the 'danger' of memory in Ireland, people constructing and appropriating versions of the Irish past that have frequently provoked separation and violent discord (cf. Garratt 2011, 81) – along these lines, Johnston also might have been grouped with the authors of the final section of this project.

Johnston was born in 1930 and grew up in Dublin as the daughter of the playwright Denis Johnston and the Abbey actress and director Shelah Richards, who were both prominently involved in the circles of the Irish Literary Revival. After settling in London for twenty years, Johnston relocated to Derry right at the outbreak of the Troubles and only then began a late but successful and prolific career as a novelist and playwright – her first work to be published, *The Captains and the Kings*, appeared in 1972. Despite her nominal Protestant and Anglo-Irish roots, Johnston identifies herself as "chiefly Irish" (Weekes 1990, 192), and throughout her career she remained "a difficult figure to pigeon-hole, either politically or culturally" (Rosslyn 2004, 104); Johnston has advocated an integrative vision of a united and diverse Ireland liberated from oppressive separatist traditions and imperatives.[83] Accordingly, a central concern of Johnston's novels are the political, religious and class divisions of Irish and Northern Irish society, Johnston creating "a comprehensive picture of the struggles and counter-struggles of British and Irish self-definition in the twentieth century" (ibid.). The Big House as a symbol of liminality and separateness represents for Johnston an intriguing and much revisited arena for such examinations. It functions in her works, as Marit Berge remarks, as "a metaphor for the failure of individuals to understand each other's motives and aspirations [...], a failure of sympathy and a breakdown of communication between people on the level of individual relationships which in turn are reflected in the wider issues of race and breeding" (Berge 1994, 14) – this frequently takes the form of friendships across class boundaries which are invariably destroyed by sectarian or class prejudice.

As a consequence of Johnston's preferred setting of the Big House, the Great War reappears in several of her works, reflecting its significance for the Anglo-Irish legacy. However, Johnston employs the Great War not just as a powerful contemporary context for the respective situation re-created in her novels – importantly, the Great War also works for Johnston as a metaphor for the political violence and sectarianism in Northern Ireland that she witnessed in the 1970s: "When I started writing prose, I had it very seriously in my mind that I wanted to write about the Troubles [...], yet I couldn't face taking them head-on. So I started to write about the First World War" (quoted in Thackray Jones 2008). Her second novel *How Many Miles to Babylon?* compellingly reflects the demarcation lines between English, Anglo-Irish and Irish identities and classes and exposes the violent regimes –

---

83 The Irish critical establishment long dismissed Johnston as an apolitical writer of Big House nostalgia and domesticity (cf. Backus 1994, 57). This view has changed which is reflected not only in more recent criticism, but also by the impressive number of literary prizes and awards Johnston received and by her membership in Aosdána.

military, economic, familial, traditional – that enforce their separation. It addresses a "crisis between difference and sameness" (Backus 1994, 57) that ends in death.

The novel is set at the estate of the Moore family in Co. Wicklow and at military locations in Northern Ireland and France before and during the Great War. The main protagonist and narrator Alexander, an imprisoned officer in the British army waiting for his execution, recounts his story of an isolated life as the only son of an unhappily married Anglo-Irish couple, Alicia and Frederick Moore. He meets and befriends Jerry Crowe, a stable boy on the Moore's estate, however, Alexander's parents forbid him to mix with the Irish and Alexander must keep up their friendship in secret. At the outbreak of the Great War, Jerry follows the example of his father and enlists to earn money for his family. Alexander initially feels no obligation to go to war despite the insistence of his hard-hearted mother. He only signs up out of despair after his mother shrewdly reveals that he is actually not the biological son of his much more congenial father. Jerry and Alexander manage to be stationed together in France. They are now divided not only by class but also by military rank and again their friendship must be kept secret as their commander Major Glendenning insists on the absolute separation of officers and common soldiers. When Jerry learns that his father is missing, he leaves his unit to search for him and is eventually arrested for desertion. Major Glendenning gives Alexander the order to command the firing squad that is to execute Jerry, yet, Alexander takes the life of his friend himself before the official sentence can be carried out. As a consequence, Alexander is arrested and sentenced to death.

Unlike the works of Hinkson and Barrington, the Big House in *How Many Miles to Babylon?* does not function as a comfortably detached and quaintly otherworldly realm and refuge for its Anglo-Irish inhabitants who have to endure the violent onslaught of the outside world of the 1910s and 1920s – the novel's main protagonist actually escapes from the Big House to the Great War. Also, compared to all the other works of this section, Johnston's novel only rather faintly evokes the sense of a lingering Anglo-Irish social decay apart from the domestic tensions created by the unhappy marriage of Alexander's parents. The imminent death of the Moores' only son as a consequence of his inappropriate conduct in the Great War of course means the end of the family line, yet, this aspect is not addressed in the novel in any way. Altogether, the estate itself is largely portrayed in a spirit of nostalgic relish, "the beautifully appointed house, the ceremony of living, the swans on the lovely lake" (Weekes 1990, 195) evoking an idyllic picture reminiscent of Yeats's vision of Coole Park – its inner life is a different matter.

Johnston also clearly exposes the strict social divisions inherent to her setting and the traditional isolationism of Anglo-Irish upper-class life, a condition upheld in differing degrees of harshness by Alexander's parents. His mother Alicia, introduced as cold, arrogant and 'English' from the beginning, detests any interaction with the Irish lower classes – for example, she resents Alexander's piano teacher for "dragging his disease and poverty into my drawing-room" (Johnston 2010, 6) and has him fired. Alexander's father Frederick is more good-natured, yet, he also insists on the separation of Anglo-Irish and Irish, based on his understanding of his paternalistic duties as a landlord: "It is a sad fact, boy, that one has to accept young. [...] The responsibilities and limitations of the class into which you are born. They have to be accepted. But then after all, look at the advantages. Once you accept the advantages then the rest follows. Chaos can set in so easily" (Johnston 2010, 29). This is the insular environment in which Alexander grows up, overprotected yet loveless, and devoid of social contacts beyond his parents and the servants. Alexander is aware of the opulence and weight of his ancestral heritage (cf. Diez Fabre 2006, 110); the splendour and generousness of his home increasingly appears to him as cold and oppressive, mirroring the distance and lack of intimacy between himself and his parents (cf. Berge 1994, 16): "I got down from my chair and left the room. I could feel their eyes watching me as I crossed miles of floor" (Johnston 2010, 8). Similarly, when Alexander later leaves for war and describes his awkward sending-off, he notes how his mother is "standing in the drawing room waiting for me. She threw out her arms as I came in with a splendidly theatrical gesture. I walked towards her. The room seemed to be a mile long" (Johnston 2010, 69) – Alexander's estrangement from his class and its imperatives here finds a striking spatial expression.

Alexander manages to find relief from his loneliness only in the accidental and illicit cross-class friendship with the Irish stable boy Jerry Crowe, a relationship he has to hide from his parents. The meetings with Jerry are liberating as they give Alexander opportunities to vent and speak his mind, being relegated to silence when at home (cf. Benstock 1982, 198). Also, against the restraining sophistication and culture of discipline of the Big House drawing-room, the relationship of Alexander and Jerry is characterised from the beginning by a liberating physical and homoerotic dimension. Their first meeting at the estate's lake, swimming together nude and wrestling in the grass, amounts for sheltered Alexander almost to a rite of passage, becoming aware of a world outside of the confines of his home and also discovering his own body and masculinity, as well as the curious attraction exuded by other bodies: "I had never seen a naked person before. He was much smaller than I was, with twig-like bones that seemed to want to burst out in various places from the white skin. Hair was just starting to grow on his body, in the same sort of lackadaisical way as on my own" (Johnston 2010, 11). It is also through their bodies that the class divide between Alexander and Jerry is communicated, an impression confirmed when Alexander describes how Jerry is transformed to premature adulthood in the following years by the effects of hard labour and the peasant lifestyle – "[i]t put years on his age. [...] [H]e no longer seemed to be a child" (Johnston 2010, 17) – while Alexander himself retains his essentially detached and well-groomed youthful innocence.

The coming of the Great War initiates the end of Alexander's sheltered youth and provokes a crisis of identity for Alexander as it magnifies and reinforces not only the personal divisions running through his family but the ideological divisions of Englishness and (Anglo-)Irishness embodied respectively by his mother and father. At first recognised only remotely by the Moores through the newspaper,[84] the Great War and the question of enlistment become more urgent issues after they learn of the death of a family friend in Flanders. Alicia Moore, flaunting a clichéd bellicose patriotic Englishness, begins to push for her son to enlist – "a moral duty, if nothing else. [...] Dulce et decorum est" (Johnston 2010, 40). Yet, it also becomes instantly obvious how her determination is centrally driven by the desire to contradict and offend the husband she does not love and to emphasise her non-Irishness. Contrary to his wife, the outlook of Frederick Moore is determined by a sense of 'Irish' Anglo-Irishness that does not necessitate the instinctive acceptance of English perspectives (cf. Weekes 1990, 195f.) – "I have never aspired to being an Englishman. Nor have I such aspirations for my son" (Johnston 2010, 40). Frederick Moore's concern is not the war, which he sees as an unnecessary wasting of lives, but his local paternalistic responsibility as a landlord and the wish for Alexander to live up to this role as well: "Here, the land must come first. You understand. It is this country's heart. It was taken from the people. We ...I must be clear ...We took it from the people. I would like to feel that it will, when the moment comes, be handed back in good order" (Johnston 2010, 42f.). This mind-set, Alexander's father being conscious of the oppressive foundations and the finite nature of the Anglo-Irish tradition he embodies, embracing an atypical sense of community spirit, is rare and it is typical of Johnston's integrative impetus, relativizing and humanising the much-disparaged stereotype of the Anglo-Irish landlord employed, as shown earlier, for example by Dowling.

Sensing Alexander's veering towards his father's position and his indifference to her pleas, Alexander's mother resorts to a drastic strategy of division. By revealing astutely that Alexander is not the biological son of Frederick Moore, Alicia effec-

---

84 "I'm glad to see that Mr Redmond is behaving at last in a responsible fashion" (Johnston 2010, 36), Alexander's mother remarks.

tively orphans her son, cutting him off from his Irish relations. As Margot Gayle Backus argues, "[s]he discursively enforces her son's status as English [...]. His life is to be hers and England's" (Backus 1994, 58f.) – and it is to be expended in England's war. Alexander is instantly devastated by the revelation. He is overwhelmed with a sense of displacement, feeling "the eyes of the ancestors on the walls, to whom I was now an intruder" (Johnston 2010, 48) as he walks away from the Big House. Deprived of the positive dimension of his genealogy, tradition and personal and national history (cf. Weekes 1990, 196), it seems that Alexander has no option but to adopt the tradition of his mother – he cannot exist beyond the two opposing concepts of nation embodied by his parents which confirms the observation of Ernest Gellner and others about the general inconceivability of the notion of a person not having a distinct nationality (cf. Anderson 2006, 5).

In an attempt to reclaim his Irish and his personal ties, Alexander reunites with Jerry, from whom he had become slightly estranged, and decides to enlist along with him. Their reunion is celebrated by a naked swim in the estate's lake just like during their first encounter, indicating a new phase of their friendship – however, the discomfort caused by the lake's mud, the icy water and the damp coldness of the grass spoils the mood and, more importantly, foreshadows the downturn of their bond that awaits them in the trenches of the Great War. The motivations of Jerry and Alexander to join up differ immensely. Alexander enlists for purely personal reasons, fleeing from his fraught former home. Jerry does not only enlist to receive the King's shilling like his father, his mother having "two envelopes arriving" (Johnston 2010, 16), he has also found interest in radical Irish nationalism and joins the British forces to be trained as a soldier, planning to use the military skills he will acquire in a coming Irish war against England: "[T]he moment's going to come when it'll be handy to have some men around who can do more than [parading with hurling sticks]. Maybe they'll make me a general" (Johnston 2010, 102).

Throughout the novel, Johnston offers a panoramic view of the variety of reasons for enlisting and attitudes to the Great War. There is Jerry's economic and republican reasoning and the personal escapism of Alexander, but there is also a presentation of constitutionalist Redmondite motivations, the frustrated socialist tendencies revealed by Jerry's and Alexander's comrade Bennett, the sense of duty of imperial English patriotism of Alicia Moore and the Irish rural disinterest in the war of Frederick Moore. Interestingly, apart from a condemnation of the militarist spirit at large, English or Irish, the novel does not subscribe to a single specific view – possibly an outcome of Johnston's proto-revisionist impetus. Moreover, the crass difference in political outlook and disposition to violence between Jerry and Alexander, which only becomes pronounced during their time at the front, does not affect their friendship. Jerry's vicious dream of a fast-paced and limitless guerrilla war against the English occupation of Ireland ("There'll be no trenches, no front lines. No waiting. Every town, every village will be the front line. Hill, rock, tree. They won't know which way to look. Even the children, for God's sake, will fight them", Johnston 2010, 111) repels Alexander; still, their personal bond and intimacy outweighs their political dissimilarity as much as the class divide: "We need each other though. Your kind and mine" (ibid.).

Nevertheless, also in the realm of the military and the Great War, the relationship of Alexander and Jerry must remain hidden. The class disparity of their peacetime identities is transferred to the army, as Alexander notes, "it never entered their heads that I should be anything but an officer" (Johnston 2010, 70). Alexander and Jerry are now divided even more officially by military rank, a formal hierarchical system much more clear-cut, discriminative and disciplining than that of landlord and peasant. Despite being reprimanded several times for violating the "[s]trict impersonal discipline" (Johnston 2010, 92) that Major Glendenning expects and facing increasingly harsh consequences, a newly isolated Alexander finds it impossible to abandon his entirely unpresentable longing to be with Jerry. In the face of the intensely physical experience of war, this longing acquires an even more intimate and tender physical dimension, demonstrated most vividly when Jerry, exhausted and chilled to the bones after illegally roaming the battlefields in search for his dead father, is welcomed in Alexander's arms and comforted in his bed: "My warmth was spreading through him, but the hand that clasped the back of my neck was still cold as a stone fresh from the sea. […] The beating of our hearts was like the cracking wings of swans lifting slowly from the lake, leaving disturbed water below. 'When we get home we'll get a place of our own'" (Johnston 2010, 141). Margot Gayle Backus argues how Alexander's relationship with Jerry is perceived as wrong by the military authorities not because of their emotional "sameness", their homoeroticism, but because of the difference in their class and rank – Alexander's desire would have been much more forgivable if it were directed at another officer – "his open interest in and friendship with a common Irish foot soldier seems to elicit in his commanders a horror of miscegenation" (Backus 1994, 59) and, consequently, it must be suppressed.

Furthermore, Alexander's illicit inclination also draws the attention of his English superiors to his national distinctiveness (ibid.), Alexander ironically being perceived as Irish by them. Major Glendenning suspects Alexander to be in the grip of what he calls "the Irish disease": "Disaffection. Disloyalty. Epidemics flare from time to time" (Johnston 2010, 121). Alexander's assumed Irishness is also linked with stereotypes of sentimentality, irrationality and emasculation: "How you damn

Irish expect to be able to run your own country when you can't control your own wasteful emotions" (Johnston 2010, 152) – leadership, fortitude and manhood, such attitudes suggest, are English. The figure of Major Glendenning here mirrors the "persistent terror of being emasculated" that Nirmala Erevelles identifies as integral in the military, fearing that an "'effeminate masculinity' might undermine loyalty and defence" of the nation (Erevelles 2011, 123). Still, it is impossible for Alexander to subscribe to any such polarities, eventually consciously locating himself in-between Irishness and Englishness, in-between classes, ranks and cruel ideals of masculinity: "They all want me to become a man. I found it hard to grasp what exactly this entailed. […] I had somehow in my head the misbegotten idea that it all had something to do with the exploration of darkness. The darkness that is inside. […] Does it matter whose son I am?" (Johnston 2010, 124). The decision to order Alexander to command the execution of Jerry is a cruel intervention against their non-conformity and aberrancy. Alexander's decisive resolution to kill Jerry himself is tragic but it represents also a final gesture of defiance, Alexander taking their future into his own hands, cheating the British military regime of its prey and his mother of a hero's funeral (cf. Backus 1994, 59; Berge 1994, 18). By means of his fatal decision, and also by the act of remembering and reaffirming his story in his final hours, Alexander effectively repossesses his identity, "fulfilling an ideal defined by himself" (Berge 1994, 18), finally achieving selfhood beyond the fixed categories defined by his class and rank.

Summing up, *How Many Miles to Babylon?* investigates the destructive and isolating imperatives of Irish and Anglo-Irish class and national affiliations magnified by the Great War, confronting them with individual experience and self-views. In its deliberately broad ideological scope and its description of a homosexual cross-class relationship, the novel represents a different approach to the Big House pattern and the presentation of the Great War within this genre. In his preface to the collection *The Essential Jennifer Johnston*, Sebastian Barry celebrates how there "is nothing official about Johnston, she is subversive, conservative, innovative and deeply traditional all at the same time. She is solitary and unique but completely integrated into the general *geist* and flavour of her time" (Barry 2000, xi) – the heart-breaking conclusion of *How Many Miles to Babylon?* very much is in tune with this contradictory character of Johnston's writing outlined by Barry. Considering his openly revisionist stance towards an Irish past perceived as contradictory and ambiguous, Barry's veneration of Johnston is unsurprising. Johnston has been lauded for the demythologising and humanising spirit in which she has addressed the Irish past (cf. Rosslyn 2004, 105) – the Troubles, the struggle for independence and, centrally, the Great War. She identified the Great War as the beginning of the sectarian violence in Northern Ireland since the late 1960s – "the failure of integration and reconciliation among Ireland's 'two nations'[,] she believed[,] stemmed from the First World War" (Ferriter 2005, 757). Johnston has been very much aware of the problematic status of the war in Irish historical consciousness – a condition that needs to be rectified, as becomes obvious in a 1984 interview:

> The First World War seemed to be happening on everybody's back door [...]. I think a rather sad thing has happened in Ireland about that war. Those men and what they did, without understanding what was happening at all, have now been turned into some sort of treachery. When they were making the film *How Many Miles to Babylon?* they had a hundred Irish soldiers marching around Co. Wicklow, dressed up in British uniforms [...]. I was talking to some of them, and I asked if their grandfathers fought in World War I. There was a very long silence while they all looked at me, and then one of them said: "Yes, my grandfather was a Connaught Ranger". Another said, "I had a great uncle", and somebody else said he had somebody in it. Suddenly you realised that they wouldn't admit it to each other. Of course they all had connections with the Great War. It didn't mean that their grandfathers were worse or better Irishmen. It meant that they were, in their own way, small heroes.
>
> (quoted in Boyce 2002, 207f.).

Stressing the value of individual memories and personal relations as opposed to the grander ideological contexts that have complicated Irish attitudes to the war, Johnston suggests that there is no need to be silent about the Irish stories of the Great War. This is a humanising attitude that characterises much of the contemporary Irish literary representations of the Great War that will be discussed in the following section.

III.3 Revisionist Perspectives – Re-Envisioning Ireland's Great War

As outlined in the contextual sections on history, culture and literature, Irish interest in the Great War only began to re-occur in the late 1960s and early 1970s. A revival of the war in Irish drama and, to a smaller extent, in Irish prose has taken place only since the 1980s. The profound transformation of Ireland in the second half of the twentieth century, which entailed a disruption of the collective nationalist forms of Irish identity institutionalised after the achievement of independence, is the decisive context for this re-discovery. The Irish and Northern Irish authors who have begun to re-envision and re-appropriate the Great War have been writing from a different Ireland and Northern Ireland. Most centrally, the eruption of the Troubles and the complex development of the peace process have initiated a questioning of Irish and Northern Irish political traditions and encouraged a search for the roots of sectarian violence – which were also found in the Great War. As D. G. Boyce notes, it was in this highly transformative period that the Great War came to be "perceived, rightly if belatedly, as central to the forging of Irish identities" (Boyce 2002, 207).

Apart from the conflict in Northern Ireland, also the social, economic and cultural changes Irish society had been undergoing invited a comprehensive re-consideration of what 'Irishness' actually means in "a country that has come of age" (quoted in Brown 2004, 405), which is how the historian Roy Foster described Ireland in 1986. The decades surrounding the turn to the twenty-first century have indeed been perceived as "a period of accelerated Irish history" (Middeke and Schnierer 2010, viii) in which concepts of Irish identity underwent radical change and diversification: Irish society has been transformed by the economic boom of the Celtic Tiger and the ensuing economic crises and stagnation of the following decades; immigration to Ireland has been changing parts of the country from monocultural to multicultural, adding a whole new dimension to the question of Irishness; new liberal social legislation and the influence of feminism have altered ideas of morality, family life and gender identities, and the Catholic Church in Ireland, "a casualty of belated secularisation and the actions of its own clerics" (O'Mahoney and Delanty 2001, vii), has been unable stop its downward spiral, successively losing its once supreme status as a moral institution and resource of orientation (cf. ibid. and Middeke and Schnierer 2010, viii). In these changing circumstances, Gerard Carruthers remarks, "Ireland's old distinctions of identity, even where these were crucially problematic before, are now witheringly viewed" (Carruthers 2005). Irish nationalism, the traditional source of identification in the twentieth century, has lost much of its monolithic hold, its codes of national identity being re-elaborated – however, it should be noted, this has not only resulted in a liberating and integrative renewal of Irishness, but these developments also entailed the formation of new reactionary strains characterised by materialism, selfish individualism, xenophobia and racism (cf. O'Mahoney and Delanty 2001, vii).

These conditions are indicative of a new identity crisis that is not a (post-)colonial one as in the first half of the twentieth century when Irish identity was constructed in an effort of counteracting British colonial dominance – it is a post-national(ist) crisis of identity, uncertainty about national belonging growing as established concepts of Irishness are coming under stress, Ireland becoming more contemporary and globalised, increasingly leaving behind established (anti-)British contexts in favour of wider European affiliations. There has been attested in late-twentieth-century Ireland a 'millennial urge', the sense of "a national eschatology, not the end of the Irish state but the end of the beginning of the Irish state – that is, the period encompassing the birth of a nation and a subsequent, insistent nationalism which takes precedence over less patriotic concerns" (Scott T. Cummings, quoted in Wehrmann 2010, 13f.).

The question of the national past as a resource for Irish identity still is crucial to this uncertainty. Despite the progressive and modernising changes outlined, the Irish past has remained potent and anchored in everyday Irish consciousness and political parties (O'Mahoney and Delanty 2001, 11). Patrick Lonergan pointedly addresses this contradictory condition: "'[W]e' may be wealthier, but it's not clear what the word 'we' refers to any more" (quoted in Middeke and Schnierer 2010, viii), and he also notes how in contemporary Ireland

> [the Irish] want to be seen as cosmopolitan but distinctive, traditional but not backward, authentic but not alien, forward-looking but not amnesiac. We want our present to be prosperous and our past to have been oppressive. And perhaps most difficult, we continue to seek a single narrative to explain an identity that has become diffuse.
>
> (Lonergan 2006, 316)

The single national narrative upon which Irish identity seems to have been centrally based is seen by Lonergan as failing to do justice to the complexities of both past and present Irish experience. Indeed, as previously outlined, there are sections of Irish history and identity that seemingly have become marginalised in the national narrative or have even been purged – Ireland's Great War history represents a prime example of such processes (cf. Decker 2015, 81), even if it has been officially rehabilitated as a meaningful episode at last, a century after the outbreak of the war.

As O'Mahoney and Delanty argue in their study on Irish history, nationalism and identity, "the future cannot be made until the past is better dealt with" (O'Mahoney and Delanty 2001, vii) – it is this very mind-set that underpins many contemporary literary efforts of dealing with Ireland's Great War history, most resonantly the war works of Tom Phelan, Sebastian Barry and Dermot Bolger. Before my investigation of these writings, starting with Frank McGuinness's *Observe the Sons of Ulster Marching Towards the Somme*, I will briefly look at the context of Irish historical revisionism and the interplay of history, memory and literary form that informs these works.

As mentioned earlier, Ireland has been frequently regarded as a culture almost pathologically obsessed with and determined by its past. As Audrey Eyler and Robert Garratt observe, "modern Irish culture insists upon recalling its ancient heritage in literature, art and music because the contemporary Irish political climate often evokes particular historical events" (Eyler and Garratt 1988, 7).

Moreover, Ian McBride remarks that, perhaps more than in other cultures, in Ireland "collective groups have expressed their values and assumptions through their representations of the past" (McBride 2001, 4). In such statements, there is a strong sense of the past as flexible and negotiable – crucially, as defined in the section on the theoretical contexts, 'history' indeed should be seen not as an unproblematic neutral or natural entity, as a stable, reliable or finished resource. Rather, history represents a retrospective narrative construction that reflects and fulfils the specific needs of those who remember and recollect bygone events, a subjective and purposeful structuring of the past.

It was not until the late 1970s, after a decade of sectarian violence in Northern Ireland, Ian McBride observes, that "the antithesis between history and memory became a common topic" (McBride 2001, 37) in Ireland, that the one-dimensional and teleological sense of and fixation on the grand narrative of the national(ist) past was substantially questioned. Irish history and historiography became strongly contested matters. Irish revisionism has focused on a re-evaluation and deconsecration of the Irish past, confronting what has been seen as the misuse of Irish history and public memory as a refuge to evade self-critical analysis of the present (cf. Ferriter 2005, 749).[85] Roy Foster, one of the leading voices of this reformed approach, summed up how "history" in Ireland "need no longer be a matter of guarding sacred mysteries. And to say 'revisionist' should just be another way of saying 'historian'" (quoted in Brown 2004, 405).

The emergence of Irish revisionism and its challenge to established but seemingly deficient master narratives can be seen in the general context of the decentring and reformulation of concepts of reality and history of post-modernism and within the pluralistic tendencies of cultural studies since the 1980s and 1990s that emphasised diversity, cultural variety and the contrast of modernity and tradition in an attempt to expose the complexity of Irish experience, identity and history (cf. Ferriter 2005, 751). Of course, the revisionist approach, which was inevitably unsympathetic to the primacy of Irish nationalism and its understanding of Irish history as a history of colonial distress, also provoked harsh reactions. Prominent commentators like Seamus Deane did not only criticise revisionism

---

85 In this vein, Declan Kiberd argued in the 1980s that "a real patriotism would base itself not on the broken bones and the accumulated grudges of the national past, but on an utterly open future. A true hero would thus be one who imagines future virtues, which would be admirable precisely because others could not conceive of them. In a land where the word 'past' is interchangeable with the word 'guilt', the idea of an uncertain future has a liberating force, as much because it is uncertain as because it is the future" (Kiberd 1988, 27).

for its 'pluralism' and its impossible claim to objectivity but even connected revisionism to partitionist, unionist or British colonialist attitudes (cf. Brown 2004, 406f.). Revisionism was accused of having "cleansed the Irish past of heroic figures, rejected the concept of an aboriginal Gaelic race, and replaced the central dynamic of nationhood with an emphasis on complexity, ambiguity and contingency" (McBride 2001, 39). Deane renounced what he understood to be a sense of standing in "servitude to history. [...] Freeing ourselves from that, we can begin to anticipate, not remember our future" (quoted in Herron 2004, 162). Nonetheless, revisionism and related concepts have remained an appealing, powerful and persistent attitude in Irish historical and political discourses.

Revisionist and pluralistic tendencies have also been reflected in Irish literature, an introspective tradition of writing, as mentioned earlier, which has always been strongly interested in exploring and recreating Ireland's past.[86] There has been a potent inclination in much Irish writing since the 1980s, particularly in drama, towards the debunking of a glorious and heroic Irish nationalist history and a deflation of nostalgic longings and melancholia for a lost past (Middeke and Schnierer 2010, x) – this is often achieved by the use of specific perspectives of memory and (historical) storytelling. The contemporary dramatic and prose works dealing with the Great War to be discussed in the following very much belong to this branch of writing, employing revisionist strategies in their re-construction of an ambiguous and long-neglected episode of Irish history. They strongly focus on acts of remembrance, operating at the intersection of official, collective and personal memory – in fact, frequently "memory, history and imagination are collapsed into one another" (Price 2015, 34). In this manner, authors like McGuinness and Barry attempt to break up the traditional polarisation of Irish history and identities – as Nicholas Grene argues, they work against the "Manichaean construction of Irish history as us and them" (Grene 1999, 244).

Altogether, the works of to be discussed in the following can be categorised as versions of the history play (and the historical novel, taking into account Barry's *A Long Long Way*).[87] They do not simply reproduce 'history' but create narratives

---

86 This preference has also provoked acerbic criticism. For example, Lynda Henderson sees in the dominance of historical themes in Irish drama "a perverse desire to remain fallen, to make no attempt to rise, to spend your life contemplating your navel [...]. Too many contemporary Irish plays bleat plaintively of old wounds" (quoted in Gleitman 2004, 218).

87 This is not to unduly equate the genres of the history play and the historical novel. Furthermore, I would like to express my awareness of the fact that also the Irish and Anglo-Irish war works of the period before the 1980s are "history" works in the sense

of the past, giving new shape to specific sections of the past (cf. Tetzeli von Rosador 1976, 31) while referring to present Irish conditions in various degrees of directness. Along these lines, these works do not only put 'historical' moments, figures and objects on stage, but also examine the very processes of how history or, rather, histories are constructed, thereby questioning the historical attitudes and beliefs of the audience (cf. Berninger 2006, 48). They attempt to revise and destabilise established historical narratives by repositioning the dramatic scope to the historical experience of people on the margins of those narratives (cf. Berninger 2006, 78f.). They re-construct history from the bottom up,[88] a concept that has also been investigated by Michel Foucault in his concept of 'popular memory', an unofficial form of remembrance which Foucault sees as the preserve of those marginalised in dominant discourse (cf. Misztal 2003, 61f.). Somewhat ironically, several of the works that re-envision Ireland's marginalised story of the Great War have since become well-integrated into reformed official discourses of remembrance.[89]

Revisionist history plays also frequently depart from conventional forms of dramatic presentation and storytelling, which is the case in all of the dramatic works to be discussed in the following. They make use of unconventional and frequently poetic and ritualistic forms of 'historical' presentation and remembrance, thereby largely eschewing the standard emblematic imagery of the Great War – in this manner, they do not only re-imagine the past but also the discourses of the past. The first two works to be covered in this chapter, McGuinness's *Observe the Sons of Ulster Marching Towards the Somme* and Reid's *My Name, Shall I Tell You My Name?*, examine fractured Northern Irish memory by means of spectral appearances and painful intergenerational discord and alienation. They are obviously rooted in the

---

that they reconstruct a specific historical situation. However, I would like to apply the genre category of the history play and historical novel rather to those more recent works as their temporal and cultural distance from the Great War is more telling regarding the notion of the "history of the history" they include and the significance of the portrayed past situation for the present. The dialectic tension between memory and history, knowledge then and knowledge now, that classically characterises the history play and the historical novel, is much more pronounced in those 'modern' texts.

88 It would be of course problematic to speak of a 'bottom up' approach, for example, when the war experiences of the declining but still privileged Anglo-Irish are addressed. In this case, 'bottom up' should be understood not in socio-economic terms but as a reference to their being rendered historically irrelevant.

89 See, for example, the 1994 performance of McGuinness's *Observe the Sons of Ulster Marching Towards the Somme* in the introductory part of section III.3.1 and, even more strikingly, Dermot Bolger's play *Walking the Road* which was commissioned by the In Flanders Fields Museum and publically funded (cf. chapter III.3.5).

revisionist spirit of the 1980s and investigate the Northern Irish legacy of the Great War in a shared effort of "breaking through silence and fanaticism" (Tylee 2001, 280), which, as will be shown, also includes challenges to the gender politics of militarism and traditional Ulster unionist militancy.

III.3.1 Frank McGuinness's *Observe the Sons of Ulster Marching Towards the Somme* (1985)

Frank McGuinness regards himself as "both a Catholic and Northern Irish writer in the broadest sense of both words" (Jordan 2010, 234). He was born in Buncrana, Co. Donegal, in 1953 and it seems as if his provenance from this northernmost county of the Republic of Ireland, geographically fairly isolated and bordering on the west of Northern Ireland, is reflected in his dramatic works which so frequently draw on experiences of liminality, marginalisation and isolation, McGuinness focusing on the perspectives of outsiders (cf. Lojek 1997, 218). McGuinness's 1985 play *Observe the Sons of Ulster Marching Towards the Somme* is representative of this dramatic interest in marginality, showing the war experiences of eight men of the 36th Ulster Division. McGuinness investigates Ulster unionism, a culture rarely presented on stage and often stereotypically regarded as cheerless, unimaginative, isolationist and scarred by negativity (cf. Lojek 2007, 82).

Observe the Sons of Ulster has attained the status of an iconic war play. It probably is the most widely received, critically acclaimed and thoroughly examined literary work addressing the Irish history of the Great War, also having seen several landmark productions in Ireland, Northern Ireland and abroad (cf. Pine 2010, 59). It was the play to establish Frank McGuinness as one of Ireland's foremost contemporary playwrights, McGuinness receiving an impressive number of awards for this work, his fourth play, which also would mark his departure from traditional realism to a fusion of dream, memory, fantasy and realism (cf. Lojek 1997, 221). With *Observe the Sons of Ulster*, McGuinness addressed a topic and area of Irish and Northern Irish experience that he felt was undeservedly underrepresented, effectively setting out to expiate the fraught history of the Great War in Irish writing. He has been outspoken about the taboo connected to the topic, embodied by the "curse [that] came upon the Irish theatre with the rejection of *The Silver Tassie*" (quoted in Grene 1999, 244), a condition that needed to be rectified – also along these lines, McGuinness's play "represents […] a new sort of imaginative reaching out in Irish drama" (ibid.).

The remarkable critical acclaim of *Observe the Sons of Ulster* is not only the result of the play's inherent qualities but it also reflects its relevance considering the political situation of its time, striking a nerve in 1980s Ireland and Northern

Ireland, a time marked by sectarian violence and tense negotiations about a way out of the conflict, about the co-existence of the two 'traditions' on the island. The play, Margaret Llewellyn-Jones notes, sympathetically represents "a historical moment in which the complexities of identity resonate with the particular Irish political context" (Llewellyn-Jones 2002, 51). It has been seen as an inspiring gesture of cross-sectarian understanding, McGuinness explaining and thereby humanising the unionist north through his play.[90] Reviewers have praised "the compassionate insight that McGuinness (a Catholic) brought to Ulster Protestantism" (Lojek 1997, 221), and McGuinness himself described working on the play as "an eye-opener for a Catholic republican, as I am, to have to examine the complexity, diversity, disturbance and integrity of the other side, the Protestant people" (quoted in Pine 2010, 59), exploring unionist identities, imaginatively engaging with the question of "what makes them them" (Grene 1999, 244).[91]

The play was first performed at the Abbey's Peacock Stage in February 1985 and the production subsequently toured Ireland and Northern Ireland with great success; new productions in London and the US followed. One of the most memorable productions of *Observe the Sons of Ulster* took place in 1994, when the play was staged at the Abbey Theatre for an audience of Ulster unionists to commemorate the IRA ceasefire (cf. Price 2015, 35) – an event that illustrates, on the one hand, the overall embeddedness of theatre in Irish political and historical discourses and, on the other hand, the increasingly acknowledged connection of the Great War and the Troubles.

The subject matter that McGuinness chose to investigate in his play, story of the 36th Ulster Division and the Battle of the Somme, represents, as explained earlier, a cornerstone of Ulster unionist identity. The narrative of the Ulstermen at the Somme is integral to the traditional national self-image and has been perpetuated

---

90 The play was turned down by the 'anti-revisionist' Field Day Theatre Company which, Graham Price argues, perhaps "reflects the nationalist strand that ran through that group. The plays that were staged by Field Day, while not exactly dogmatic, certainly did not attempt to grapple with the alternative to Catholic nationalism that exists in the North" (Price 2015, 36).

91 However, more recent criticism has also confronted the play for reinforcing historical divisions instead of dismantling them, McGuinness essentially repeating the partitioned memory of the Great War by exclusively focusing on the unionist experience instead of depicting the shared suffering of soldiers from Ireland, regardless of their political or religious affiliations. In this vein, Seamus O'Malley suggests that "McGuinness tries to make a sympathetic gesture across a partisan divide but this very gesture actually creates division where need be none: the war itself was a shared experience" (O'Malley 2012, 120) – "McGuinness – and his critics – do not bridge that gap" (O'Malley 2012, 121).

in Northern Ireland in a large variety of forms, albeit not extensively through literature. It has become a vital part of the rituals and imagery of the Orange Order and the British Legion, just as it has been featured in paramilitary displays, in popular songs and in murals, while the Somme Association and Somme Heritage Centre continue to provide official information on the topic (cf. Officer 2001, 161).

The tradition of the Somme upon which these groups, activists and institutions draw is longstanding. Within days after its beginning, the Battle of the Somme was integrated into a rich and complex web of unionist and imperial narratives. This was centrally driven by an effort to make sense of the traumatic losses that the Ulster Division suffered, approximately 6,000 Ulstermen being killed only on the first day of battle. In Ulster public discourses, the Somme was instantly contextualised within a history of Ulster sacrificial patriotism, along with such feats as the Siege of Derry of 1688 and the Battle of the Boyne of 1690 – consequently, the Ulster Division quickly became a paradigm of patriotic martyrdom. This sense of continuity and tradition becomes specifically obvious in the powerful image of Ulster soldiers allegedly storming into battle shouting "No surrender!" (a reference to the Siege of Derry) and "Remember the Boyne!", a myth popularised in the British and Northern Irish press that would underscore the organic relationship of the Ulster Division, the Ulster Volunteer Force and the Orange Order (cf. Officer 2001, 168; 180).

The Ulster Division was seen as practically identical with Ulster itself in public discourses of the time. As a commentator in the *Belfast Newsletter* of 8 July 1916 glories, also revealing the isolationism of Ulster unionism, "no other Division can stand for any other section of the people of the United Kingdom. It typifies us in all that we cherish and stand for, and all that we are in the eyes of the rest of the nation, whatever view they take of us" (quoted in Officer 2001, 170). In this manner, the Ulster Division was constructed to embody the northern unionist community as a whole, being envisioned as a force of good not only directed against the evil of German aggression against Britain but also against the evil of Irish nationalism (cf. Officer 2001, 166). Of course, these allegiances were understood within a context that surpassed the immediate situation of the Great War. Consequently, the Ulster Division was ascribed the status of a "transhistorical being in the world which would demand an obligation from those who came after" (Officer 2001, 173), being presented "not only as unambiguously displaying a transcendental essence which united past generations but also as a model for future generations" (Officer 2001, 171). It is exactly this transhistorical condition which is taken up and scrutinised in McGuinness's play: The notion of a violent history of sacrifice and separatism that painfully underpins Ulster unionism and determines its future, the play's protagonists being torn between the inherited violent imperatives of their collective identities as Ulster unionists and soldiers, and their individual perceptions and urges in the moments of crisis to which they are exposed in the Great War.

Observe the Sons of Ulster is episodic in structure and begins with an invocation of memory. In the first act, entitled "Remembrance", the main protagonist Kenneth Pyper, an old man, is haunted by the ghosts of his fallen comrades, prompting him once again to reluctantly remember their service in the Great War. The second act, "Initiation", shows the arrival of young Pyper at an army training camp along with seven other volunteers from all over Ulster. While his comrades enlisted for King and Country and for their Protestant beliefs, eccentric Pyper, a sexually ambiguous upper-class drop-out from a prominent Northern Irish family, joined up in a rare act of class defiance with the goal of being killed. The third act, "Pairing", shows the men home on leave, appearing as pairs in symbolic Ulster locations. Marked by their experiences at the front and having lost their faith in the war, now only their friendship, intimacy and the suffering they collectively endured matter. Returning to the front, the fourth and final act, entitled "Bonding", shows how despite their disillusionment the Ulstermen, including Pyper, are united by personal solidarity and how they are ready to fight, storming off into the Battle of the Somme. The play ends in a ritualistic encounter of young and old Pyper that concludes this cycle of Pyper's remembrance.

From the start, the play establishes a mode of sceptical retrospection, a sentiment of uncertainty concerning the authenticity and reliability of memory that takes up and radicalises the retrospective narrative situation established in Johnston's *How Many Miles to Babylon?*. Incessantly tortured by the images of the past and by survivor's guilt, old Pyper angrily confronts the ghosts of his past:

> I do not understand your insistence on my remembrance. I'm being too mild. I am angry at your demand that I continue to probe. Were you not there in all your dark glory? [...] There is nothing to tell you. Those willing to talk of you that day, to remember for your sake, to forgive you, they invent as freely as they wish. I am not one of them. I will not talk, I will not listen to you. Invention gives that slaughter shape. That scale of horror has no shape, as you in your darkness have no shape.
>
> (McGuinness 1996, 97)

Old Pyper, Tom Herron observes, is trapped in "a condition of past-present, in equal parts monotonous and urgent" (Herron 2004, 136). He has no choice but to talk and remember, and he is torn between having to acknowledge the scandalous artificiality of Ulster myths of war and embracing the same myths in order to find some meaning, to find a reason for the slaughtering and for his existence, particularly now, in the present, when Pyper is distressed by a modern, partitioned Ulster in decline, an Ulster that appears to him to have "grown lonely" (McGuinness 1996, 99), lying "in rubble at our feet" (McGuinness 1996, 100). Centrally, it is subjective personal remembrance that shapes the play, the above quoted opening monologue setting the play's tone. As Emilie Pine argues, McGuinness's fundamental concern is "how to put shape on the Unionist experience of the First World War, culminating in the Battle of the Somme, and how that experience should be remembered [...]; what the audience sees is always viewed through the lens of memory" (Pine 2010, 60) – and Pyper varies his recollection between triumphalism, playfulness and utter despair (ibid.). The question of identity, Pyper rejecting, transcending and appropriating the established categories of "Ulsterman", "unionist", "soldier", and "man", is integral to the play's agenda. McGuinness's introduction of the split self – the simultaneous appearance of old Pyper and young Pyper on stage – reveals a profound sense of fractured identities (cf. Llewellyn-Jones 2002, 50).

Old Pyper begins the painful process of the re-construction of his Great War experience by looking back at the days of training, his arrival and reception in the army. Throughout this part, Young Pyper functions as a disruptive element in the community of the eight Ulster volunteers who inhabit the makeshift barracks on stage. Significantly, McGuinness designed Pyper's comrades as to reflect the variety of Ulster identities and backgrounds, representing the six counties of Ulster as well as different classes and temperaments. McGuinness thus resists the stereotypical homogenisation of Ulstermen into the single emblematic image of radical Belfast working-class men (cf. Grene 1999, 247). However, the play's Ulstermen, apart from Pyper, are also united even before they meet by their unionism and their rejection of Catholics and "Fenian rats" (McGuinness 1996, 122), almost all of them having joined the army in a spirit of Carsonite duty (cf. Gleitman 2004, 220). It is this ideological foundation of his comrades' identities that Young Pyper, more intelligent, experienced and daring than his peers and quickly identified as an outsider, "a bit of a mocker" (McGuinness 1996, 104), "a madman" (McGuinness 1996, 106) and a "rare boyo" (McGuinness 1996, 110), sets out to destabilise. Almost delightfully, Pyper creates unease, doubt and suspicion among the other men through his cynicism and role-playing, recognising the gravity of their situation (cf. Backus 1994, 53), undermining the unity of the group, with which he cannot bond at this point. Pyper derides the hopes and expectations of his comrades, confronts them with fierce official military discourse and challenges their motivations:

PYPER: You are here as a volunteer in the army of your king and empire. You are here to train to meet that empire's foe. You are here as a loyal son of Ulster, for the empire's foe is Ulster's foe. You are here to learn, Mr Millen. Learn to defend yourself and your comrades, and while you are here, you will learn to conduct yourself with respect, respect for this army, respect for your position in this army, and respect for all other positions above you. Since there are no ranks beneath you, you will never be at ease again until you leave this army. Do you understand that clearly?

(McGuinness 1996, 107)

PYPER: Why spend your time here?
CRAIG: It goes without saying.
PYPER: Say it.

(McGuinness 1996, 115)

MILLEN: We'll all survive. This is the best army on God's good earth.
PYPER: But we're the scum of it. We go first.
CRAIG: Not if we fight together.
PYPER: We will go first, David.

(McGuinness 1996, 135)

The unsettling of his comrades' convictions also extends to religious certainties and, very expressively, aspects of masculinity and sexual orientation. Pyper's parading of effeminate qualities and frequent homoerotic innuendo in the first part of the play disturbs and bewilders the other men, just as his provocative anecdote of having been married to a French Catholic whore, and the act of punching one of his companions in the groin to punish him for his aggressive macho antics (cf. Gleitman 2004, 221). In such moments, Pyper's role as a trickster figure becomes obvious. As Helen Gilbert and Joanne Tompkins note, "the trickster evades and disrupts all conventional categories, including those corporeal hierarchies upon which various forms of discrimination are based. [...] [T]he trickster's androgyny breaks down binary definitions of gender and thus defers, rather than defers to, gender-based authority systems" (Gilbert and Tompkins 1996, 235). Pyper's ostensible defeatism indeed can be seen as related to his non-uniform masculinity and the increased sense of self-awareness it seems to have forced upon him. It is this non-conformity that enables him to gain a detached viewpoint from which to examine and criticise the sectarian culture in which he was raised and which shaped his comrades and drove them into the British army (cf. O'Malley 2012, 112).

Consequently, Pyper's decision to enlist at first appears paradoxical; it is only explained and resolved in the following act. It becomes apparent that Pyper is a "gay man grappling with multiple identities formed in relation to Northern Irish political realities" (Cadden 2006, 560). He discloses that he comes from a prominent Protestant upper-class family which he left behind for a more independent life as an artist in Paris. Interestingly, like the other upper-class Anglo-Irish figures in the war works covered in this study, Pyper must find out that, eventually, it is impossible for him to escape his confining original identity and to resist the role imposed on him by family tradition, by history itself – yet, his departure into war is not entirely involuntary:

> I escaped Carson's dance. I got out to create, not to destroy. But the gods wouldn't allow that. I could not create. [...] I couldn't look at my life's work, for when I saw my hands working they were not mine but the hands of my ancestors, interfering. [...] I was contaminated. I smashed my sculpture and I rejected any woman who would continue my breed. [...] And I would destroy my own life. I would take up arms at the call of my Protestant fathers. I would kill in their name and I would die in their name. To win their respect would be my sole act of revenge, revenge for the bad joke they had played on me in making me sufficiently different to believe I was unique [...].
>
> (McGuinness 1996, 163f.)

Pyper's enlisting thus becomes an act of defiance and self-destruction. His initial goal is to subvert the values, myths and identity concept for which his family stands (cf. Grene 1999, 246), and to die, effectively ending his family line and its inherited lust for bloodshed. In Pyper's confessions, McGuinness foregrounds both the constructedness of sectarian traditions and their irresistible destructive force, something that McGuinness himself once addressed when he called memory "a lethal cultural weapon" (quoted in Lojek 1988, 64). Pyper does acknowledge his complicity in this process, when he admits that "I turned my ancestors into Protestant gods. [...] So I could rebel against them. I would not serve. [...] But the same gods have brought me back" (McGuinness 1996, 150f.).

The workings, failures and inescapability of such myths and their effects on group identities and self-perception dominate the rest of the play. In the third act, "Pairing", the soldiers return home on leave to a strangely empty Ulster, obviously transformed by their war experiences and estranged from their pre-war selves. McGuinness arranges the soldiers as pairs who visit different Ulster locations, a Protestant church, Boa Island at Lough Erne, a suspended rope bridge, and the Field, an Orange marching ground. The pairing suggests that it has become impossible for the men to leave the war context and reclaim individual identities, to exist on their own beyond their military identity – tellingly, there is no interaction with non-military characters and there are also no female figures in the play. In this act, each man experiences something akin to an epiphany (cf. Kiberd 2005, 287): Pyper becomes aware of the futility of his rebellion but also of his love for his comrades, while the others must realise that their service in the war really is not a crusade in the name of the King and a Protestant god but that they will be needlessly sacrificed. The men no longer feel encouraged by the coherent world view which previously sustained them and they recognise that they have nowhere to turn to but to themselves (cf. Gleitman 2004, 221). As Crawford muses, "What am I? I'll tell you. I'm a soldier that risks his neck for no cause other than the men he's fighting with. I've seen enough to see through empires, kings and countries. I know the only side worth supporting is your own sweet self" (McGuinness 1996, 152) – an affirmation of the power of private unions over public ones energised by myths of pride, violence and hatred.

The increasingly questionable stability of unionist identities and myth in the second half of the play becomes most pronounced in several failed unionist rituals of commemoration, even unsettling the play's most radical advocates of Ulster Protestantism, McIlwaine and Anderson. The two soldiers attempt to stage an Orange parade to celebrate the "Twelfth", the anniversary of the Battle of the Boyne on 12 July, which they missed at the front. However, instead of demonstrating their pride and determination, their re-enactment tilts and turns into a symbol of their despair and of the integral hollowness of public ritual that manifests itself when taken out of its communal context:

> McIlwaine: It is no good here on your own. No good without the speakers. No good without the bands, no good without the banners. Without the chaps. [...] Why did we come here, Anderson?
> Anderson: To beat a drum.
>
> (McGuinness 1996, 148)

What follows is a hesitant performance on the traditional Lambeg drum by McIlwaine and Anderson's imitation of the Grand Master of the Orange Lodge, delivering a manic speech abounding in hateful anti-Catholic clichés and the demand to die for Ulster, ending in a physical as well as spiritual collapse and the admission that "Pyper the bastard was right, it's all lies. We're going to die for nothing" (McGuinness 1996, 167).

The play denies a way out. Ulster's cult of sacrifice, how contradictory and vulnerable it might seem at this point, has trapped the men (cf. Boyce 2002, 210). None of them has the capacity to reformulate their position, to resist the certain downfall awaiting them and to escape the regime and cult of death to which they have been inevitably submitted as Ulster unionists. The final act, entitled "Bonding", shows the group in the trenches on the morning of the first day of the Battle of the Somme, preparing their attack. In two further moments of failed remembrance, originally intended to psych the soldiers up for combat, the play again underlines the mutability and unreliability of myth and historical narratives. First, McIlwaine's recounting of the Easter Rising turns out to be ineffective burlesque propaganda, denigrating, also in a highly gendered fashion, the efforts and ideals of the nationalist rebels (cf. O'Malley 2012, 114). In McIlwaine's story, Patrick Pearse is ridiculed as a "boy who took over a post office because he was short of a few stamps" (McGuinness 1996, 175), and who is later shot by his own mother. The story fails to fortify the group's damaged spirit of unionist superiority, just as the other reconstruction of the past orchestrated by the soldiers, an absurd re-enactment of the Battle of the Boyne. Since there are not enough men to depict the Boyne in the trenches, McIlwaine and Anderson decide to re-enact the Battle of Scarva instead, a popular mock-battle of the Boyne presented every year on 13 July in a small village in Co. Down. As Emilie Pine notes, the "instability of the myth is already implicit within the fact that the men are performing a version of a version" (Pine 2010, 62), and despite Anderson reminding his fellow actors to keep to the result of a Protestant victory, Pyper, who plays the horse of William of Orange, trips and the Protestant king on his shoulders, destined to win, crashes to the ground – a failure interpreted by the men as "not the best of signs" (McGuinness 1996, 188) for the things to come.

Facing imminent carnage, a sentiment of pragmatism and fatalistic joking takes over, yet, in the final moments of the play, the disillusioned soldiers manage to re-establish a fighting spirit. This, however, is achieved not as much through another invocation of unionist mythology and narratives but rather by the men's conscious appreciation of their loyalty, their intimate group identity, acknowledging the closeness to each other beyond their differences, effectively forming a community of fate – unionist discourses only provide a loose thematic framework for these unifying processes. This new condition is exemplified most vividly by the integration of the former eccentric and iconoclast Pyper, who accepts the Orange sash given to him by Anderson before battle, "so we'll recognise you as one of our own" (McGuinness 1996, 193). The ritualistic exchanging of Orange sashes among the eight men that follows further equalises the group and bolsters communal spirit – importantly, the separatist ideology implied by the sashes remains unexpressed in this moment, the sashes function first and foremost as markers of belonging, not as markers of belligerent unionism.

Similarly, in his final prayer before going into battle, a newly empowered Pyper, now assuming the leading role for which he was originally determined, does resort to Unionist discourse, inevitably invoking the "Protestant" god to make "this day at the Somme [...] as glorious in the memory of Ulster as that day at the Boyne" (McGuinness 1996, 196) – however, the emphasis of his prayer is not on bloodshed, sacrifice and hateful separatism, but on survival, protection and love for his companions and his "personal" Ulster:

Lead us back from this exile. To Derry, to the Foyle. To Belfast and the Lagan. To Armagh, to Tyrone. To the Bann and its banks. To Erne and its islands. Protect us. Protect me. Let us fight bravely. Let us win gloriously. Lord, look down on us. Spare us. I love –. Observe the sons of Ulster marching Towards the Somme. I love their lives. I love my own life. I love my home. I love my Ulster. Ulster. Ulster. Ulster. Ulster [...].

(McGuinness 1996, 196)

Significantly, there is only little notion of the inherited hatred and violence of "No surrender!" in Pyper's prayer – it is not just a straightforward "warmongering sermon" (Pine 2010, 64) as which Emilie Pine has assessed it, and Pyper's identity in these concluding moments, I would suggest, has not really been transformed from liminal sceptic to a "righteous scourge of unionism" (Gleitman 2004, 223) as Claire Gleitman argues – Pyper's late adoption of unionist discourses could rather be seen as driven by his formal acceptance of homosocial (and, considering Pyper's special bonding with Craig, homosexual) collectivity and, Graham Price argues, of "his role as private individual within a broader community and tradition" (Price 2015, 43). Pyper's new found love for Ulster could also be seen as the result of a sublimation of his love for companions (cf. Cadden 2006, 562). The sense of unification evoked in these scenes, interspersed by modified Ulster rituals, corresponds to the observations of Gilbert and Tompkins in their study of metamorphic bodies in post-colonial drama, who argue that "[t]raditional enactments such as ritual and carnival demonstrate that the performing body can help to regenerate and unify communities despite the disabilities, disintegrations, and specific disconnections of the individual bodies involved" (Gilbert and Tompkins 1996, 231).

The men storm off to fight, Pyper's "Ulster" chant "turn[ing] into a battle cry, reaching frenzy" (McGuinness 1996, 196), yet, the play ends on a sombre note: Old Pyper, the lone survivor of the battle, reappears on stage and confronts Young Pyper – a ghostly converging of different temporalities in the 'hauntological' sense of Derrida mentioned earlier. Contrasted with his younger self, the old man embodies Ulster's entrapment in the past – old Pyper is the disillusioned result of the failure of the Ulster imagined, remembered and ritualised in the decades after the war and of the demise of the homosocial/homosexual bond that once gave meaning to his existence. This is confirmed in the ritualistic exchange that concludes the play: "The house has grown cold, the province has grown lonely. [...] You'll always guard Ulster. [...] Dance in this deserted temple of the Lord" (McGuinness 1996, 197). Pyper is left only with the burden of his memories.

To conclude, with *Observe the Sons of Ulster*, McGuinness provides an intriguing perspective on the Great War and its interplay of public and personal identities. He constructs a view that reflects marginality and distance in multiple ways (cf. Kosok 2012, 234): A Catholic author from the Republic of Ireland, McGuinness sympathetically depicts the Great War experiences of Protestant Ulster unionists, a milieu rarely dramatized, and within this presentation he confronts and destabilises the identity-defining certainties of the group portrayed by means of a homosexual main protagonist; furthermore, writing almost seventy years after the Somme, McGuinness employs a subjective perspective of memory, underlining the variability of remembrance and the dangers of partisan uses of the past. McGuinness's re-imagining of the mythically burdened story of the Ulstermen at the Somme also represents a comment on the condition of Ulster, as well as Ireland, at the time of the play's creation. It reveals the conditional, contradictory and performative nature of unionism (cf. O'Malley 2012, 112), how unionist identity is "constructed around lack" (Kiberd 2005, 296) and negativity, and how the "rhythm of myth is out of step with the rhythm of life" (Pine 2010, 62), the play presenting the distressing entrapment of Ulster identities founded on a mythical past. The play's exposure of the manipulative powers of memory and ideology represents a warning and a critique that is also directed at McGuinness's own side, the Catholic Irish from the Republic and their myths – as Eamonn Jordan notes, the play "chimes with nationalist commemorations of the Easter Rising" (Jordan 2010, 238). McGuinness hints at the possibility of a more humane sense of community and identity surpassing partisan definitions and embracing intimacy. Finally, as Declan Kiberd remarks, the play "proposes that all fixed identities are dangerous and deathly, but that to live without some form of identity is impossible" (Kiberd 2005, 296) – this is the dilemma of Pyper that underscores his entrapment among the ghosts of the past and that encourages not only Irish and Northern Irish audiences to rethink inherited positions and self-views.

The next work to be discussed, Christina Reid's *My Name, Shall I Tell You My Name?* (1987) shares many aspects with McGuinness's play despite its extended scope and its different dramatic setup as a short radio play. Again, the destructive grip of a violent and militant past, particularly the memory of the Battle of the Somme, on Northern Irish identities and the Northern Irish present is investigated, however, this time it is not only the troubled veteran trapped in his memories which takes centre-stage but also his granddaughter and her memories of him, Reid providing an explicitly female and essentially pacifist response to war.

III.3.2 Christina Reid's *My Name, Shall I Tell You My Name?* (1987)

While McGuinness's *Observe the Sons of Ulster* represents an imaginative and symbolic act of a Catholic from the Republic of Ireland reaching out to the 'foreign' rival culture of Ulster unionism, Christina Reid's *My Name, Shall I Tell You My*

Name? comes from the very heart of this milieu. Reid (1942–2015) was born into a Belfast working-class family described as "fiercely Protestant" (Delgado 1997, vii) and "utterly unionist" (Große 2010, 285), her father acting as the head of an Orange lodge. It is this environment that dominates Reid's dramatic oeuvre, including *My Name*, depicting Northern Irish family life at the intersection of public and private life, of domesticity and politics. Reid's works reflect how in Northern Ireland, as Christian Große notes, "every action, even a seemingly private one [...], is political, and public conflicts are often dealt with at home" (Große 2010, 398). As a dramatist, Reid has been located in the tradition of Sean O'Casey as a chronicler of the life and desperation of the urban working class and the poor of Northern Ireland, frequently evoking the mock-heroism but also the humour and musicality of O'Casey (cf. Tylee et al. 1999, 211; Tylee 2001, 281f.). Like O'Casey, Patrick Lonergan notes, Reid employs a "gendered perspective to think about heroism, military sacrifice, cycles of violence, and the legacies of the past" (Lonergan 2015).

A central concern of Reid's works is the omnipresence of these legacies – national, regional, religious or familial – and the confrontation of her female protagonists with the past while seeking a coherent and sustaining self-vision, frequently finding themselves at odds with the powerful narratives and memories that define family life and their position within Northern Irish unionist culture (cf. McDonough 1997, 300f.; Große 2010, 396). Along these lines, Reid sets out to expose the fissures of her community, deconstructing the traditional dichotomies that have fuelled sectarian conflict and restricted personal freedom by employing intersecting storylines, "merging past and present, dreams and memories, oral traditions and visual metaphors" (Delgado 1997, xvi).

Within these schemes, the experiences of women are of vital importance. Through her concentration on traditionally disenfranchised female perspectives, Reid can be seen to add a matrilineal narrative of Northern Ireland to the traditional patrilineal one (Große 2010, 398; 402). This female view frequently is more complex and compassionate than the dominant male one and, unlike their male counterparts, Reid's dynamic female protagonists often have the capacity to rethink inherited beliefs and roles and to seek compromise in a static and destructive environment created by a male fixation on traditionalism in Northern Ireland (cf. McDonough 1997, 301; Große 2010, 297). "Northern Ireland," as Elizabeth Shannon noted in the late 1980s, "is like a secret society for men – they belong to all-male clubs, invent childlike mysterious handshakes, march to loud drumbeats, make deals, stir up hatreds – and try to find solutions to problems men have created" (quoted in Tylee 2001, 285) – Reid's works both illustrate the consequences of this condition as well as women's responses to it.

These patterns are also prominent in *My Name, Shall I Tell You My Name?*, Reid's intergenerational and cross-gender investigation of the determining and destructive power of memory and tradition in Northern Ireland. Like many of Reid's works, the play includes autobiographical elements, most centrally in the character of the Great War veteran Andy, the grandfather of the main protagonist – as Reid recalls,

> [m]y grandfather was like that. When I asked him about the Somme he talked about valour, patriotism, loyalty. He won't question it. He couldn't because to question war would have meant questioning his peacetime allegiances too, King and Country, God and Ulster. Everything he'd lived and survived by.
>
> (quoted in Liddy 2010, 64)

Another precursor to the figure of Andy can be found in Reid's earlier play *Tea in a China Cup* (1983) where the unnamed "Grandfather", a minor character, is also a proud veteran who cannot leave behind the old belligerence and needs to be contained by his level-headed wife:

> GRANDFATHER: I was in the trenches in France when I was little more than a lad. It never did me no harm.
> GRANDMOTHER: Oh, aye, I suppose you were born with that bit of shrapnel in your leg.
> GRANDFATHER: I'd do it again gladly, if they'd have me, for my King and Country.
> GRANDMOTHER: But they won't have you, will they, because your oul chest is still full of gas from the last great war.
>
> (Reid 1997a, 11)

This is exactly the pattern of harmful and persistent male patriotic intransigence and a female response to it that underpins the conflict portrayed in *My Name*.

My Name was originally written as a radio play for two voices and premiered in 1987 on BBC Radio 4. It was subsequently re-arranged for the stage for the 1989 Dublin Theatre Festival and transferred to the Young Vic Studio in London in the following year.[92] While some contemporary critics found fault with the overly wide range of issues discussed in the play – unionism, republicanism, sectarianism, feminism, racism, the Great War, the Falklands War and contemporary politics, pacifism – others praised the fierce poignancy of the work (cf. McDonough 1997, 305), the play distinctively echoing the tense and increasingly transformative condition of Northern Ireland during the 1980s, a period marked by terrorism and sectarian

---

92 Still, none of Reid's works have been staged at a major venue in the Republic of Ireland to this day (cf. Große 2010, 286).

violence as well as by more substantial efforts of ending the Troubles, such as the 1985 Anglo-Irish Agreement, which was ferociously attacked by unionists.

The one-act memory play takes the form of a complex episodic confrontation of the memories of Andrea, aged twenty-four, and Andy, her 93-year-old grandfather, Andrea reworking their eventual estrangement. The year is 1986. The two characters are separated from each other on stage, Andrea sitting in a London prison cell while Andy is in his room in an old people's home in Derry. The indirect dialogue of Andrea and Andy that evolves from their separate retrospective reflections is interspersed with recordings of them from Andrea's childhood in Northern Ireland, resulting in an intriguing and suggestive interplay of past and present perspectives. The play begins with Andrea's memories of her affectionate upbringing as "Granda's pet" (Reid 1997, 253), being Andy's favourite grandchild. However, Andrea also has since become aware of Andy's unionist radicalism, of his obsession with military discipline, his fierce sense of paternal authority and, centrally, his distorted but unrestrained pride as a veteran of the Battle of the Somme. Shunning the grim and divided realities of the war, Andy would insist on recounting the glorious sacrificial feats of the Protestant Ulstermen at the front and on drilling his seven year old granddaughter to learn the names of his comrades by heart, making sure that Andrea is brought up in his bellicose and nostalgic spirit. Andrea proceeds to recount her much-resented move to London as a young woman to become an artist and study drama, where she soon fell in love with Hanif, who is half-Pakistani. The only instance of direct on-stage interaction between Andrea and Andy in the play is a re-enactment of Andrea's last visit to her grandfather in the days of the Falklands War. When Andrea admits to Andy that her boyfriend is not white and that she is pregnant, Andy promptly expels his granddaughter and cuts all ties with her. In the final moments of the play, an angered and defiant Andy is getting ready to attend the 70th Derry Somme Commemoration Parade, while Andrea explains how she ended up imprisoned. After Hanif had been injured and traumatised in a racist attack, Andrea had gone to the Greenham Common Women's Peace Camp and was arrested, a policeman recognising her Irish accent, calling her "a stupid IRA cunt" (Reid 1997, 274). Facing several weeks of imprisonment, Andrea cannot help wishing for the lost comfort of being with her grandfather, longing for reconciliation: "I miss you. I need you. I need to make my peace with you. [...] I love you, even though I have grown to loathe everything you believe in" (Reid 1997, 275). The play ends with this call for a personal truce.

The central issue of *My Name* is identity (cf. Kosok 2007, 58), which is reflected in the title and in the eponymous nursery rhyme that introduces the play:

ANDY (*V. O.*)[93]: My name, shall I tell you my …
ANDREA (*V. O.*): Name.
ANDY (*V. O.*): It's hard, but I'll …
ANDREA (*V. O.*): Try.
ANDY (*V. O.*): Sometimes I forget it, that's when I'm …
ANDREA (*V. O.*): Shy.
ANDY (*V. O.*): But I have another, I never forget. So …
ANDREA (*V. O.*): Easy.
ANDY (*V. O.*): So …
ANDREA (*V. O.*): Pretty.
ANDY (*V. O.*): And that's …
ANDREA (*V. O.*): Granda's Pet.

(Reid 1997, 253)

This little song playfully indicates the central predicament of Andrea, who is caught in-between finding an adequate sense of self and being dependent on and determined by her lineage, her family and the dominant socio-political context of her family. The song and the ritualistic way in which it is conveyed – Andy not just expressing his love for his granddaughter but essentially conditioning her to feel attached to him and, in effect, to represent him – signify the weight and the power that he claims for himself and his legacy from which Andrea eventually cannot wean herself. Thus, the song is crucially concerned with Andy's identity just as much as with Andrea's. The issue of naming is repeatedly addressed in the play, underlining the power of tradition in Northern Irish society: By means of names, tradition is maintained, generations are symbolically tied together, family lines are unified and consolidated and identities are effectively pre-determined. In the case of Andrea's family, the naming processes specifically emphasise the inherited patriarchal authority of Andy and the primacy of masculinity in the family portrayed: To compensate for having "only" daughters and no son and heir, Andrea's mother was christened "Annie", "the nearest we'll get to Andy" (Reid 1907, 255); similarly, when she was born on Andy's sixty-ninth birthday, Andrea's name was chosen "to please him" (Reid 1997, 255). Andrea, falsely remembered by Andy as the "cleverest child in the street" and "the best lookin'" (Reid 1997, 254), was chosen to embody his heritage. Accordingly, coming from such an environment, it is difficult for Andrea to imagine herself in a context other than that of her family.

The naming song is part of an arsenal of ritualistic practices, invocations and narratives, as well as symbolic artefacts (Andy's box of photographs, his medals, the ivory-topped walking stick given to him on the day of his retirement), that Andy

---

93 "V. O.", voice-over, indicates the use of the recorded voices of Andrea and Andy.

employs to define, cement and secure, on the one hand, his assertive "narrative of the self" (Hall 1995, 598) and, on the other hand, the relations to his family and community. Centrally, Andy's self-image is determined by his political identity as an unwavering Protestant Ulster Orangeman and as a proud and respected veteran of the Great War. This orientation is continuously re-confirmed by Andy and transferred unforgivingly to every facet of his life, including his family and private life. Along these lines, Andy does not only fully embrace his traditional role as a patriarch, insisting on unquestioned male authority and female obedience – he also combines this role with a staunch sense of patriotic duty and an insistence on military discipline. For example, he accepts his wife's announcement of wanting to have no further children only because "[s]he'd had five, so she'd done her bit. Even if they were all girls" (Reid 1997, 255). It is this spirit of 'doing one's bit', of fulfilling one's duty and respecting the demands and orders of authorities, which governs Andy's life and, consequently, the lives of those subjected to his own authority. Accordingly, when it is later suggested to Andy to make use of the council's elderly care services, Andy reacts with indignant pride:

> I have five daughters. They were brought up to know where their duty lies. [...] That's the trouble with the world today. People thinkin' they're entitled to charity from the cradle to the grave. [...] From the day I came back from the Great War, till the day I retired from the Linen Mill, I never went sick once. [...] Not even when the oul knee was that sore I could hardly walk, let alone work. I never used my war wound as an excuse to lie in my bed and live off the State. [...] My country gave me medals. Honoured me. I never demeaned that by lookin' for a hand-out.

> (Reid 1997, 260)

Accepting help from the council, the scene suggests, would not only violate Andy's soldierly self-image of being a deferential and self-restrained servant to the state, it is also seen by him as undermining his patriarchal power, as an emasculating admission of weakness and dependency.

Andy's crude concepts of masculinity and femininity are principally guided by the idealisation of masculine military resilience and female subservience and passivity. Andy's much repeated mantra is that it was the army that "made [him] a man" (Reid 1997, 255) and that it is natural and necessary for men to "go off to war, and the weemin' and the children stay behind and keep the home fires burnin' 'till the men get back" (Reid 1997, 259). In this manner, Reid's play mirrors a view established in feminist criticism of war writing – as Judith Stiehm summarises, "[t]hree ideas are fundamental to military enterprise: 1) War is manly 2) Warriors protect 3) Soldiers are substitutable. [...] Women do not seem irrelevant at all. In fact, they seem to be absolutely essential to the military. Their essentialness, though, lies in their absence" (Stiehm 1989, 224; cf. Peach 2000, 211). Andy resolutely adheres to these simplistic principles, never letting down his masculinist façade of unfazed strength and rejection of female weakness. For example, for his former friend and comrade Edward Reilly, who still struggles with the horrors witnessed in the war, Andy has nothing but contempt: "Like an oul woman. Nobody never seen me cry" (Reid 1997, 262). Similarly, there is not a jot of sadness or regret in Andy after cutting all ties with his once so beloved granddaughter – all Andy worries about is that his reputation might suffer because of Andrea's arrest at Greenham Common: "I'll go to the Somme Parade the day. Wear my medals with pride. Hold my head high, despite what she has done. And well dare anybody mention her name in the same breath as mine" (Reid 1997, 272).

The inescapable conflation of public and private life, the latter clearly overpowering the former, in the society portrayed by Reid is obvious. Andy cannot exist as a private individual, the play suggests, he cannot picture himself beyond his fixed identity as a soldier and Orangeman, and he extends this condition to his family. When Andy lectures seven year old Andrea that the most important thing in life is "[k]nowin' who ye are, an' what ye come from" (Reid 1997, 258), he does not mean the family's individual history but its embeddedness in the Protestant unionist tradition – "[c]arryin' on the tradition. [...] That's what life's about, child" (ibid.). It is mandatory in Andy's eyes to continuously reassert one's belonging and reverence to "tradition", against "[p]opery. Bad Blood. Nationalism. Communism" (Reid 1997, 261).

The Great War and Andy's contribution to it of course are integral to tradition and, consequently, also Andrea's childhood is steeped in battle lore (cf. Liddy 2010, 64). From an early age, she remembers, Andrea had been confronted with Andy's belligerent patriotism and Ulster cult of sacrifice and duty. The litany of the names of Andy's comrades of the Great War has become part of Andrea's imaginative repertoire and is repeated by her throughout the play in different contexts. The first painting Andrea ever saw in her life is entitled "The Battle of the Somme. Attack by the Ulster Division. First of July 1916" and hangs in the City Hall of Belfast: "We went there on a train from Derry when I was about seven, to visit his eldest daughter. But his real reason for going was that he wanted to stand with me in front of that painting ...and teach me another poem" (Reid 1997, 256). In this way, Andy worked to immerse and integrate his granddaughter in Ulster unionist ideology and myths, perpetuating "tradition".

However, already as a young girl, Andrea begins to notice the darker sides of her grandfather's glorifications and of the culture in which she is to be raised. In one of her most poignant and uneasy memories, the violence and sacrificial nature of Orange culture becomes obvious to her. Andrea recalls being taken by Andy to a ceremony of the local branch of the Orange Order, watching a fanatic performance on the Lambeg drum by Wee Billy Matchett, whose family line of identically named Orangemen epitomises Andy's obsession with sacrificial soldierly tradition, Wee Billy's grandfather having fallen at the Somme and his father at Dunkirk during World War II. Andrea remembers:

> Wee Billy Matchett was a huge, fat, sweaty man. [...] He had been beating the drum for a long time, and his hands were bleeding. The blood trickled over the tattoos on his arms ...'Ulster is British'; 'No Surrender'; 'Remember the Somme'/ 'Dunkirk'/ 'the Relief of Derry'. Billy's little sparrow of a wife kept darting forward with a sponge soaked in whiskey and water to cool his parched mouth and his burning face. She didn't attempt to sponge away the blood on his hands. That was sacred. I was more curious than frightened. I couldn't make sense why the great fat man was hurting himself like that. And why was his silly little wife so pleased about it?

> (Reid 1997, 258)

The scene does not only underline the unhealthy fixation on a history of war and violent resistance that underpins Orange culture, its rituals and symbolism, it also strikingly reveals its gendered nature, its idolisation of male sacrifice and patriotic suffering while women remain "loyal steadfast servicer[s] and nurturer[s] of men willing to die for Queen and country" (Delgado 1997, xiv). Wee Billy Matchett's body here serves as a performative site of ideology, it becomes "theatrical" as defined by Gabriele Klein (cf. Klein 2005, 40). The blood and sweat shed by the 'flagellant' Billy connect him and his enthusiastic spectators to the masculine narratives of unionist struggle. Furthermore, the scene exemplifies the notion of Jay Winter, informed by Halbwachs's theories, of the complex overlapping of individual and collective, private and public processes of remembrance (cf. Winter 2011, 426). The figure of Wee Billy Matchett embodies the concept of collective memory as "the sound of voices once heard by groups of people, afterwards echoing in an individual who was or is part of that group. It is a form of individual memory, socially constructed and maintained" (Winter and Sivan 1999, 24).

Hearing her grandfather join in the ceremony, young and puzzled Andrea eventually understands that the entire spectacle "was about war" (Reid 1997, 259). In a climactic and highly symbolic moment of the ceremony, Andrea is lifted off her grandfather's shoulders and held up high by Wee Billy Matchett, presenting her to the cheering spectators – she is used by Billy to represent the vitality, the purity and the future of Orange culture. While Andy is smitten with pride about the iconic involvement of his granddaughter, Andrea is disturbed as the blood from Wee Billy Matchett's ruined hands is running over her dress – this is perceived by her not as sanctifying but as an invasive pollution. In this highly contradictory image, the uneasy notion of Orange culture's conflation of violence, sacrifice, patriotism and masculine authority is highlighted most strikingly. Andrea's discomforted reaction foreshadows the eventual failure of her integration into this culture – it reveals the same sense of anxiety that the flawed Orange rituals in McGuinness's play evoke.

As she grows older, Andrea begins to question her grandfather's values; her image of him – and by that her own understanding of herself – begins to change. Learning about the story of Edward Reilly, Andrea realises how her grandfather has been distorting his war experiences to suit the unionist myths of wartime glory and unity around which his identity revolves. It is revealed to Andrea that Edward Reilly once was Andy's best friend, had fought beside him and returned from the Great War decorated with medals like Andy – however, after the war, he became a socialist and pacifist and sent back his medals. Consequently, in Andy's eyes, Edward Reilly "[t]urned traitor. [...] Betrayed all the brave men who fought and died so that we could be British and free" (Reid 1990, 261). Andy subsequently did not only turn his back on his best friend, he also cut him out of the much cherished photograph of his comrades taken during the war. Yet, since Andy and Edward embrace on the picture, Andy had to cut out himself as well – a striking symbol of the self-destructive effects of Andy's radicalism and the mutability of remembrance: Previously, Andrea had had no idea Edward Reilly even existed, Andy explaining his absence on the photograph by claiming to have taken the picture himself.[94] Furthermore, learning about the grim war memories of Edward Reilly, Andrea is confronted with a counter-narrative to Andy's propaganda that lets her see things in a different light:

> ANDREA: Eddie's grandfather [...] lay in the mud for three days, listening to Billy Matchett screaming and sobbing and moaning. He could hear Billy, and he could see him. But he couldn't help him, because his own legs were broken, and he was half-buried in an avalanche of mud and blood and bits of the bodies of Joseph Sloan, Isaac Carson, Samuel Thompson, Hugh Montgomery ...
> ANDREA (V. O.): Hugh Montgomery, Frederick Wilson, James Elliott, John Cunningham, Edward Marshall.
> ANDREA: And Edward Reilly. Who survived and wept every time he told that story to his grandson.
>
> (Reid 1990, 261f.)

---

94 When Andrea moves to London and stays at the home of relatives of one of Andy's former Great War comrades, she recognises that it is not only her grandfather who has repudiated the dissenter Edward Reilly, underlining the harsh and unforgiving insistence on uniformity that characterises Ulster Orangemen and veteran circles: "The Sloans hadn't cut their photo, they'd blanked out Edward Reilly's face" (Reid 1997, 266).

Most poignantly, the established heroism of the litany of Andy's comrades is deflated here as it is converted to victimhood and contextualised in a spirit of mourning. This moment of the play is also crucial because it highlights Andy's dilemma. In contrast to Edward Reilly's genuine and level-headed confrontation of the past, Andy's commemoration is almost impersonal, completely ritualised and dominated by well-established official discourses, Andy regurgitating over and over again propagandistic imagery – "the lads in France. Real Men. Heroes. Ulster Protestant Orangemen" (Reid 1997, 255), "a glorious victory. Their finest hour" (Reid 1997, 256). Andy has failed to enter into a more personal and potentially healing process of mourning, his exclusively heroic commemoration of his lost companions "displac[ing] the emotional complexities of bereavement" (Peach 2000, 211). Andrea eventually recognises how hopelessly Andy is lost in his 'official' veteran persona, how mercilessly he shuts himself off by his distorted invocations of the past, and how he seeks security in hazy memories of heroism and strength (cf. Liddy 2010, 67) that must not be questioned in order to keep up his identity: "Did you ever cry, I wonder, when there was nobody there to see? Perhaps you didn't dare, in case you could never stop" (Reid 1997, 262). And she wonders, "[y]ou must have moments of doubt. You must have. You're stubborn and you're proud, but you're not a fool" (Reid 1997, 275).

Importantly, leaving Northern Ireland and gaining a more distanced perspective, Andrea recognised how Andy is a victim of his culture and tradition and how they both have been shaped by a destructive permanent state of war and aggression: "I was brought up in a city with armed police and soldiers on the streets [...]. I don't remember Derry without barbed wire. Checkpoints. The war was always there, a part of everyday life. [...] An acceptable level of violence" (Reid 1997, 273). At the Greenham Common Women's Peace Camp, Andrea's insight is expanded. Inspired by the protest of other women, for the first time Andrea leaves her position of submissiveness and passive suffering behind, articulating her opposition to a (self-)destructive masculine ideology of war:

> I lit twelve more candles. Held them in a bunch in my hand, and walked towards the policeman. It was as if we were the only two people in the world. I held out the candles, and I said to him, "These are for Joseph Sloan and Billy Matchett and Isaac Carson and Samuel Thompson and Hugh Montgomery and Frederick Wilson and James Elliott and John Cunningham and Edward Marshall" [...]. The other three candles were for Edward Reilly and my grandfather and Hanif. But I didn't get to say their names. [...] Perhaps I'll say it in court.
>
> (Reid 1997, 273f.)

By means of Andrea's gesture of protest, the play approaches war as a more collective phenomenon, blurring boundaries between wars (cf. Peach 2000, 210), Reid "identifying an underlying pattern of colonial aggression" (Tylee 2001, 275), establishing a link of the Great War, World War II, the Troubles and the Falklands War within a history of male violence.

Yet, by the end of the play, Andrea has to admit that she cannot maintain her more active and politically conscious role as she simply cannot completely renounce her connection to Andy and live without him. She longs for a collaborative arrangement in which Andy's and her own belief systems can co-exist (cf. Liddy 2010, 72). This wish hints at a crisis of identity which essentially is a question of heritage – how can she adequately define herself within the hostile and bellicose but inescapable context of Andy? This problem remains unsolved, yet, at least it is grasped and can be articulated by Andrea. The image which Andrea chooses to illustrate her dilemma poignantly belongs to the imaginative resources of the Great War, the discourse of Andy. This choice does not simply indicate Andrea's entrapment in Andy's world – it should rather be seen as a concession to Andy, a sign of good will, in Andrea's attempt to achieve reconciliation: "They say that one Christmas Day, during the First World War, a group of British and German soldiers called a halt to the fighting, and declared a truce. Just for an hour. There must be an hour, a place, where he and I can meet. A piece of common ground. A no man's land" (Reid 1997, 276). The notion of the "no man's land" here of course does not only imply a neutral space but centrally one devoid of belligerent masculinity, a place in which Andy's identity as a veteran is overpowered by his identity as a loving family man (cf. Delgado 1997, xiv).

Summing up, *My Name, Shall I Tell You My Name?* illustrates a female response "to the ways in which masculine identity is constituted by violence and national identity by war" (Tylee et al. 1999, 211) in Northern Ireland, Reid centrally addressing the relevance of the Great War for these concepts of identity. The response presented is the refusal of a new generation of women to condone an oppressive and inflexible masculine tradition of nationalism, bigotry and violence (cf. Tylee 2001, 284). Reid's play specifically calls out and challenges the distorting and destructive partisan uses of the past that underpin private and public, personal and collective processes of Northern Irish identification – as Wei H. Kao summarises, she shows how dominant myths like the one of the Somme "gloss over the horrors of war, cover up problems of unionist patriotism, simplify history, [and] aid in the making of male heroism" (Kao 2010, 218). Against these simplifications, Reid suggests by means of Andrea's story the existence of multiple narratives in revising Northern Irish nationhood (cf. ibid.).

The next work to be discussed, Nicola McCartney's *Heritage* (1998) has also been categorised, apart from its classification as a war work (cf. Kosok 2007, 59), as a history play and Troubles play (cf. Headrick 2009, 64; McKean 2011). Again, a dominant female perspective and a concentration on the destructive power of memory and fixed identities are offered. However, unlike Reid who directly addresses contemporary developments in Northern Ireland and Britain in her play and connects them with the legacy of the Great War, McCartney distances and complicates her investigation of Irish identities and conflicts by setting her play in the milieu of Irish immigrants in Canada in the years of the Great War – a substitutive strategy that has been likened to the approach of Arthur Miller in *The Crucible* (cf. Headrick 2009, 64).

III.3.3 Nicola McCartney's *Heritage* (1998)

Like Christina Reid, Nicola McCartney (*1972) was born and grew up in Belfast. However, as a daughter of parents of different religious backgrounds, her personal history, as much as her dramatic work, is much less informed by Northern Ireland and Protestant unionist uniformity than Reid's. McCartney was happy to leave behind Belfast and the Troubles, an environment that she experienced as suffocating and oppressive (cf. McKean 2011), at the age of eighteen. She went to study English and drama at the University of Glasgow, a city that would become her home; her professional life as a prolific playwright and director has since been split mainly between Scotland and (Northern) Ireland (cf. Maguire 2013, 69). Along these lines, McCartney resists easy national categorisation as an author. She has recognised a degree of insecurity about her credentials herself, being seen by some critics as a Scottish playwright while others have positioned her within the Irish dramatic tradition (cf. McKean 2011; Headrick 2009, 65). Yet, McCartney is comfortable with being placed in either category, confidently identifying as Irish, Northern Irish, Scottish and European (cf. McKean 2011), claiming her heritage from multiple traditions.

McCartney has been counted among the practitioners of the 'new' Troubles play, which includes authors like Owen McCafferty, Marie Jones, Joseph Crilly and Dave Duggan, whose works frequently engage directly with the past, employ perspectives conventionally marginalised, and break with realism in favour of direct narration to the audience (cf. Maguire 2013, 67f.). The question of identity within an unsettled and problematic Northern Irish culture and society is a key concern of these authors. In McCartney's plays, this issue is often linked to representations of memory which are characterised by a "fracturing of space and a palimpsestic vision of time" (McKean 2011). This is also the case in *Heritage*, which probably is McCartney's best known play. *Heritage* was first produced in 1998 by the Traverse Theatre Company in Edinburgh and was revived in 2001. In 2006, the play was produced at the Royal Scottish Academy of Music and Drama in Glasgow and it also saw its American premiere at the American College Theatre Festival. *Heritage* was generally favourably received by critics, who praised, for example, the "complex and evocative" 1998 production; the American productions won several awards. Furthermore, the play was added to the Scottish school curriculum (cf. Headrick 2008, 65; McKean 2011).

Admittedly, the Great War is not the main concern of *Heritage* – nonetheless, as will be argued in the following, it represents a vital and suggestive element in the play's contextual backdrop. The relevance of the Great War in the play has hardly been addressed in the small amount of academic criticism dedicated to *Heritage*. For example, in his survey of English and Irish Great War drama, Heinz Kosok only briefly touches on the play, considering it "a complex analysis of Irish as well as international conflicts" and "a specifically Irish play about the war" (Kosok 2007, 59). Charlotte Headrick's more extensive reading of *Heritage* includes only a few fleeting references to the Great War (Headrick 2009, 76; 77f.), while Kathy McKean focuses exclusively on the play's use of memory (cf. McKean 2011).

Before discussing the play's approach to the Great War and Irish identities, it seems reasonable to briefly elucidate the fairly uncommon historical setting McCartney chose, Irish immigrant communities in Canada, and the significance of the Great War for Canada. *Heritage* has been called an "extremely well researched" (Gifford and Robertson 2002, 59) play, covering the historical complexity of identities and allegiances in the Canadian Irish immigrant milieu during the 1910s. McCartney carefully re-constructs a period of crisis and transition not only for Ireland but also for Canada and Canadian national consciousness, at the same time mirroring the transitions Northern Ireland experienced during the mid-1990s.

In the first two decades of the twentieth century, more than 750,000 immigrants from the British Isles came to Canada (cf. Thompson 2008, 91), represented in McCartney's play by the Scots-Ulster Protestant McCrea family. Yet, the history of Irish immigration to Canada is much older. Already in the 1830s and 1840s, large waves of immigrants had arrived from Ireland, trying to escape poverty, overcrowding and the catastrophe of the Great Famine – this older generation is represented in the play by the Ulster Catholic Donaghues.[95] The early Irish immigrants contributed substantially to the progress of Canada – as Desmond Morton

---

95 Interestingly, more than half of the Irish immigration to Canada originated from Ulster (Headrick 2009, 69).

remarks, they formed "that huge, anonymous, forgotten army of labourers who dug the canals and who would build the railways, the mines, and the cities of a developing Canada" (Morton 1994, 54). However, they also brought with them "the old country quarrels of Orange and Green" (ibid.), transferring the Irish tensions of Catholicism vs. Protestantism and nationalism vs. loyalism across the Atlantic. This shows, for example, in the prominent role of the Canadian branch of the Orange Order, which grew to become the largest and most important voluntary society in Canada by the late nineteenth century, at some point including nearly a third of all English-speaking Protestant males. While its ethnic Irish roots faded in the course of the century, the Canadian Orange Order's aim of keeping Canada British and Protestant was upheld throughout (cf. Buckner 2008, 83).

The different original identities of the immigrants from Ireland essentially persisted in Canada well into the twentieth century and many of the conflicts and developments in the mother country were reflected in or even directly transferred to Canada. Yet, of course, the immigrant communities did not remain completely unchanged in the long run. Loyalist Protestant Irish immigrants to Canada, along with those with English and Scottish roots, increasingly began to embrace a sense of national belonging that was comfortable with both imperial Britishness and being Canadian (cf. Buckner 2008, 82; Thompson 2008, 88), many seeing themselves as 'British Canadians'. The Catholic Irish minority, just as the French-speaking Catholic population, frequently retained a stronger sense of separateness, particularly considering the dominant ties of Canada to Britain – however, by the end of the nineteenth century, also the Catholic Irish were beginning to be gradually incorporated within a larger sense of a new Canadian identity (Buckner 2008, 83). This included leaving behind much of their anti-British heritage, a process that has been labelled the "Waning of the Green" (Thompson 2008, 91). Importantly, this does not mean that all Irish Catholics in Canada eventually turned into advocates of the Empire, but that there was a shared appreciation of "the liberties received by Canadians under the British flag" (Thompson 2008, 91f.).[96]

The outbreak of the Great War occurred in a tense domestic situation for Canada, the country struggling with a large-scale economic crisis, high rates of unemployment and a severe drought in the summer of 1914. Due to its status as a Dominion of the Empire, Canada automatically had to enter the conflict upon King George V.'s declaration of war – yet, there were only few voices of dissent. Even Wilfrid Laurier,

---

96 A much more pronounced and pressing conflict in Canadian society was the discord between French and British Canadians, which, like the Irish conflicts, also ran along the lines of the religious divide of Catholicism and Protestantism.

Liberal leader of the opposition and strong advocate of Canadian autonomy within the Empire, emphasised Canada's absolute willingness to contribute to the war effort, to "answer to the call of duty, 'Ready, aye, ready!'" (quoted in Thompson 2008, 96). At the outset, the war enjoyed great popularity and the initial response of the British-Canadian majority in Canada to the war was enthusiastic, British and Protestant Irish immigrants rushing to arms in large numbers. Significantly, the contribution of Catholic (i. e. French and Irish) Canada was much smaller: Altogether, less than five percent of all Canadian recruits of the Great War came from French Canada, while two thirds of the recruits were British born. This discrepancy became even more prominent as the Great War, against initial expectations, was dragging on and the number of volunteers began to decrease, leading to the upheavals of the 1917 Canadian conscription crisis. The contradictory colonial implications of the Great War surfaced particularly in this moment, when enlistment was made obligatory, and, most centrally, it was the Catholic French Canadian minority that voiced that their only loyalty was to Canada and not to Britain (or to France) (cf. Morton 1994, 173f.). Still, despite these divisions, the Great War quickly came to be seen as a cornerstone for the development of Canadian nationhood, a dominant view to this day,[97] the Great war still being assessed as "Canada's 'war of independence' even if it was fought at Britain's side against a common enemy" (Moyles and Owram, quoted in Thompson 2008, 96f.). For many Canadians, the Great War was a crusade for democracy and civilisation in which, for the first time, Canada acted as Britain's ally, not as a subservient colony (cf. ibid.).

In total, Canada sent five divisions to Europe. More than 670,000 Canadians (out of a population of about eight million) served in the Great War, 61,000 of which were killed and more than 170,000 wounded (ibid.). Canadian troops participated in iconic battles of the war, among them Ypres, the Somme and Passchendaele, acquiring a reputation of outstanding discipline and courage. The most famous Canadian operation of the war was the Battle of Vimy Ridge of 1917, an important allied success. This battle would enter Canadian national consciousness and become a widely lauded symbol of national sacrifice as it was the first concerted effort of all Canadian divisions – in McCartney's play, John McCrea,[98] the brother of the main protagonist, takes part and is wounded in this battle. As Desmond Morton summarises, taking up Renan's classic concept

---

97 The highly regarded status of the Canadian contribution to the Great War in public consciousness is reflected, for example, by the inclusion of parts of John MacCrea's famous 1915 war poem "In Flanders Fields" on Canadian bank notes.

98 McCartney's choice of name, linking the character with the celebrated Canadian soldier poet, connects the character with the notion of national sacrifice, pride and gratefulness

of nation-building through narratives of collective triumph and suffering, Vimy was "one of those great deeds, done together, which have created nations. French and English [Canadians] could take equal pride in their victory" (Morton 1994, 169). The narrative of Vimy contributed massively to the post-war sense of a new Canadian national self that both united and eventually transcended established unilateral traditions and inherited conflicts. The essence of this new Canadian spirit, even if it does not prevail at the play's conclusion, is also evoked in McCartney's play, albeit in a distinctively non-belligerent way.

Heritage is set in the farmlands surrounding the fictional township of Stanley, west of Yorkton, in Saskatchewan, Canada. The play covers the period from spring 1914 to spring 1920. It interweaves a Romeo-and-Juliet narrative of a tragic and illicit love with the upheavals of the period: the enduring antagonism of Irish nationalism and loyalism and the accompanying dispute about Catholicism and Protestantism, the Great War, and, more remotely, the conscription crisis and the long-distance effects in Canada of the War of Independence in Ireland. In this manner, the love relationship of the play also amounts to "an allegory for some kind of national romance" (Maguire 2013, 70f.). The main protagonist and 'narrator' of Heritage is Sarah McCrae, aged 14 at the beginning of the play. Sarah, born in County Antrim, comes from an Ulster Protestant farmer family which had immigrated to Canada only a few years earlier. She befriends and eventually falls in love with Michael Donaghue, the son of the neighbouring family, third generation Canadians of Ulster Catholic descent. The love story is framed and metaphorically underpinned by Sarah and Michael playfully recounting and performing the Irish folktale of Deirdre and Naoise (or Deirdre of the Sorrows), which is part of the Ulster cycle, throughout the play. From the beginning, the antagonism of the two Irish traditions embodied by the McCraes and the Donaghues overshadows both the relationship of Sarah and Michael and the co-existence of the two neighbouring families. There are small steps towards conciliation between the families in the new country, however, heightened by the polarising political backdrop of the Great War and other developments, the traditional hostilities that divide the two Irish cultures eventually prove insurmountable. The separation of Sarah and Michael is enforced and the unfortunate couple subsequently have to meet in secret. They plan to elope together, yet, Michael, who is increasingly influenced by Irish radical nationalism, despite his love for the Ulster Protestant girl Sarah, dies in a self-inflicted arson attack on the

- however, as will be shown, this is not a positive association: the John McCrea of the play is a belligerent and radical young Orangeman.

McCrea's barn. At the end of the play, a devastated Sarah leaves behind her family and the traditions – the sectarian heritage – that troubled Sarah's and Michael's love and that led to the death of her lover.

Like McGuinness and Reid, also McCartney makes use of a memory perspective which works on multiple levels. The play starts with a "dream" (McCartney 2002, 66), a ritualised flashback to the play's conclusion, showing a boy dancing to the beat of a drum before being consumed by fire, followed by silence and the weeping of a woman. In the ensuing scene, the play's main protagonist Sarah enters the stage covered in ashes and dirt – a link to the fire at the play's ending, underlining the play's retrospective point of view – drifting "ghost-like into the light" (ibid.). She delivers a prologue, sketching the vastness and variety of Canada, "the wheat country" (McCartney 2002, 67) to which her family had come for a better life, and she announces the telling of the story of how she met and lost her lover Michael: "I will tell you the story / By the big river / I met him / My boy / Mine / All mine / [...] I will tell you the story / Listen / I will tell the story to you / As I have been told it" (ibid.). The prologue ends with Sarah being joined by Michael on stage, the two reciting a section of the Deirdre myth together. The following scene jumps back again to the day Sarah and Michael first met and only at this point the chronological recapitulation of their ill-fated love story begins. This complex overlapping of flashbacks and flash-forwards at the play's outset, creating different temporalities (cf. McKean 2011), evokes a sense of story-telling and memory as subjective, changeable and disordered. It also expands the play's temporal scope and elevates the play above the level of a mere period piece. With regard to the issue of identity, as Kathy McKean argues, the play's complex beginning directs attention to the notion that "in memory, in different representations of the self in history, there are many layers and competing narratives" (McKean 2011) – and, as the play shows, the rivalry between inherited narratives, individual selves and actual needs can end in disappointment and destruction.

Memory, history and, most significantly, the related concepts of tradition and heritage are at the heart of the play's investigation of Irish-Canadian identities. The events of the play's present are determined by the characters' relationship to their dissonant cultural, political and historical heritage, by their embeddedness in their communities which exist within inherited sectarian demarcation lines. Crucially, these divisions and loyalties are based on conceptions of an Ireland that exists only in memory, in tradition and in imagination (cf. McKean 2011), an Ireland that is actually twice removed, by temporal and by geographical distance. This condition is destructive – as Sarah muses in an interlude in the first act, speaking to the audience, "[h]eritage / A brand burned deep / Through skin of centuries. / Scarring forever / The soul / The land / The memory / The future. / Carried across deathbeds / Across oceans / To a faraway land" (McCartney 2002 94), straightforwardly evoking the notion of the inevitable, comprehensive and harmful grip of heritage, of partisan versions of the past.

A telling example of this uneasy condition, the contradictory simultaneous remoteness and imminence of the influential mental concept "Ireland", can be found in the first meeting of Sarah and Michael. Michael recounts to Sarah an earlier punch-up with Sarah's belligerent brother, John, who had called him, the third-generation Irish-Canadian who lives in the middle of the Canadian nowhere, "a Papist bastard" (McCartney 2002, 71). In the scene, Michael, the soon-to-be self-appointed Canadian Irish nationalist, also asks Sarah to describe Ireland for him as he has never seen it: "Is Ireland very green?" (ibid.). Similarly, for Sarah's family, 'home' still means Protestant loyalist Ulster – this culture remains their central point of reference, even if they settled down on another continent years ago, and even if Sarah's father, Hugh, once explains to his daughter that they are "Scots Irish Canadian British subjects" (McCartney 2002, 94). This suggests an awareness of the hybridity of their situation (cf. Gifford and Robertson 2002, 63), yet, with the exception of Sarah, the McCrea's reality is different. Sarah's mother, Ruth, for example, longs for their old-fashioned Ulster stone cottage and feels unsafe in their wooden Canadian house – a foreshadowing of the fire at the end of the play. Also, in a letter home, Hugh sends for flower and wheat seeds from Ulster – they turn out to be unsustainable in the Canadian soil, a potent symbol of the failure of the integration of the intransigent McCreas. In the letter, Hugh also proudly announces the participation of him and his son John in the local Orange parade on the "Twelfth", expressing his gratefulness for the "certificate of transfer" (McCartney 2002, 79) that eased his move to the Orange Order in Canada or, as he calls it, "British North America" (ibid.).

On the other side of the sectarian divide, in the Donaghue family, it is Michael's grandmother, Emer, who is the driving force in perpetuating the family's Catholic Irish history. For example, she teaches Michael how the Great Famine drove them out of Ireland:

> EMER: My daddy / Poor cottier / Lost foot on the land. / The British! / Not even a crust of bread to chew upon / They give us / Ship off cattle and grain we've raised / To serve up on English dinner tables / While our children / Perish. / Protestant Ministers / They dishing out bowls of free soup / But you must recant / Must throw away soul. / So we live on / Grass, seaweed and shellfish.
> MICHAEL [joining in with her]: "Grass, seaweed and shellfish."
> EMER: That was the beginning of the great disease that destroyed Ireland, Mihal.
>
> (McCartney 2002, 85f.)

This scene very much resembles the indoctrination young Andrea is subjected to by her grandfather Andy in Reid's *My Name, Shall I Tell You My Name?* and, in fact, throughout McCartney's work, Emer plays a similar if slightly less radical part. Another central marker of heritage within the Donaghues is the use of Gaelic between Emer and Michael, or "Mihal" as Emer calls him,[99] which also directly underlines the division that runs through the Irish immigrant communities portrayed (cf. McKean 2011).

Nonetheless, there is also a counterweight to the inherited and imported sectarian polarisation in the figure of Peter Donaghue, Michael's Father. Peter is the only character in the play who can see through the destructiveness of the ancient divisions and who straightforwardly defines himself as Canadian, leaving behind his Irish heritage.[100] Consequently, he insists on Emer and Michael speaking English at home, tries to discourage Michael from joining radical nationalist groups and blames himself for letting Emer fill his impressionable son's head "with romantic nonsense about the Old Country and the coffin ships and martyred rebels" (McCartney 2002, 138). In open opposition to his environment, Peter rejects the sweeping reliance on tradition and calls "history [...] more dangerous a friend than an enemy" and "[n]othing but a load of lies and bitterness" (McCartney 2002, 88).

Peter is also the driving force behind the few moments of mutual exploration and conciliation between the two families and traditions. These moments evoke a promising sense of appeasement, hinting at a new and integrative notion of Canadian identity. For example, in a cheerful and relaxed moment at the end of the first act, the culture-crossing Ulster Protestant Sarah is taught a traditional Irish dance at the home of the Donaghues – "[i]t's only a start. Only a start" (McCartney 2002, 112), Peter remarks ambiguously at the end of the scene. More expressively, in an earlier scene, a new barn is being built by the McCreas and several hired immigrant labourers, and Peter selflessly offers his and Michael's expert help. As Sarah reports to the audience, "[m]en from Italy / Doukhobours and Ruthenians / Irish

---

99   In the scene quoted above, Emer is speaking English because Sarah is present, confronting her with the suffering caused by the British to whom Sarah's family feels connected by tradition.

100   This attitude is the result of Peter's personal experiences with the bigotry of his culture. Towards the end of the play, it is revealed that Michael's mother, who is absent in the play, actually was a Protestant divorcee – "mistreated, deserted, divorced. Mine to marry by law" (McCartney 2002, 139), as Peter remarks. Yet, Peter's marriage to that woman was recognised neither by the Church nor by his family which led to his profound disillusionment with his culture.

Men / Orange men / To build the new barn / Log on log / Plank on plank / Up and up / Tower of Babel" (McCartney 2002, 96) – and Hugh McCrea must admit that "Donaghue's a polite, quiet sort of fella. The Cathelickes here is of differ'nt nature to the Irish ones" (McCartney 2002, 97), perceiving Peter as a Canadian local, not as a representative of a rival Irish tradition. However, Sarah's reference to the Tower of Babel in her description of the building process already hints at the looming failure of the multicultural cooperation as, eventually, the old hostilities still prove too strong to be overcome – at the end of the play, as mentioned before, the barn, a symbol of cross-national and cross-sectarian conciliation, is burnt down by Irish republican radicals and Michael dies in the fire.

The issue of the Great War is instrumental in highlighting the contrasts between the concepts of Irish, Ulster and Canadian identity presented in the play. The conflicting attitudes to the war are indicative of how the Donaghues and the McCreas define their position both to their cultural and historical heritage and to the new country in which they live. Importantly, the Great War is referred to on two levels in the play. On the one hand, the war and, again, particularly the question of enlistment are debated conventionally by the characters as a topical issue within Sarah's story. On the other hand, acting as a guide to the political and historical context of the period portrayed, Sarah describes the Great War and its wider impact on the play's communities to the audience in vignettes, in a heightened but fairly fragmented, minimalistic and frequently onomatopoeic way (cf. McKean 2011). This approach to the war by Sarah provides a female and essentially pacifist perspective from the home front. Sarah's focus is mostly on the aspect of death, destruction and loss and she subsumes the complex network of allegiances and identities that underpins the Great War under the theme of heritage:

[Summer 1915] Heritage / [...] Running deep into the soil / Blood in the veins / And fire in the blood / What fire! / Sixty thousand miles from here / Big guns go / Boom Boom / Boom Boom / At Ypres / Canadians / French / British / Irish / All / Defending the Empire / Boom Boom / Sixty thousand miles away / They harvesting and reaping / And counting the dead / Sixty thousand miles from / Planting and harvesting and profit.
(McCartney 2002, 94)

[Spring 1916] Letter from home tells / More warriors in battle / Red Hand / Defending Ulster / Green Hand / Defending Ireland / Rise up / All / Defending / Heritage.
(McCartney 2002, 105)

[November 1916] Long deserted roads that will soon be / Flowing rivers of mud / Driving rain and sleet / Then frozen under snow. [...] / Big engine / Belching steam / Green carriages / New and shiny / Not to carry our cheap cheap wheat / But our men / On the platform / Tears / Embraces / Farewells / Engine blasts / One two / One two / And he's gone / My brother John / Not yet seventeen years / Off to fight / The enemy / Sixty thousands miles away.

(McCartney 2002, 113f.)

[Spring 1918] America turns its hand / To a different plough / War Machine / To dig it up / Plough it up / Churn it up / Europe / More guns / More mines / More dead / All along the Western Front / Boom Boom / Boom Boom.

(McCartney 2002, 117)

In these vignettes, Sarah relies heavily on the rural imagery associated with her Canadian home. They evoke the sense of an almost absurd remoteness ("Sixty thousand miles away"), contrasting the rural prosperity and calmness of Canada with the destruction of the war ("Boom Boom [...] / They harvesting and reaping"), also revealing to some degree Sarah's difficulty of giving expression to the conflict. This condition is not only the outcome of the geographical distance between Canada and Europe but also of the distance of Sarah from the realities of war as a young woman, witnessing passively how the men are sent off to fight, trying to make sense of the situation – similarly to Reid's play, the war is constructed here as a hermetic arena for male aggression.

The reasoning that Sarah offers in her vignettes for the men's war service appears contradictory and ambiguous: Some go off to fight in defence of the British Empire, some fight for Home Rule for Ireland and, effectively, against the Empire, and some fight against Home Rule – however, ironically, all serve on the same side. The recruits, in Sarah's view, are united beyond their respective contradictory allegiances in another all-encompassing way: they fight in the name of heritage, their war service is the outcome of the inescapable force of tradition. Sarah pictures the soldiers as attempting to live up to the sense of obligation posed by the respective traditions to which they belong – it is the call of heritage that stirs up the "fire in the blood" (McCartney 2002, 94) and leads them into war.

Sarah's brother John, a proud young Orangeman fully immersed in his belligerent heritage, can be seen as the prime example of these processes. Tellingly, John, who never appears on stage and only exists in the accounts of the other characters, is described from the beginning as driven by an almost pathological sense of sectarian militancy and violence, which shows in several complaints by Michael of having been assaulted by John, even during the superficially harmonious building of the McCrea's barn. Similarly, when Sarah and Michael first discuss the Great War, Michael reckons that John will gladly enlist because he "enjoy[s] killing people. [...] Running Huns through the ribs with his bayonet" (McCartney 2002, 82). Indeed, John joins up promptly after reaching the minimum age, is shipped off to Europe and participates in the Battle of Vimy – however, he is wounded and he returns shell-shocked, a broken man:

> SARAH: Half come home / Of those who went / And some of them / Are only half / Of what they were. / Brother John returns / But not to harvest. / Hollow as reed / Pale as milk / All a-tremble / Screaming / Terror / Sweat lashing / She rock-a-byeing him in her arms / Sayin
> RUTH: There, there my son. You're alright now. You're home.

> (McCartney 2002, 124)

Still, John's harrowing war experiences and his trauma do not seem to affect his earlier militancy in a permanent way. John, at least on the surface, has not been fundamentally transformed by the war – on the contrary, despite the brief post-deployment breakdown described by Sarah, John embodies a sense of continuity in which the earlier violence of Orange radicalism and the war are embedded: His war service can be effortlessly accommodated within his militant pre-war identity, there is no substantial break, it is all part of 'heritage' – tellingly, the next reference to John in the play pictures him in 1920, Michael falling victim to John's extremism once again as he reports having been beaten up by John and fellow Orangemen after visiting a meeting of Irish republicans.

Importantly, the distinct view on the war provided in Sarah's vignettes is a retrospective one, formed after having lived through the war at the home front, fearing for John, and having suffered the loss of Michael. However, in the play's actual story, young Sarah initially does not really know how to assess the war. She merely mirrors the attitudes of her environment, which, as mentioned before, are indicative of how the respective Irish groups define themselves and how they relate to Canada:

> SARAH: Mr Rutherford said that it is Canada's duty to give whatever help she can to the efforts of the Allies on the Western Front.
> MICHAEL: Russia?
> SARAH: You can volunteer.
> MICHAEL: I don't want to.
> SARAH: Why not? You're old enough. Our John will go as soon as he is sixteen. […]
> MICHAEL: I won't fight. For it is not our war.
> SARAH: It's a threat to the British Empire.
> MICHAEL: And this is Canada.

> (McCartney 2002, 82)

Here, the issue of the war underlines the gulf between the traditions embodied by Sarah and Michael and the different concepts of their integration into the new country. While Sarah parrots the popular notion of Canada as a part of or indebted to the Empire and of the self-evident duty of volunteering, Michael argues for the opposite – "it is not our war". This divisive dichotomy is spelt out even more directly in a later and fairly uneasy conversation of Ruth and Emer:

> RUTH: [John] goes off to do his duty. So we must be proud of him. I wonder at your grandson's not going.
> EMER: I do not. Why would he be fighting for the British?
> RUTH: I think we come from different stock.
>
> (McCartney 2002, 115)

The most striking manifestation effected by the Great War of how the McCreas and the Donaghues "come from different stock" can be found in an exchange between Hugh and Peter that introduces another approach to the war and the divided situation:

> HUGH: We thought we had lost [John], he was wounded at Vimy.
> PETER: That's honourable.
> HUGH: Aye. He is a brave lad. How is it your boy doesn't go?
> PETER: He doesn't want to.
> HUGH: He's one of the few young lads his age about here not volunteered yet. Does he sicken or something?
> PETER: No. He just has his own mind.
> HUGH: His own? [...]
>
> [They inspect Hugh's rotten crops.]
> PETER: We must stick together. I wonder that you don't join the League of Farmers.
> HUGH: We never had such things in Antrim. Sure we had meetings, but not organised demonstrations. [...] It smacks of socialism to me.
> PETER: What else are we to do? This government's sympathy lies not in people but in profit.
> HUGH: We must all get behind the war effort, that's what I told our John.
> PETER: If the new settlers want to go, let them go. They are still wedded to the old country. We Canadians have other business.
> HUGH: You don't back the war?
> PETER: Oh, it's not the war that bothers me. Let them fight it – it's a just enough war. It's the conscription business I don't like.
> HUGH: You Catholics is all opposed to it.
> PETER: Nothing to do with being Catholic. Canada's a nation on her own, free to fight her own wars, not the rest of the world's.
> HUGH: That's Fenian talk where I come from.
> PETER: Where you come from maybe. Here, it's just progress.
>
> (McCartney 2002, 118–20)

In this dialogue, Hugh's complete immersion in the heritage of the "old country" is called out by Peter as oppressive, self-destructive and outdated – Hugh can imagine neither himself nor can he assess his environment or the contemporary situation beyond the sectarian categories he inherited and brought with him to Canada. In stark contrast to Hugh, Peter has moved on from the confinement of heritage and embraced an attitude that is not determined by a perpetual look back but by pragmatism and the question of how to cope with the Canadian present and build a future. Canadians, he argues, "have other business" than catering to displaced traditions by joining in a foreign war and they "must stick together", regardless of their origins. Peter confidently resists the call of heritage which makes Hugh a supporter of the war, which automatically led John into the carnage of European battlefields, and which has been contaminating local communal life. Importantly, this resistance also distinguishes Peter from his son Michael. When Michael explains to Sarah in the scene quoted earlier that "it is not our war", "our", or the implicit "we" Michael uses, does not chime with the integrative notion of Hugh's ideas of a unified Canadian society – it is informed by Michael's adoption of Irish republican sectarianism, in which the Great War is an affair of the British colonial oppressor.

Tragically, at the play's conclusion, also the voices of moderation and progress, Peter and, increasingly, Sarah, are overpowered by the grip of heritage. The official separation of Sarah and Michael is enforced and Hugh subjects his daughter, who disgraced the purity of his Protestant family line, to a severe beating. Moreover, Michael's fully formed identification with Ireland and sectarian traditions, Charlotte Headrick notes, "leads him away from the path of peace" (Headrick 2009, 67) and to his pointless death. Michael is oblivious to the positive energy of Sarah and the wisdom of Peter. Ignorant of his hybrid situation as a third-generation Canadian in love with a Protestant girl from Ulster, and fuelled by martial Pearsean rhetoric that had belatedly reached Canada, Michael announces that "[e]ach generation has risen up to free our land of the British. It's tradition" (McCartney 2002, 108). His fatal involvement in the arson attack on Hugh McCrea's barn is the outcome of his ambitions to do his bit for Ireland's freedom and live up to tradition.[101]

The position of Sarah at the end of the play is challenging. Having witnessed the destructive consequences of the fixation on heritage on either side of the sectarian divide, Sarah is at a liminal point in her existence – as Tom Maguire

---

101   Interestingly, in Sarah's shocked account of seeing her lover burn to death, Michael is described as "[i]n the fire / Man / *Orange Man* / Leaping / Flinging arms up down" (McCartney 2002, 145, my emphasis), evoking the sense of how the two opposing radical forces of Irish nationalism and Orangeism are in fact exchangeable and united considering the violence and destruction they cause.

observes, Sarah "must cross over from the world which she has been bequeathed by her parents with its nineteenth-century customs and limitations into the new land of Canada in a new century with its challenges and opportunities, where what she is and will become is not yet settled" (cf. Maguire 2013, 72). Unlike Andrea in Reid's *My Name*, at the end of *Heritage*, Sarah is eventually able to walk away and leave her home behind:

> Bitter / Not me / It is old / Old / So old / Not beautiful / Sharp shins wheeling / Turning / Will I / Home / Not home / Not beautiful / No more / Shouldnae be remembered / Sludge heavy boots / Through soil / Sun bleeds / Awake / Township of Stanley / Six road ends / Which / Nearly day
>
> (McCartney 2002, 147)

Sarah cuts her ties with the tradition in which she was raised; significantly, she also rejects the nationalist vision of her dead lover. Sarah takes on personal responsibility for forging her identity beyond inherited values in a new and open country (cf. Maguire 2013, 73). The telling of her story represents a way of coming to terms with her past and in the case of Sarah, in contrast to Pyper in McGuinness's *Observe the Sons of Ulster* and Andrea in Reid's *My Name*, there is a sense of closure and the possibility of progress.

Summing up, McCartney's play focuses on the question of identity and how identity is determined by heritage, the confining traditions and myths of the culture in which the individual is brought up, founded upon memory and imagination. Centrally, heritage is associated with separateness and division. Heritage is what keeps the Irish immigrant communities of the play apart and what prevents them from recognising the possibilities of peaceful multicultural co-existence (cf. Gifford and Robertson 2002, 63f.) – with harrowing consequences. The Great War in the play strikingly accentuates the demarcation lines between the traditions and respective identities and allegiances. Furthermore, the Great War is retrospectively constructed by Sarah, who has managed to cross cultures and surpass tradition, in a more abstract sense as a destructive culmination of the effects of tradition – the soldiers of the Great War, regardless of their individual allegiances, have gone to fight in response to the obligations of heritage.

Of course, the concern of McCartney's play, problematising the pull of tradition, of tribal allegiances, religion and the past (cf. Headrick 2009, 64), resonates with the shifting situation in Northern Ireland in the 1990s. *Heritage* premiered in the year of the Good Friday Agreement, a monumental step ending decades of sectarian violence in Northern Ireland and establishing a *modus vivendi* between rival cultures, heralding a new phase in Irish relations. The notion of coming to terms with the past was integral to these conciliatory processes – McCartney once personally suggested that "one needs to know one's history and then forget it" (Headrick 2009, 75) in order not to be a prisoner of the past.

Switching from Northern Ireland to the south and away from the immediate context of the Troubles back to wartime Ireland, the final authors of this section, Tom Phelan, Sebastian Barry and Dermot Bolger, also engage with such ideas, however, their view is almost exclusively male and their interest lies not in forgetting but in a pluralisation of Irish history and memory, setting out to challenge imbalances established by the long dominance of nationalist perspectives and discourses.

III.3.4 Tom Phelan's *The Canal Bridge* (2005)

Among the authors of this section, Tom Phelan is probably the least prominent one – still, his 2005 novel *The Canal Bridge* represents an intriguing example of the reformed attitudes towards the First World War in 21st-century Ireland and of the interest of contemporary authors in providing alternative views on Irish history that bring marginalised aspects of the past, like the involvement of Catholic Irishmen in the Great War, back into focus. Born in 1940, Phelan grew up on a small farm in Mountmellick, Co. Laois, in the Irish Midlands. In the 1960s, he went to St. Patrick's Seminary in Carlow and became a Catholic priest, serving in England and the United States. He abandoned the priesthood in the mid-1970s, studied at Seattle University and then went on to work in the public school system of Long Island, where he still lives today. Although Phelan had started to write in the 1970s, his literary career only took off in the 1990s, when his first novel *In the Season of the Daisies* (1993) was published by Lilliput Press in Dublin. Since then, he has written five novels, most recently *Lies the Mushroom Pickers Told* (2015). Furthermore, Phelan has commented on Irish topics in American newspapers and media outlets such as *Irish Echo* and *Newsday*. Although his works, including *The Canal Bridge*, were warmly received by critics and readers, and he was awarded several prizes and fellowships,[102] Phelan has remained mostly under the radar as an Irish author to this day. This is also the case considering scholarly attention to his works. At the time of writing, Marzena Sokolowska-Paryz's 2014 essay on *The Canal Bridge* (cf. Sokolowska-Paryz 2014) seems to be the only substantial academic approach to Phelan's novels.

Diverging views on the Irish past and questions of Irish identity are of key importance for Phelan. His novels are frequently built around historical Irish settings, for

---

102 E. g. fellow of the Christopher Isherwood Foundation (2008–2009), writer-in-residence at Princess Grace Irish Library, Monaco (Ireland Fund of Monaco, 2012).

example, his debut *In the Season of the Daisies* is about an IRA killing of a young boy in 1921, while *Derrycloney* (1999) explores Irish country life during the 1940s. Furthermore, the perspective of the returned Irish emigrant, who is re-confronted with the past and the Ireland that was once left behind, is a recurring feature in his works (*Iscariot* (1995), *Lies the Mushroom Pickers Told*). Phelan's approach to this complex field clearly has been shaped by personal experience, his upbringing in a staunchly nationalist environment and the reforming experience of emigration, gaining a sobering external perspective on his home country in the process. In a 2016 article on the legacy of the Easter Rising, Phelan describes his childhood in a rural Irish culture infused with nationalist fervour that nourished anti-English feelings in him to the point that by the age of sixteen he "had been sufficiently radicalised to die for Ireland" (Phelan 2016). Young Phelan was also aware of the "muted presence" ("Forgotten Heroes" 2007) of destitute Irish veterans of the Great War on the streets of Mountmellick in the 1940s and 50s, who were, as he later recognised, "pushed to the edge of society" (Smith 2014) – back then, however, they were only a subject of ridicule for him. Only after leaving Ireland, living abroad as a young priest in England, did Phelan begin to recognise the negativity and extremism of the attitudes he had internalised, and he also became aware of the divisive effects of partisan myths. He realised that the English around him actually were "kind and polite and every bit as human as the Irish" (Phelan 2016) and he was surprised how most did not care much about the age-old animosities between Ireland and England that had so greatly influenced his own upbringing. He began to see the interconnections of Irish and English lives that he had once regarded as incompatible, long-established individual ties being obscured by the polarising nationalist narrative of Ireland.[103]

This recognition and the corresponding desire to rectify what Phelan perceives as a disruptive partisan bias of Irish historical consciousness play a central role in several of his works. Accordingly, when Phelan remarks that his novels "are based to some degree on fact" (Smith 2014), he means that their depiction of the Irish past is consciously positioned against what he has identified as the 'non-factual' nature of nationalist "propaganda" (Phelan 2016), such as the heroic narratives surrounding the Easter Rising and the connected image of the treacherous Irish soldiers of the Great War. This is also the conceptual framework within which *The Canal Bridge* is embedded. The novel is dedicated to the "men of Mountmellick who were in uniform during World War I" (Phelan 2005, v) and preceded

---

103   In his 2016 article, Phelan also observes that ironically this narrative is now more powerful and widely accepted among "virulently anti-English" (Phelan 2016) Irish-Americans than among the majority of people in Ireland.

by an affectionate "salute to [...] the delegation from 'the North'" (Phelan 2005, vii) that Phelan once met at the Menin Gate memorial in Ypres in 1999, former members of the security forces in Northern Ireland, who honoured the war dead "not because of where they had come from, but because of where they were" (Phelan 2005, viii). As Marzena Sokolowska-Paryz observes, *The Canal Bridge* "serves the evident purpose of recovering the memory of Irishmen serving in the Great War from 'national amnesia'" (Sokolowska-Paryz 2014, 341), Phelan attempting to restore them to their rightful place in Irish national memory and historical consciousness (cf. ibid.).

However, this does not mean that Phelan, like other authors of this section, argues from a more or less elaborately theorised, 'de-centred' postmodern or post-national angle – as will become apparent in the discussion of *The Canal Bridge*, he is not really immune to the appeal and the certainties of traditional discourses of heroism, (military) bravery and the nation. This is also evident in his journalistic writing where Phelan has phrased his plea for a more balanced approach to Irish history in traditional terms, stressing that to remember the national past 'truthfully' is "our duty to our forefathers" (Phelan 2016), and that it is time "for the Irish to demand that the guards at the gates of the pantheon of Irish heroes stand aside and admit their grandfathers and great-grandfathers who fought in the Great War" (Phelan, "Notebook", 2005). *The Canal Bridge* operates along similar discursive lines – as will be shown, Phelan eventually lionises his Irish soldier characters, who had "fought for Ireland in Europe" and then were "consigned to Ireland's ash pit" (Phelan, "Notebook", 2005), while scathingly condemning zealous nationalists and Easter Rising propagandists, not transcending but reversing established stereotypes.

The Canal Bridge offers a panoramic view on the Irish history of the Great War and the post-war phase, including the interplay of Irish, Anglo-Irish and English identities. The novel is structured into three parts, "Going Away", "The War" and "Coming Home", consisting of short subchapters presented from the perspectives and memories of individual characters – again, the war period is approached in a personal and retrospective mode. Set mostly in the small town of Ballyrannel in the Irish Midlands during the 1910s and early 1920s, *The Canal Bridge* traces the story of the Hatchel triplets: Con and his sister Kitty Hatchel, as well as the adopted orphan Matthias "Matt" Wrenn. The three share the memory of a humble but essentially happy and unworried childhood spent together on the banks of the Ballyrannel canal, a vital point of reference for them throughout the novel. In 1913, the Irish Catholic peasants Con and Matt enlist in the British forces to see the wonders of the world. Their promising journey with the army to exotic outposts of the Empire ends prematurely when the First World War breaks out and their ship is redirected back to Europe. The two soon find themselves as stretcher-bearers in the gory turmoil of French and Belgian battlefields. While Matt and Con are away, Kitty manages to get work at Enderly, the local Big House, and befriends Mrs. Hodgkins, the landlord's benevolent wife. Only Matt survives the carnage of the war, yet, he comes home as a shadow of his former self to a country deeply changed. Kitty, who finally realised during Matt's absence that she is in love with him, works hard to restore Matt's former mental and physical strength. She is worried about his intimate connection to Mrs. Hodgkins's daughter, Sarah, who served in the war as a VAD nurse and was traumatised herself, yet, it is eventually this friendship with Sarah that helps Matt overcome his own war trauma. Eventually, Kitty and Matt marry, have a child, and live on the treasured Hodgkins estate. Their happiness together is short-lived – during the War of Independence, Matt is killed trying to defend Enderly from an attack by radical republicans. The novel ends with a section narrated by Kitty in 1970, looking back at her troubled life in Ballyrannel.

One of the central contrasts that Phelan depicts in his novel is the shift from a materially poor but essentially harmonious and fairly apolitical pre-war social situation in Ballyrannel to a condition of political tension and divisiveness brought about by the Easter Rising and the subsequent rise of more radical forms of Irish nationalism. In the process, the issue of Irish identity comes into focus more strongly than before, extending into a political dimension that had previously been more or less irrelevant – "Are you an Irishman or what?" (Phelan 2005, 105) increasingly becomes a crucial question after 1916. Pre-war and pre-Rising Ballyrannel, on the contrary, is constructed by Phelan as a narrow and simple but idyllic and peaceful world, inhabited mostly by good-humoured peasants and overseen by the kind-hearted and overall respected Anglo-Irish Hodgkins family, with whom the lower-class Catholic Irish main characters freely interact. The looming Home Rule conflict is only faintly noticeable in Ballyrannel through the presence of some men and women "who wanted to be Fenians" (Phelan 2005, 21); the only truly disruptive element, the radical nationalist Johnjoe Lacy, is constructed as a miserable and marginal figure at the fringes of the community, universally despised for his aggressive fanaticism.

Accordingly, the 1913 enlistment of Matt and Con in the British forces is generally met with approval and even admiration in Ballyrannel. The departure of "the adventurers, as we all thought of them" (Phelan 2005, 19), "laughing and waving and shouting" (Phelan 2005, 18), and blessed by the local priest Father Kinsella, is portrayed as a cheerful and optimistic send-off, notwithstanding few critical remarks about taking the King's shilling (cf. Phelan 2005, 22) by sulky nationalists. Importantly, the decision of Matt and Con to become soldiers is the outcome of an innocent fascination with the British Empire and the attractive exoticness of places like "India and Kenya and Australia and Rhodesia and Jamaica and Malaya and Burma and Ceylon and Borneo too, and New Zealand. [...] Kilimanjaro. The Himalayas. The Khyber Pass. Cotopaxi. Chimborazo. Oh God!" (Phelan 2005, 44) – a fascination shared by many Irishmen at the time (Sokolowska-Paryz 2014, 337). Matt and Con were more or less seduced to join up by the imperial propaganda in the books of Mr. Hodgkins and the suggestions of his son Lionel, yet, Phelan never directly problematises their fascination. Throughout the novel, Matt and Con remain indifferent to the fact of their own colonial status as Catholic Irishmen and of Britain's role as coloniser of Ireland. For them, the British army neither is a tool of imperial oppression, nor a mere source of income as for many Irishmen. Until the outbreak of the Great War, it is seen rather naïvely as a sort of travel agency that provides an opportunity for the curious young men to leave behind the cherished and safe but also humble and confining world of Ballyrannel for the promise of a more exciting and, ironically, more self-determined life (cf. Phelan 2005, 58).

The transformation that the two Irish peasants undergo in the first year of their service is profound, amounting to a spiritual and physical rite of passage that practically renders their pre-army selves obsolete. Similar to the case of Shaw's Dennis O'Flaherty, the British army opens up completely new perspectives to Matt and Con: For the first time, they experience urban life in Dublin, interact with people from unfamiliar social and regional backgrounds, enjoy the unknown warmth of the Mediterranean sun and get a glimpse of the vastness of the world. Life in the rugged community of soldiers also leads to a maturation towards adult sexuality and confidence, Matt and Con overcoming existing boundaries of intimacy, privacy and morality.[104] The two Irishmen revel in their new lives as soldiers and enjoy the "newly acquired imperial masculinity" (Sokolowksa-Paryz 2014, 338) that their smartly uniformed bodies emanate. Well-fed, rigorously trained and fully equipped, they experience army life as intensely empowering as opposed to their previous peasant existence. Phelan phrases this in almost Brookean tones of martial exuberance: "Bulging with energy in every muscle, we were brimming with life, young as the sun, invincible, indestructible,

---

104 "The sergeant [...] ordered us to put our hands over our heads, to spread our legs, to move our hips so that our mickeys swung back between our legs and then slapped against our bellies. Then he shouted at us to look at the swinging mickey in front of us. The laughing started, and that was the end of being shy" (Phelan 2005, 57).

immortal [...]. The pure joy of it all – of being young, of being together, of trying to outdo each other" (Phelan 2005, 54). The two Ballyrannel men change from "country bumpkins [...] into golden-skinned warriors; peasants turning into knights who could look any man anywhere in the eye; paupers we had been, but now we were men with a jiggle in our pockets" (Phelan 2005, 56). This transformation neatly matches Elaine Scarry's observation of how upon entering the disciplining and unifying corporeal regime of the army, men become "inextricably bound up with the men and materials of [their] labor" (Scarry 1985, 83). Yet, importantly, Matt and Con's adoption of soldiership in the service of the Empire again remains apolitical in the sense that they do not at all conceive of themselves as representatives or enforcers of any specific political agenda. They turn into soldiers, but not into imperial patriots; their pride in their uniforms is pride in their new soldier selves, i. e. in what they perceive as 'soldiership'. Also, as they fully merge with the military collective, glorying in the prospect of an easier life in foreign lands, their distinctive Irishness becomes increasingly irrelevant. In their interaction with their comrades, their being Irish only becomes a factor again as English and Irish soldiers begin to keep to themselves in the aftermath of the Easter Rising, much to the dismay of Matt and Con (cf. Phelan 2005, 102).

The outbreak of the war puts an abrupt end to Matt and Con's long-cherished fantasies of tropical adventures with the British army. It means a disillusioning return to much bleaker European realities:

> Even though the sun was shining hotly on the backs of our legs and necks, we could feel the return of chilly winds and rains of England. A dark cloud of disappointment descended on the ship and it did not stir for two days as we all tried to get used to two new terrible ideas: we were not going to India and we were going to war. It was like we'd had a double-barrelled, rotten trick played on us. [...] The magic of the possibilities had turned out to be an illusion after all.
>
> (Phelan 2005, 74f.)

Importantly, the war, just as their service in the British army, is perceived not as a political or ideological matter by the two Irishmen. Phelan never has his two Irish soldiers work up any political enthusiasm by referring, possibly, to the eventual realisation of Home Rule, the rights of small nations, the containment of German aggression or any other of the established political reasons for contributing to the war effort. Instead of a confrontation of such concrete political positions, Phelan concentrates on something else. He puts forth a more universal, humanising and rather depoliticised view of the war, evoking an impartial sense of solidarity and respect in the novel that is extended to all soldiers involved in this "rotten trick" of a war waged by irresponsible statesmen. This includes "the lads from Ulster [who] got farther than anyone else" (Phelan 2005, 92) while being mercilessly sacrificed in the Battle of the Somme, as well as the German soldiers who, "without their helmets on, [...] looked just like us, same height, same coloured skin, same coloured hair, same age, every bit as dirty" (Phelan 2005, 144). The powerful claim that Phelan makes here (cf. Sokolowska-Paryz 2014, 341) – even if this is a well-established theme, not just in Irish war literature – is that all combatants are united across national and political divisions through their hardships, united as suffering human beings, deserving acknowledgement and sympathy. Considering Phelan's revisionist impetus and the divisive Irish legacy of the Great War, this view is of specific relevance.

Consequently, Phelan centrally focuses on the harshness of Matt and Con's individual experience. First and foremost, the war quickly and entirely shatters the powerful new self-image that Matt and Con had adopted. Amid the industrialised mass slaughtering of the battlefields, exalted ideas of heroic "golden-skinned warriors" and peasants turned into "knights" are completely out of place. Instead, serving as stretcher-bearers, not as fighters, Marzena Sokolowska-Paryz observes, Matt and Con are confronted on a daily basis with the most revolting results of combat, "the degradation of men to sheer corporeality" (Sokolowska-Paryz 2014, 338), death, mud, mutilation and victimhood: "heads in the muck, or legs, or arms" (Phelan 2005, 90). The grimmest facet of their service is Matt's administration of the *coup de grâce* to thousands of lethally wounded or abominably mutilated soldiers from all nations, "English, Irish, French, German, Indian, Senegalese" (Phelan 2005, 91). Matt, who acts out of heartfelt compassion, refers to this heavy task only euphemistically, possibly out of a sense of self-protection. He personalises his killing tool as "Knifey", the razor-sharp blade offering a quick way out of mortal agony, "kiss[ing] all the pain away if that's what's wanted" (ibid.).

As the war is dragging on, the outrage of the two Irishmen at the obscene human cost of the war and the apparent insanity of the entire undertaking grows. This culminates in an improbable scene in which Con antagonises the Commander in Chief of the British forces at the Western Front, Field Marshall Douglas Haig – a courageous gesture of protest on behalf of all suffering soldiers that eventually earns Con a death sentence. Covered in filth and smelling "like an open grave" (Phelan 2015, 194), Con introduces himself as a message "from all the lads" (Phelan 2015, 195) and mockingly invites a stunned Haig to visit the trenches and take a look at the actual results of his orders: "[T]he muck, and the rats, and the shite, and the piss, and the rotten corpses, and rotten horses" (ibid.). Phelan reproduces here the popular image of Haig as the "Butcher of the Somme", one of the villains in the 'Lost Generation' narrative. However, apart from illustrating the protest of common soldiers against the continuation of a disastrous war, the main purpose of the scene is encapsulated in another aspect of Con's accusations. Shortly before being arrested, Con declares that "[s]urely they'll make a statue of you on a horse after the War to pretend to themselves how great the War was, and when all the people are cheering you, Mr. Haig, it's not cheering you will hear but the hisses of the men you sent to hell" (Phelan 2005, 198). In this manner, Phelan highlights the problematic combination of power, politics and commemoration that enables the establishment, embodied by Haig, to popularise deceptive historical narratives and to legitimise senseless violence (cf. Sokolowska-Paryz 2014, 340f.). In the context of Phelan's concern with the long distorted approach to the Irish past and his anti-nationalist attitudes, this pattern also applies to the Irish situation of the idolisation of the Easter Rising rebels and the concomitant marginalisation of Irish soldiers of the Great War.

Interestingly, as Matt and Con are exposed to the horrors of the war and as "India" has long vanished as a viable prospect, their Irishness and their personal ties to their former home manifest themselves again. Matt and Con try to cope with the unspeakably violent reality of their daily lives by reframing their experiences in familiar terms and images they had essentially abandoned upon entering the army. For example, Con tries to imaginatively convert the unprecedentedly horrific sights of the battlefield into soothing familiar images from home:

> [B]loated horse-bodies floating in dark shell-holes were hippopotamuses in pictures in Mister Hodgkins's books; the muck was ploughed fields in Ireland on a tired Sunday evening after hunting rabbits on a miserable wet day; [...] the men going over the top by the thousands were little boys playing King of the Hill; the acres of dead bodies under a low-slung black sky, with lightning flashes on the horizon, were sheaves of barley before stoking.
>
> (Phelan 2005, 96)

Similarly, in a way foreshadowing the coming loss of Con and his own difficult return home, Matt begins to dream of the Ballyrannel canal, which now seems "[m]illions of miles away, so far away I'll never ...And then I imagine I'm on my way and it's only two more miles. Cork Corcoran's house is in sight on the bog road I have walked a million miles – walked and marched and run and crawled and crept and cried. Con with me everywhere. Con" (Phelan 2005, 89). However, these strategies inevitably prove futile in the face of the overwhelmingly appalling experience of the war and turn out to be counterproductive – as Con remarks, eventually, "reality smashed my defences [...], took my imagination and worked it against me" (Phelan 2005, 97). For example, the flares that light up the night sky over the trenches begin to remind Matt of the nightly shine of the fire that once killed his family in their hatch, orphaning him when he was just a boy (Phelan 2005, 133). Through this imaginary re-confrontation with their home, Phelan reaffirms Matt and Con's Irishness and the inseparability of their roots while being stranded in the international arena of the war. Yet, he also foreshadows that a possible return to Ballyrannel will not be unproblematic, that a restoration of pre-war selves and certainties is impossible considering the transformative dehumanising experience of the war. As Con realises, "if I lived to be a hundred, my body and mind would never be free again. My memory was being scarred forever and I knew it" (Phelan 2005, 116).

Apart from such more personal and psychological aspects, the return of the survivor Matt to his former life and his reintegration into his home community are compounded by the political changes in Ireland since 1916. Matt does not go back to find a "condition of the unitary" (Scarry 1985, 87f.), as Elaine Scarry describes the state of societies in the immediate post-war phase – Ireland in late 1918 is not an entity ideologically homogenised through the war effort that welcomes its returning soldiers in a spirit of gratitude. In the subchapter that introduces the novel's final part, "Coming Home", a Ballyrannel man named Jer Meaney describes the new atmosphere of hostility against the Irish involvement in the Great War that developed in the aftermath of the Easter Rising – and that crucially was linked to the issue of identity:

> Of course, [returning Matt] wasn't wearing the uniform. I wouldn't have been wearing it myself neither, if 'twere me, never knowing when you'd run into a Fenian or some bugger who'd give you hell for joining the army [...]. Ireland had changed since Matthias went off to join up. Those lads in 1916 had seen to that; suddenly you weren't a real Irishman if you'd fought in the English army. It was a terrible mix-up – most of the lads out in the trenches fighting for a daily wage on the English side, and suddenly at Easter, the English soldiers in Dublin shooting the yobs in Kilmainham. If you ask me, they got what they deserved. Of course, I'd never say that out loud, or I'd get hit by someone sooner or later, most likely in the back in the dark.
>
> (Phelan 2005, 165)

This rather sudden and fairly irrational turn, as well as the resulting dilemma of Irish veterans being perceived as traitors by radicalised sections of the public, is a central element in the third part of the novel. Yet, as apparent in the excerpt above, Phelan emphasises strongly in his revisionist construction of post-Rising rural Ireland that the condemnation of Irish soldiers and the idolisation of the Easter rebels was not as all-encompassing as often imagined. Not everybody, Phelan suggests, was instantly swept away by republican fervour after 1916; by 1918, the novel still evokes the impression that the supporters of the Rising and its anti-English aims were a minority, albeit a vocal and disruptive one. None of the different voices that make up the novel, including the nationalist ones, actually commends the Rising; both in the more contemporary and the retrospective views offered, it is regarded as an essentially foolish and futile episode that did more harm than good. The only truly passionate supporter of the Rising, Johnjoe Lacy, does not even get a voice in the novel and is only spoken about by the other characters although he plays an important role in the plot (cf. Sokolowksa-Paryz 2014, 344).

This distanced approach to the Easter Rising is a vital, even if at times awkwardly and slightly implausibly constructed, aspect of Phelan's concern with the Irish history of the 1910s and 1920s and the afterlife of that period. As Marzena Sokolowska-Paryz notes, "in order to restore the Irish soldiers of the Great War to their rightful place in national memory, it was necessary [for Phelan] to rewrite W. B. Yeats's version of the Easter Rising as the spiritual triumph of men whose willing sacrifice gave birth to a new Ireland" (Sokolowksa-Paryz 2014, 314) – for Phelan, the deconsecration of the event of the Easter Rising and the deflation of the influential discourses connected to it are prerequisites for an adequate approach to Ireland's Great War and its legacy. Accordingly, in *The Canal Bridge*, Phelan relativises and undermines images and narratives of heroic republican martyrdom in several ways. Through Matt, he contrasts the few mythologised dead of the Rising with the bloodbath of the Somme: "Twenty-seven thousand lying in the muck in front of us, many of them from Ireland, but all that Ireland could think of was twelve bastards who stabbed in the back every Irishman fighting against the Germans. Couldn't they have waited? Did they need to be heroes that badly?" (Phelan 2005, 93). Also, Patrick Pearse, the Rising's most iconic figure, is harshly criticised and ridiculed by several characters as an unmanly suicidal fanatic out of touch with reality, who "read too much poetry" (Phelan 2005, 85) and vainly threw away his life for fame – "a few hours in a trench in France on a wet day would have knocked the illusions out of that lad" (Phelan 2005, 102).

The most exemplary addressee of Phelan's demolition of republican radicalism in the novel is Johnjoe Lacy. As mentioned before, the ugly[105] and belligerent loud-mouth Lacy is a universally despised figure in the Ballyrannel community, even after the Easter Rising. Through him, Phelan points out the self-serving processes of myth-making and the delusional nationalist rhetoric of Irish martyrdom that for

---

105 Phelan stresses the contrast between the malicious figure of Lacy and the blameless Irish soldiers Matt and Con also on the level of appearances. Lacy is a dirty and bruised "skinny fecker" (Phelan 2005, 22) with a crooked nose and jawline, while Matt is "tall and long-armed with a head of black hair above a well-put-together face" and Con is "blond and within a hair's breadth of being too good-looking for a man" (Phelan 2005, 18).

some has become instrumental in discerning who is an 'Irishman' and who is not, and that actually is rather insignificant compared to the real dimensions of Irish (and non-Irish) suffering at European frontlines that Matt and Con witnessed. Ralphie Blake, a naïve street sweeper who was talked into participating in the deadly raid on Enderly, recounts about Lacy how

> [e]veryone in the town knew that Dan Griffin left Johnjoe nearly dead in the cowshite of the Fair Day. But many times from the wingboard of my cart, Johnjoe told me he had risen up out of the cowshite and it was this rising that had proved he'd been right to tell Dan Griffin he wasn't an Irishman at all. Johnjoe was proud of his injuries, he believed the nose and the jaw made people think that if only he'd had the chance he would have got the same wounds in Dublin in 1916, that he would have been out there in the frontlines laying down his life for Ireland twenty times over. He always managed to put his scars in front of the burning General Post Office with guns shooting all over the place.
>
> (Phelan 2005, 238f.)

Through the awkward exchanges between Lacy and an unwilling but weak Blake, Phelan also specifies the alienating or, at worst, treacherous transformation that Irishmen who joined the British forces undergo in the eyes of the nationalist part of the public. Blake notes how "there was something about all the lads who'd been in the War. It was like they'd seen things, had apparitions like the girl at Lourdes and been changed, made different from the rest of us. [...] [N]one of them giving a shite about the IRA or about what happened in Dublin at Easter in 1916" (Phelan 2005, 237). To please Lacy, Blake also confirms how they are "not Irish anymore after being in the English army so long. Some of them talk like they're English. They don't believe in God anymore and they don't care if the Hodgkinses are Protestants or Catholics or pagans" (Phelan 2005, 239). The willing acceptance of the foreign culture of the English army and the violation of the boundaries between Irish, English and Anglo-Irish identities, Blake suggests, has anglicised people like Matt. Back in their Irish communities after the war, they are seen as occupying dangerously liminal positions and cannot be safely placed in either category of the sharp Irish-English binary that dominates the nationalist world view. In Lacy's view, this is an unnatural condition for an Irishman and, ludicrously, Phelan has him assume that deep inside, "traitors" like Matt are actually longing for a repatriation to 'true' Irishness, all "panting, all waiting for the chance to fight the English to get forgiveness from the real Irish – the anti-English, patriotic and Catholic Irish" (Phelan 2005, 240).

The actual process of Matt's homecoming is of course more complex than that. It neither results in a happy reunion and the restoration of his light-hearted pre-war self, as hoped by Matt's friend and lover Kitty, nor in the ultimate adoption of a completely alienated 'English' veteran identity. Apathetic and almost mute, Matt initially is frustratingly unresponsive to Kitty's efforts, the harrowing loss of Con becoming all too obvious to him upon returning to Ballyrannel. Only after coming back to the canal, the quintessential site of his pre-war existence, does Matt begin to slowly reconnect with the world he left behind for the army. Phelan integrates this in a highly evocative scene in which a fully clothed Matt lowers himself into the water of the canal and asks Kitty to wash him, Kitty symbolically scrubbing off the muck of the trenches in a ritual of reunion. In this moment, Matt's helplessness and his emasculation resulting from his war experiences specifically become apparent – as a perplexed Kitty notes, "there was no response from his adult body. [...] I dried and dressed him as if he were a three-year-old" (Phelan 2005, 181).

Importantly, Matt's eventual recovery to mental and physical stability after many months is achieved not principally by means of Kitty's loving efforts of reintegration. In fact, it is the cross-class friendship of Matt and Sarah Hodgkins that enables him to re-enter civilian life. Phelan here revisits the theme of unification across social and national boundaries in war through shared suffering – Matt can connect with the traumatised Anglo-Irish VAD nurse Sarah on a level that is inaccessible to the non-combatant Kitty. Together, Matt and Sarah can process their experiences of fear and guilt more honestly and effectively to find working forms of closure. Interestingly, at the same time, the concept of shared suffering beyond nominal constraints is also at work in the case of Kitty and Mrs. Hodgkins, Sarah's mother. As self-declared "sisters in anxiety" (Phelan 2005, 205), the Irish domestic servant and her upper-class Anglo-Irish employer bond over the shared worry about the recovery of their war-damaged loved ones.

Matt manages to come to terms with the burden of his war experience by the end of the novel, living and working in the liberal environment of the Hodgkins's estate, married to his childhood friend Kitty. Still, he remains profoundly changed, the war has become an irremovable facet of his self. Most impressively, in the novel's concluding moment of crisis, the IRA attack on Enderly, 'English' soldierly qualities Matt apparently acquired[106] in the war make a drastic and fairly uncanny comeback. Outnumbered in a standoff with six aggressors from his own Ballyrannel community, Matt unflinchingly kills one of his opponents, who was about to rape his friend Sarah, with a hammer. In this tense moment, Phelan even has the reawakened soldier Matt recall the heavily mythologised medieval Battle of Agincourt, a staple element of English patriotic propaganda not only during the Great War. Facing

---

106 Matt's combat skills and demonstration of military authority in the scene actually seem slightly implausible considering his original role as a stretcher-bearer in the war.

the destruction of the home they share, Matt explains to Kitty and Sarah that "[a]n English army once beat a French army six times as big" (Phelan 2005, 264), reassuring them and himself that he will handle the situation. Stunned by his display of unbridled brutality, fearlessness and military authority, the amateurish IRA attackers led by Johnjoe Lacy actually give in to Matt's commands – however, only to turn on him and Kitty at the first opportunity. Matt, the war-hardened heroic defender of Enderly, is cowardly murdered by the republican zealots.

Significantly, the site of Matt's violent death is the Hodgkins's machine shed, which was previously introduced by Con as a symbol of peaceful pre-war country life and the possibility of harmonious Irish and Anglo-Irish co-existence, although within traditional paternalistic hierarchies. As Con remembers, Mr. Hodgkins's annual "blessing of men and machine was a pleasant little ceremony that had developed over the years in the shadow of the Machine Shed, Catholics and Protestants praying together in a farmyard when they weren't allowed to pray together in a church, the unspoken defiance uniting the participants" (Phelan 2005, 137f.) – an image that reminds of the unifying collaborative project of the barn in McCartney's *Heritage*. This pre-war ideal is destroyed by the delusional hatred of Irish republicanism embodied by Lacy and a few other Ballyrannel men, as is the promising example of a more open and humane cross-class community set by Matt, Kitty, and the Hodgkins family. As in the other works covered in this study which construct harmonious Irish-Anglo-Irish relations or positive visions of the Big House, also *The Canal Bridge* eventually disappoints these hopes.

Taking up again the commemorative framework set by Phelan's dedication and acknowledgements, and rounding off the novel's collection of voices, the last chapter of *The Canal Bridge* is presented from Kitty's perspective in 1970, looking back at her worrisome life and her loneliness as the only remaining member of the ill-fated Hatchel-Wrenn-Hodgkins bond. For a long time, the now seventy-four-year-old woman has been an odd figure in her community, gossip about her still circulating among the people of Ballyrannel, who apparently have adopted mainstream nationalist values: "She never goes to Mass", "She lives with Protestants", "She was a terrible one when she was young, always in fights" (Phelan 2005, 273). Kitty is aware of her outsider status, yet, true to the confident and energetic image of her created earlier in the novel, she is unfazed by the rumours. What really does concern her in the final years of her life is the feeling of her story slipping away – the certainty that her personal memories of Matt, Con and the others and what they stood for will be lost one day:

> The dead people who were once so important to us quickly become mere lines in a
> closed book when we who remember them pass from the scene. [...] When I die, gone

forever will be the pain created by the loss of Lionel and Con and Matt, and now Sarah and her husband Phillip. There will be only knowledge. History books cannot pass on the pain endured, the anguish, the terror of the times. I suppose it's good that they can't. Even a headstone in a cemetery, leaned on and wept at for years, becomes just one more piece of cold granite when the final rememberer dies.

(Phelan 2005, 278)

Like the remaining bridges over the now dried up canal, still standing but "leading to nowhere" (Phelan 2005, 277) and irrelevant for modern Ballyrannel, the tragic story of the Hatchel triplets will survive, if at all, only as an isolated episode that no one can relate to as deeply and meaningfully as Kitty. Phelan addresses here a central problem of commemoration, the discrepancy of individual and collective memory and the absorption of the former by the latter, inevitably being transformed into "knowledge" or, as in the case of the Irish history of the Great War, into functional politicised narratives detached from the important original emotional dimension of the event. This is what Phelan tries to point out in *The Canal Bridge*. He suggests, as Marzena Sokolowksa-Paryz argues, that the "path to understanding the Irish past, beyond the contending political interpretations of the Great War and the Easter Rising, leads through the thoughts and emotions of the people of that particular time, even if these people are only figments of the authors imagination" (Sokolowska-Paryz 2014, 345).

Summing up, *The Canal Bridge* represents an attempt to extract the story of Irishmen serving in the British forces during the Great War from the divisive politicised nationalist framework within which it has long been seen, instead promoting a view of national history determined by "historical empathy" (ibid.). Phelan works against the reductive negative stereotype of Irish soldiers as traitors or mercenaries of the British Empire by portraying them as valuable members of their home community beyond political demarcation lines, as blameless victims of a horrific conflict that was not their making, and as men who heroically take a stand for others. Phelan also concentrates on the complexity of processes of identity transformation his Irish soldiers undergo, eventually highlighting the essential inseparability of their Irish roots. Phelan's efforts of rehabilitation are paralleled by a scathing critique of radical Irish nationalism and its discourses of martyrdom and anti-English aggression. In Phelan's revisionist re-construction of wartime rural Ireland, it is a minority of republicans that poisons a once peaceful community with a divisive ideology and identity politics, destroying the beginnings of a more liberal form of Irish and Anglo-Irish coexistence that was centrally shaped by the shared experience of the Great War.

The Canal Bridge is not free of occasional implausibilities of plot as well as some other aspects that may be regarded as imbalances and simplifications.[107] While essentially sharing Phelan's concern of a re-envisioning of Ireland's Great War history, the final two authors covered in this study, Sebastian Barry and Dermot Bolger, are slightly more sensitive in their approach than Phelan, offering a less polarised perspective on the war and Irish identities, particularly in their reference to the context of Irish nationalism and the Easter Rising.

III.3.5 Sebastian Barry's *A Long Long Way* (2005)

Born in Dublin in 1955 as the son of the well-known actress Joan O'Hara, Sebastian Barry came into contact with theatre from an early age, the Abbey Theatre "forming an important background to his childhood" (Wehrmann 2010, 1). He began his literary career in 1982 as a poet but soon also turned to the writing of novels and plays. Since then, Barry has been recognised as a distinguished and popular voice in contemporary Irish literature, which also shows in a number of literary awards he received, among them the James Tait Black Memorial Prize and nominations for the Man Booker Prize.

The issue of Irish history and memory informs many of his works. This interest is connected to a specific motivation of Barry – almost from the beginning of his career, Barry has been outspoken about the need for a reformed approach to Irish history in order to overcome parochialism and false nationalist nostalgia. For example, in *The Inherited Boundaries*, his 1986 anthology of young Irish poets, Barry calls for modern Ireland to find its own literary expression while pleading for radical cultural pluralism (cf. Wehrmann 2010, 10f.), rejecting – fairly ironically, considering Barry's own fixation on re-writing Irish history – the "philosophy of cultural back-track" (ibid.) that he identifies as dominating Irish cultural and political life. Edna Longley has seen *The Inherited Boundaries* as heralding the developing southern revisionism of the period (cf. Longley 1994, 47), and since the late 1980s, Barry's works indeed have been frequently labelled 'revisionist' – of course, with varying degrees of approval. Some critics have accused Barry of merely reversing the traditional nationalist dichotomies of heroism and villainy, or of casting a view on historical figures and situations that reserves compassion and understanding only for those who were not part of the nationalist mainstream (cf. Kenny 2005, 10; Wehrmann 2010, 10ff.; Harte 2012,

---

107 As Marzena Sokolowska-Paryz notes, Phelan is not primarily interested in producing an entirely accurate reconstruction of the war period but in changing the perception of this period in the present (cf. Sokolowska-Paryz 2014, 345).

104ff.) – in the case of Barry's 2005 novel *A Long Long Way*, as will be shown shortly, such charges are unwarranted.[108]

Barry tries to open up alternative narratives of Irish history in his writings, shedding light on aspects and identities of the Irish past previously dwarfed or obliterated by the dominant nationalist view, thereby elucidating also the problematic processes of how history and memory have been constructed and used in Ireland. In the words of Fintan O'Toole, the Irish history Barry presents in his works is a "history of anomalous people" (O'Toole 1995, v) and "of countercurrents, of lost strands, of untold stories. Against the simple narrative of Irish history as a long tale of colonisation and resistance, Barry releases more complex stories of people who are, in one way or another, a disgrace to that history" (O'Toole 1995, vii). This disgrace, Roy Foster remarks, frequently is the outcome of "religious exclusion, or a change of regime, or a redefinition of loyalty" (Foster 2006a, 183) – in *A Long Long Way*, it is the latter that effects the downfall and historical obliteration of Barry's soldier protagonist Willie Dunne. In this manner, Barry also underlines the connection between political, cultural and religious allegiances and identity in his works, exposing how "those who cannot keep up with the speed of change" (Wehrmann 2010, 14) remain left behind. Altogether, Barry creates a framework of a more comprehensive and heterogeneous view of Irish identity which he understands as the outcome of a "collective history that must [...] be considered [...] as plural, made up of a multitude of individual histories that are not necessarily convergent but often painful" (Seree-Chaussinand 2010, 60) and that necessitates reconciliation.

Barry's approach to Irish history is an individual and private one set against the grand narratives. It is inspired by the obscure parts of his own family history, which also shows in the "involved sense of urgency" (Kenny 2005, 10) that characterises his works. For example, the character of Thomas Dunne, the main protagonist of Barry's seminal play *The Steward of Christendom* and an important figure in *A Long Long Way*, is based on Barry's great-grandfather, who was a Catholic unionist and a superintendent in the Dublin Metropolitan police. "[T]hese people", Barry once remarked, "survive in me somewhere, in a corner of the brain, in the heart, wherever, and somehow or other release their stories", however, at the same time, in the Irish cultural and political mainstream, they represent an unwanted past – they

---

108   I have addressed the subject of Irish history and marginalised Irish identities in Barry's *A Long Long Way* in an earlier essay entitled "'I'm at home, you little bastards' – Re-Envisioning the Marginalised Irish Soldier in Sebastian Barry's *A Long Long Way* and Dermot Bolger's *Walking the Road*" (cf. Decker 2015). Several of the ideas outlined in the following can be found in a more comprehensive form in that essay.

"are not spoken about because the truth about them cannot be admitted to. [...] A silence grew around them. So we have a censored past, censored individuals, and a country whose history is erased" (quoted in Kenny 2005, 10).

Focusing on the Irish dimension of the Great War, *A Long Long Way* represents an attempt to reconstruct a slice of the history of such censored identities and to reposition and re-contextualise them in Ireland's national or, as has been argued, post-national narrative (cf. Decker 2015, 84). The novel was very well received both by critics and readers, also being shortlisted for the 2005 Man Booker Prize, and it has also attracted considerable academic attention. Eugene McNulty praises *A Long Long Way* as "the most sustained attempt by a modern Irish novelist to engage with the visceral horrors endured by (southern) Irish soldiers in the trenches of Europe. It is also [...] a subtle exploration of the conditions that have made such a direct engagement difficult in the past" (McNulty 2010, 76). This dual interest is also reflected in the novel's title, which is borrowed from the most iconic of soldiers' songs of the Great War, "It's a Long Way to Tipperary", a music hall piece initially popularised by the Connaught Rangers in August 1914. The image of the "long, long way" home does not only evoke the general sentiment of homesickness, of the soldiers' painful distance from home as they are serving abroad, but it also hints at the more specific notion of the post-war alienation of Irish soldiers from the transformed state and society to which they returned, a condition only rectified many decades later, when most Irish veterans had already passed away.

Moreover, Barry straightforwardly embeds his work in the discourses of rediscovery and rehabilitation of Ireland's part in the Great War in Irish historiography that have developed since the 1980s (cf. Foster 2006a, 191), providing a bibliography of the works of Jeffery, Denman, Hennessey and others in the acknowledgements in the back of the novel. In an almost didactic manner, *A Long Long Way* meticulously covers the variety of views on the war, illustrates the reasoning behind different allegiances and identities, including a brief look at the Anglo-Irish (cf. Foster 2006a, 190), and addresses insightfully almost all the developments relevant to the Irish experience of the Great War, Barry sending his main protagonist through a series of emblematic situations and scenarios.

Many of Barry's works are thematically and personally interrelated, presenting different facets and sections of the history of two families, the Dunnes and the McNultys. Across several of Barry's novels and plays, characters reoccur at different stages of their development and family story lines are played through various perspectives and settings. This also applies to *A Long Long Way*, which expands the tragic story of Private Willie Dunne that had already been alluded to in an earlier and much lauded play of Barry's, *The Steward of Christendom* (1995). Before discussing the novel, I will briefly look at this play, in some way the sequel to *A Long Long Way*, which provides an intriguing retrospective angle on Willie Dunne: the regretful view of Willie's father on the war service of his late son. The play is also relevant for my reading of *A Long Long Way* as it prefigures the novel's desire to humanise the image of Irishmen associated with a shunned chapter of Irish history, without bluntly justifying or sanctioning their political positions (cf. Wehrmann 2010, 5).

The Steward of Christendom is a memory play set in a county home for the mentally ill in Baltinglass, Co. Wicklow, in 1932. It shows the struggle of Thomas Dunne, a former chief superintendent of the Dublin Metropolitan Police and Catholic unionist in his seventies, with his problematic personal past and with the loss of the Ireland to which he had dedicated his entire life, 'Victorian' colonial Ireland. Importantly, in Thomas, the realms of both personal experience and public allegiance are inextricably intertwined (cf. Gleitman 2004, 226). The sense of how Thomas's political identity has become outdated and unacceptable in the new Irish state of the early 1930s is unmistakable from the beginning. Right at the outset of the first act, Smith, the nurse who takes care of Thomas, leaves no doubt that the tables have turned in Ireland and aggressively turns on the senile man:

Dublin Metropolitan Police, weren't you, boyo? In your braid. The DMP that are no more. Oh, la-di-da. Look at you. [...] Castle Catholic bugger that you were. But you're just an old bastard in here with no one to sponge you but Smith. [...] Chief Superintendent, this big gobshite was [...] that killed four good men and true in O'Connell Street in the days of the lock-out. [...] His men it was struck down the strikers. (*A gentle hit with the drying cloth.*) Baton-charging. A big loyal Catholic gobshite, killing poor hungry Irishmen. If you weren't an old madman we'd flay you.

(Barry 1996, 75)

While not all staff members of the county home are as downright abrasive as Smith, the placing of Thomas in this state institution still chimes with the notion of independent Ireland disposing of unwanted elements. In the words of Jürgen Wehrmann, the county home might be seen as "an instrument of the new state's exclusion and disciplining of groups and historical narratives that cannot be contained in national identity and remembrance" (Wehrmann 2010, 5).

Like the outsider Kenneth Pyper in McGuinness's *Observe the Sons of Ulster*, also the outsider Thomas Dunne is trapped in-between past and present, being continuously haunted by the ghosts of the past and tortured by his memories: "(*Thomas kneels at the end of his bed and grips the metal tightly*) I must not speak to shadows. When you see the shadows, Thomas, you must not speak. Sleep in the afternoon, that's the ticket. How did I get myself into this pickle, is it age just?" (Barry 1996, 84). One of the "shadows" that keeps visiting Thomas is the ghost of Willie, his son, who was killed in the Great War. Willie only briefly appears in three moments of the play and, apart from a short exchange with his father and some singing, he remains mute. Yet, his ghostly presence is crucial as it underlines one of Thomas's greatest regrets – having encouraged his son to enlist:

> (*His son, Willie, neat and round, comes in and sits on the end of his bed and sings to him Schubert's* Ave Maria. *At the end, Thomas looks over the sheet. Willie wears his uniform.*)
> THOMAS: Hello, child. Are you warm?
> WILLIE: It's cold in the mud, Father.
> THOMAS: I know child. I'm so sorry.

(Barry 1996, 85)

Later, in the presence of ghostly Willie, Thomas remembers the day he received the harrowing news of Willie's death: "Why do they send the uniforms to the fathers and the mothers? I put it over my head and cried for a night, like an owl in a tree. I cried for a night with your uniform over my head, and no one saw me" (Barry 1996, 115). These shattering experiences are the grave personal consequences of Thomas acting on his public political identity. As a unionist and public servant, it was natural and self-evident for Thomas to send Willie off to serve in the Great War, yet, the price was painfully high – regardless of his political convictions, Thomas is unable to elicit a sense of pride or at least the notion of a necessary and meaningful sacrifice from the war death of his son. Now, in the present of the play, there is only despair.

The play ends with Thomas telling Willie about a touching incident from his own childhood, the story of a troublemaking but much-loved dog on the Dunne's farm, who had killed a ewe and was about to be put down in retaliation. To save his life, Thomas ran away with the dog but since it was winter, he could not stay away long and ultimately had to go home again. Upon return, surprisingly, instead of being punished and the dog being killed, Thomas was embraced by his worried father, who was greatly relieved by the safe return of his son; also, the dog's crime was never spoken of again. Through this story of devotion, love and forgiveness, the play ends on a consoling note of empathy. This call of course is also directed at the fate of the outmoded class of Thomas, "that most erased of figures, the Catholic loyalist" (Grene 2006, 170). The tender presence of Willie, who brings his father over to his bed, sits next to him in his uniform while listening to his story and then lies close to him, the two falling asleep,[109] extends this call for compassion also to

---

109   This image also strongly resembles the final embrace of Old Pyper and Young Pyper in McGuinness's *Observe the Sons of Ulster*, two characters embodying the problematic relationship of the present and the past.

the "erased" figure of the Irish Great War soldier. In this manner, partisan views on people like Thomas and Willie Dunne as little more than malicious and wilful accomplices of a tyrannical colonial regime are countered and humanised by Barry. He constructs the unionist Irishmen Thomas and Willie as vulnerable and caring individuals and he lets Thomas speak for himself, evoking the image of a misled but principally decent and well-intentioned "servant of a protective matriarchy" (Grene quoted in Brown 2004, 404), who is worthy not only of the audience's but also modern Ireland's empathy and recognition.

Many aspects of the ill-fated story of Thomas and Willie Dunne reappear in *A Long Long Way*, however, this time the focus is on the son. The novel is set in Dublin and at various military and battle locations in England and at the Western Front during the Great War. Willie Dunne's childhood and adolescence, which are outlined concisely at the outset of the novel, are characterised by his admiration for his serious, elegant and awe-inspiring father Thomas, a Catholic unionist and high-ranking officer of the Dublin Metropolitan Police, and by Willy's frustration about his physical weakness and, specifically, his insufficient height. Officially not tall enough to follow the example of Thomas and join the DMP, Willie decides to volunteer in the British army right at the outbreak of the First World War, at the age of seventeen. As a soldier of the Royal Dublin Fusiliers, he fairly naïvely lives through typical experiences of the Great War and army life. During his first visit home, Willie has to contribute to the crushing of the 1916 Easter Rising, an event that he does not understand and that leaves him deeply confused as he soon goes off to war again. The ensuing public division in Ireland about the Rising and the role of the Irish in the Great War soon also reaches the troops at the front. Willie's increasing doubts about his part in the whole affair lead to a fundamental rift between him and his angered father, who feels his formerly powerful status slipping away. On his second visit home, Willie gets a taste of his coming displacement as an Irish soldier in the British army. "Dublin was no longer a city intent on the war" (Barry 2006, 253), the novel's third-person-narrator notes, and Willie is subsequently physically attacked in public for serving with the "fucking Tommies" (Barry 2006, 254). Willie is forced to leave his home; furthermore, he finds out that Gretta, the woman he loves, has married another man. Disappointed, bewildered and helpless, Willie returns to the front. In another intense battle he is wounded and wakes up shell-shocked in an English military hospital. Despite his utter disillusionment and mental fragility, Willie returns to his decimated unit after his recovery. He is finally killed on the battlefield by a single shot in a calm autumn night in 1918 and buried on the spot. His father's moving letter, apologising to Willy and expressing his love, arrives too late (cf. Decker 2015, 84).

A crucial concern of Barry's approach is to challenge the simplifying and polarising processes of identity politics connected to the nationalist narrative of Ireland – the story of heroic Easter rebels and misguided Irish Great War soldiers. As Barry once remarked, "a game is played with our history and our society, of cops and robbers, goodies and baddies. But there is no such thing" (quoted in Kenny 2005, 10), and with *A Long Long Way*, he sets out to paint a more differentiated picture. In the novel, Barry determinedly portrays Irish soldiers as complex individuals with individual and, at times, contradictory motivations and expectations (cf. Decker 2015, 84). He exemplarily covers the complexity of reasons and aims that motivated Irishmen to enlist, also introducing an individualising note that keeps his characters from functioning as mere signifiers of the major political identities of the age.

Considering Willie Dunne, despite coming from a staunchly politicised unionist background, his reasons for volunteering at first appear fairly ambiguous and vague:

> [M]uch against Gretta's desires, he wanted to go to war. It was difficult for him to explain to her why it was so, because it was difficult to put it into words for himself. He told her it was because he loved her he had to go, that there were women like her being killed by the Germans in Belgium, and how could he let that happen? Gretta did not understand. He said he would go to please his father also and though she did understand that, she thought it a poor enough reason. [...] But he knew he must play his part, and when he came home he would not be remorseful, but content in his heart that he had followed his mind.
>
> (Barry 2006, 13)

The most central impetus to join up for Willie is more personal than political: Willie's volunteering represents a much desired initiation to manhood and adulthood,[110] a quest for masculinity (cf. Mosse 1985, 115) and a huge step towards being able to live up to the example set by his father. Soon after entering the army, Willie, just as the soldier protagonists in Phelan's novel, indeed recognises how military training and the new experience of living in a rough community of adult men have been transforming him: "He could think of only one word to describe everything, bloody manhood at last" (Barry 2006, 21). Not having seen combat yet, Willie is easily swept away with euphoria and completely adopts his new soldier persona, including the propaganda:

---

110 This was a common sentiment among young soldiers of the Great War (cf. Roper 2004, 309).

[H]e imagined for a moment that he had grown those wanting inches, and might go now after all and be a policemen if he chose, astonishing his father. The men of the decent world had been asked by Lord Kitchener to go and drive back the filthy Hun, back where they belonged, in their own evil country beyond the verdant borders of Belgium. [...] It was this country he had come to heal, he himself, Willie Dunne.

(Barry 2006, 22)

Yet, Willie's exuberance is instantly deflated the moment he sets foot on the battlefield for the first time – again, Barry refers to Willie's height to illustrate his disillusionment: "When they came into their trench he felt small enough. The biggest thing there was the roaring of Death and the smallest thing was a man" (Barry 2006, 24).

Against Willy's nominally unionist innocence, Barry positions other Irish characters, whose war service is more complex and problematic considering their class affiliations and political allegiances. In his first appearance, Willy's foulmouthed commanding officer, Christy Moran, a middle-class Irish nationalist, delivers a passionate diatribe against "[t]his fucking British army" that is run by "English bastards", serving "the [...] fucking King" (Barry 2006, 25f.), while it is a known fact among his platoon that Moran actually comes from an Irish family with a long history in the British military.[111] Later, it is revealed that it was actually a terrible accident of his wife in which she lost a hand that made Moran continue the family tradition and join up – not only in order to be able to support her financially, but "because he could not live with such trouble. The distress of his wife was worse to him than any charging Hun or gas attack" (Barry 2006, 31).

An even more intriguing example of conflicting allegiances is Jesse Kirwan. The constitutional Irish nationalist Kirwan originally volunteered in support of John Redmond, going off to war to ensure Home Rule for Ireland. However, after the Easter Rising, he begins to refuse to follow the orders of his superiors and when Willie visits him in his improvised prison, Kirwan faces capital punishment. Strikingly, Kirwan actually wants to be killed:

They do have to shoot me. I want them to. [...] [A]n Irishman can't fight this war now. Not after those lads being executed. [...] I won't serve in that uniform that lads wore when they shot those other lads. I can't. I'm not eating so I can shrink, and not be touching the cloth of this uniform, you know? I am trying to disappear, I suppose.

(Barry 2006, 154f.).

---

111 Roy Foster notes how the figure of Moran represents "one of several points where Barry's work chimes with recent preoccupations of Irish historiography: the many ways in which Irish Catholics, often middle-class nationalists, made their careers through imperial channels" (Foster 2006, 9) – another facet of Irish experience previously overlooked.

Kirwan's renunciation of his earlier allegiance is not just driven by a sudden veneration of the 'martyrs' of the Rising but also by the recognition that his original goal of Home Rule has become impossible: The rebels "have ruined everything. Now we won't have a country at all. Now everything you and me and the others were trying to do is useless. But then they started shooting those poor men, and that was a filthy business" (Barry 2006, 156). Kirwan's refusal to obey and his wish for self-elimination, "to disappear", also foreshadow the similar predicament of Willie at the end of the novel, as well as, Eugene McNulty argues, "the fissures that will open up in Irish history in the wake of 1916. Kirwan's Kafkaesque act of shrinking enacts his future historiographical erasure on his still living body [...]. His tragedy is that he already knows he will be rejected by the historical forces that he in fact feels loyalty towards" (McNulty 2010, 79).

Despite their political, sectarian and national differences, there are very little animosities between Barry's men at war. The collective identity of the men as soldiers, as a community sharing a historical moment of danger, fear, deprivation and death in a strange environment, actually surpasses the harsh divisions that separate them at home. This also extends to the divide of Ulster unionists and Irish nationalists, even after the Easter Rising. For example, when Willie and his comrades receive the news of the devastating losses of the 36th Ulster Division on the first day of the Battle of the Somme, they are not indifferent or smug but shocked and compassionate: "There was odd love there for the brave Ulstermen; what could a man do against that love? Nothing at all, only add to it by thinking and weeping privately" (Barry 2006, 150). This view, by the way, is not a wishful retrospective harmonising fantasy of Barry. Among the Irish soldiers of the Great War, even if they were separated by political outlook, there generally was mutual respect. As Keith Jeffery notes, "the sombre truth remains that the nationalist and unionist Irish casualties of the Great War became more divided in death than they had ever been in life" (Jeffery 1993, 153) – the sense of polarisation that has surrounded the narratives of Ireland's Great War very much is a retrospective construction (cf. McNulty 2010, 78).

Along these lines, Barry casts a different view on the Irish participants of the Great War. He constructs Willie Dunne and his comrades not to live up to or compete against but to reach beyond conceptions of heroism, valour, strength and determination. In fact, the novel is underpinned by a comprehensive deflation of any notion of patriotic self-sacrifice, embracing instead, like Phelan, the well-established pacifist and distinctively internationalist view on the Great War that highlights shared experiences of suffering and loss (cf. Harte 2012, 111). This sentiment is introduced right at the outset of the novel, when Barry positions

Willie Dunne within a global generation preordained to be senselessly sacrificed, consciously reinserting the commonly forgotten "Irish bodies [...] into the network of participants in the 1914–18 conflict" (McNulty 2010, 77):

> And all those boys of Europe born in those times, [...] Russian, French, Belgian, Serbian, Irish, English, Scottish, Welsh, Italian, Prussian, German, Austrian, Turkish – and Canadian, Australian, American, Zulu, Gurkha, Cossack, and all the rest – their fate was written in a ferocious chapter of the book of life, certainly. [...] [H]uman stories told for nothing, for ashes, for death's amusement, flung on the mighty scrapheap of souls, all those million boys in all their humours to be milled by the mill-stones of the coming war.
>
> (Barry 2006, 4)

Willie learns to fully embrace this view by the end of the novel, his initial naivety and innocence overpowered by the experience of death and destruction both at the Western Front and at home:

> Some of his new thoughts offended even him. It had nothing to do with kings and countries, rebels or soldiers. Generals or their dark ambitions, their plus and their minus. It was that Death himself had made those things ridiculous. Death was the King of England, Scotland, and Ireland. The King of France. Of India, Germany, Italy, Russia. Emperor of all the empires. He had taken Willie's companions, lifted away entire nations, looked down on their struggles with contempt and glee. [...] And his old loyalty, his old faith in the cause, as a man might say, a dozen times so sorely tested, was dying in Willie Dunne. An ember maybe only remaining, for his father's sake.
>
> (Barry 2006, 279)

Willie finally becomes aware of his alienation and the eventual pointlessness and inhumanity of any form of violent patriotism (cf. Decker 2015, 85). His insight challenges not only the unionist certainties, the "old faith in the cause", within which Willie was raised and which provided the context for his enlistment – through Willie's critique, Barry also challenges the nationalist ideal of self-sacrifice and martyrdom upon which the new Ireland was founded.

Barry's project of humanisation and his deconstruction of nationalist and imperialist discourses of heroism also extend to the closely connected aspect of masculinity. The depiction of Willie's confusing experience of the Easter Rising represents one of the most striking subversions of these concepts (cf. ibid.). Barry denies the fighters of the Rising the masculinist qualities of strength, determination and fearlessness traditionally attributed to them. Accordingly, moving into battle, Willie's captain nonchalantly predicts that the upcoming fight against the insurgents will by no means be a dangerous confrontation with unrelenting, ferocious revolutionaries: "We won't be long mopping these lads up" (Barry 2006, 90). In a similar vein, Willie's face-to-face encounter with one of the rebels turns out distinctly unimpressive: Willie, who actually thinks he is facing a German, is briefly held at gunpoint by an insurgent, who assumes that Willie is an Englishman. The insurgent is described not as a hyper-masculine Irish Volunteer bent on martyrdom for Ireland but as "a very young shivering man in a Sunday suit and a sort of military hat, and an ancient-looking revolver held in both his hands" (Barry 2006, 92). His voice trembling, the young man declares Willie arrested ("I need you for prisoner, Tommy" (ibid.)) – only to be casually shot in the neck seconds later by Willie's captain: "'Rifle jammed, Private?' [...] The captain issued a sardonic laugh and pulled away again" (ibid.).

Importantly, Barry's subversion of masculine heroism also includes the Irish soldiers. Barry undermines military ideals of masculine purity and strength by unglamorously documenting the fearful struggle for survival on the battlefield in graphic detail. In moments of deadly peril, Barry has his protagonists lose control of their bodies, soldiers involuntarily crying, urinating and defecating:

> At least six lads now were entirely blinded and Captain Sheridan moved them roughly back to the parados side of the trench [...]. Willie Dunne had just shat his pants, he could not help it, no more than a man who was hanged could help the stiff pecker he showed to the mocking crowds.
>
> "Oh Jesus," he said to himself, "Oh Jesus, protect us."
>
> He wished his father's lot could rush up now with batons drawn and dispel this horrible unruly gas, drive it off the page of the world.
>
> "Papa, Papa," he said. Then he found a picture in his mind of the gates of his grandfather's house in Lathaleer [...]. "Grandpa, Grandpa," he whispered, "protect us."
>
> (Barry 2006, 114)

> Of the twelve hundred, how many remained? How many hearts stopped beating, how many souls to their allotted places, how many in the crowds now also clogging up the way under St. Peter's gate, and did the saint wonder at these sudden hordes advancing on him with their Irish accents from the Four Green Fields to beseech the mercies of heaven? The shit he had shat in his pants was hardening, making Willie Dunne's backside devilishly itchy. It was Easter Thursday in that realm of myriad deaths.
>
> (Barry 2006, 116)

In the latter quotation, Barry connects the sorrowful aftermath of a particularly vicious gas attack with the ongoing fighting in Dublin. As opposed to Phelan's *The Canal Bridge*, the novel's treatment of the Irish experiences of *both* the Great War and the Easter Rising is determined by the aim of a humanisation and de-politicisation of their protagonists, highlighting the unacceptable human cost of political violence, whatever the ideology. In this manner, Barry frees both the figure of the soldier and of the Easter rebel from ideologically burdened perspectives, and he challenges the hold of traditional identity constructions (cf. Decker 2015, 85).

The connection of the Easter Rising and the Great War, as well as the Rising's historical significance for the marginalisation of Ireland's Great War experience, is reflected extensively in the novel. Barry's depiction of the fighting in and around the General Post Office through the eyes of an Irish soldier is a rare perspective.[112] Willie Dunne's utter incomprehension of the background and of the implications of the very event in which he is ordered to take part allows Barry to provide a vivid synopsis of the Rising and its links to the Great War in the form of a history lesson from Jesse Kirwan (cf. Foster 2006a, 188f.), creating a more complex image than the one offered in *The Canal Bridge*. Kirwan explains to a perplexed Willie the differences between the Ulster Volunteer Force, the Redmondite National Volunteers, the Irish Volunteers of the Rising and the volunteers of the Great War – "England's difficulty is Ireland's opportunity. Did you never hear that, Willie?" (Barry 2006, 96). Willie's reaction to the lecture unwittingly prefigures the displacement of the Irish soldiers of the Great War that would evolve from the situation described by Kirwan: "'So where does it leave you, Jesse?' – 'I don't know, do I, Willie? Where does it leave you?'" (Barry 2006, 95). A little later, in an equally telling scene, Willie gets ready to leave Dublin for the Western Front after his deployment in the Rising, finding his British uniform "badly stained with blood. It was the blood of that young man dying. [...] [H]e tried a few scrubs at the cloth [...] [b]ut he had no yellow soap and he had no ammonia. He tried again in the morning but in the main he carried the young man's blood to Belgium on his uniform" (Barry 2006, 97) – a powerful image that underlines the tragic and ill-fated connection of the two events, embodying a plangent clash of concepts of Irishness.

Images of uncleanliness and pollution actually abound in *A Long Long Way* – and they often serve as metaphors for the social, political and historical transformations and interconnections the novel addresses. For example, for Willie's unionist father Thomas, a fervent advocate of hygiene and order, the Easter Rising

---

112 Thomas Hennessey mentions an anonymous soldier's poem entitled "Easter Monday" that addresses the situation from such a point of view – however, the speaker here is an Irish nationalist in the British army and he is very aware of the contradictory implications of his part in quelling the Rising: "So I helped to put down the Sinn Feiners / My God it was a pitiful work ..../ Invading my own native town / Where my Mother + Father were living / And shooting my Countrymen down / I was proud of the boys while I fought them / For I knew to a surety they / Were true in their hearts to the old land" (quoted in Hennessey 1998, 143f.).

has "put a mark on Dublin that can never be wiped away, a great spreading stain of blood" (Barry 2006, 247). Also, Barry's central concern, the origins and the process of the marginalisation of Irish soldiers, is strikingly expressed in images of impurity and contamination (cf. Decker 2015, 86). For instance, Willie's comrade Pete O'Hara suffers from gonorrhoea and discovers "a rash the shape of fucking England" (Barry 2006, 66) running down his leg. An even more expressive stigma is the blemish Willie acquires as a consequence of the blast of a German shell. An army nurse discovers a strange stain on his chest that has the shape of a harp and a crown – the heat of the explosion had seared into Willie's skin the medal of Christy Moran which he had kept for him in his pocket. The reaction of the nurse again is telling, foreshadowing the coming marginalisation of Irishmen like Willie who are "tainted with the stain of collaboration" (Gregory and Paseta 2002, 5): "You'll carry that to your grave. I have no oil to wipe it off" (Barry 2006, 276).

At that point, Willie Dunne has finally overcome his childlike perplexity about his situation. He has become aware of how the tables have turned and how his identity as a unionist Catholic Irishmen in the British army has been rendered unacceptable and embarrassing – the harp and the crown must no longer be united and Willie now carries on him an irremovable mark of British collaboration. Broken and disillusioned, he imagines the life that awaits him in the Ireland to come:

> He knew he had no country now. He knew it well. [...] All sorts of Irelands were no more, and he didn't know what Ireland there was behind him now. But he feared he was not a citizen, they would not let him be a citizen. [...] They may stone him too when he returned, or burn the house of himself to the ground, or shoot him, or make him lie down under the bridges of Dublin and be a lowly dosser for all the rest of his days. [...] How could a fella go out and fight for his country when his country would dissolve behind him like sugar in the rain? How could a fella love his uniform when that same uniform killed the new heroes [...]? How could a fella like Willie hold England and Ireland equally to his heart, like his father before him, like his father's father, and his father's father's father, when both now would call him a traitor, though his heart was clear and pure, as pure as a heart can be after three years of slaughter?
>
> (Barry 2006, 286f.)

Willie's identity is based on a version of Ireland that has been made obsolete by history, manoeuvring him and many others out of the national community – a process that leaves him helpless and confused (cf. Decker 2015, 86). Willie has to acknowledge that the ties to his home have been cut – he can no longer insist that he is "at home, you little bastards" (Barry 2006, 254), as he did on his last visit to Dublin, when a group of rowdy boys threw stones and yelled at him, the "fucking Tomm[y]" (ibid.), to go home.

Yet, Willie Dunne actually never returns home and, unlike his father,[113] he does not live to witness his disgrace. The larger context of an Irish 'lost generation' within which Barry has placed his main protagonist from the beginning also frames Willie's death: Willie is one of "[s]ome thirty thousand souls of that fell country [that] did not register in the scales of God. Under that heaving swell of history was buried Willie and all his kindred soldiers, in a forgotten graveyard without yews or stones" (Barry 2006, 290). As Eugene McNulty observes, "the final image of Willie's make-shift grave establishes his dead body as the site of a much-needed cultural archaeology" (McNulty 2010, 80) – the lost and forgotten bodies of the war constitute a rupture in Ireland's national identity that needs to be resolved.

Summing up, *A Long Long Way* represents an attempt to re-envision and thereby to humanise and pluralise Irish identities within the context of the Great War – beyond the essentially dehumanising and de-individualising concepts of nationalism, unionism and militarism, and against the hold of polarising partisan narratives of the Irish past. This extensive humanisation is paralleled by a pronounced internationalist contextualisation of the novel's subject matter, Barry thereby also rejecting the notion of Irish exceptionality (cf. Seree-Chaussinand 2010, 60). Barry's view on the Irish history of the Great War is strongly informed by the historiographic rediscovery of the period; he elucidates the origins of the processes that led to the marginalisation of the war and the figure of the Irish veteran. While passionately calling for empathy and understanding, foregrounding the complex circumstances that led Irishmen from all kinds of backgrounds into the Great War, Barry does not 'collaborate' with his characters – apart from showing their victimhood, he is also unafraid to show their shortcomings and harmful self-deceptions (cf. Gleitman 2004, 229f.).[114] Instead of the retrospective reversal of polarisation that Phelan offers, Barry insists "on 'the gap between the two things': between the reassuring power of a static and self-affirming view of the past, and the more various, conflicting, confounding and contestable stories which combine to form that fluid phenomenon we call 'history'" (ibid.).

---

113 Making the connection to *The Steward of Christendom*, Barry mentions at the end of *A Long Long Way* how "Willie's father's world passed entirely away in the coming upheavals. In the upshot, he lost his wits and died a poor figure indeed in the County Home in Baltinglass" (Barry 2006, 291).

114 This is seen differently by Liam Harte, who criticises Barry for "exalting the sacrifice of the ordinary Irish volunteer in World War One" (Harte 2012, 106), also taking issue with the enduring innocence of Willie Dunne that eventually seems to him "more reprehensible than pitiable" (Harte 2012, 115).

The final work to be discussed, Dermot Bolger's experimental 2007 play *Walking the Road* (2007), straightforwardly takes up McNulty's aforementioned notion of "a much-needed cultural archaeology" of the stranded bodies of Ireland's Great War. Bolger reimagines the life, war death and, significantly, the commemorative resurrection of the Irish war poet Francis Ledwidge, who epitomises the contradictions and complexities of Irish identities and allegiances magnified by the Irish involvement in the Great War.

III.3.6 Dermot Bolger's *Walking the Road* (2007)

A prolific, versatile and popular dramatist, novelist, poet, as well as editor and publisher,[115] Dermot Bolger (*1957) is one of the most active and prominent figures in Irish cultural life. Much of his work is dedicated to themes of identity and questions of belonging, particularly the exploration of identities and spaces at the margins of Irish society and public consciousness. He frequently concentrates on the depiction of Irish urban and suburban working-class life, sections of Irish society that are not extensively acknowledged in traditional nationalist discourses. This interest in marginality very much is the outcome of his own upbringing in the Dublin suburb of Finglas, "a creation of the expansionist 1960s" (Harte 1997, 18). As Bolger notes, "I am fascinated by people on the edge of society outside the general flow, and that comes from my own experiences of trying to explore what it was like to grow up in Finglas on the edge of the Dual Carriageway and being told that you weren't truly Irish in terms of your interests and occupations" (quoted in Murphy 2010, 181) – what Bolger addresses here is a sentiment of estrangement from inherited dominant definitions of Irishness determined by a monolithic, anti-modern and distinctively rural nationalism (cf. Harte 1997, 18): The traditional concept of a rural Irish nation, he suggests, does not incorporate in its collective vision people from 'no-places' like Finglas, places "without the accumulated resonance of centuries" (Fintan O'Toole, quoted in ibid.).

The sense of alienation and rootlessness that results from this situation resonates in Bolger's works and it determines many of his characters. The quest for 'home', in various contexts, consequently is the central motif that informs Bolger's writings (cf. Wald 2010, 32). As Christina Wald argues, Bolger depicts "the soothing, strengthening impact of experiencing a sense of home and the tormenting,

---

115 Bolger founded the Raven Arts Press in his early twenties and published the early works of authors like Sebastian Barry, Roddy Doyle, Colm Tóibín and Fintan O'Toole, works that would frequently address contemporary social issues in Ireland such as unemployment, drug abuse and emigration (cf. Murphy 2010, 181).

deadening effect of clinging to a vision of home that cannot be achieved" (ibid.). Importantly, the past and the grip of 'history' on the present play a central role in these processes (cf. ibid.) – yet, in Bolger's outlook, which has been described as post-national (cf. Harte 1997, 17; Pelletier 2009, 253), the constraints of the past and the historical continuity on which Irish identities seem to depend frequently can be overcome (cf. Pelletier 2009, 252), which distinguishes him from the works of McGuiness, Reid, McCartney and Barry previously covered in this section. As will be shown shortly, it is exactly this condition of marginality, 'homelessness' and an internationalist and post-national outlook that is evoked in *Walking the Road*,[116] even if the play does not exactly operate within Bolger's trademark setting.

Even more intensely than Barry's *A Long Long Way*, which meticulously processes the reformed historiographical rediscovery of Ireland's Great War experience, *Walking the Road* is embedded in official discourses of remembrance and revision. Marking the ninetieth anniversary of Francis Ledwidge's death in the Third Battle of Ypres, the play was commissioned and funded by the In Flanders Fields Museum in Ypres, the South Dublin County Council and the Axis Art Centre in Ballymun, Dublin. The play premiered at the Axis Art Centre in June 2007 and was subsequently transferred to the Ypres Town Theatre before returning to several other venues and festivals around Ireland. The centenary of the Great War was accompanied by new productions of *Walking the Road*, including one in Bolger's home town of Finglas; also, a radio version of the play was broadcast on RTÉ Radio 1 – altogether, a production history that mirrors the new interest in and the reformed and more integrative attitudes towards the Great War in twenty-first-century Ireland, as well as the expanded European context in which Ireland has positioned itself in recent times. The play has been credited for its discrete poetry (cf. Crawley 2007), yet, generally, it has not attracted very much attention among reviewers. Also, academic criticism on *Walking the Road* – as on Bolger's oeuvre in general[117] – is scarce. Even within the context of Irish war

---

116 I have addressed *Walking the Road* in an earlier essay entitled "'I'm at home, you little bastards' – Re-Envisioning the Marginalised Irish Soldier in Sebastian Barry's *A Long Long Way* and Dermot Bolger's *Walking the Road*" (cf. Decker 2015). Several of the ideas outlined in the following can be found in a more comprehensive form in that essay.

117 Despite his prolific literary output and prominent position in Irish cultural life, Bolger has received only limited critical attention in academic circles. As Martine Pelletier summarises, many scholars "either ignore or dismiss him as a member of the new generation of depressing and crude working-class realist writers" (Pelletier 2009, 249). Another point of disagreement are the ideological implications of Bolger's works, influential critics like Christopher Murray and Declan Kiberd dismissing Bolger as

literature, the play has not been more than namechecked, and to my knowledge, at the time of writing, my 2015 reading of *Walking the Road* (cf. Decker 2015) remains the only extended scholarly analysis of the play.

Before investigating the play's approach to liminal Irish identities, the Great War and the role of memory, I will take a brief look at its subject, the Irish (war) poet Francis Ledwidge, whose life and death are traced in *Walking the Road*. Bolger has been interested in and fascinated by Ledwidge since the 1970s, long before the major rediscovery of Ireland's Great War experience and Ledwidge's rediscovery as an Irish poet of the war (cf. Barry 2007, 7). Early in his literary career, Bolger wrote an affectionate poem about Ledwidge and made a 'pilgrimage' to Ledwidge's cottage in Slane (cf. Bolger 2007a). In 1992, he edited and published a collection of Ledwidge's poetry, which was reissued in 2007 with an introduction by Seamus Heaney. Ledwidge was not only an inspiring role model for Bolger as a young poet, his attraction also lies in his short and contradictory life, corresponding to Bolger's preoccupation with marginality. Ledwidge really lived in-between the conflicting demarcation lines of class, politics, nation, and the pastoral beauty of poetry and the destruction of war (cf. Decker 2015, 87). He is "our dead enigma" in whom Ireland's "strains / Criss-cross in useless equilibrium" (Heaney 2008, 345, ll. 41f.), as Seamus Heaney poignantly describes him in his 1979 poem "In Memoriam Francis Ledwidge".[118] In the figure of Ledwidge, the complexity and contradictions of the Irish involvement in the Great War, as much as its burdened legacy, become apparent, consequently, he has become something like "a revisionist icon" (Dugan, quoted in Haughey 2002, 95). Ledwidge, Terry Phillips observes, "is representative of the relationship and tension between cultural inheritance and politics" (Phillips 2008, 400), and Jim Haughey argues that "part of Ledwidge's appeal is how he transcends Ireland's political fault lines and demonstrates the extent to which British and Irish identities overlap" (Haughey 2002, 95).

Ledwidge was born as the second youngest of eight children of a poor Catholic agricultural labourer's family in Slane, Co. Meath, in 1887. After the early death of his father, Ledwidge had to toil hard from a young age to contribute to the family's survival, working in the fields, in copper mines, as a road ganger and

---

essentially conservative and lost in a deceptive nostalgia for better times. However, this view is not shared among the majority of the small amount of academic criticism dedicated to Bolger, arriving instead at the opposite of Murray's and Kiberd's notion, seeing Bolger's works as an invitation to overcome individual and national nostalgia (cf. Wald 2010, 32f.).

118 For a discussion of Heaney's poem and of the treatment of Ledwidge in Eavan Boland's "Heroic", see Lojek 2006.

as a grocer's apprentice. In his mining days, he first became involved in trade union politics and was soon appointed the secretary of the Slane branch of the Labour Union. He also shared the revolutionary republican aspirations of the radical Irish nationalists of the time and joined the Irish Volunteers right after their formation in 1913 (cf. Johnson 2003, 127f.; Phillips 2008, 392). Ledwidge began to write pastoral poetry in his early twenties and his blossoming talent was strongly supported by the local unionist peer, Lord Dunsany, a poet himself, who acted as his patron, giving Ledwidge access to his library, providing him with financial aids and contacts, and eventually editing and publishing his works – "it was as poets that Dunsany and Ledwidge shared their most common interest" (Johnson 2003, 127), beyond political and class divisions.

These divisions became sharply apparent at the outbreak of the Great War. In accordance with their respective classes and allegiances, Dunsany instantly rushed to arms while Ledwidge railed against Ireland's involvement, also quitting the Irish Volunteers in protest at Redmond's call for recruitment. At a council meeting in the early days of the war, Ledwidge was outspoken about how he felt Irishmen were deceived into volunteering against their actual allegiances: "In the north of Ireland the recruiting sergeants have been saying to the men 'Go out and fight with anti-papal France'. In the south of Ireland they will say, 'Go out and fight for Catholic Belgium'" (quoted in Johnson 2003, 129) – however, he met considerable opposition, being called a coward and pro-German. Surprisingly, only five days after his anti-war speech, Ledwidge enlisted. This sudden and fairly mysterious turn was probably caused, apart from an awakening notion of duty and identification with 'Gaelic' heroism, by the disappointment at a failed relationship and by the lack of perspectives at home (cf. Bolger 2007, 11; Phillips 2008, 392f.). Ledwidge himself later explained his decision to enlist referring to a sense of patriotic duty: "I joined the British Army because she stood between Ireland and an enemy common to our civilisation and I would not have her say that she defended us while we did nothing at home but pass resolutions" (quoted in Phillips 2008, 393).

As a member of the Royal Inniskilling Fusiliers, Ledwidge participated in major battles of the Great War, including Gallipoli,[119] the Somme and Ypres. He continued to write poetry during his deployment, at times expressing a sense of loneliness in his still majorly pastoral works.[120] The 1916 Easter Rising threw Ledwidge – and many other Irish nationalists in the British army – out of kilter,

---

119 "It was a horrible day and a great day. I would not have missed it for worlds" (Ledwidge in a letter to Lord Dunsany, quoted in Phillips 2008, 393).

120 Only a few poems of Ledwidge directly address the war experience.

forcing him to re-confront his political identity and his actual position in the current state of affairs. Ledwidge fully identified with the Easter rebels, his "friends [...] shot by England" (quoted in Phillips 2008, 394), and was soon deeply troubled by the feeling of having missed his true hour by enlisting (cf. Phillips 2008, 395), having chosen the wrong side of history, the side which executed Ireland's liberators (cf. Devine 1999, xf.). Tellingly, it is "Lament for Thomas MacDonagh", an Easter Rising elegy, written after a stay in Dublin in the immediate aftermath of the insurrection, that would become Ledwidge's most famous work.[121] Still, Ledwidge remained in the army and was killed by a stray shell in July 1917, during the Battle of Ypres, while building a road behind the frontlines, leaving behind some 230 poems (cf. Phillips 2008, 392).

Ledwidge's status as a Catholic Irish nationalist serving in the British forces was long seen as problematic. In the epilogue to *Walking the Road*, Bolger recalls the hostile climate of his youth, more than six decades after Ledwidges' death, in which "even Francis Ledwidge's name could provoke an argument", and he mentions how "the copy of Curtayne's biography of Ledwidge in one library near me was covered in graffiti – Republican readers having doctored the text to scribble slogans on the margins" (Bolger 2007a, 122). Writing in 2007, Seamus Heaney notes that Ledwidge still is "a political phenomenon [that] represents conflicting elements in the Irish inheritance which continue to be repressed or unresolved. There is still minimal acknowledgement in Ireland of the part played by Irish soldiers in the First World War, although their devotion to the ideal of independence was passionate in its day" (Heaney 2007, 14) – even if Heaney's assessment of contemporary Ireland is possibly slightly too harsh, Ledwidge remains representative of an unwanted part of Irish history. Bolger's *Walking the Road* represents an attempt to work against this condition by reimagining his life.

Remembrance is the central strategy of the short one-act drama. *Walking the Road* is typical of Bolger's approach to the memory play and historiographic metadrama, frequently radicalising psychic realism and integrates poetic devices, privileging subjective perceptions, imaginations and realities over more objective or 'official' ones (cf. Wald 2010, 33). Bolger's self-described "theatre of evocation" (quoted in Wald 2010, 34) is largely uninterested in verisimilitude and linearity:

---

121 The 1998 monument for Ledwidge in Boezinge, a village near Ypres, includes on a plaque the first two lines of Ledwidge's poem for MacDonagh: "He shall not hear the bittern cry / In the wild sky, where he is lain" (Ledwidge 2008, 80, ll. 1–2). This choice also underlines the new Irish understanding of the period of the war, acknowledging the connections between Irish nationalism and the Great War embodied by people like Ledwidge.

His plays freely switch between locations and times, also not distinguishing between the dead and the living, his stages being frequented by ghosts and imaginary figures that signify loss and unresolved conflicts (cf. Wald 2010, 33). Accordingly, *Walking the Road* is not a chronological dramatization of Ledwidge's biography. The play is set in a "dreamlike continuum of time" (Bolger 2007, 5) and it shifts between an uncanny present, the locations of Ledwidge's impoverished pre-war life at the beginning of the twentieth century, the battlefields of the Great War, and a timeless limbo inhabited by the forgotten dead of the war who were prematurely cut from life (cf. Decker 2015, 87). The cast consists of only two characters, the restless ghost of Francis "Frank" Ledwidge and a second ghostly figure, Frank's "Companion", who switches between multiple roles in every scene. Interrupted by harsh frontline flashbacks, the two re-visit key moments from Frank's life: Frank's loving but destitute upbringing, his early days as a poet, his failed love interest, his abrupt decision to volunteer in the Great War, and his death during the Battle of Ypres in 1917.

The impetus that underpins Frank's remembering of his former life is a similar one as in McGuinness's *Observe the Sons of Ulster*. Frank's past is revisited in an attempt – at times playful, at times hesitant, desperate and eventually therapeutic – to make sense of his present situation and, more importantly, to find some form of finality, to find a way 'home', out of a ghostly existence that is unfinished and trapped. Like Pyper, Frank is initially pushed to reconstruct his identity: "Such a long walk, Frank, such a long time you've been walking home. [...] You should be able to remember, Frank. Try" (Bolger 2007, 15). An uneasy sense of dislocation and disconnection is established right at the outset of the play, pervading its atmosphere throughout. In his first appearance, Frank, wearing "a uniform so faded that it is impossible to distinguish any features" (ibid.), proclaims that he has "[n]o sense of where I am or who I am. I just know that I'm walking home" (ibid.). Along these lines, Bolger instantly defines the soldier identity embodied by Frank as liminal and blurry, literally placing his protagonist in a distressing state of incompletion between life and death and in a historical no-place that mirrors the conflicted legacy of the Great War in Ireland (cf. Decker 2015, 87). Frank's ghostliness, his undead presence, underlines how the latter condition still remains an unresolved issue.

The subjective imaginative reconstruction of Frank's life that follows his initial proclamation brings about a de-anonymisation and re-individualisation that eventually reconnects him with the culture and society from which he has found himself permanently alienated – the interrupted and forgotten narrative of Frank Ledwidge is told. As in the case of Barry's novel, the polarised and heated condition of Ireland in the years before and during the Great War is reflected in Bolger's play. Frank's position, like the one of the "Castle Catholic" Willie Dunne, is problematic even before he enlists in the British army. Marked by his very humble upbringing, Frank's contradictory political commitments and his interest in the creation of poetry, mentored by the unionist aristocrat Lord Dunsany, do not only add to Frank's insecurity about himself, worrying that he is "pretending to be someone he wasn't" (Bolger 2007, 46). Frank is also perceived by his environment as violating the political imperatives of the moment and transgressing codes of class and gender:

> [T]hey don't come more common than this road worker lecturing us about Ireland's right to be free. If the pro-German traitor loves freedom, he can show it by fighting for other small nations, like Catholic Belgium. But for all his Socialist talk, this coward seems better with *limp* poems than *stiff* resolve.
>
> (ibid., italics in the original)

As a poet and idealist, Frank is deemed not man enough to be fully accepted among his working-class peers, which is further promoted by his failure to protect Ellie, the woman with whom he is in love, from the approaches of a stronger and bolder man (cf. Decker 2015, 87): "Pouncing about like a Dublin dandy, yet he can't keep his hands on a girl" (Bolger 2007, 49).

It is this experience of frustration and isolation that prompts Frank to leave his home and volunteer in the British army, against his earlier convictions:

> FRANK: It's too small, Joe, don't you understand?
> COMPANION [*as Joe, kneeling beside him*]: What's too small, Frank?
> FRANK: My life in this goldfish bowl of a place. I thought that poetry would earn me respect, Joe, but all I earn here is mockery. Every man has a label for me: pro-German, coward, traitor, failed lover. I've no hope of a job except mending roads. [...] They laughed at me in *The Drogheda Independent* when I turned up, looking for a reporter's job. [...] Know my place, they meant. There's no place for me here except on the roads. I'm going up to Dublin, Joe; I'm going to enlist. [...]
> COMPANION [*as Joe*]: But Frank, after all your talk ...
> FRANK: Can't you see, Joe? All anyone in Ireland does is talk and pass resolutions. All I did with Ellie was talk and, see where that got me. She took me for a coward, without an acre of land or a stir in my hand to chance my luck.
> COMPANION [*as Joe*]: Going to war won't win Ellie back, Frank.
> FRANK: I'm not trying to win her back, Joe; I'm trying to forget her.
>
> (Bolger 2007, 50f.)

By going to war, Frank effectively leaves behind a contradictory self-image, an identity that is at odds with a parochial and unsympathetic home community.

His decision to enlist is an impulsive escapist switch from talk to action, from the idealistic and spiritual to the physical and the pragmatic – however, his departure to war is anything but political or patriotic, Frank never directly mentions Home Rule, the protection of Belgium or the common enemy of Germany as his motivation. In this manner, Bolger reworks Ledwidge's volunteering into a personal act of defiance, in some way an unwilling liberation and also a rite of passage into manhood. This personal and fairly apolitical view is extended when Bolger goes on to recast Frank's retreat to the Great War within an international context, envisioning an entire lost generation of young men from all over Europe who naïvely go to war to escape and forget (cf. Decker 2015, 88): "The world had an awful lot of forgetting to do, because half the young men in Dublin were queuing up in that barracks. Queuing to forget or queuing to find work or blindly following their pals. They were queuing up too in Glasgow and Birmingham, in Hamburg and Düsseldorf and cities I'd never heard of" (Bolger 2007, 52).

Initially, Frank finds distraction, an opportunity to vent his anger and a new sense of community in army life and war, Frank fully merging with the "we" of his platoon, fighting and suffering collectively:

> We charged through cheering crowds on the Dublin quays. We charged up the beaches at Suvla Bay into the teeth of Turkish guns at Gallipoli. We crouched in crumbling holes in the sand and rose and charged and then retreated amid the slaughtered bodies. We charged and charged as the battlefronts changed. What never changed were our screams during each bayonet charge. [...] One continuous scream emanating from our throats as the dying flashed past and two years flashed past.
>
> (Bolger 2007, 54)

Frank extends this notion of soldierly collectivity and solidarity also to the enemy. In an earlier scene, he reminisces about an incident in which a rat dropped a severed and mutilated hand at his feet: "Were the fingers German or French, English or Irish? Had they once stroked a girl's cheek like I stroked Ellie's cheek [...]? [...] I knelt to pray for whomever once owned those fingers, whatever age or nationality or religion. Because we're all trapped here like insects under glass" (Bolger 2007, 36f.). Here, Bolger repeats the well-established but powerful humanising notion of a dissolution of national identities in war, the collective war experience of the ordinary ranks uniting them in distress, across the pettiness of the national divide and prescribed political hostilities – an internationalist view that, as mentioned before, can be found in much war writing, including many of the texts featured in this study.

At war, Frank also experiences a new creative impulse: "I'd sworn to finish with poems during the war, but the poems were not finished with me. Waking at strange hours to scribble down verses" (Bolger 2007, 55). Yet, this poetic urge is also indicative of the strength of the connection to his home, his original identity as a peasant, poet and family man, which proves indissoluble no matter how far he escapes from home and how strongly he recasts himself within an international context. The poems Frank creates chime with an intense longing to be reunited with his home[122] – for example, Bolger has the Companion whisper lines from Ledwidge's "Home": "This is a song a robin sang / This morning on a broken tree, / It was about the little fields / That call across the world to me" (Bolger 2007, 55, cf. Ledwidge 2008, 84). Frank is continuously haunted by what he left behind in anger and a profound sense of homesickness tortures him even after his untimely death which left the narrative of his life unresolved: "Is this No Man's Land or the Promised Land? Why am I standing here so long, trapped in the eternity of one second? I can't go forward, yet I can't go home. I'm twenty-nine years old; I'm nineteen, I'm nine. I'm continually walking back through time, seeking that moment when I'll feel safe" (Bolger 2007, 56). Out of his mortal form, Frank is trapped in the dilemma of being unable to "fully let go of the world of the living" (Bolger 2007 57), the personal memory of his unfinished life, at the same time being buried by 'history' like Barry's Willie Dunne, by communal memory, leaving him longing for "someone to find my remains – a splintered skull and some buttons, two rows of teeth biting into a rusted identity tag" (Bolger 2007 59).

Unlike McGuinness and Barry, Bolger provides a solution to the predicament of his protagonist at the end of the play. Again, the Companion pushes Frank – "[i]t's time [...] to try and walk this road home" (Bolger 2007, 59) – it is time to finally re-unite Frank with his home, to reconcile his unresolved personal history with communal memory (cf. Decker 2015, 88), a process that reflects the Halbwachsian idea of the need of the individual to have its fragmented and ephemeral memories validated and complemented by its community. This is achieved by Frank joining a complex procession of the dead, a ceremonial march of countless soldiers returning home:

FRANK: For ninety years now I have been walking home. My name is Wolfgang and I am walking home. My name is Hans and Gunter and Gabriel ...
COMPANION: [overlapping with him] My name is Alasdair and Alexander and Dirk and Dieter.
FRANK: My name is Frederick and Flavio and Fritz and Felix. [...] My name is forgotten by every living being. I have lost my legs and arms.

---

122   Another telling example, even if it is not directly mentioned in the play, is Ledwidge's poem "In France": "Whatever way I turn / The hills of home are in my mind / and there I wander as I will" (quoted in Brown 2008, 36).

COMPANION: The mustard gas in my lungs still burns, even though my lungs were eaten by worms. [...] You are not walking home alone, Frank.

FRANK: No, I sense thousands walking, a great host in tattered uniforms. Who are you? Why are you following me?

COMPANION: [...] I'm not following you, Frank, I'm Edmond Chomley Lambert Farran, my body missing in the Ypres Salient. I'm walking to Knocklyon House, Templelogue. This is Hastings Killingley beside me, aged twenty-one, of the Vicarage Rathfarnham. Remember the lime tree in his garden?

FRANK: And I'm Joseph Whelan of Whitechurch Road, Rathfarnham. [...] And Patrick Emmett here, [...] both of us having fallen, both keeping you company as far as Finglas village, with John McDonagh, whose mother's house is on the Green.

COMPANION: And John Dillon of Kelly's Cottage, Rathfarnham, sharing your road. [...] And your friend and fellow poet, Thomas MacDonagh, walking towards St. Edna's in Rathfarnham, divided by uniforms, united by dreams.

(Bolger 2007, 60–63)

The dominant aspect of naming in this scene highlights, as in Reid's play discussed earlier, the issue of identity, more precisely, the discrepancy between individuality and the inextricable public (national, ideological, political) context in which the individual is placed: By giving names to the war dead, by 'identifying' them, they are re-personalised and humanised, extracted from the uniformity of the war and of its remembrance. The narrative of Frank is recast by the ceremony, on the one hand, again within an international context, and, on the other hand, in Ireland's conflicted history of the Great War. Significantly, the mentioning of Thomas MacDonagh – "divided by uniforms, united by dreams" – stresses the connection between the Great War and the Easter Rising, the reformed notion of the 'seamless robe' of Irish experience in this period (cf. Ferriter 2005, 132). Furthermore, Frank is reintegrated in and reconciled with the more obscure personal history of his own local community of Rathfarnham (cf. Decker 2015, 88). This communal reunion, contesting Frank's burdened historical status as "other", is later complemented by a personal reunion in which Frank finally reaches his home and meets his younger self and his (equally ghostly) brother Joe, recovering his identity and his sense of self. Thus, Frank is again, in the sense of Stuart Hall's concept of cultural identity, "sutured" into the story, the narrative of Ireland, "chaining [...] the subject [back] into the flow of discourse" (Hall 1996, 5f.). All of this is achieved by the conscious act or even 'work' of remembering, *Erinnerungsarbeit* in Freudian terminology (cf. Zamorano 2010, 119). This deliberate confrontation and re-examination of the past, emphasising the crucial role of remembrance and forgetting for the formation of individual and collective identities (cf. Halbwachs in Zamorano 2010, 120), is used by Bolger as a tool against the ideological imbalances of collective memory (cf. ibid.).

Summing up, in this manner, Bolger insists on the acknowledgement of people like Frank, whose stories and identities have been obliterated within various contexts. As Bolger himself notes,

> *Walking the Road* is only in part about Ledwidge. The Ledwidge within it is filtered through my own reimagining to hopefully become a sort of Everyman, a representative of the thousands of Irishmen who walked the same road as him [...]. Hopefully in some way he also represents all the young men from every nation who died ninety years ago in that nightmare battle for Ypres

> (Bolger 2007, 11)

With his play, Bolger traces the "political and cultural disorientation" of Ledwidge that culminated in the Great War and that reveals "the futility of subscribing to identity politics within the Irish context" (Haughey 2002, 95). He works against historical and cultural homogeneity, emphasising the fluidity of memory and the co-existence of different 'nation-views' (cf. Duara 1996, 151), and he suggests a more integrative and humane form of communal existence, unburdened by parochial categorisations of nation, class or political allegiance (cf. Decker 2015, 88f.) – the ideal of a pluralist and, effectively, a post-national Irish identity.

IV. Conclusion

The Great War and its Irish history and contested legacy represent an intriguing arena in which the complicated and disparate processes and pressures of Irish identity politics have become visible for more than a century. The multiple and changing ways in which Ireland and Northern Ireland have responded to the Great War and its legacy – official and unofficial, public and private, collective and individual – have magnified the fraught interrelations between Irishness and Englishness and between the defining forces of nationalism and unionism in Ireland. Furthermore, they have highlighted the sense of an overall instability of Irish identity and nationhood, 'nation' remaining a source of identification that necessitates constant re-confirmation, re-interpretation and re-appropriation. Apart from these concerns of national belonging and national self-conceptions, the Great War also brought about various related transformations considering more personal dimensions of identity, such as masculinity and femininity, mental and physical integrity, familial relations and traditions, and the adoption of militaristic and belligerent attitudes – changes that have affected not only those who actively participated in the war, but also those at the home front and those who had to or, perhaps, in some way, still have to live with the heritage of the war.

All of these conditions are reflected extensively in Irish literary responses to the Great War, from the outbreak of the conflict to the present. Altogether, these texts form only a fairly small and heterogeneous collection, which is mostly the outcome of the ambiguous and long marginalised status of the Great War in Ireland that has only been recovered in the last couple of decades. As a consequence, it is difficult to make out a single dominant development or attitude considering the representation of Irish identities that unites these texts – instead, they rather need to be seen in the light of the different situations in which they were written as their treatment of the Great War also centrally responds to the respective conditions in Ireland and Northern Ireland at the time of their creation.

The Irish war plays by George Bernard Shaw and Sean O'Casey, *O'Flaherty V. C.* (1915) and *The Silver Tassie* (1928), respond to different historical situations, wartime and post-war Ireland, yet, they both belong to a phase in which the immediacy of the war was still given, a condition that compounded the staging of both plays, thereby revealing the uneasy and contested status of the war in Ireland. The two works are radically different in dramatic approach and tone, yet they are united in their essentially socialist outlook. Both texts eschew the nation as a source of identification, both with regard to the allegiances underpinning the Irish involvement in the Great War and the rival culture of Irish nationalism and its identity concepts. Like many other Irish war works, they focus on the depiction of the home front. Shaw and O'Casey's representation of the war service of their protagonists foregrounds harsh and materialist socio-economic conditions at home, characterised, respectively, by greed and the idolisation of the heroic male body and masculinist hierarchies. The archetypal notion of the gulf in experience and outlook between men and women in war is very pronounced in both works. Women are cast in a very unfavourable light in both plays, even if the conditions produced by the war, particularly in O'Casey's work, lead to female empowerment, liberation and a transformation of pre-war female identities. Against these ghastly conditions at home, the socialists Shaw and O'Casey suggest, in differing degrees of directness, internationalist sensibilities in which the experience of soldierly community and shared suffering leads to a new sense of the self and critical new views of home – a motif that reoccurs in many of the texts covered in this project.

A considerable number of texts, written during the long period in which Ireland's amnesia about the Great War was most pronounced, the late 1920s to the late 60s, reflects the war experiences of a section of Irish society that had come under stress even before the era of the Great War and that experienced its ultimate downfall during the war and in its immediate aftermath. This group, the traditional leading class of the Anglo-Irish, embodies a profound sense of liminality, occupying a position in-between Irishness and Englishness. In these texts, the Big House, the Anglo-Irish country mansion, once a prominent signifier of Anglo-Irish identity and supremacy, plays a central role. For example, the novels of Pamela Hinkson and Margaret Barrington, *The Ladies' Road* (1932) and *My Cousin Justin* (1939), construct the Big House as an attractively detached and remote but inevitably endangered and moribund refuge from the crude realities of the war on the Continent and in wartime England – a telling allegory by means of which the liminal position of both Ireland and the Anglo-Irish in this period becomes apparent. In plays such as Lennox Robinson's benevolent *The Big House* (1926) and Sean Dowling's acerbic *The Bird in the Net* (1960), the Big House serves as a venue for the interplay of different identity concepts, classes and allegiances – the gradations of Protestant Anglo-Irish, Catholic Irish and English identities – culminating in confrontations centrally triggered by the divisive issue of the Great War in connection with related domestic Irish conflicts such as the Easter Rising, the War of Independence and the Irish Civil War. The overall image of Anglo-Irishness produced in all of those works reflects the constraints and, centrally, the eventual demise of this 'anomalous' Irish class. It seems impossible for male Anglo-Irish characters to resist the obligations of their tradition and refuse to enlist and die for Britain. War service here appears as a natural consequence of their heavily politicised public identity. Interestingly, female Anglo-Irish characters such as Robinson's Kate Alcock or Barrington's Loulie Delahaie frequently prove more confident and flexible considering their sense of belonging, hopes for socio-cultural co-existence and the way they relate to the war and their soldiering male peers – yet, eventually, they are also unable to transcend their origins and their dependency on the utterly transformed Anglo-Irish and Irish men who have managed to return from the battlefields.

Jennifer Johnston's *How Many Miles to Babylon?* (1974) represents a shift towards a conscious humanisation and general demythologisation not only of Anglo-Irish perspectives on the Great War. Johnston anticipates with her Big House novel the reformed attitudes towards the Irish history of the Great War that have underpinned more recent literary and historiographic efforts of dealing with the subject. Providing a panoramic view of the complexity of allegiances of the war period, Johnston's novel exposes the isolation and destruction caused by the quasi-official imperatives of both Irish and Anglo-Irish class and national affiliations, which are positioned against the private realm of a fulfilling but doomed homosexual cross-class relationship transferred to the Western Front.

The examination of Irish identities in literary works about the Great War since the 1980s is very strongly determined by the question of how to (re-)construct and relate to the legacy of the conflict in the light of contemporary conditions in Ireland and Northern Ireland. This retrospective orientation shows in the dominance of memory-themed works and in straightforwardly revisionist approaches. This is the outcome, on the one hand, of the general rediscovery of the Great War as a crucial context for and ideological source of the sectarian violence of the Troubles that had begun in the late 1960s, and, on the other hand, of the increasingly waning authority of traditional nationalist concepts of history and identity in Ireland since the late twentieth century. It is the former context that informs Frank McGuinness's seminal war drama *Observe the Sons of Ulster Marching Towards the Somme* (1985). The play represents an innovative and influential gesture of a Catholic author from the Republic of Ireland reaching out to a diametrically opposed culture: McGuinness depicts sympathetically the war experiences of Protestant Ulster unionists, humanising a milieu rarely dramatized and usually perceived as immovable and embittered. He destabilises the belligerent identity-defining 'Orange' certainties of the soldiers by means of an eccentric homosexual main protagonist. The play develops a less politicised sense of community and identity that transcends partisan definitions and instead values personal intimacy and understanding. Moreover, it exposes the manipulative powers of public memory that have determined identity politics in Northern Ireland just as in the Republic, encouraging audiences

271

to become aware of the omnipresent grip of the past and to reconsider inherited positions and self-views – a concern that McGuinness shares essentially with all of the subsequent Irish and Northern Irish texts relating to the Great War.

This concern is crucial also for the war works of Christina Reid and Nicola McCartney, *My Name Shall I Tell You My Name* (1987) and *Heritage* (1998). Both texts have been categorised not only as war plays but also as Troubles plays, emphasising the inherited nature of the sectarian violence in Northern Ireland, tracing, like Johnston and McGuinness, the origins of the conflict majorly to the period of the Great War. The two plays centrally address the issue of identification and belonging across generational and gender boundaries, staging the collisions of monolithic belligerent traditions with changing environments. Reid's work, set in 1980s Derry, represents a distinctively female challenge to the constitution of dominant and inflexible Northern Irish masculine identities through violence and war, specifically by the mythologised and memorialised sacrifice of Ulstermen in the Battle of the Somme. Reid emphasises the troublesome discrepancy between politicised public and intimate private dimensions of identity, the family in Northern Ireland being envisioned as both an ideological battleground and a source of personal identification. McCartney's play shares many of these aspects, even if her investigation of the identity-defining powers of partisan versions of the past is distanced by moving the setting to the milieu of Ulster immigrants in rural Canada during the 1910s. The Great War in *Heritage* represents the central vehicle to illustrate rival concepts of Irishness, sharply divergent attitudes to the war reflecting the inherited demarcation lines between Irish cultures as well as the fairly fraught relations to the new home Canada. McCartney shares with Reid as with the other authors of this period an interest in the question of how to overcome the pitfalls of tradition as a source of identification – *Heritage* suggests the adoption of progressive ideas of a new multicultural sense of belonging, consciously leaving the past behind. This is a remedy chiming with the progress made in the Northern Irish peace process at the time of the play's creation.

The three most recent Irish works to address the Great War and its legacy, Tom Phelan's *The Canal Bridge* (2005), Sebastian Barry's *A Long Long Way* (2005), both historical novels, and Dermot Bolger's experimental memory play *Walking the Road* (2007), largely transcend the direct context of the Troubles. From a more or less openly revisionist or even post-nationalist stance, they aim for a pluralisation of Irish historical experience and identity concepts by telling the multi-layered and long marginalised stories of Irish volunteers in the Great War. This concern is embedded in a larger interest, particularly by Barry and Bolger, in 'anomalous' Irish identities, i. e. forms of Irishness at odds with the nationalist mainstream and its fixation on insular rurality, Catholicism and anti-Britishness. Phelan's novel straightforwardly challenges the negative nationalist stereotypes of Irish soldiers of the Great War, on the one hand, by heroising his soldier protagonists and emphasising their inseparable ties to their home, and, on the other hand, by a full-blown attack on radical Irish nationalism, exposing the harmful effects of its discourses of martyrdom and of its integral divisiveness. Calling for sympathy and understanding, Barry sends his protagonist, a young unionist Catholic Irishman – thus already occupying a liminal position even before joining up – through emblematic situations of the Irish history of the Great War, including the 1916 Easter Rising. Barry's protagonist anticipates the imminent obliteration of his class in an Ireland changed utterly, as well as the purging of his story from the national narrative. These concerns also inform Bolger's experimental memory play, which reconstructs the equally liminal life and war death of the Irish poet Francis Ledwidge, again a highly contradictory figure that reflects the complexities of Irish identity politics magnified by the Great War. The ghostliness of the soldier character "Frank" in Bolger's play underlines not only the sense of a worldly existence prematurely terminated but also a convergence of different temporalities that exposes the instability of the Irish presence in the sense of Derrida's "hauntology" (cf. Jameson 1999, 38f.) – a spectral condition that occurs in several of the war works covered in this project. In Bolger's play, this instability actually can be alleviated by new forms of remembrance, reuniting the disparate strands of Irish history and identity, and re-contextualising Ireland's Great War within a larger and more humane international framework.

As Keith Jeffery observes of the more recent Irish discourses in which the subject of the Great War is embedded, introducing a sceptical note, "the Irish dead of the conflict have today been conscripted [...] to serve in a very political, if well-meaning project of mutual communal understanding and reconciliation" (Jeffery 2008, 274). The contemporary literary responses to the Great War in drama and fiction obviously are part of this project. Their politicised approach to the contested categories of Irishness and Irish identity is deliberately wide-ranging and inclusive, trying to find ways of coming to terms with the national self – or, more precisely, selves – after a century of vicissitudes in a country "obsessed with difference" (Jeffery 2000, 3) that now faces new challenges and transformations such as immigration, globalisation, economic turbulences, austerity and secularisation. However, significantly, it is not just this more recent phase in Irish writing in which views on the Great War and Irishness have been pluralised and unfolded. Looking at the entirety of texts discussed in this project and the manifold perspectives they offer, a multi-layered narrative of Irish identities emerges, expanding, altogether, the "single narrative to explain Irish identity" (Lonergan 2006, 216) that Patrick Lonergan has made out as insufficient, doing justice to an area of national and personal experience and belonging that is much more diffuse and complex than conventionally imagined.

List of Works Cited

Primary Works

Æ [George Russell]. "Salutation. To the Memory of Some I Knew Who Are Dead and Who Loved Ireland." *Earth Voices Whispering. An Anthology of Irish War Poetry. 1914–1945.* Ed. Gerald Dawe. Belfast: Blackstaff, 2008. 20.

Asquith, Herbert. "The Volunteer." *The Oxford Book of War Poetry.* Ed. Jon Stallworthy. Oxford: Oxford University Press, 2008. 163.

Barry, Sebastian. *A Long Long Way.* London: Faber, 2006.

Barry, Sebastian. "The Steward of Christendom." *Three Plays by Sebastian Barry.* London: Methuen, 1996. 67–133.

Barry, Sebastian. "White Woman Street." *Three Plays by Sebastian Barry.* London: Methuen, 1996. 135–81.

Birmingham, George A. *Gossamer.* New York: George H. Doran, 1915. *Project Gutenberg EBook.* <http://www.gutenberg.org/files/24394/24394-h/24394-h.htm>. Accessed 29 November 2014.

Boland, Eavan. "A Soldier's Son." *Earth Voices Whispering. An Anthology of Irish War Poetry. 1914–1945.* Ed. Gerald Dawe. Belfast: Blackstaff, 2008. 372.

Bolger, Dermot. *Walking the Road.* Dublin: New Island, 2007.

Dowling, Sean. *The Bird in the Net.* Dublin: James Duffy, 1961.

Dunsany, Lord [Edward Plunkett]. "To the Fallen Irish Soldiers." *Earth Voices Whispering. An Anthology of Irish War Poetry. 1914–1945.* Ed. Gerald Dawe. Belfast: Blackstaff, 2008. 38.

Ervine, St. John. *Changing Winds.* New York: Macmillan, 1917.

French, Percy. "The Letter from the Front." *Prose, Poems and Parodies.* Dublin: Talbot Press, 1959. 157–63.

Heaney, Seamus. "In Memoriam Francis Ledwidge." *Earth Voices Whispering. An Anthology of Irish War Poetry 1914–1945.* Ed. Gerald Dawe. Belfast: Blackstaff Press, 2008. 343–45.

Hinkson, Pamela. *The Ladies' Road.* Harmondsworth: Penguin, 1946.

Johnston, Jennifer. *How Many Miles to Babylon?.* London: Penguin, 2010.

Ledwidge, Francis. "Thomas MacDonagh." *Earth Voices Whispering. An Anthology of Irish War Poetry. 1914–1945.* Ed. Gerald Dawe. Belfast: Blackstaff, 2008. 80.

Ledwidge, Francis. "Home." *Earth Voices Whispering. An Anthology of Irish War Poetry. 1914–1945.* Ed. Gerald Dawe. Belfast: Blackstaff, 2008. 84.

Longley, Michael. "Wounds." *Earth Voices Whispering. An Anthology of Irish War Poetry. 1914–1945.* Ed. Gerald Dawe. Belfast: Blackstaff, 2008. 334.

MacGill, Patrick. *The Red Horizon.* London: Herbert Jenkins, 1916.

MacGill, Patrick. *The Amateur Army.* London: Herbert Jenkins, 1915.

McCartney, Nicola. "Heritage." *Contemporary Scottish Plays for Higher English and Drama.* Ed. Anne Gifford and Jane Robertson. London: Hodder & Stoughton, 2002. 59–147.

McGuinness, Frank. "Observe the Sons of Ulster Marching Towards the Somme." *Plays I.* London: Faber, 1996. 91–198.

O'Brien, Flann. "Thirst." *Stories and Plays.* Harmondsworth: Penguin, 1977. 99–114.

O'Casey, Sean. "The Silver Tassie." *Collected Plays.* Vol. 2. London: Macmillan, 1964. 1–111.

O'Flaherty, Liam. "The Alien Skull." *The Collected Short Stories of Liam O'Flaherty.* Vol. 2. Ed. A. A. Kelly. Dublin: Wolfhound Press, 1999. 49–54.

O'Flaherty, Liam. *The Return of the Brute.* London: The Mandrake Press, 1929.

Pearse, Patrick. "The Mother." *The Literary Writings of Patrick Pearse.* Ed. Séamas Ó Buachalla. Dublin: Mercier Press, 1979. 27.

Phelan, Tom. *The Canal Bridge.* Dublin: Lilliput Press, 2005.

Reid, Christina. "My Name, Shall I Tell You My Name?." *Plays: 1.* London: Methuen Drama, 1997. 251–76.

Reid, Christina. "Tea in a China Cup." *Plays: 1.* London: Methuen Drama, 1997a. 1–66.

Rickard, Mrs. Victor [Jessie Louisa Rickard]. *The Fire of Green Boughs.* New York: Dodd, Mead and Company, 1919.

Robinson, Lennox. "The Big House." *Selected Plays of Lennox Robinson.* Ed. Christopher Murray. Gerrards Cross: Colin Smythe, 1982. 137–98.

Sassoon, Siegfried. "They." *The Oxford Book of War Poetry.* Ed. Jon Stallworthy. Oxford: Oxford University Press, 2008. 176.

Shakespeare, William. *King Henry V.* Ed. Andrew Gurr. Cambridge: Cambridge University Press, 2005.

Shaw, George Bernard. "O'Flaherty V. C.: A Recruiting Pamphlet. With 'Censorship and Recruiting.' 'Brawling in the Theatre.'" *The Bodley Head Bernard Shaw. Collected Plays with Their Prefaces.* Vol. 4. London: Max Reinhardt, The Bodley Head, 1972. 983–1019.

Yeats, William Butler. "On Being Asked for a War Poem." *Earth Voices Whispering. An Anthology of Irish War Poetry. 1914–1945.* Ed. Gerald Dawe. Belfast: Blackstaff, 2008. 9.

Yeats, William Butler. "An Irish Airman Foresees His Death." *Earth Voices Whispering. An Anthology of Irish War Poetry. 1914-1945.* Ed. Gerald Dawe. Belfast: Blackstaff, 2008. 8.

Yeats, William Butler. "Reprisals." *Earth Voices Whispering. An Anthology of Irish War Poetry. 1914-1945.* Ed. Gerald Dawe. Belfast: Blackstaff, 2008. 13-14.

Yeats, William Butler. "Easter 1916". *The Major Works.* Ed. Edward Larrissy. Oxford: Oxford University Press, 2001. 85-87.

Secondary Works

Allison, Jonathan. "The Reception of Yeats in Ireland since 1950." *The Reception of W. B. Yeats in Europe.* Ed. Klaus Peter Jochum. London: Continuum, 2006. 231-54.

Anderson, Benedict. *Imagined Communities. Reflections on the Origin and Spread of Nationalism.* Rev. Ed. London: Verso, 2006.

Backus, Margot Gayle. "Homophobia and the Imperial Demon Lover: Gothic Narrativity in Irish Representations of the Great War." *Canadian Review of Comparative Literature* 21 (1994): 45-63.

Barry, Sebastian. "Introduction." *Walking the Road.* Dublin: New Island, 2007. 7-8.

Barry, Sebastian. "Preface." *The Essential Jennifer Johnston.* London: Headline, 2000. ix-xi.

Benjamin, Walter. "Über den Begriff der Geschichte." *Erzählen. Schriften zur Theorie der Narration und zur literarischen Prosa.* Ed. Alexander Honold. Frankfurt am Main: Suhrkamp, 2007. 129-42.

Benstock, Shari. "The Masculine World of Jennifer Johnston." *Twentieth-Century Women Novelists.* Ed. Thomas F. Staley. London: Macmillan, 1982. 191-217.

Berge, Marit. "The Big House in Jennifer Johnston's Novels." *Excursions in Fiction. Essays in Honour of Professor Lars Hartveit on His 70th Birthday.* Ed. Andrew Kennedy and Orm Overland. Oslo: Novus Press, 1994. 11-31.

Bergonzi, Bernard. "The First World War: Poetry, Scholarship, Myth." *English Literature of the Great War Revisited: Proceedings of the Symposium on the British Literature of the First World War.* Ed. Michel Roucoux. Amiens: University of Picardy Press, 1986. 7-18.

Berninger, Mark. *Neue Formen des Geschichtsdramas in Großbritannien und Irland seit 1970.* Trier: WVT, 2006.

Bolger, Dermot. "Author's Note." *Walking the Road.* Dublin: New Island, 2007. 9-12.

Bolger, Dermot. "Milestone to Monument: A Personal Journey in Search of Francis Ledwidge." *The Ledwidge Treasury. Selected Poems of Francis Ledwidge.* Ed. Dermot Bolger. Dublin: New Island, 2007a. 72-128.

Bonikowski, Wyatt. *Shell Shock and the Modernist Imagination. The Death Drive in Post-World War I British Fiction.* Farnham: Ashgate, 2013.

Bowman, John. "Time for Ireland to remember those who lost their lives in first World War." *Irish Times Online.* 02 August 2014. <http://www.irishtimes.com/culture/heritage/time-for-ireland-to-remember-those-who-lost-their-lives-in-first-world-war1.1885 196>. Accessed 10 August 2014.

Bourke, Joanna. "The British Working Men in Arms." *Facing Armageddon. The First World War Experience.* Ed. H. Cecil and P. H. Liddle. Barnsley: Pen and Sword, 2003. 336–52.

Bourke, Joanna. *Dismembering the Male. Men's Bodies, Britain and the Great War.* London: Reaktion Books, 1996.

Boyce, D. G. "'That party politics should divide our tents': Nationalism, Unionism and the First World War." *Ireland and the Great War. 'A War to Unite Us All?'.* Ed. Adrian Gregory and Senia Paseta. Manchester: Manchester University Press, 2002. 190–216.

Brearton, Fran. *The Great War in Irish Poetry.* Oxford: Oxford University Press, 2000.

Brown, Terence. *The Literature of Ireland. Culture and Criticism.* Cambridge: Cambridge University Press, 2011.

Brown, Terence. "Writing the War." *Our War. Ireland and the Great War.* Ed. John Horne. Dublin: RIA, 2008. 233–47.

Brown, Terence. *Ireland. A Social and Cultural History. 1922–2002.* London: Harper Perennial, 2004.

Brown, Terence. "Who dares to speak? Ireland and the Great War". *English Studies in Transition.* Ed. Robert Clark and Piero Boitani. London: Routledge, 1993. 226–37.

Buchanan, Ian. *Fredric Jameson: Live Theory.* London: Continuum, 2006.

Buckner, Phillip. "The Creation of the Dominion of Canada, 1860–1901." *Canada and the British Empire.* Ed. Phillip Buckner. Oxford: Oxford University Press, 2008. 66–86.

Cadden, Michael. "Homosexualizing the Troubles: A Short Query into Two Derry Airs by Frank McGuinness." *Princeton University Library Chronicle* 68 (2006): 560–71.

Caherty, Therese. *More Missing Pieces. Her Story of Irish Women.* Dublin: Attic Press, 1985.

Calnan, Denise. "Politician criticises An Post's 'contradictory' WW1 commemoration stamps." *The Irish Independent.* 15 August 2014. <http://www.independent.ie/irish-news/politician-criticises-an-posts-contradictory-ww1-commemoration-stamps-30510796.html>. Accessed 20 August 2014.

Campbell, Mary. "No Picnic." *Books Ireland* 151 (1991): 117–8.

Carpenter, Andrew. "Double Vision in Anglo-Irish Literature." *Place, Personality and the Irish Writer*. Ed. Andrew Carpenter. Gerrards Cross: Colin Smythe, 1977. 173–90.

Carruthers, Gerrard. "Fictions of Belonging: National Identity and the Novel in Ireland and Scotland." *A Companion to the British and Irish Novel 1945–2000*. Ed. Brian W. Shaffer. Malden: Blackwell, 2005. Blackwell Reference Online. Accessed 12 February 2014.

Cole, Sarah. "People in War." *The Cambridge Companion to War Writing*. Ed. Kate McLoughlin. Cambridge: Cambridge University Press, 2009. 25–37.

Collins, Stephen. "First World War was a 'horrific event', says President Higgins." *The Irish Times*. 4 August 2014. <http://www.irishtimes.com/news/politics/first-world-war-was-a-horrific-event-says-president-higgins-1.1887087>. Accessed 20 August 2014.

Crawley, Peter. "*Walking the Road*, Axis, Dublin." *The Irish Times*. 8 June 2007. <http://www.irishtimes.com/culture/reviews-1.1209512>. Accessed 27 May 2015.

Culleton, Claire. "Irish Working-Class Women and World War I." *Representing Ireland: Gender, Class, Nationality*. Ed. Susan Shaw Sailer. Gainesville: University Press of Florida, 1997. 156–80.

Curtayne, Alice. *Francis Ledwidge. A Life of the Poet (1887–1917)*. London: Martin Brian & O'Keeffe, 1972.

Dawe, Gerald. "Introduction." *Earth Voices Whispering. An Anthology of Irish War Poetry. 1914–1945*. Ed. Gerald Dawe. Belfast: Blackstaff, 2008. xvii–xx.

Decker, Martin. "'I'm at home, you little bastards' – Re-Envisioning the Marginalised Irish Soldier in Sebastian Barry's *A Long Long Way* and Dermot Bolger's *Walking the Road*." *Anglistik* 26.1 (2015): 81–91.

Decker, Martin. "'You half-baked Lazarus' – Masculinity and the Maimed Body in Sean O'Casey's *The Silver Tassie*." *Gender and Disease in Literary and Medical Cultures*. Ed. Iris M. Heid and Anne-Julia Zwierlein. Heidelberg: Winter, 2014. 117–32.

Dederich, Markus. *Körper, Kultur und Behinderung. Eine Einführung in die Disability Studies*. Bielefeld: transcript, 2007.

Delgado, Maria M. "Introduction. 'Beyond the Troubles': The Political Drama of Christina Reid." *Plays: 1*. London: Methuen, 1997. vii–xxii.

Denman, Terence. *Ireland's Unknown Soldiers. The 16th (Irish) Division in the Great War, 1914–1918*. Dublin: Irish Academic Press, 1992.

Devine, Kathleen. "Introduction." *Modern Irish Writers and the Wars*. Gerrards Cross: Colin Smythe, 1999. ix–xix.

Diez Fabre, Silvia. "Jennifer Johnston's *How Many Miles to Babylon?* Questioning the Past Among Echoes of Literary History." *Back to the Present: Forward to the Past. Irish Writing and History since 1798.* Vol. 1. Ed. Patricia A. Lynch, Joachim Fischer and Brian Coates. Amsterdam: Rodopi, 2006. 109–17.

Dooley, Thomas P. *Irishmen or English Soldiers? The Times of a Southern Catholic Irish Man (1876–1916) Enlisting in the British Army during the First World War.* Liverpool: Liverpool University Press, 1995.

Doyle, Jacqueline. "Liturgical Imagery in Sean O'Casey's *The Silver Tassie.*" *Modern Drama* 21 (1978): 29–38.

Duara, Prasenjit. "Historicising National Identity, or Who Imagines What and When." *Becoming National. A Reader.* Ed. Geoff Eley and R. G. Suny. New York and Oxford: Oxford University Press, 1996. 151–77.

Eagleton, Terry. "Revisionism Revisited." *Irish Writing in the Twentieth Century. A Reader.* Ed. David Pierce. Cork: Cork University Press, 2000. 1156–58.

Eisen, Kurt. "Lennox Robinson (1886–1958)." *Irish Playwrights 1880–1995. A Research and Production Sourcebook.* Ed. Bernice Schrank and W. W. Demastes. Westport: Greenwood Press, 1997. 308–21.

Eliot, T. S. "Letter to A. D. Peters, 26 April 1928." *The Letters of T. S. Eliot.* Vol. 3. *1926–28.* Ed. Valerie Eliot and John Haffenden. New Haven: Yale University Press, 2012. 144–5.

Erevelles, Nirmala. "The Color of Violence: Reflecting on Gender, Race, and Disability in Wartime." *Feminist Disability Studies.* Ed. Kim Q. Hall. Bloomington: Indiana University Press, 2011. 117–35.

Erll, Astrid. *Gedächtnisromane. Literatur über den Ersten Weltkrieg als Medium englischer und deutscher Erinnerungskulturen in den 1920er Jahren.* Trier: WVT, 2003.

Eyler, Audrey S. and Robert F. Garratt. "Preface." *The Uses of the Past. Essays on Irish Culture.* Ed. Audrey S. Eyler and Robert F. Garratt. Newark: University of Delaware Press, 1988. 7–9.

Feltmann, Guy. "An Historical Survey." *The Big House in Ireland. Reality and Representation.* Ed. Jacqueline Genet. Dingle: Brandon, 1991. 15–18.

Ferriter, Diarmaid. *The Transformation of Ireland. 1900–2000.* London: Profile Books, 2005.

Fitzpatrick, David. "Commemoration in the Irish Free State: A Chronicle of Embarrassment." *History and Memory in Modern Ireland.* Ed. Ian McBride. Cambridge: Cambridge University Press, 2001. 184–203.

Fitzpatrick, David. "The Logic of Collective Sacrifice: Ireland and the British Army, 1914–1918." *The Historical Journal* 38.4 (1995). 1017–30.

Fitzpatrick, David. "Home Front and Everyday Life." *Our War. Ireland and the Great War.* Ed. John Horne. Dublin: RIA, 2008. 133–42.

Ford, Madox Ford. *Joseph Conrad: A Personal Remembrance.* Boston: Little, Brown & Company, 1924.

"Forgotten Heroes." *Irish Echo.* 28 February 2007. <http://irishecho.com/2011/02/forgottenheroes/>. Accessed 20 July 2015.

Foster, John Wilson. "Introduction." *The Cambridge Companion to the Irish Novel.* Ed. John Wilson Foster. Cambridge: Cambridge University Press, 2006. 1–21.

Foster, Roy. "A tale of two halves. Roy Foster acclaims Diarmaid Ferriter's gripping account of the making of the Celtic Tiger, The Transformation of Ireland." *The Guardian.* 13 November 2004. <http://www.theguardian.com/books/2004/nov/13/featuresreviews.guardian review3>. Accessed 17 November 2014.

Foster, Roy. "'Something of us will remain': Sebastian Barry and Irish History." *Out of History. Essays on the Writings of Sebastian Barry.* Ed. Christina Hunt Mahony. Dublin: Carysfort Press, 2006a. 183–97.

Fussell, Paul. *The Great War and Modern Memory. The Illustrated Edition.* New York: Sterling, 2009.

Garratt, Robert F. *Trauma and History in the Irish Novel. The Return of the Dead.* Basingstoke: Palgrave Macmillan, 2011.

Gilbert, Helen and Joanne Tompkins. *Post-Colonial Drama. Theory, Practice, Politics.* London: Routledge, 1996.

Gilbert, Sandra M. "Soldier's Heart. Literary Men, Literary Women, and the Great War." *Signs* 8 (1983). 422–50.

Gleitman, Claire. "Reconstructing History in the Irish History Play." *The Cambridge Companion to Twentieth-Century Irish Drama.* Ed. Shaun Richards. Cambridge: Cambridge University Press, 2004. 218–30.

Gonne, Maud. "The Famine Queen." *Irish Writing. An Anthology of Irish Literature in English 1789–1939.* Ed. Stephen Regan. Oxford: Oxford University Press, 2004. 183–85.

Grayzel, Susan. "Liberating Women? Examining Gender, Morality and Sexuality in First World War Britain and France." *Evidence, History, and the Great War. Historians and the Impact of 1914–18.* Ed. Gail Braybon. New York: Berghahn, 2003. 113–33.

Gregory, Adrian and Senia Paseta. "Introduction." *Ireland and the Great War. 'A War to Unite us All?'.* Manchester: Manchester University Press, 2002. 1–7.

Grene, Nicholas. "Out of History: From *The Steward of Christendom* to *Annie Dunne.*" *Out of History. Essays on the Writings of Sebastian Barry.* Ed. Christina Hunt Mahony. Dublin: Carysfort Press, 2006. 167–82.

Grene, Nicholas. *The Politics of Irish Drama. Plays in Context from Boucicault to Friel.* Cambridge: Cambridge University Press, 1999.

Große, Christian. "Christina Reid." *The Methuen Drama Guide to Contemporary Irish Playwrights.* Ed. Martin Middeke and Peter Paul Schnierer. London: Methuen, 2010. 385–404.

Hall, Stuart. "Introduction: Who Needs Identity?" *Questions of Cultural Identity.* Ed. Stuart Hall and Paul du Gay. London: Sage, 1996. 1–17.

Hall, Stuart. "Ethnicity: Identity and Difference." *Becoming Nation. A Reader.* Ed. Geoff Eley and R. G. Sury. New York and Oxford: Oxford University Press, 1996a. 339–49.

Hall, Stuart. "The Question of Cultural Identity." *Modernity. An Introduction to Modern Societies.* Ed. Stuart Hall, David Held, Don Hubert and Kenneth Thompson. Malden: Blackwell, 1995. 596–632.

Harkness, Marguerite. *"The Silver Tassie:* No Light in the Darkness." *The Sean O'Casey Review* 4.2 (1978): 131–37.

Harris, Susan Cannon. *Gender and Modern Irish Drama.* Bloomington: Indiana University Press, 2002.

Harte, Liam. "The Politics of Pity in Sebastian Barry's *A Long Long Way.*" *The South Carolina Review* 44.2 (2012): 103–16.

Harte, Liam. "A Kind of Scab: Irish Identity in the Writings of Dermot Bolger and Joseph O'Connor." *Irish Studies Review* 20 (1997): 17–22.

Haughey, Jim. *The First World War in Irish Poetry.* Lewisburg: Bucknell University Press, 2002.

Haughey, Jim. "Partitioned Memories: The Great War and Irish Poetry." *LIT* 10 (1999): 181–91.

Headrick, Charlotte J. "Shattering Irish Dreams: Nicola McCartney's *Heritage.*" *Visions of the Irish Dream.* Ed. Marguerite Quintelli-Neary. Newcastle upon Tyne: Cambridge Scholars, 2009. 64–84.

Heaney, Seamus. "Introduction." *The Ledwidge Treasury. Selected Poems of Francis Ledwidge.* Ed. Dermot Bolger. Dublin: New Island, 2007. 3–14.

Hennessey, Thomas. *Dividing Ireland. World War I and Partition.* London: Routledge, 1998.

Herron, Tom. "Dead Men Talking: Frank McGuinness's *Observe the Sons of Ulster Marching Towards the Somme.*" *Eire-Ireland* 39 (2004): 136–62.

Hinkson, Pamela. "War-time Ireland." *The English Review* 62.3 (1936): 378–9.

Horne, John (ed.). *Our War. Ireland and the Great War.* Ed. John Horne. Dublin: RIA, 2008. 133–42.

Horne, John. "Our War, Our History." *Our War. Ireland and the Great War.* Ed. John Horne. Dublin: RIA, 2008a. 3–14.

Horne, John. "Masculinity in Politics and War in the Age of Nation-States and World Wars, 1850–1950." *Masculinities in Politics and War: Gendering Modern History.* Ed. Stefan Dudink, Karen Hagemann and John Tosh. Manchester: Manchester University Press, 2004. 22–40.

Humphreys, Joe. "Centenary commemorations should not distort history, says President Higgins." *The Irish Times.* 16 January 2014. <http://www.irishtimes. com/culture/ stage/centenary-commemorations-should-not-distort-history-says-president-higgins-1.1658033>. Accessed 27 April 2014.

Hynes, Samuel. *A War Imagined. The First World War and English Culture.* London: Pimlico, 1990.

Innes, Christopher. "Defining Irishness: Shaw and the Image of Ireland on the English Stage." *A Companion to Irish Literature.* Vol 2. Ed. Julia Wright. Oxford: Blackwell Press, 2010. 35–49.

Jameson, Fredric. *The Political Unconscious. Narrative as a Socially Symbolic Act.* Ithaca: Cornell University Press, 1981.

Jeffery, Keith. "'Writing out of opinions': Irish Experience and the Theatre of the First World War." *Race, Empire and First World War Writing.* Ed. Santanu Das. Cambridge: Cambridge University Press, 2011. 249–64.

Jeffery, Keith. "Echoes of War." *Our War. Ireland and the Great War.* Ed. John Horne. Dublin: RIA, 2008. 263–75.

Jeffery, Keith. *Ireland and the Great War.* Cambridge: Cambridge University Press, 2000.

Jeffery, Keith. "Irish Prose Writers of the First World War". *Modern Irish Writers and the Wars.* Ed. Kathleen Devine. Gerrards Cross: Colin Smythe, 1999. 1–17.

Jeffery, Keith. "Irish Culture and the Great War". *Bullán* 1 (1994): 87–96.

Jeffery, Keith. "The Great War in Modern Irish Memory." *Men, Women and War.* Ed. T. G. Fraser and Keith Jeffery. Dublin: Liliput Press, 1993. 136–57.

Johnson, Nuala C. *Ireland, the Great War and the Geography of Remembrance.* Cambridge: Cambridge University Press, 2003.

Jordan, Eamonn. "Frank McGuinness." *The Methuen Drama Guide to Contemporary Irish Playwrights.* Ed. Martin Middeke and Peter Paul Schnierer. London: Methuen, 2010. 234–50.

Kao, Wei H. "Remapping Protestant Women and Interracial Minorities in Christina Reid's War Dramas." *Irish Women at War. The Twentieth Century.* Ed. Gillian McIntosh and Diane Urquhart. Dublin: Irish Academic Press, 2010. 205–21.

Kelly, Bernard. *Returning Home. Irish Ex-Servicemen after the Second World War.* Dublin: Merrion, 2012.

Kenny, John. "'His Heart Is There.'" *The Irish Times.* 26 March 2005. 10.

Kiberd, Declan. "Frank McGuinness and the Sons of Ulster." *The Yearbook of English Studies* 35 (2005): 279–97.

Kiberd, Declan. *The Irish Writer and the World.* Cambridge: Cambridge University Press, 2005a.

Kiberd, Declan. "1916: The Idea and the Action." *Modern Irish Writers and the Wars.* Ed. Kathleen Devine. Gerrards Cross: Colin Smythe, 1999. 18–35.

Kiberd, Declan. "From Nationalism to Liberation." *Representing Ireland: Gender, Class, Nationality.* Ed. Susan Shaw Sailer. Gainesville: University Press of Florida, 1997. 17–28.

Kiberd, Declan. *Inventing Ireland. The Literature of the Modern Nation.* London: Vintage, 1996.

Kiberd, Declan. "Fathers and Sons: Irish-Style." *Irish Literature and Culture.* Ed. Michael Kenneally. Gerrards Cross: Colin Smythe, 1992. 127–143.

Kiberd, Declan. "The War Against the Past." *The Uses of the Past. Essays on Irish Culture.* Ed. Audrey S. Eyler and Robert F. Garratt. Newark: University of Delaware Press, 1988. 24–54.

Klein, Gabriele. "Körper und Theatralität." *Diskurse des Theatralen.* Ed. Erika Fischer-Lichte, Christian Horn, Sandra Umathum and Matthias Warstat. Tübingen: Francke, 2005. 35–47.

Korte, Barbara and Ralf Schneider. "Introduction." *War and the Cultural Construction of Identities in Britain.* Ed. Barbara Korte and Ralf Schneider. Amsterdam: Rodopi, 2002. 1–8.

Kosok, Heinz. *Inszeniertes Irland. Geschichte des irischen Dramas und Theaters.* Trier: WVT, 2012.

Kosok, Heinz. "Ireland, Yeats and World War I." *Explorations in Irish Literature.* Trier: WVT, 2008. 153–64.

Kosok, Heinz. "Two Irish Perspectives on World War I: Bernard Shaw and Sean O'Casey." *Explorations in Irish Literature.* Trier: WVT, 2008. 165–77.

Kosok, Heinz. "The Battle of the Somme versus the Easter Rising: The First World War in Irish Drama." *Explorations in Irish Literature.* Trier: WVT, 2008. 179–96.

Kosok, Heinz. *The Theatre of War. The First World War in British and Irish Drama.* Basingstoke: Palgrave, 2007.

Kreilkamp, Vera. "The Novel of the Big House." *The Cambridge Companion to the Big House.* Ed. John William Foster. Cambridge: Cambridge University Press, 2006. 60–77.

Laird, John Tudor. (ed.) *Other Banners. An Anthology of Australian Literature of the First World War.* Canberra: Australian War Memorial and Australian Government Publishing Service, 1971.

Larkin, Hilary. *A History of Ireland, 1800–1922. Theatres of Disorder?* London: Anthem Press, 2014.

Leed, Eric J. *No Man's Land. Combat and Identity in World War I.* Cambridge: Cambridge University Press, 1979.

Leonard, Jane. "Facing 'the Finger of Scorn': Veterans' Memories of Ireland after the Great War." *War and Memory in the Twentieth Century.* Ed. Martin Evans and Ken Lunn. Oxford: Berg, 1997. 59–72.

Leonard, Jane. "Survivors." *Our War. Ireland and the Great War.* Ed. John Horne. Dublin: RIA, 2008. 211–23.

Llewellyn-Jones, Margaret. *Contemporary Irish Drama and Cultural Identity.* Bristol: Intellect Books, 2002.

Löschnigg, Martin. "'… the novelist's responsibility to the past': History, Myth, and the Narratives of Crisis in Pat Barker's *Regeneration* Trilogy (1991–1995)." *ZAA* 47.3 (1999): 214–28.

Lojek, Helen. "*Observe the Sons of Ulster*: Historical Stages." *Echoes Down the Corridor. Irish Theatre – Past, Present, and Future.* Ed. Patrick Lonergan and Riana O'Dwyer. Dublin: Carysfort Press, 2007. 81–94.

Lojek, Helen. "Man, Woman, Soldier: Heaney's 'In Memoriam Francis Ledwidge' and Boland's 'Heroic.'" *New Hibernia Review* 10.1 (2006): 123–38.

Lojek, Helen. "Frank McGuinness (1953-)." *Irish Playwrights, 1880–1995. A Research and Production Sourcebook.* Ed. Bernice Schrank and William W. Demastes. Westport: Greenwood Press, 1997. 218–30.

Lonergan, Patrick. "Christina Reid." *Scenes From the Bigger Picture.* 2 June 2015. <https://patricklonergan.wordpress.com/2015/06/02/christina-reid/>. Accessed 2 June 2015.

Lonergan, Patrick. "Introduction." *The Methuen Drama Anthology of Irish Plays.* London: Methuen 2008. viii–xv.

Lonergan, Patrick. "McDonagh, Globalisation and Irish Theatre Criticism." *The Theatre of Martin McDonagh. A World of Savage Stories.* Ed. Lilian Chambers. Dublin: Carysfort Press 2006, 295–323.

Longley, Edna. *The Living Stream. Literature and Revisionism in Ireland.* Newcastle: Bloodaxe Books, 1994.

Luckhurst, Mary. "A Wounded Stage: Drama and World War I." *A Companion to Modern British and Irish Drama.* Malden: Blackwell, 2006. 301–15.

Lyons, J. B. *The Enigma of Tom Kettle: Irish Patriot, Essayist, Poet, British Soldier.* Dublin: Glendale Press, 1983.

MacAodha, Breandán. "Distribution, Function and Architecture." *The Big House in Ireland. Reality and Representation.* Ed. Jacqueline Genet. Dingle: Brandon, 1991. 43–57.

Maguire, Tom. "Northern Irish Drama: Speaking the Peace." *A Concise Companion to Contemporary British and Irish Drama.* Ed. Nadine Holdsworth and Mary Luckhurst. Malden: Blackwell, 2013. 66–84.

Malkki, Liisa. "Citizens of Humanity: Internationalism and the Imagined Community of Nations." *Diaspora* 3.1 (1994): 41–68.

Malone, Maureen. *The Plays of Sean O'Casey.* Carbondale: Southern Illinois University Press, 1969.

Martin, Peter. "Dulce et Decorum: Irish Nobles and the Great War, 1914–1919." *Ireland and the Great War. 'A War to Unite us All?'.* Ed. Adrian Gregory and Senia Paseta. Manchester: Manchester University Press, 2002. 28–48.

Maurer, Michael. *Kleine Geschichte Irlands.* Stuttgart: Reclam, 1998.

McAteer, Michael. "Expressionism, Ireland and the First World War: Yeats, O'Casey, McGuinness." *Irish Modernism: Origins, Contexts, Publics.* Ed. Edwina Keown. Oxford: Lang, 2010. 65–79.

McBride, Ian. "Memory and National Identity in Modern Ireland." *History and Memory in Modern Ireland.* Ed. Ian McBride. Cambridge: Cambridge University Press, 2001. 1–42.

McClintock, Anne. "'No Longer in a Future Heaven': Nationalism, Gender, and Race." *Becoming National. A Reader.* Ed. Geoff Eley and R. G. Sury. New York and Oxford: Oxford University Press, 1996. 259–84.

McDonald, Ronan. *Tragedy and Irish Literature: Synge, O'Casey, Beckett.* Basingstoke: Palgrave, 2002.

McDonough, Carla J. "Christina Reid (1942-)." *Irish Playwrights 1880–1995. A Research and Production Sourcebook.* Ed. Bernice Schrank and William W. Demastes. Westport: Greenwood Press, 1997. 300–7.

McKean, Kathy. "'Listen I will tell the story to you / As I have been told it': Memory and Identity in the Plays of Nicola McCartney." *International Journal of Scottish Theatre and Screen* 4.1 (2011). <http://journals.qmu.ac.uk/index.php/IJOSTS/article/ view/113>. Accessed 12 September 2014.

McLoughlin, Kate. "War and Words." *The Cambridge Companion to War Writing.* Ed. Kate McLoughlin. Cambridge: Cambridge University Press, 2009. 15–24.

McMinn, Joe. "Language, Literature and Cultural Identity." *Styles of Belonging: The Cultural Identities of Ulster.* Ed. Jean Lundy and Aodán MacPóilin. Belfast: Lagan Press, 1992. 56–63.

McNulty, Eugene. "Incommensurate Histories: The Remaindered Irish Bodies of the Great War". *Conflict, Nationhood and Corporeality in Modern Literature. Bodies-at-War.* Ed. Petra Rau. Basingstoke: Palgrave Macmillan, 2010. 64–82.

Meyer, Bruce. "Introduction." *We Wasn't Pals. Canadian Poetry and Prose of the First World War.* Ed. Barry Callaghan and Bruce Meyer. Toronto: Exile Editions, 2001. xix–xxvii.

Meyer, Jessica. *Men of War. Masculinity and the First World War in Britain.* Basingstoke: Palgrave Macmillan, 2009.

Middeke, Martin and Peter Paul Schnierer. "Introduction." *The Methuen Drama Guide to Contemporary Irish Playwrights.* Ed. Martin Middeke and Peter Paul Schnierer. London: Methuen, 2010. vii–xix.

Misztal, Barbara. *Theories of Social Remembrance.* Maidenhead: Open University Press, 2003.

Mitchell, David and Sharon Snyder. "Disability Studies and the Double Bind of Representation." *The Body and Physical Difference. Discourses of Disability.* Ann Arbor: University of Michigan Press, 1997. 1–31.

Mortimer, Mark. "Jennifer Johnston and the Big House." *The Big House in Ireland. Reality and Representation.* Ed. Jacqueline Genet. Dingle: Brandon, 1991. 209–214.

Morton, Desmond. *A Short History of Canada.* Toronto: McClelland and Stewart, 1994.

Mosse, George. *Nationalism and Sexuality. Respectability and Abnormal Sexuality in Modern Europe.* New York: Howard Fertig, 1985.

Moulton, Mo. *Ireland and the Irish in Interwar England.* Cambridge: Cambridge University Press, 2014.

Murphy, Paula. "'Scattering us like seed': Dermot Bolger's Postnationalist Ireland." *Redefinitions of Irish Identity. A Postnationalist Approach.* Ed. Irene Nordin and Carmen Zamorano Llena. Bern: Lang, 2010. 181–199.

Murray, Christopher. "O'Casey at War." *Modern Irish Writers and the Wars.* Ed. Kathleen Devine. Gerrards Cross: Colin Smythe, 1999. 81–101.

Murray, Christopher. "Lennox Robinson, *The Big House, Killycregs in Twilight* and 'the Vestigia of Generations'." *Ancestral Voices. The Big House in Anglo-Irish Literature.* Ed. Otto Rauchbauer. Hildesheim: Georg Olms Verlag, 1992. 109–119.

Murray, Christopher. "Lennox Robinson: The Abbey's Anti-Hero." *Irish Writers and the Theatre.* Ed. Masaru Sekine. Gerrards Cross: Colin Smythe, 1986. 114–34.

Murray, Christopher. "Introduction." *Selected Plays: Lennox Robinson.* Ed. Christopher Murray. Gerrards Cross: Colin Smythe, 1982. 7–21.

Murtagh, Peter. "Protesters heckle at Cross of Sacrifice ceremony." *The Irish Times*. 1 August 2014.<www.irishtimes.com/news/ireland/irish-news/protesters-heckle-at-cross-of-sacrifice-ceremony-1.1884233>. Accessed 20 August 2014.

"Novel Notes. *Harvest*. By Peter Deane." *The Bookman*. January 1927. 244.

Novick, Ben. *Conceiving Revolution. Irish Nationalist Propaganda during the First World War*. Dublin: Four Courts Press, 2001.

O'Casey, Sean. *The Letters of Sean O'Casey. Vol. 4. 1959*-1964. Ed. David Krause. Washington: Catholic University of America Press, 1992.

O'Casey, Sean. *The Letters of Sean O'Casey. Vol. 1. 1910*-*1941*. Ed. David Krause. London: Cassell, 1975.

Officer, David. "'For God and for Ulster': The Ulstermen on the Somme." *History and Memory in Modern Ireland*. Ed. Ian McBride. Cambridge: Cambridge University Press, 2001. 160-183.

O'Flaherty, Gearóid. "George Bernard Shaw and Ireland." *The Cambridge Companion to Twentieth-Century Irish Drama*. Ed. Shaun Richards. Cambridge: Cambridge University Press, 2004. 122-35.

O'Mahony, Patrick and Gerard Delanty. *Rethinking Irish History, Nationalism, Identity and Ideology*. Basingstoke: Palgrave, 2001.

O'Malley, Seamus. "Amnesia and Recovery of the Great War in Plays by McGuinness and Barry." *New Hibernia Review* 16 (2012): 110-26.

O'Riordan, John. "The Garlanded Horror of War: Reflections on *The Silver Tassie*." *The Sean O'Casey Review* 5 (1978): 23-28.

Orr, Philip. "200,000 Volunteer Soldiers." *Our War. Ireland and the Great War*. Ed. John Horne. Dublin: RIA, 2008. 65-77.

O'Toole, Fintan. "John B. Keane and the Ireland of his Time." *'Come All Good Men and True'. Essays from the John B. Keane Symposium*. Ed. Gabriel Fitzmaurice. Dublin: Mercier, 2004. 28-60.

O'Toole, Fintan. "Introduction: Grace and Disgrace." *Three Plays by Sebastian Barry*. London: Methuen, 1996. v-ix.

Ouditt, Sharon. "Myths, Memories and Monuments: Reimagining the Great War." *The Cambridge Companion to the Literature of the First World War*. Ed. Vincent Sherry. Cambridge: Cambridge University Press, 2005. 245-60.

Ouditt, Sharon. *Women Writers of the First World War. An Annotated Bibliography*. London: Routledge, 2002.

Owens, Coílín D. and Joan N. Radner. "Lennox Robinson, 1886-1958." *Irish Drama, 1900-1980*. Washington: The Catholic University of America Press, 1990. 285-87.

Peach, Linden. *The Contemporary Irish Novel. Critical Readings*. Basingstoke: Palgrave Macmillan, 2004.

Pearse, Patrick. "The Coming Revolution." 1913. *University College Cork Corpus of Electronic Texts*. <http://www.ucc.ie/celt/online/E900007-003/text001.html>. Accessed 19 April 2013.

Pelletier, Martine. "Dermot Bolger's Drama." *Theatre Stuff. Critical Essays on Contemporary Irish Theatre*. Ed. Eamonn Jordan. Dublin: Carysfort Press, 2009. 248–55.

Pennell, Catriona. "Going to War." *Our War. Ireland and the Great War*. Ed. John Horne. Dublin: RIA, 2008. 35–48.

Petter, Martin. "'Temporary Gentlemen' in the Aftermath of the Great War: Rank, Status and the Ex-Officer Problem." *The Historical Journal* 37.1 (1994): 127–52.

Phelan, Tom. "Remembering 1916 and moving on from it." *Irish Echo*. 27 April 2016. Transcript on Phelan's Facebook site <https://www.facebook.com/laois press/posts/ 982055871890515>. Accessed 15 May 2016.

Phelan, Tom. "Notebook." *Newsday*. 12 November 2005. <http://www.newsday.com/opinion/ notebook1.596246>. Accessed 20 July 2015.

Phillips, Terry. "Shaw, Ireland, and World War I: *O'Flaherty V. C.*, an Unlikely Recruiting Play." *Shaw* 30 (2010): 133–46.

Phillips, Terry. "The Wisdom of Experience: Patrick MacGill's Irishness Reassessed." *Sub-Versions. Trans-National Readings of Modern Irish Literature*. Ed. Ciaran Ross. Amsterdam: Rodopi, 2010a. 29–52.

Phillips, Terry. "No Man's Land: Irish Women Writers of the First World War." *No Country for Old Men: Fresh Perspectives on Irish Literature*. Ed. Paddy Lyons and Alison O'Malley-Younger. Oxford: Lang, 2009. 265–79.

Phillips, Terry. "Enigmas of the Great War: Thomas Kettle and Francis Ledwidge." *Irish Studies Review* 16 (2008): 385–402.

Phillips, Terry. "'No World Between Two Worlds': Liminality in Anglo-Irish Big House Literature, 1925–1932." *Mapping Liminalities. Thresholds in Cultural and Literary Texts*. Ed. Lucy Kay, Zoe Kinsley, Terry Phillips and Alan Roughley. Bern: Peter Lang, 2007. 69–91.

Pierson, Ruth Roach. "Nations: Gendered, Racialized, Crossed with Empire." *Gendered Nations. Nationalism and Gender Order in the Long Nineteenth Century*. Ed. Ida Blom, Karen Hagemann and Catherine Hall. Oxford: Berg, 2000. 41–61.

Pine, Emilie. "The Tyranny of Memory: Remembering the Great War in Frank McGuinness's *Observe the Sons of Ulster Marching Towards the Somme*." *Irish University Review* 40.1 (2010): 59–68.

Price, Graham. "Memory, Narration and Spectrality in Brian Friel's *Faith Healer* and Frank McGuinness's *Observe the Sons of Ulster Marching Towards the Somme*." *Irish Studies Review* 23.1 (2015): 33–47.

Rée, Jonathan. "Internationality." *Radical Philosophy* 60 (1992): 3–11.

Renan, Ernest. "What is a Nation?" *The Collective Memory Reader*. Ed. Jeffery K. Olick, Vered Vinitzky-Seroussi and Daniel Levy. Oxford: Oxford University Press, 2011. 80–83.

Roper, Michael. "Maternal Relations: Moral Manliness and Emotional Survival in Letters Home During the First World War." *Masculinities in Politics and War. Gendering Modern History*. Ed. Stefan Dudnik et al. Manchester: Manchester University Press, 2004. 295–315.

Rosslyn, Felicity. "'The Nonsense about Our Irishness': Jennifer Johnston." *Contemporary British Women Writers*. Ed. Emma Parker. Cambridge: D. S. Brewer, 2004. 104–22.

Rudd, Joy. "'Cast a Cold Eye': A Sociological Approach." *The Big House in Ireland. Reality and Representation*. Ed. Jacqueline Genet. Dingle: Brandon, 1991. 31–42.

Scarry, Elaine. *The Body in Pain. The Making and Unmaking of the World*. Oxford: Oxford University Press, 1985.

Seree-Chaussinand, Christelle. "Irish Man, No Man, Everyman: Subversive Redemption in Sebastian Barry's *The Whereabouts of Eneas McNulty*." *SubVersions. Trans-National Readings of Modern Irish Literature*. Ed. Ciaran Ross. Amsterdam: Rodopi, 2010. 53–64.

Shaw, George Bernard. *What I Really Wrote about the War*. London: Constable, 1930.

Shaw, George Bernard. "Common Sense about the War." *The New York Times Current History. A Monthly Magazine. The European War*. Vol. 1. New York: New York Times Company, 1915. 11–59.

Sheffield, Gary. *Forgotten Victory. The First World War. Myths and Realities*. London: Review, 2002.

Shuttleworth, Russell, Nikki Wedgwood and Nathan J. Wilson. "The Dilemma of Disabled Masculinity." *Men and Masculinities* 15.2 (2012): 174–94.

Siebers, Tobin. *Disability Theory*. Ann Arbor: University of Michigan Press, 2009.

Sluga, Glenda. "Masculinities, Nations, and the New World Order: Peacemaking and Nationality in Britain, France and the United States after the First World War." *Masculinities in Politics and War. Gendering Modern History*. Ed. Stefan Dudnik et. al. Manchester: Manchester University Press, 2004. 238–54.

Smith, Wendy. "Talking with Tom Phelan, author of 'The Canal Bridge'." *Newsday*. 21 May 2014. <http://www.newsday.com/entertainment/books/talkingwith tomphelanauthorofthecanalbridge1.8096578>. Accessed 20 July 2015.

Sokolowska-Paryz, Marzena. "The Great War and the Easter Rising in Tom Phelan's *The Canal Bridge*: A Literary Response to the Politics of Commemoration in Ireland." *The Great War in Post-Memory Literature and Film*. Ed. Martin Löschnigg and Marzena Sokolowska-Paryz. Berlin: de Gruyter, 2014. 335–47.

Starkie, Walter. "Sean O'Casey." *The Irish Theatre*. Ed. Lennox Robinson. London: Macmillan, 1939. 147–76.

Stevenson, Randall. *Literature & the Great War 1914–1918*. Oxford: Oxford University Press, 2013.

Stiehm, Judith H. *Arms and the Enlisted Woman*. Philadelphia: Temple University Press, 1989.

Stubbings, Diane. *Anglo-Irish Modernism and the Maternal. From Yeats to Joyce*. Basingstoke: Palgrave, 2000.

Sullivan, Robert. "Ervine, St. John G. (St. John Greer) (1883–1971)." *Modernist Journals Project*. <http://modjourn.org/render.php?view=mjp_object&id=mjp. 2005.01.015.> Accessed 16 March 2014.

Taithe, Bernard and Tim Thornton. "Identifying War: Conflict and Self-Definition in Western Europe." *War. Identities in Conflict 1300–2000*. Ed. Bernard Taithe and Tim Thornton. Phoenix Mill: Sutton, 1998. 1–18.

Tate, Trudi. "The First World War: British Writing." *The Cambridge Companion to War Writing*. Ed. Kate McLoughlin. Cambridge: Cambridge University Press, 2009. 160–74.

Taylor, David. *Memory, Narrative and the Great War. Rifleman Patrick MacGill and the Construction of Wartime Experience*. Liverpool: Liverpool University Press, 2013.

Tetzeli von Rosador, Kurt. *Das englische Geschichtsdrama seit Shaw*. Heidelberg: Winter, 1976.

Thackray Jones, Rachel. "Jennifer Johnston." *British Council. Literature*. 2008. <http://www.literature.britishcouncil.org/jennifer-johnston>. Accessed 20 April 2013.

Thompson, John Herd. "Canada and the 'Third British Empire', 1901–1939." *Canada and the British Empire*. Ed. Phillip Buckner. Oxford: Oxford University Press, 2008. 87–108.

Tosh, John. "Hegemonic Masculinity and the History of Gender." *Masculinities in Politics and War: Gendering Modern History*. Ed. Stefan Dudink, Karen Hagemann and John Tosh. Manchester: Manchester University Press, 2004. 41–58.

Tylee, Claire. "First World War Literature." *Men and Masculinities. A Social, Cultural, and Historical Encyclopaedia*. Ed. Michael Kimmel and Amy Aronson. Santa Barbara: ABC Clio, 2004. 304–6.

Tylee, Claire. "'Name Upon Name': Myth, Ritual and the Past in Recent Irish Plays Referring to the Great War." *Dressing Up for War. Transformations of Gender and Genre in the Discourse and Literature of War.* Ed. Aránzazu Usandizaga and Andrew Monnickendam. Amsterdam: Rodopi, 2001. 271–87.

Tylee, Claire M., Elaine Turner and Agnès Cardinal. *War Plays by Women. An International Anthology.* London: Routledge, 1999.

Tylee, Claire M. *The Great War and Women's Consciousness. Images of Militarism and Womanhood in Women's Writings, 1914–64.* Iowa City: University of Iowa Press, 1990.

Vance, Jonathan. *Death So Noble: Memory, Meaning, and the First World War.* Vancouver: University of British Columbia Press, 1997.

Vormann, Hartmut. *The Art of Lennox Robinson. Theoretical Premises and Theatrical Practice.* Trier: WVT, 2001.

Waite, John. "Why Irish soldiers who fought Hitler hide their medals." *BBC News UK.* 28 December 2011. <http://www.bbc.co.uk/news/uk-16287211>. Accessed 17 November 2012.

Wald, Christina. "Dermot Bolger." *The Methuen Drama Guide to Contemporary Playwrights.* Ed. Martin Middeke and Peter Paul Schnierer. London: Methuen, 2010. 19–36.

Weekes, Ann Owens. *Irish Women Writers. An Uncharted Tradition.* Lexington: The University Press of Kentucky, 1990.

Wehrmann, Jürgen. "Sebastian Barry." *The Methuen Drama Guide to Contemporary Irish Playwrights.* Ed. Martin Middeke and Peter Paul Schnierer. London: Methuen, 2010. 1–17.

Wehrmann, Jürgen. "Revising the Nation: Globalisation and Fragmentation of Irish History in Sebastian Barry's Plays." *Global Challenges and Regional Responses in Contemporary Drama in English.* Ed. Jochen Achilles, Ina Bergmann and Birgit Dähres. Trier: WVT, 2003. 203–16.

Welch, Robert. *The Abbey Theatre. 1899–1999. Form & Pressure.* Oxford: Oxford University Press, 1999.

Widmann, Andreas Martin. *Kontrafaktische Geschichtsdarstellung. Untersuchungen an Romanen von Günter Grass, Thomas Pynchon, Thomas Brussig, Michael Kleeberg, Philip Roth und Christoph Ransmayr.* Heidelberg: Winter, 2009.

Wills, Clair. *Dublin 1916. The Siege of the GPO.* London: Profile, 2009.

Winter, Jay. "Remembering War: The Great War between Memory and History in the Twentieth Century." *The Collective Memory Reader.* Ed. Jeffery K. Olick, Vered Vinitzky-Seroussi and Daniel Levy. Oxford: Oxford University Press, 2011. 426–29.

Winter, Jay and Emmanuel Sivan. "Setting the Framework." *War and Remembrance in the Twentieth Century*. Ed. Jay Winter and Emmanuel Sivan. Cambridge: Cambridge University Press, 1999. 6–39.

Winter, Jay. *Sites of Memory. Sites of Mourning. The Great War in European Cultural History*. Cambridge: Cambridge University Press, 1995.

Winter, Jay. *The Great War and the British People*. Basingstoke: Macmillan, 1986.

Wisenthal, J. L. and Daniel O'Leary. "Introduction: Shaw's Theatre of War." *What Shaw Really Wrote About the War*. Ed. J. L Wisenthal and Daniel O'Leary. Gainesville: University Press of Florida, 2006. 1–15.

Woollacott, Angela. "'Khaki Fever' and its Control: Gender, Class, Age and Sexual Morality on the British Home Front in the First World War." *Journal of Contemporary History* 29 (1994): 325–47.

Yeats, William Butler. *The Letters of W. B. Yeats*. Ed. Allan Wade. London: Hart-Davis, 1954.

Zamorano, Carmen Llena. "Contemporary Redefinitions of Irishness: Revisiting the Past from a Postnationalist Perspective in Dermot Bolger's *The Family on Paradise Pier*." *A Review of International English Literature* 38 (2007): 115–38.

Regensburger Arbeiten zur Anglistik und Amerikanistik
Regensburg Studies in British and American Languages and Cultures

Band 1 Karl Heinz Göller: Romance und Novel. Die Anfänge des englischen Romans. Unter Mitarbeit von Manfred Markus und Rainer Schöwerling. 1972.

Band 2 Eberhard Griem: Form und Funktion der Englischen Geburtstagsdichtung im Klassizismus. 1971.

Band 3 Manfred Markus: Moderne Erzählperspektive in den Werken des Gawain-Autors. 1971.

Band 4 Thomas Ross: A Book of Elizabethan Magic. Thomas Hill's Natural and Artificial Conclu-' sions. 1974.

Band 5 Alfred Becker: Franks Casket. Zu den Bildern und Inschriften des Runenkästchens von Auzon. 1973.

Band 6 Kurt-Michael Pätzold: Historischer Roman und Realismus. Das Erzählwerk Thomas Deloneys. 1972.

Band 7 Evelyn B. Jolles: G. A. Bürgers Ballade Lenore in England. 1974.

Band 8 Anton Bauer: Das melanesische und chinesische Pidginenglisch. Linguistische Kriterien und Probleme. 1974.

Band 9 Philip A. Luelsdorff (Ed.): Linguistic Perspectives on Black English. 1975.

Band 10 Ludwig Rothmayer: Der Mensch und das Schicksal in den Romanen Herman Melvilles. 1977.

Band 11 Hans-Martin Braun: Prototypen der amerikanischen Kriminalerzählung: Die Romane und Kurzgeschichten Carroll John Dalys und Dashiell Hammetts. 1977.

Band 12 Günter Tschöpl: Zur Identitätsthematik bei Robert Penn Warren: Die Ermittlung des Ich in All the King's Men. 1978.

Band 13 Henning Thies: Namen im Kontext von Dramen. Studien zur Funktion von Personennamen im englischen, amerikanischen und deutschen Drama. 1978.

Band 14 Wolfgang Riedel: Die Arbeit der Dichter. Vergleichende Studien zur dichterischen Subjektivität in der englischen Romantik und Moderne. 1979.

Band 15 Jochen Achilles: Drama als problematische Form. Der Wandel zu nichtrealistischer Gestaltungsweise im Werk Sean O'Caseys. 1979.

Band 16 Renate Haas: Die mittelenglische Totenklage. Realitätsbezug, abendländische Tradition und individuelle Gestaltung. 1980.

Band 17 Jean Ritzke-Rutherford: Light and Darkness in Anglo-Saxon Thought and Writing. 1979.

Band 18 Rainer Schöwerling: Chapbooks. Zur Literaturgeschichte des einfachen Lesers. Englische Konsumliteratur 1680-1840. 1980.

Band 19 Anke Janssen: Francis Godwins The Man in the Moone. Die Entdeckung des Romans als Medium der Auseinandersetzung mit Zeitproblemen. 1981.

Band 20 Michael Thomas: Studien zur Short Story als fiktional-narrative Textform und die Möglichkeiten einer Typenbildung. 1982.

Band 21 Werner Huber: James Stephen's frühe Romane. Rezeption - Text - Intention. 1982.

Band 22 Claus Gadau: How to write a Short Story. Zum historischen Wandel der Kurzgeschichtentheorie in amerikanischen Leitfäden zum Verfassen kurzer Prosaerzählungen. 1984.

Band 23 Reinhard Gleißner: Die 'zweideutigen' altenglischen Rätsel des Exeter Book in ihrem zeitgenössischen Kontext. 1984.

Band 24 Peter Lenz: Klerus, Gesellschaft, Literatur. Die moderne irische Erzählprosa zwischen innerem und äußerem Exil. 1985.

Band 25 Johann Aßbeck: Why are my Country-Men such Foes to Verse? Untersuchungen zur schottischen Dichtung des frühen 18. Jahrhunderts in ihrem Verhältnis zum englischen Klassizismus. 1986.

Band 26 Michael Baumann: Milton's Arianism. 1987.

Band 27 Thekla Zachrau: Mythos und Phantastik: Funktion und Struktur der Cthulhu-Mythologie in den phantastischen Erzählungen H.P. Lovecrafts. 1986.

Band 28 Manfred Pütz: Ralph Waldo Emerson: A Bibliography of Twenthieth-Century Criticism. With the assistance of J.K. Adams and J. Böck. 1986.

Band 29 Marion Soceanu: Das Federal Theatre Project und seine Dramen über amerikanische Geschichte. 1987.

Band 30 Wilhelm Bomke: Die Teufelsfiguren der mittelenglischen Dramen. 1990.

Band 31 Richard J. Utz: Literarischer Nominalismus im Spätmittelalter. Eine Untersuchung zu Sprache, Charakterzeichnung und Struktur in Geoffrey Chaucers Troilus and Criseyde. 1990.

Band 32 Markus Preußner: Poe und Baudelaire: Ein Vergleich. 1991.

Band 33 Ulrike Dirscherl: Ritterliche Ideale in Chrétiens Yvain und im mittelenglischen Ywain and Gawain. Von "amour courtois" zu "trew luf", vom "frans chevaliers deboneire" zum "man of mekyl myght". 1991.

Band 34 Paul Neubauer: Die Rezeption der US-amerikanischen Literatur der Postmoderne im deutschsprachigen Raum. 1991.

Band 35 Franz Meier: Die frühe Ding-Lyrik William Carlos Williams'. Genese und Poetologie. 1991.

Band 36 Christoph Houswitschka: Politik und Liebe in der Literatur des englischen Spätmittelalters am Beispiel von Thomas Malorys Morte Darthur. 1991.

Band 37 Klaus-Dieter Groß: Zwischen Romantik, Naturalismus und Moderne. Strömungen des Realismus in amerikanischen Romanen und Gemälden der Zeit zwischen 1920 und 1940. 1992.

Band 38 Paul Neubauer: Die Diskussion der US-amerikanischen Erzählliteratur der Postmoderne in der deutschsprachigen Amerikanistik. 1994.

Band 39 Helge Nowak: "Completeness is all". Fortsetzungen und andere Weiterführungen britischer Romane als Beispiel zeitübergreifender und interkultureller Rezeption. 1994.

Band 40 Vera Hölzl: His Motto is Service. Die Herr-Diener-Problematik in der englischen Literatur seit dem 18. Jahrhundert. 1999.

Band 41 Rainer A. Wirth: Welt / Spiegel / Buch: Theorie der Fiktionalität und James Joyces Prosa. 2000.

Band 42 Eva Hofmann: Decadence Revisited: F. Scott Fitzgerald und das europäische Fin de siècle. 2000.

Band 43 Karsten Fitz: Negotiating History and Culture. Transculturation in Contemporary Native American Fiction. 2001.

Band 44 Elmar Singer: Moving Beyond Nativism. Eine Betrachtung des irischen Gegenwartsromans aus dem Blickwinkel postkolonialer Theorien. 2002.

Band 45 Christin Galster: Hybrides Erzählen und hybride Identität im britischen Roman der Gegenwart. 2002.

www.peterlang.com